THE HUMANITARIAN
CONSCIENCE

Also by W. R. Smyser

Refugees

The German Economy

From Yalta to Berlin

THE HUMANITARIAN
CONSCIENCE

CARING FOR OTHERS
IN THE AGE OF TERROR

W.R. SMYSER

First published 2003 by
PALGRAVE MACMILLAN™
175 Fifth Avenue, New York, N.Y. 10010 and
Houndmills, Basingstoke, Hampshire, England RG21 6XS.
Companies and representatives throughout the world.

PALGRAVE MACMILLAN is the global academic imprint of the Palgrave Macmillan division of St. Martin's Press, LLC and of Palgrave Macmillan Ltd. Macmillan® is a registered trademark in the United States, United Kingdom and other countries. Palgrave is a registered trademark in the European Union and other countries.

ISBN 0–312–23296–9 hardback

Library of Congress Cataloging-in-Publication Data
Smyser, W. R., 1931 –
The humanitarian conscience : caring for others in the age of terror / W. R. Smyser
    p.   cm.
  Includes bibliographical references and index.
  ISBN 0–312–23296–9
  1. Humanitarian assistance.   2. War relief.   I. Title.

HV640.S653   2003
363.34'988—dc21

2003053576

A catalogue record for this book is available from the British Library.

Design by Letra Libre, Inc.

First edition: December 2003
10 9 8 7 6 5 4 3 2 1

Printed in the United States of America

CONTENTS

PREFACE

EVERY BOOK BEGINS WITH AN IDEA, an experience and a sense of mission. So did this one.

The idea is that human beings deserve to be protected from the effects of war and other forms of conflict. It holds that the human race can and should act on the basis of common innate standards of humanism and decency that people understand and appreciate, although governments often do not follow them. That idea originated at the dawn of organized human existence. It has always been under challenge, even more now than in the past, but it must ultimately prevail.

In this book, I call that idea the humanitarian conscience.

The experience is personal. It includes travel to over 50 countries to witness and to guide humanitarian care during my years of international humanitarian and refugee work as Director of the U.S. State Department Refugee Program, as Deputy U.N. High Commissioner for Refugees, and as author on humanitarian programs. The countries range across every continent except Antarctica and include, most recently, Bosnia and Kosovo in the Balkans. I have seen of what I write and I know that it matters.

The sense of mission arises because I fear that the United States and the West as a whole are disregarding the humanitarian conscience and may abandon it. They have, of course, not said so. In fact, almost every government in the world constantly proclaims its commitment to humanitarianism. But, even after the experiences of the twentieth century, governments in the new century do not act on the basis of the humanitarian conscience as they should and as they have acted at other times.

The world paid dearly for this on September 11, 2001. If governments do not change their attitudes, we will pay even more dearly and for much longer than a day.

The book tells how we got where we are today, after a century and a half of modern humanitarian action. I will describe how the humanitarian conscience arose, how it showed itself and how we risk abandoning it. I will also describe the problems that it faces and will suggest some steps to overcome them.

I will present the record of humanitarian action over 150 years, concentrating on the last few decades, and will write about the people and the organizations that perform the work. I will sometimes go into detail to illustrate particular points and will at other times paint with a broader brush. I cannot cover everything but will describe what I believe matters most. I will try to give the reader a sense for the humanitarian experience and show where it has succeeded, where it has fallen short and why.

I will end with very concrete proposals. The world, especially the West, does not need more humanitarian speeches. It needs to take very specific steps that will express the humanitarian conscience, advance the humanitarian response to tragedy and save lives and societies.

I have lived and worked in both the world of humanitarian action and the world of strategic thought. Many people believe that these two worlds are doomed to eternal mutual opposition. I do not believe that, and this book will show why.

I offer my deep thanks to the Ford Foundation for a generous grant that made it possible for me to dedicate the time and effort necessary for writing this book. Susan Berresford, the President of the Foundation, and Mary McClymont, then the Senior Director of the Peace and Social Justice Program at the Foundation and now President of InterAction, made it possible, giving me not only financial but also intellectual support.

A number of persons have contributed facts, ideas and comments, and some have read the manuscript and offered helpful suggestions. Without them, I would have faltered and perhaps failed. I owe them thanks as well. The main ones have been Pamela Aall, Kofi Asomani, Omar Bakhet, James Bishop, John Borton, Claire Bourgeois, Margie Buchanan-Smith, Dawn Calabia, Patrick Cronin, Robert DeVecchi, William Durch, John Fredriksson, Hans-Peter Gasser, Douglas Hunter, Jacques Klein, Ruud Lubbers, Brunson McKinley, Dennis McNamara, Edward Mortimer, Poul Nielson, James Purcell, Mercedes Rose, Christopher Russell, Daniel Serwer, Frank Sieverts, Richard Solomon, Shashi Tharoor, Sergio Vieira de Mello, George Ward, Roy Williams, Roger Winter and Mary Ann Wyrsch. They deserve credit for any strengths this book may have but no blame for its flaws.

I especially thank my wife Sally for the patient and unstinting support that made everything possible.

For Cameron

THE CLASH OF PRINCIPLES

THE WORLD TODAY FACES A CLASH between two irreconcilable principles.

One principle, that of the humanitarian conscience, has its origins in the ideals of Greek, Roman and Medieval philosophers as well as in the beliefs of the great world religions.

The other principle, that of absolute sovereignty, has its origins in the nationalist doctrines laid down by the kings of England, France and Spain over 500 years ago.

The humanitarian conscience and those who serve it have helped tens of millions of people to survive the brutal wars and political upheavals of the modern world. Every day they jointly affirm the right of individuals to receive protection and support.

For their part, sovereigns dismiss the humanitarian conscience. Instead, they have always mobilized massive power in the search for glory, and they still do.

This seems an uneven struggle, with the sovereigns seemingly stronger, but it is not. For even the most powerful states must recognize that they cannot violate the humanitarian conscience without paying a price. That has, paradoxically, become ever more true even as national power appears to have grown.

The two principles can sometimes be reconciled. But right now they are not. That is why Americans and others feel insecure, for the clash of principles led to the tragedy of September 11, 2001, and to much of what has gone wrong since then.

The modern humanitarian movement arose after national abuses of sovereignty became even more extreme than usual during the middle of the nineteenth century.

Caring men and women found ways to protect at least some of their fellow humans from the gruesome catastrophes perpetrated by sovereigns.

Those men and women combined idealistic principles with practical sense. They wanted to change the world but they did not ignore the reality in which they lived.

The humanitarians could not abolish the state. But they fought tenaciously to force or to persuade states to change their ways and to respect human existence even in the midst of carnage.

The humanitarians had a stubborn persistence. They faced the horror of war and destruction every day. But they built an architecture of laws and institutions to express and implement their convictions. Over decades of war and tragedy, they mobilized thousands of organizations and tens of thousands of humanitarian workers to help men, women and children in over a hundred states all over the world.

The humanitarians had major successes, especially during the second half of the twentieth century after the horrors of the two world wars. Many Western states saw it in their interest to support humanitarian action during the Cold War.

After the end of the Cold War, however, and contrary to widespread hopes, states that had supported humanitarian action turned away. They said the right things but did not do the right things. Humanitarian principles and the humanitarian conscience found themselves on the defensive, whether in the Balkans, throughout Africa or all along the vast southern arc of the Eurasian heartland from the Middle East to the two Koreas.

States, and especially the states of the West, became ever more ambivalent. They continued to support humanitarian agencies and refugees. But they cut their support steadily. Moreover, they failed to deal with the crises that had caused humanitarian emergencies in the first place.

Humanitarian agencies and humanitarian helpers could still carry out a humanitarian response, but the states that claimed to support them did not put humanitarian purposes high on their own agendas. They ignored the humanitarian conscience and they let countless millions and entire societies suffer. They wanted the humanitarian organizations to repair the damage, but that was not always possible.

The terrorist attacks on the World Trade Center towers and the Pentagon on September 11, 2001, represented a massive failure of states neglecting the humanitarian conscience. The attacks exacerbated the dilemma facing the world and especially the United States.

The September 11 attacks actually made humanitarian action and humanitarian principles more essential then ever. But the states responded by raising questions about the relevance of the humanitarian conscience in the age of terror.

The rulers of the sovereign states may, therefore, continue to turn their backs on the humanitarian conscience. If they do, they will fail to build the world order they want. They will, in fact, destroy that world order.

The world will sink into chaos as states become ever more powerful but ever less secure.

We face a silent, invisible emergency that Western publics do not even recognize except when one or another crisis boils over and American or other Western soldiers get killed in Afghanistan, Iraq or elsewhere. But we must face it, for it will continue to disrupt our lives and our safety.

Traditional meanings of sovereignty have become irrelevant after September 11. If the states want to survive and prosper, they must introduce the humanitarian conscience into their policies as a fundamental goal, not as an afterthought.

Every political crisis inevitably leads, sooner or later, to a humanitarian emergency. By the same token, every humanitarian emergency leads, sooner or later, to a political crisis. All too often, the humanitarian emergency becomes a humanitarian tragedy. States must make real efforts to solve both the political problems and the humanitarian emergencies. They cannot really solve one without the other, and they usually cannot solve either without help. They do not need to surrender their sovereignty. But they must moderate it and learn when not to proclaim it as their governing principle.

Humanitarian action cannot become a makeup kit, hiding reality. It must be central to what the states do.

Some U.S. officials have taken to interpreting the Greek philosopher Plato's notion of the philosopher king to buttress their concept of absolute sovereignty and the free right to use force. But Aristotle and other philosophers and religious teachers—as well as Plato himself—proclaimed humanism, not state sovereignty as these officials like to interpret it. The philosophers helped to found and to expand the existence of the humanitarian conscience, and that part of their teaching also deserves a careful hearing (chapter 2).

Humanitarian action and the humanitarian conscience have truly transformational power. The world can neither ignore nor neglect them.

This book will begin by showing what humanitarians do today. It will then review how humanitarian action has changed the world over the past century and a half, and especially during the Cold War. It will conclude by stating what the West must do now, not only for the humanitarian conscience but for Western and global safety and survival in the age of terror.

Most of all, the book will show that the West and the world have more at stake in the humanitarian conscience than their leaders may realize.

ONE

HUMANITARIANS AT WORK

CARLOS CACERES-COLLAZO, AN AMERICAN LAWYER who had hoped to save the lives of others, suddenly found his own life in danger. He and two colleagues, Samson Aregahegn from Ethiopia and Pero Simyndza from Croatia, could hear soldiers of the advancing Indonesian militia shouting for their death.

They had come to help refugees in Timor, a large island near the coast of Australia. The refugees had fled East Timor to escape the punishment that Indonesian militia were meting out to those who had dared to vote for independence from Indonesia.

The East Timorese had been promised a chance to vote freely in August, 1999, for or against independence. But when the overwhelming majority chose independence, the militia had gone on a rampage. With the support and connivance of the Indonesian military, they had slaughtered over 1,000 East Timorese and had incinerated almost every building. Within a few days, they had emptied the capital city of Dili. Many people had fled to West Timor, where they hoped to find safety.

Carlos Caceres-Collazo and his two colleagues worked for Mrs. Sadako Ogata, the United Nations High Commissioner for Refugees (UNHCR). She had sent them to try to arrange protection for the refugees so that they would be safe in West Timor and could later freely return to their home towns and villages. Caceres-Collazo had come to help argue that the refugees should be left in peace on the basis of important international legal conventions and should be able to go back when they wanted. The two others had been sent to help arrange food relief for the refugees.

But the Indonesian militia wanted to kill anybody who helped refugees. And so they came after the three men.

Caceres-Collazo had time to send a quick e-mail that the militia were "on their way" and that "we sit here like bait, unarmed, waiting for the wave to hit."[1] Those were the three men's last words to the outside world.

After they had killed the three, the militia searched every house where any United Nations or other relief worker had been staying. Fortunately, all had fled.

Nine months later, in May, 2001, an Indonesian court pronounced a verdict of guilty on the six militia members who had killed the three UNHCR humanitarians. Although the six expressed no regret, the court sentenced them to mild prison terms of only 10 to 20 months. Ogata labeled the sentences a "mockery" that was "deeply disturbing."[2] But other militia received equally mild punishment, with many killers walking away scot-free.

The three were not the only humanitarians who had to reckon with the risk of death. Even as the lenient verdict was pronounced against their killers, six members of an International Red Cross relief team were killed in the Congo. Two were women: Rita Fox, a Swiss citizen, and Véronique Saro, a Congolese. The men were Julio Delgado from Colombia and three more Congolese, Aduwe Boboli, Jean Molokabonde and Unen Ufoirworth.[3] They had been trying to help Congolese and Rwandan refugees caught in the middle of a civil war in northeastern Congo.

Fred Cuny, a well-known American humanitarian relief worker who had saved literally thousands of lives during various crises in Africa, the Balkans and elsewhere, also paid for his efforts. He disappeared without a trace in the snowy mountains of Chechnya on March 31, 1995. Neither he nor his remains have ever been found, despite massive search efforts by his family and others.

Cuny had been labeled "the man who tried to save the world" and had probably done more than anyone else to call attention to the humanitarian crisis in the Russian province fighting for freedom. He had entered Chechnya to help those trapped in the war. Russian and Chechen civilian or military officials to this day deny any knowledge of what might have happened to him.[4]

The list goes on. The Taliban in Afghanistan had nothing but contempt for the United Nations (U.N.) and for agencies trying to bring relief and support to the citizens of Afghanistan. On July 20, 1998, Taliban members killed Muhammad Habibi, who had been helping refugees as a member of the UNHCR office in Kabul, and Mohammed Bahsaryar, another Afghan who had been bringing food on behalf of the United Nations World Food Program (WFP).[5]

The Setting; the Risks; the Purpose

Humanitarian workers risk death whenever they enter war zones to help the hungry, the homeless, the dispossessed, the wounded and the dying. And they risk it ever more frequently because they now need to go to ever more places in the midst of war. Front lines have become blurred if indeed they exist at all.

Almost 200 United Nations relief workers lost their lives during the decade of the 1990s, when the world was supposed to be safer after the end of the Cold War. Because governments take no responsibility for relief workers, no government investigates the murders closely. Only one of every ten cases involving the violent death of a U.N. relief worker is ever solved.[6] The killers rarely suffer any punishment.

Many of the humanitarian workers who have been killed did not even work directly for the United Nations but worked for voluntary agencies that helped the United Nations. Some of those agencies, such as Catholic Relief Services and World Vision, now train their relief workers in special conflict zone survival tactics.[7] All agencies have become more cautious. But, like soldiers, humanitarians cannot do their jobs without facing risk. And they must often go where soldiers do not.

This is the world of the humanitarian, a world both old and new, constantly changing and never at rest. A world known to most Americans and Westerners only in occasional newspaper or television photos of war, massacre or famine, but very real to those who are in it.

At any given moment, as many as 65,000–75,000 civilian professionals work full-time in the middle of crises on various humanitarian tasks, whether protection, relief, post-conflict reconciliation or rehabilitation. They receive headquarters support from at least an equal number of administrative, legal and logistical officials, making a total of perhaps 150,000 or more full-time civilian humanitarians. Since the end of the Cold War, tens of thousands of soldiers have been supporting humanitarian operations in peacekeeping roles. They help to bring the total of persons engaged directly or indirectly in humanitarian operations to perhaps 250,000 civilians and military operating full-time in over 100 different states. Tens of thousands of other civilians perform humanitarian tasks on a part-time basis.[8]

The number of 65,000–75,000 civilian professionals working in humanitarian crisis zones may not seem large in a world population of billions, but it represents the equivalent of what four to six U.S. Army divisions could put on line at any given moment in a ground combat operation. Few national armies can match it with their forces.

The Soviet dictator Josef Stalin once asked rhetorically and scornfully: "How many divisions has the Pope?" He might be impressed to know that the international humanitarian community has as many divisions as it does. And those divisions, unlike many current Western military forces, do not hesitate to go into danger.

Richard Holbrooke, the former U.S. Ambassador to the United Nations, in 2000 described the Saint Demetrius bridge between the Serb and Albanian sectors of the Kosovo city of Mitrovica as the most dangerous bridge in the world. Yet Claire Bourgeois, a French woman working for the U.N. High Commissioner for Refugees, crossed the bridge almost every day at that time in an easily targetable white Land Rover. She was helping to shield Albanians living in Serb ethnic areas and Serbs living in Albanian ethnic areas, earning both the enmity and the gratitude of both groups. If she was afraid, she did not show it.

Humanitarians have come to recognize their world with painful familiarity:

- The barren, often empty, land, whether in Afghanistan, Sudan, Somalia, Eritrea or Angola.
- The roofless, often charred, houses, whether in Bosnia, Chechnya or Nicaragua.
- The red clay or brown mud trails called roads, whether in Cambodia or Uganda.
- The triple canopy jungle, whether in Colombia or Rwanda.
- The snow-blocked mountain passes, whether in Bosnia, Kurdistan or Afghanistan.
- The flies, the mosquitoes, the roaches and the scorpions everywhere.
- The low-rent rooms in the big cities where asylum seekers huddle, whether in Frankfurt, London or New York.
- And, all too often, weather that is either too hot or too cold, with people suffering from drought or from freezing.

In those settings, the humanitarians can see those they have come to help:

First, they see the children, always many more than one expects. They often cry. They sometimes, but rarely, play. Mainly, they look, trying to understand what is happening to them and to their world and to their parents if those parents are still alive and around. And they try to hang on to something, anything, that might protect them.

Many children are ill, undernourished or crippled. They have stepped on mines and they walk on one leg with a makeshift crutch. They have become accustomed to sleeping within a hollow in the earth or very close together for warmth. They have also become accustomed to living by the dozen or more in a room—if there is a room.

Then, the old. They say little, if anything. They rarely look around. Instead, they look at nothing in particular. They huddle silently and move as little as possible, saving their strength, and they seem very thin and very tired.

The women, in contrast, are usually much too busy. They are often looking for their children or, if they are lucky, trying to care for them. They appear overwhelmed, as they almost always are. They look first for any medical tent that they should visit with the children. They also look for the food line or for any other line in which they should be standing to get relief or clothing. They live at the outer edge of anxiety, exhaustion and despair, often famished and cold because they give their food allotment and their warm clothes to their children.

Some men may be around as well, but not as many. Few of those in any humanitarian camp are ablebodied and healthy. For those must be elsewhere, either fighting or trying to protect whatever may be left of their land or of their possessions. They are too proud or too independent to be comfortable in camp or relief surroundings. Only the old, the sick or the lame stay in the camps for more than a few days unless they cannot go anywhere else.

One cannot help but notice the eyes. They reflect exhaustion and fear. If they meet the eyes of any humanitarian helper, they look either pleading or hopeful at any sign of attention. And the eyes are often closed. Or they appear to be turned inward, seeing nothing that they do not absolutely need to see for survival.

Then one notices the other relief workers. In the tropics, they wear shorts and light blouses, jeans that have become shapeless over time, or faded safari suits. In the highlands, they wear bulky sweaters and jackets. Nothing that will need cleaning or care. They all too often live where there are no houses, no doors, no beds, no showers, no toilets, no comforts and very little sleep.

Some, middle-aged, have seen it all before. Tanned, even in winter, from long exposure to the sun and the air, they try to get things organized. They give quiet instructions or bark out orders. They help where they can and try to straighten out the mess around them. They complain that nothing is where it should be and that supplies have not arrived on time—as indeed they never have. But they go on.

Few have become cynical, though all might well have. They act and think as if everything will work out. Like old army sergeants, they know that not everybody around them will still be alive in a week. But they do not speak of it.

Many have become "ex-pats," or expatriates, who long ago left either England or Germany or Denmark or Australia or India or Japan or Minnesota or Massachusetts or California or wherever they once thought they belonged. They do go home from time to time, but many have moved almost permanently to Geneva or to wherever their organization's headquarters may be.

Humanitarians spend much of their time in what they call "the field," which can be anywhere in the world, although some work at agency headquarters in Geneva, New York, Atlanta, London, Tokyo, Islamabad, Nairobi or elsewhere. Many even prefer the field because they can help real people instead of filling out forms, wearing suits and ties, attending meetings and soliciting funds.

Some of the Western humanitarian workers are young Americans, Europeans, Canadians, Scandinavians or Australians, just out of school or college, often on their first or second job. They show enthusiasm and genuine concern. They try to help. They do not mind the heat or the cold or the vermin or the disease around them, but they do mind the tragedy of what they see.

A few suffer burnout after one or two tours in the field, having seen too much pain and too much death too early in their lives. But most are able to continue, believing that the help they offer can alleviate the suffering they witness.

Most are not Westerners. They may be African, whether Kenyan, Ethiopian or Nigerian. They may be Asian, perhaps Indian, Thai, Pakistani, Japanese or Indonesian. Many come from the Middle East, be they Jordanian, Egyptian, Israeli or Turkish. Some come from Latin America. Many are local hires or belong to a local organization. They increasingly fill the humanitarian ranks with a kind of multiculturalism that did not exist in the decades right after World War II but that has helped to make the relief organizations more understanding of what they face.

Often, in peacekeeping operations, soldiers from many countries may temporarily become humanitarians. They wear many different uniforms, be they American, British, French, Nigerian, Scandinavian, Indian, Pakistani, Jordanian or from any one of dozens of different states.

The peacekeeping forces often wear heavy armored jackets weighing up to 40 pounds to protect themselves from small-arms fire or bombs and to protect those who sent them from criticism. They try to keep order. These military humanitarians represent a new but growing category, with relatively few deployed during the Cold War but many more since its end.

All get around in the well-known four-wheel vehicles that can go wherever needed: ambulances, Land Rovers, trucks, or whatever one can find or scavenge. And in some crises, as in Bosnia, Kosovo or Afghanistan, armored personnel carriers.

The vehicles have foot-high black letters stenciled on their sides and backs, such as ICRC, INTERFET, IOM, IRC, ISAF, KFOR, MSF, SFOR, UN, UNHCR, UNICEF, WFP, etc.[9] They reflect the alphabet soup of humanitarian agencies or of military commands supporting humanitarian action. Those letters once offered protection but they have recently become targets as well.

Those who have served in humanitarian crises know all those initials and many others by heart. For all the major agencies appear in any crisis, especially at the beginning. Some have symbols, like sheltering or giving hands or a large red cross or red crescent, to help show who they are and what they do.

Humanitarian Care

In all these settings, what do the humanitarians do?

More than can be asked and yet less than is needed.

Most important, they try to offer immediate help: clean water, food, shelter, medicine, safety.

As soon as possible, they try to find out who is who and where they come from, and whether they know where their families might be. They try to register everybody and to let others know where they are, perhaps by sending messages or letters or calls for help.

They also try to protect new arrivals, either from those who might attack them because they fled or from those who want to send them back. They especially try to shield them from those who want to recruit them to return and fight.

They work with local authorities, trying to arrange for land or resources for refugees and other displaced persons. They try to get the police to respect the rights of those whom the police have captured or those the police want to expel. They try to prevent gangs from seizing food supplies and they try to get things done without paying bribes. They often need their headquarters to appeal to a central government, if that central government has any authority where they are. If not, they negotiate as best they can to save their charges from death, rape or capture. Even when the central government supports the humanitarian cause, nothing comes easy.

At the beginning, the humanitarians usually find themselves totally overwhelmed. They drive or run from place to place, from group to group, constantly behind the needs.

All too often, they have nothing to offer except their support. Food, water, clothing and building materials always seem to arrive at the wrong time or at the wrong place or in the wrong form. Lots of things are "on the way" but not yet available, especially during the rainy season or the winter months. And there is never enough money to do what needs to be done.

Humanitarians often do not work in camps but in towns. They need to find people who were lost long ago. Or they go to hospitals or to prisons. Or they protect people from mobs of different ethnic groups. They carry letters to or from families. Sometimes they can deliver the letters and wait for replies. Sometimes, not.

At other times, they write letters themselves. Either to their own home offices, asking others to review files of the dead and missing to try to unite families or at least to let them write to each other. Or they enter names onto paper pads or laptop computers to sort them and pass them on. Or they may write to tell families what they do not want to read.

The humanitarians especially hate some kinds of days. When there is too little to do because there is nothing that can be done. There may be no food or medicine. Or an asylum application has not yet been approved. Some wounded may die. Some may live. Everybody waits.

Humanitarians do not work without authority. They act on the basis of a large collection of international treaties and conventions termed humanitarian law, the laws of war or refugee law. They follow widely accepted principles of relief and rehabilitation. The laws and principles apply in war, in other forms of conflict, in flight or in asylum situations. The rules protect civilian victims of conflict but also protect soldiers. They govern behavior in many crisis situations. They overlap human rights law in some instances but stand mainly on their own.[10]

Under those laws, and under the humanitarian principles and standards that have grown up over 150 years of humanitarian action, the humanitarians try to relieve suffering. Whether the suffering is physical, from wounds, illness, or hunger, or whether it is deeper, from loss of children, loss of wife or husband, loss of other family or friends, or loss of home and country and identity.

They can do some things very well. They can usually relieve hunger and thirst once food and water arrive. They can hand out medicines, give injections, ease dysentery, provide sanitation. They can take names and addresses and try to find relatives. They can provide building materials.

They try to provide security. They can offer some physical protection in a camp. They can try to prevent rival gangs or clans from killing each other in or around the camps. They try, often successfully but sometimes not, to block local terrorist attacks or pressures. They try to enforce some rules of behavior. They try to provide legal protection more than physical protection. They sometimes get military or police support, but all too often they are defenseless.

Military humanitarians do provide physical protection. They prevent hostile groups from attacking those who want to meet for reconciliation. They make sure that election sites are functioning. They may shield a minority that is under threat. They may protect the homes or the churches of that minority. Or they may walk some threatened families to grocery stores, to church or to school.

The soldiers could often use protection as well. Almost 600 military peacekeepers were killed between 1948, when U.N. peacekeeping began, and early 2003. Keeping the peace can sometimes be as dangerous as fighting a war.

But both the civilian and the military humanitarians have their limits. They cannot rebuild shattered lives. They cannot bring back the dead, although they can often help to reunite the living.

Nor can humanitarians act on a government's behalf. They cannot release a prisoner of war or a person falsely accused. They cannot let a refugee stay in a foreign country. They are not even fully in control of the camps that they may administer.

The humanitarians do not command. The politicians do that, sometimes to good effect and sometimes to horrible effect. The humanitarians follow, trying to undo or to repair the damage that others have done. And to save what can be saved.

To say "humanitarian action" or "humanitarian care," therefore, is to speak of many things in many places and with many people. But they have one thing in common: the humanitarian conscience, the wish to help people who fear for their lives, for their families and for their future.

Theirs is a hopeless task in many ways. Yet a deeply rewarding one.

Even as they help others, the humanitarians have a war of their own to fight. That war is not against one or another state. Nor is it against any particular group. It is against the mindset that human beings do not matter in war or crisis, that they are expendable instruments to be used, abused and cast away rather than helped and sheltered.

Humanitarians have fought that war for centuries. They will not win it in a day or in a week or in a year or even in a decade. Sometimes, like now, they appear to be losing. But the humanitarians do not surrender.

The war began a long time ago, in the realms of philosophy, religion and law.

TWO

FROM NATURAL RIGHTS
TO NATIONAL RIGHTS

FRED CUNY, LIKE CARLOS CACERES-COLLAZO or Véronique Saro or others like them, may not have realized that their service and their sacrifice followed rules and principles that had first emerged in ancient Greece and Rome. They lived—and died—in the present, but their ideals had first found voice more than two thousand years ago in the Greek philosophers Socrates, Plato and Aristotle.

Greek philosophers had originated the concept of natural right. They believed that man was by nature a social being and that the state of nature was a social state. In that state of nature, natural right and natural law prevailed. Humans had to act in accordance with the principles of nature in order to function in harmony with society and with their inner social being.[1]

Natural Law: From Aristotle to Aquinas

The Greek philosophers linked natural right to the ideal political society. Natural right would prevail in that society. The order of nature would combine with the order of justice to produce a perfect environment for all men and women to live in harmony.

Normally, the philosophers believed, people would act in ways that preserved civil society and civic virtue. They would find peace, tranquility and security as rewards. Justice would prevail. All would exercise restraint, following rules that reflected and protected natural and universal rather than sectarian or destructive values.

To Aristotle, rights did not arise out of human law but out of nature. Justice existed in nature, not only in society. He and Plato believed that humans had a being independent of state authority. All were equal, and their mutual relationships did not depend on a state. Within a system of universal justice, an individual had his or her own place. And thus the law of nature applied, at one and the same time, both universally and individually.[2]

Greece fell and Rome rose in its place as the core of Western civilization. From the time before Jesus Christ until almost the middle of the first millennium, the Roman Empire ruled what most Europeans then considered the entire world. Rome set universal standards and universal rules.

The Roman philosopher Marcus Tullius Cicero shared the ideals and ideas of the Greek philosophers. He believed that all human law had to conform to a natural concept of justice and that morality existed above politics. To him, as to the Greeks, the law of nature was also the law of reason. Together, those laws ranked higher than the laws of a city or of a state. When the latter laws did not conform to the laws of reason, the city or the state would fall.

For Cicero, universal justice transcended all. Persons living in different political systems should and would share common values and common rules. Although Cicero himself had to take poison because he opposed the rise of the Roman emperors, his thinking gradually permeated the legal principles of the Roman Empire. Increasingly, Roman law tried to mirror the ideals of natural law.[3]

When Alaric, the ruler of the Visigoths, sacked Rome in the year 410, he doomed Europe to darkness and confusion. Plundering hordes roamed the continent from east to west and north to south, killing, raping, looting and pillaging. The civilized society introduced by Greece and Rome faded as Europe became a tangled mass of competing warlords. The Dark Ages began, and were to last for centuries.

Some institutions, yearning for the kind of stable order once imposed by imperial Rome, tried to establish new frameworks for civilization and society even as chaos prevailed all around them. The Catholic Church, seen as the universal church, set a common framework of faith, reason and organization. The papacy in Rome tried to hold Christendom together, combining a spiritual mission and a common order of humanity. Catholic philosophers tried to set universal norms. Philosophers linked with the Catholic Church looked again at natural law and natural rights.

St. Augustine, writing at the beginning of the fifth century, merged Platonic and Aristotelian thought with Catholicism. He linked the heavenly city of God with the earthly city of Rome, giving the Pope authority over the temporal as well as the spiritual realm. Natural law joined with religious law, striving to unite the fractured lands of Europe under common norms of thought, belief and action.

Other civilizations had advanced even earlier concepts of a higher order and of universal law. The Chinese philosopher Meng-tzu believed that governments needed to conform to the noble principles of human nature and to the well-being of their people in order to retain what he termed "The Mandate of Heaven." King Hammurabi of Babylon believed in universal principles of justice and developed a legal code to guide and govern ethical behavior.[4]

The notions of humanism and of natural law and universal principles voiced by Greek, Roman, European and other philosophers seized the imagination of those who heard them. Those notions responded—and still respond—to deeply felt human wishes for a community of peace, order and tranquility. They had a powerful idealistic impact in a chaotic world.

But they did not prevail, especially in Europe. The rules of natural law envisaged by St. Augustine could not protect the people of Europe against the armies ravaging the continent. The people needed to find a governing authority to do that.

The Emperor Charlemagne tried at the end of the eighth century A.D. to establish such a governing authority. He founded the empire of the Franks, an empire that covered the part of Europe that now includes France, Belgium, Luxembourg, western Germany and northern Italy. Charlemagne, who called himself the "most serene, Augustus, crowned by God, great and pacific emperor, governing the Roman Empire," wanted to create a united Europe under a single temporal ruler to complement the spiritual authority of the Pope. To establish and to protect Europe, he fought along his southern border against the Moors who were then advancing into Spain after the death of Mohammed. He also fought along his eastern border against marauding tribes from central and eastern Germany.

Charlemagne's work did not long outlive him. His heirs divided the empire. The core of Europe split into hundreds of petty entities ruled by local lords. The land and the people remained divided into myriad pieces, in a society and an economy based on agriculture and livestock. Nothing happened without some feudal master's consent, no matter how large or small the realm of that particular lord.[5]

The philosophers of the Middle Ages tried to bring reason into this chaotic world. Often working and writing in monasteries, they expanded on the original Greek and Roman concepts of natural law and natural right. Saint Thomas Aquinas, writing during the thirteenth century, declared natural law to be universally valid, universally obligatory and linked to the divine. He endorsed St. Augustine's belief that the natural law was "written in the hearts of men" and could not be blotted out.[6]

Aquinas believed and wrote that men and women were religious creatures as well as social creatures, and that natural law linked them not only with a perfect social order but with a sublime and overarching order of God. Rules did not need to be specifically ordained. The human mind could understand and appreciate that civil society needed universally given and accepted mandates of behavior. Men and women would act according to those principles.

Aquinas thus gave natural right and natural law the highest possible authority. He also gave them a reach that went beyond any temporal rule, for all men and women had to obey natural law and respect natural right.

But the philosophy of Aquinas, like that of his predecessors, did not prevail. Even as he wrote of a natural law that transcended human law, the world of a universal church collapsed. Secular lords, and especially kings, began to gather greater power. They claimed a more immediate authority than the Pope's. They not only rejected universal natural law but imposed their own separate laws. They fought each other for land, wealth and power.

The mercenaries and vassals whom the kings and lords called upon to fight their wars acted as brutally as they could. They served any master but they mainly served themselves. They postured fiercely but engaged sparingly. They heaped suffering mainly on innocent civilians who could not resist. They based their tactical movements not on strategic goals but on the search for places that had not yet been looted dry. They sacked, pillaged and stole whatever they could and wherever they could. They seized food, ornaments, cattle, slaves, women and anything else that they could take. Entire armies formed and melted away according to the wealth of their master and the plunder that he and his soldiers could amass.[7]

The ever-expanding arts of war demanded ever greater resources. The feudal lords could not protect their lands or even their castles against such new weapons as the musket and the cannon. New fighting units of hundreds and even thousands of armed men could attack and destroy castles and cities. Wars became ever larger and more deadly, and they could only be won by those who had greater resources than the traditional feudal masters.

The peasants and the townspeople had no protection. Some rulers and Catholic bishops tried to introduce what they called "the Peace of God" or "a truce of God" to protect noncombatant civilians, but they had little success. Soldiers, usually unpaid, had to attack peasants to get food; they had to attack merchants and markets to get booty. Avoiding battles with opposing armies, they preferred to sack farms and towns in order to survive.[8]

During the Hundred Years' War, which continued from 1337 to 1453, both English and French continually raided the other's farms and towns on what is now French soil. The kings on both sides increasingly saw such raids as part of a strategic plan. One English captain, Sir John Fastolf, even recommended a deliberate strategy of targeting towns and farms instead of wasting time, lives and resources attacking enemy troops or fortified installations.[9]

Honoré Bouvet, prior of a Benedictine monastery in southern France around 1389, recognized as well as challenged this reality in his book *L'Arbre des Battailles:*

> If, on both sides, war is decided and begun by the councils of the two kings, the soldiery may take spoils from the kingdom at will and make war freely; and if sometimes the humble and innocent suffer harm and lose their goods, it cannot be otherwise. . . . Valiant men and wise, however, who follow arms should take pains, so far as they can, not to bear hard on simple and innocent folk, but only on those who make and continue war, and flee peace.[10]

The attacks on unarmed civilians provoked an angry but powerless reaction, especially among the French who suffered the greatest depredations from English armies that roamed the countryside. People protested in writings and demonstrations. But they could do little.

The great humanist Erasmus, surveying the scene, wrote in disgust that *"Dulce bellum inexpertis"* (War is sweet to those who do not know it).

The Sovereigns: Henry VIII and Louis XIV

Kings and their sovereign states took over and expanded the range of warfare. The kings first established their authority over their own subjects and then tried to establish that authority over any others they could conquer.

England, being an island and thus less subject to foreign invasion than a continental nation, in the thirteenth and fourteenth centuries became the first state to develop a national government, under the rule of the Plantagenets and later of the Tudors.

France followed within a century. Only a king commanding national resources could pull together the forces needed to fight off the English invaders during the Hundred Years' War.

During the reign of Ferdinand and Isabella and after Christopher Columbus had discovered the Americas, Spain became the next national state in the late fifteenth and early sixteenth centuries.

Sweden and Russia and other states joined the new club, as did some of the smaller European countries. Only Italy and Germany had to wait until after the middle of the nineteenth century.

Henry VIII made clear to the Pope when he divorced his queen and instituted his own church that kings and their armies were putting an end not only to the Roman and the feudal systems but to any universal concept of law. The new sovereignty of the monarch could brook no restraint of any kind and certainly no universal principles that the king found inconvenient. English nationalism rang more immediately attractive than universal principles, no matter how much those principles might appeal to a common humanity.

The principles that Plato and Aristotle had espoused in ancient Greece and that Cicero, St. Augustine and St. Thomas Aquinas had carried forward to Rome and beyond could not survive the physical power of the kings' challenge, especially as the kings claimed divine right for themselves.

Four European political philosophers challenged universal notions and instead justified the new national states and governments that the kings were forming.

Niccolò Machiavelli, the Florentine administrator and philosopher who lived from 1469 to 1627, rejected the notion of an idealist order of society or of natural law. In his main work, *The Prince,* he accepted neither an ideally nor a divinely ordained world order. Instead, he described a world of constant struggle in which one had to prevail to survive. Men and women acted as they had to act within such a world, not as they might choose to act in a perfect world. An immoral world justified immoral means.

Thomas Hobbes, the English philosopher who wrote his major works more than a hundred years after Machiavelli, went even further. He rejected Plato's and Aristotle's notion that men and women by nature inclined toward society. He rejected even more categorically Thomas Aquinas' notion that such a society reflected the will of God. Instead, he wrote, people chose society because it was better than the brutish state of nature. In his main work, *Leviathan,* he proclaimed that only a powerful national sovereign could bring peace to his people and that he could do so only through military conquest and dictatorial rule. The subjects had an obligation as well as an interest to obey a ruler and a state. Reversing the Greek and Roman priorities, Hobbes argued that even a tyrannical ruler was better than the state of nature.

Another English philosopher, John Locke, softened the edges of Hobbes' argument. He did not describe the mythical state of nature in the same murderous terms that Hobbes had used. Instead, he defined it as "an ill condition" to be avoided, but not at all cost. Therefore, while supporting the concept of the nation-state, he favored limited government rather than absolute government. Civil society had superseded anarchy, but had to give its members some rights beyond self-preservation. Nonetheless, while asserting some limits on a king's powers over his own subjects, Locke placed no limits on a ruler's right to act on the basis of raw national interest. The state could behave callously abroad if not at home.

Jean Bodin, writing in France, made arguments similar to those put forth by Machiavelli and Hobbes. He particularly joined Hobbes in justifying the existence of standing armies, large forces trained and exercised continually under the rule of a national monarch.

The new kings and their new wars brought ever greater forms of human cruelty. Whether fighting for territorial, dynastic or commercial advantage, the kings wreaked destruction wherever they went. They killed, burned and looted because that was the way they fought and that was the way that soldiers and sailors behaved.

Violent wars raged across Europe as the continent faced both religious and political upheaval and as the new nation-states fought for position. In the Thirty Years' War (1618–1648), France and Sweden—representing the new national powers—imposed a bitter defeat upon the Papacy and the Holy Roman Empire. They devastated the center of Europe and especially the German lands over which they fought. The war killed an estimated 40 percent of Germany's population, perhaps as many as six million, and left no farm or town untouched.

The Peace of Westphalia, which ended the Thirty Years' War in a series of agreements signed in the German cities of Münster and Osnabrück in 1648, formally put an end to the Pope's and the Holy Roman Emperor's universal claims. It gave all rulers, whether kings or lords, full authority within their domains. It put an end to any hopes for a common universal order, whether of divine law or natural law. Secular rulers could decide the laws and even the religions that would govern their subjects.

The new doctrine has come down to the present as the principle of sovereignty. Under that principle, each national government has total authority within its own borders. It can do as it pleases within those borders. Any attack from any other state against or across those borders is an act of war.[11]

With the Peace of Westphalia, the states assumed power over the world. They established the far-reaching modern system based on the authority of a sovereign ruler and—later—of a sovereign government. The Peace of Westphalia formally recognized that authority and gave it legal sanction, initially in Europe and then across the world.[12] Natural law and divine law yielded to sovereignty and national law.

The Westphalian system did not prescribe how states were to deal with each other. Some eminent theoreticians thought that the modern state could and would exercise restraint, respecting other states and functioning within a system of commonly accepted laws. The Dutch philosopher Hugo Grotius believed that states would recognize that they shared an interest in cooperating within some areas even as they might fight in others. In *De Jure Belle ac Pacis,* published in 1625, before the Peace of Westphalia, he laid down foundations for an international law that could govern relations between sovereign and independent entities. He believed states would see some advantage in exercising restraint for the sake of mutually beneficial relations.

Grotius, who had experienced decades of war between Spain and the Netherlands, condemned the practice of conflict:

> War of which even barbarous nations would have been ashamed; recourse was had to arms for slight reasons, or for no reason; and when arms were once taken up, all reverence for divine and human laws was thrown away; just as if men were henceforth authorized to commit all crimes without restraint.[13]

But Grotius could not change state behavior in conflict. Whatever he or others may have thought, war became ever more the pattern of the world. And virtually each new state in western Europe began its existence by launching aggression against its neighbors and beyond.

The new nation-state fully committed itself to the systematic propagation of violence, whether by war, by the slave trade or by colonization. Most kings regarded war as their principal occupation. By expanding his realm, a king could amass more wealth for his nation, more soldiers for his army, more taxes for his government and more power, glory and resources for himself. War advanced the business of the state and of the kings.

Louis XIV, known as *Le Roi Soleil* (The Sun King), set ever higher standards, conducting a systematic campaign of killing, looting and destruction over major portions of the Holy Roman Empire. In the greatest campaign of sheer destruction since the Huns, the French army put about 1,000 towns and villages to the torch. Bodin and Hobbes, who had written that the nation-state had no restriction on its behavior abroad, had been proven right.[14] Louis XIV also originated a new concept and a new word, "refugees," by revoking his grandfather's Edict of Nantes, which had granted religious tolerance to Protestants. More than 50,000 persecuted Protestants fled and became refugees in Prussia.[15]

Men and women had left behind them the chaos and the ravages of the Dark Ages only to find the chaos and the ravages of the nation-state.

The French philosopher Abbé Saint-Pierre in the middle of the eighteenth century observed the monstrosities perpetrated by the new nation-states and predicted that change would come, but not for at least a hundred or two hundred years:

> We must endure more than a hundred years yet of war in Europe, and in consequence more than two hundred years of Sovereignty, before all rulers become fully

convinced that no League, no Alliance, can be lasting without a permanent system of arbitration, and that therefore no power can have any security . . . unless the general Association of the Sovereigns of Europe guarantees it.[16]

The American Declaration of Independence of 1776, with its famous phrase "We hold these truths to be self-evident," reflected the principle of natural law that some matters did not require logical proof because they were universally understood. But at the end of the eighteenth century the principles of universal and natural rights no longer existed in Europe except in occasional essays or speeches.[17]

Napoleon and the *Levée en Masse*

In the French Revolution, on July 14, 1789, the people of France seized control of their state. They then forever changed how France and the world would fight.

The new revolutionaries served the new ideals of "Liberty, Equality and Fraternity." War ceased to be a profession and became a cause. Although the soldiers of the revolutionary army had originally been recruited to defend the new French regime against a royalist counterrevolution from abroad, they quickly turned to the attack. The French revolution brought forth the Declaration of the Rights of Man and Citizen, extolling the worth of every individual, but it also brought forth the *Levée en Masse,* universal conscription on an unprecedented scale. From a largely professional army that might at times assemble 300,000 men under arms, France moved to a conscript army of one million.

The French army no longer belonged to the king but to the "people." And the people did not declare peace. Neither did the foreigners who feared the effects of radical new French ideas. The French revolution thus set off a period of virtually uninterrupted killing that was to last for 25 years and was to reach new levels of carnage, destruction and suffering all over Europe as far as the gates of Moscow.

Lazare Nicolas Carnot, who organized French revolutionary armies, wrote that: "We must exterminate! Exterminate to the bitter end!" He added that French armies had to *"agir en masse,"* to move with massed force so as to overwhelm by sheer force of numbers.[18]

The revolution might have put an end to royal totalitarianism but it brought forth an even fiercer breed, popular totalitarianism. Most of all, the revolution brought terror to France's neighbors. The huge French army could survive only as a mercenary army had survived: off the fat of the land and preferably of foreign land. The army had to fight abroad because no state could want or afford to keep it at home.

Napoleon Bonaparte, who became First Consul in 1799 and then Emperor after the revolution had lost its momentum, took the army ever further. He began 15 years of war against the other states of Europe and—more tellingly—against their peoples. Virtually all of Europe suffered under the French army as well as under the armies that opposed the French.

The emotions aroused by the new regimes produced some remarkable paradoxes. When Napoleon had finished his 1812–1813 campaign against Russia, his invading force of 422,000 had been reduced to an emaciated remnant of 10,000 that hobbled back to France. If any foreign ruler had been responsible for the deaths of more than 400,000 Frenchmen, all of France would have erupted in rage against him. Yet Napoleon became, and still remains, a hero in France. And no historian recorded how many civilians his army killed. Such were the popular fascinations of the sovereign revolutionary state.

Henry Dunant and the Red Cross

The new nation-states fought with ever-growing firepower throughout the nineteenth century. But soldiers remained as vulnerable as before. At the end of any battle, thousands of bodies remained on the field, dead or mutilated—sometimes beyond recognition—while groaning or screaming with pain.

The victorious army might perhaps care for its own wounded if it did not pursue the defeated enemy. But nobody cared for the losers. They were left to die, often an agonizing death that might take hours and even days to reach them in a twisted act of mercy.

A battle during the Italian war of unification was to change that. Led by Count Cavour from northern Italy and Giuseppe Garibaldi from the south, the Italians had united most of their peninsula by 1858 and had then set about to expand their realm toward the north. This brought them into war with the Emperor of Austria, the young Franz Joseph, and with forces determined to defend the Alpine regions that had been part of Austria for centuries. The Italians could not have defeated the Austrian army on their own, but they had a powerful ally in Emperor Napoleon III of France, who wanted to become a renowned military commander like his namesake.

Napoleon III and his Italian allies defeated Franz Joseph and his army in one battle after another on the north Italian plain during the early summer of 1859. Finally, in a battle that was to set the course of European history, they scored a decisive victory over the Austrian Emperor near a small village called Solferino. After a long hot day of pitched battles, the Austrian army retreated and rain turned the battlefield into a sea of mud laced with the bodies of the dead and the wounded.[19]

Henry Dunant, a young Swiss businessman from Geneva, had come to Solferino to do business with Napoleon III. He happened to arrive just as the battle had ended. He recoiled in horror at what he saw. He quickly went around to nearby towns to assemble some local doctors, nurses and volunteers in a frantic if futile effort to help the wounded. He could not forget the experience.

Two years later, Dunant wrote a small book about the battle and about what he had seen. He published it under the title *A Memoir of Solferino*, pouring into it the anguish and shock that he had felt as well as his frustration at not having been able to do more to help.

Dunant's graphic descriptions must have come as a shock to the tender sensibilities of those who had tried to shield themselves from the reality of the wars that they applauded at a safe distance. He wrote of "swollen faces, green and black," of expressions "distorted in the grip of the death-struggle," of "bodies blotched with ghastly spots, their eyes staring wildly," of heads separated from their shoulders, of limbs torn away and lying in the mud, and of open wounds seething with worms and flies. He wrote of brains spattered in every direction by the hoofs of horses galloping across the wounded. And he wrote of the swaggering contempt that the victors showed toward their helpless victims.[20]

Dunant concluded the book with an appeal for the world to take two steps:

- To form associations of volunteers who would be available to help the wounded when war broke out;
- To draw up some internationally accepted principles on the basis of which those associations could do their work.[21]

Dunant had not been the first to describe the suffering of wounded soldiers and to appeal for help. During the Crimean War (1854–1856), British journalists had described the ghastly conditions of the wounded in English military hospitals. England had sent teams of nurses led by Florence Nightingale, a woman who combined a sense of mercy for the wounded with a tough-mindedness that enabled her to win support for her hospital work not only from the London *Times* and its readers but also from the English government. Another nurse, Mary Seacole from the West Indies, performed what many wounded men described as "miracles of healing." But these nurses' work did not have the widespread public impact of Dunant's book, largely because the soldiers they helped had already reached a hospital.[22]

Two other women also raised their voices about the plight of the wounded on the battlefield. The Grand Duchess Elena Pavlovna of Russia had organized a group of 300 women, who became known as the Sisters of Mercy, to help relieve the suffering of Russian soldiers in the Crimean War. And Clara Barton, an American, became widely known as "the Angel of the Battlefield" for helping wounded soldiers during the American Civil War (1861–1865).[23]

Dunant's account of the horrors of battle shocked countless members of royal and aristocratic families as well as writers. Most important, it moved some of Geneva's prominent citizens to act. Meeting on February 9, 1863, four of them and Dunant decided to form what they called an International Committee for Relief to the Wounded. Two members of Geneva's most prominent families, General Guillaume Henry Dufour, who had himself been a prisoner of war, and Gustave Moynier, a Geneva lawyer and philanthropist, became president and vice-president of the committee, with Dunant becoming secretary.

As Dunant spoke with members of his committee and with others throughout Europe who shared his revulsion at the abominations of war, he had an even bolder thought: to create a medical personnel corps sworn to neutrality in battle and serving only to help the wounded and the dying. He also thought that they should carry special identification to distinguish them from soldiers. Dunant and his friends called a conference in Geneva to present the proposals to delegates from various European states who had shown some interest. Somewhat to Dunant's and Moynier's surprise, 16 states as well as some of Europe's main philanthropic institutions sent representatives to a planning meeting in 1863.

A more formal international conference met in Geneva in August 1864, with the same major European powers and the United States of America represented. The atmosphere remained generally friendly despite skepticism from Florence Nightingale, who wondered whether the noble intentions being expressed all around her would mean anything. Several states questioned whether neutral doctors and nurses were really needed because they had their own national medical services, but they finally accepted the spirit of the congress in favor of providing additional help for the wounded.

The conference adopted both of Dunant's ideas as well as most of the concrete proposals drafted by Moynier. Committees were to be formed to organize and offer medical services to wounded in the field. Doctors and nurses were to be neutral and were to be respected as such. The Geneva committee would coordinate the work of the others.

Louis Appia, one of the five original members of the Geneva committee, proposed that international medical personnel should wear a white band around one arm with a red cross in the middle. He suggested that design because it seemed simple and easily recognizable. It was not a Christian cross because all its arms were to be of equal length. The conference accepted that proposal. Many agreed because it had the reverse colors of the Swiss flag (a white cross on a red field) and they saw it as an honor they could pay to the Swiss for suggesting the idea.

The conferees also agreed that the volunteer doctors and nurses would not displace national military medical staff but would support their efforts. While the conference did not try to draft a formal treaty, the international representatives agreed informally on a resolution containing some basic principles that would permit neutral medical forces to operate in a battle zone.[24]

On August 22, 1864, most delegates to the conference signed the Convention for the Amelioration of the Condition of the Wounded in Armies in the Field. It became the first formal international legal agreement regulating the conduct of warfare on a humanist or humanitarian basis.

The Geneva Convention, as it often came to be known, provided for care and respect for wounded soldiers whatever their nationality. It also provided that states would honor the neutrality of ambulances, military hospitals and hospital staff. And a red cross on a white background became the universally recognized symbol, whether on a flag or on an armband, for neutral medical facilities and personnel. Twelve delegations signed. The British and Americans did not because they lacked the authority, but they did not oppose the proposal. All agreed that they had shared in a genuine breakthrough.

The conferees had achieved more than anybody could have originally expected. As Appia put it:

> To humanize war, if that is not a contradiction, is our mission. . . . Once we have voiced our undisguised rejection of war, we must take it as it is [and] unite our efforts to alleviate suffering.[25]

Appia had put his finger on the central paradox, which was to haunt the International Committee of the Red Cross (ICRC) and all that were to join in its work or in other humanitarian action even to the present: to hate war but to help those who fought it; to remain objective no matter what one might see or feel; and to preserve a spirit of humanity in the most inhumane surroundings.

Dunant's ideal sounded simple and direct, but carrying it out could become excruciatingly difficult and unimaginably tortuous. For humanitarians would have to adhere to their ideals of compassion and neutrality while violent and even cataclysmic struggle surged all around them. They were not to stop the struggle but only to try to overcome its worst effects.

Dunant's ideal also failed to address the suffering of civilians, which had actually been a greater problem over the centuries of European wars. Dunant had happened upon a battlefield and had seen the suffering of wounded soldiers. He had reacted with justifiable compassion. But civilians had often suffered even more than soldiers in the long history of war. The Geneva Convention would not help them.

The world would begin to help soldiers wounded in battle. But it had not helped the civilians who had suffered under the artillery bombardment of Sevastopol during the Crimean War. Nor would it help the civilians caught by General Tecumseh Sherman's march through Georgia during the American Civil War. It was to be a long time before any international instrument would help civilians at all. Nonetheless, helping soldiers gave humanitarian action its start.

Dunant's ideas spread far and wide. Because of growing awareness of soldiers' plight, many governments decided to act on their own even while granting the International Committee of the Red Cross significant authority. Every major state in

Europe began to establish its own national committee of the Red Cross. Many of them remained playgrounds for rich and titled dilettantes. Dukes, duchesses, counts and countesses, and even an odd prince or princess, joined the boards of the new societies. As amateurs, they could not be expected to work in field hospitals, but their involvement brought funds and support. Others worked hard to prepare for field duty or at least to collect food and medicines and clothing for their own potential casualties and perhaps even for enemy soldiers. Dunant's book had launched a movement.

The new societies and the horrors that had brought them into being did not stem the lust for conflict. Warclouds gathered over Europe. At the Paris Universal Exhibition of 1867, the German cannon-maker Krupp displayed its newest models not too far from the exhibition stands full of newly designed first aid equipment for soldiers and civilians. And the recently invented dum-dum rifle bullet, which split on impact and could turn every minor wound into a major laceration, made its way quickly into national arsenals. States were doing what they could to make war more brutal and terrible even as the Red Cross was introducing some measure of human conscience.

Dunant had brought back into international relations a small element of the spirit of universal natural law. His ideals transcended the rules of state sovereignty by appealing to a higher notion of universal humanity. They did not get very far, as they protected only one of many groups that suffered from war. But he had made an important start toward the revival of the humanitarian conscience.

Humanitarian Ideals in Practice

The Red Cross movement was to meet its first real test, the Franco-Prussian War, in 1870. As one battle followed another, and as the Prussian army advanced toward Paris, both sides began suffering heavy casualties.

The International Committee of the Red Cross met hurriedly in Geneva to decide on the steps it could take to help. Red Cross personnel began bringing to the battlefields those items on which they and others had agreed: from the simplest matters, such as medical and first aid equipment or name tags that would permit the Red Cross to identify wounded soldiers, to the most complicated, such as arrangements for the repatriation of soldiers too badly wounded to fight again. Perhaps most important, the Red Cross pioneered ways for prisoners of war to be put in touch with their families at home. Soon thousands of letters between soldiers and their families were passing through Red Cross offices in Geneva.

Dunant, Moynier and Appia had reason to believe that all their effort had borne some fruit. The Franco-Prussian War had become a successful test case for the application of the new rules of war and of the role of Red Cross societies. They learned with delight that the respective armies were, with only a few exceptions, recognizing and respecting the neutrality of Red Cross doctors and nurses. The armies were also respecting the function of an "ambulance," first used on a wide scale in the Franco-Prussian War to carry the dead, the sick and the wounded. And other national Red Cross societies came to help wherever they could, making the relief effort truly international.

The German Red Cross, relatively well organized and financed, could help its own casualties and even some of the French army's. The French Red Cross, still shaking off the top-level figureheads who complicated its operations, had some success as well. Both often played their roles with a remarkable display of neutrality even if their sympathies lay with Prussia or France. They gave signs that they wanted to take the humanitarian movement beyond national rivalry, which was not easy in the heat of battle.

Colonel Robert James Loyd-Lindsay, head of the British Red Cross, marveled that the spirit of the Geneva Convention permitted him to pass through Prussian lines to help wounded French soldiers. Dunant himself had some of his finest hours helping the sick and wounded during the siege of Paris that followed the French defeat at Sedan. He could see to his delight that the fundamentals of the Geneva Convention had held.

Moynier later said that the Red Cross had passed a "baptism of fire."[26] It had been able to help hundreds of thousands of wounded soldiers and prisoners of war, easing the burdens of the conflict not only for the soldiers but for their families. It had shown that neutral doctors and others had a role to play. It had not challenged the sovereignty of the fighting states but had brought a modest measure of international humanitarianism.

The International Committee of the Red Cross saw the Franco-Prussian War as an auspicious beginning for its mission. Dunant and Moynier and their colleagues had created institutions and rules that they could view with satisfaction and that others could view with thanks. They had plainly found a role and they had begun to establish the principle of neutrality as a respected watchword.

More important, however imperfect the success of the Red Cross might have been, its very presence could give some credibility to the humanitarian spirit that it represented. For Dunant and his movement carried more than nurses and doctors into the field. They carried the hope that the sense of a common humanity could make war, as terrible as it was, more merciful at the edges.

The next two wars showed both the limits and the possibilities of humanitarian action. Both occurred outside Europe. One reached new levels of cruelty but the other carried out the Red Cross ideal at least in part.

In the first, the Boer War in Southern Africa, the Red Cross movement came face to face with two vexing problems: first, the refusal of national forces to accept any Red Cross role; second, its lack of authority to help civilians. The war lasted from 1899 to 1902 and pitted half a million British regular forces against a much smaller Boer force and a largely Afrikaaner civilian population. To win it, the British Army introduced practices that were to mark military operations against civilian populations throughout the twentieth century.

Lord Kitchener, the British commander, chose to isolate the Afrikaaner forces and insurgents by a scorched earth policy. His army systematically burned Boer homes and farms. He built the first of what came to be known as "concentration camps" to hold captured Boers. He ordered the British Army to force thousands of Boer women and children to travel to those camps and to remain in them for the duration of the war. Many women and children died from starvation and disease on the way to the camps, and were often abandoned for weeks in railroad cars in the middle of nowhere. The camps themselves were little better, offering few facilities and little food until various English charitable societies protested to the British Parliament and forced an end to what became known by the newly minted term of "genocide."[27]

The International Committee of the Red Cross could not function in the Boer War. Lord Kitchener had no sympathy for the notion of neutrality or for any new conventions. He once tried to attach his personal military railway carriage to a Red Cross train. And the Red Cross had no authority to help the civilians who were the principal victims of British strategy and tactics. It could offer some general support and aid but it could not intervene to stop Kitchener or even to complain about his practices.

Moynier proposed an international tribunal to investigate and punish atrocities, the first time any national or international official had made such a proposal. But the proposal got nowhere against British opposition. The International Committee thus confined itself to publishing reports of British atrocities in its *Bulletin,* but it did not protest or try to encourage other protests.

The Red Cross knew very well that its mandate extended only to wounded and captured soldiers. It decided to remain within that mandate. It also had to remain neutral if it was to carry out even the limited functions for which it was authorized. Therefore, it did not intervene to put an end to the concentration camps and the inhumane practices followed there. Nor did it raise its voice to condemn Lord Kitchener's policies. The precedent of its failure to do so was to haunt the International Committee of the Red Cross well into the next century.

Within three years, however, the Red Cross ideal could claim what seemed a triumph, in the Russo-Japanese War of 1904–1905. For the Japanese Red Cross Society, based on the International Committee's principles and modeled after European

Red Cross societies, performed minor miracles in helping Japanese casualties and even more in helping Russian casualties and prisoners of war. Sponsored by the Emperor and by the full aristocracy of Japan, the Japanese society had attracted more than a million members—making it the largest in the world—and it set out to show that Japan could carry out humanitarian ideals as well as any Western nation.[28]

Tens of thousands of Russians became Japan's prisoners of war as the Russian army and navy suffered one after another major humiliation in the battles of Mukden, Port Arthur and Tsushima. Many Russians suffered from terrible wounds. The Russian Red Cross, disorganized and demoralized, could do nothing for them, leaving their fate to the Japanese military medical services and to the Japanese and International Red Cross staff. And the Japanese played their role to perfection. They saved thousands of Russian lives.

Louis Livingstone Seaman, an American military surgeon, wrote that "no prisoner of war has ever been so comfortable or so free."[29] For Japan went well beyond its obligations under the Geneva Convention. It took good care of prisoners of war and helped the Red Cross in its efforts to keep contact between the prisoners and their families. Sir Frederick Treves, a British surgeon, said that the "business-like organization" of Japanese Red Cross hospitals "is the most remarkable and efficient of its kind in the world."[30]

Gustave Moynier and the ICRC could thus enter the twentieth century with some faint glimmer of hope. They had become the first humanitarians. And the nascent international humanitarian movement, which included not only the ICRC but the national Red Cross societies, could also feel some pride and satisfaction. They could discern, not only in Europe but around the world, some early signs of what they could interpret as humanitarian understanding. They could legitimately hope that men and women might treat each other with a measure of decency even in the most horrible circumstances and the most bitter battles.

Not everything had gone as they might have hoped. Wars went on, as did killing. Not everybody followed the rules of the Geneva Convention. Armies continued to target civilians, who had no organized protection. But some consciousness of a common humanity appeared to be stirring. As the new century advanced into its second decade, there might have been at least some reason to believe that the human race might restrain its worst instincts and that nation-states would recognize that some common humanity linked even enemies.

Nothing fundamental had changed since Westphalia, however. Perhaps the ICRC and the national Red Cross societies could alleviate some suffering at the margins.

But states still controlled the international system. Those states might permit some groups to carry out harmless humanitarian activities, but only to the limited extent that the states would permit. The world had witnessed the rebirth of the common humanitarian conscience of Aristotle and the humanists. But states still monopolized the means of violence, and the coming decades were to reveal how brutally they would exercise that monopoly.

THREE

HUMANITARIAN FRUSTRATION IN TWO WORLD WARS

GAVRILO PRINCIP, A BOSNIAN SERB NATIONALIST, had the great honor to be one of the six hit men chosen to kill the Archduke Francis Ferdinand, heir to the throne of Austria-Hungary, when the Archduke paid a visit to Sarajevo on June 28, 1914. Bosnian Serbs, like many other Balkan peoples, had long fought against foreign domination, but they had fallen under Austrian rule when Austria annexed Bosnia in 1908. The Archduke's visit offered a chance to strike at the Habsburg crown.

The day began badly for the plotters. Francis Ferdinand and his staff had heard of assassination plans. They had decided to go ahead with the visit but had changed their route. The plot appeared to have failed. Four plotters did not even fire their weapons. Then, by one of those bizarre twists of fate that often dictate the course of history, the driver of the Archduke's carriage became separated from the escorting security force because not everybody had got news of the new route. Nor did the driver know the new route himself. He missed a turn and had to stop and pull back.

Princip suddenly found himself virtually face to face with Francis Ferdinand. He pulled out his pistol, fired, hit and killed the Archduke. Then, by accident, his second shot hit the Archduke's wife.

This act of terrorism shocked and galvanized Vienna. The Austrian government and public demanded revenge against its traditional Balkan enemy Serbia, although Serbia claimed that it had nothing to do with the assassination. The Austrians issued a 48-hour ultimatum full of onerous conditions. One of those conditions, a major attack on Serbian sovereignty, would have permitted Austrian intelligence agencies to enter Serbia and to have freedom of movement for a full investigation of the Archduke's assassination. Serbia could not accept all the demands and had not been expected to do so. Austria mobilized and, with encouragement from German Kaiser Wilhelm II, attacked Serbia. With that, it launched what came to be called the Great War.[1]

Within days, all of Europe was in flames. The so-called Central Powers of Germany, Austria-Hungary and Turkey fought against the so-called Entente Powers of France, Great Britain and Russia, later joined by Italy and still later by the United States of America. The war lasted four years, to be followed by a 20-year armistice and by another conflict that did not end until 1945, 31 years after the assassination of the Archduke.

Gustave Ador, the new President of the International Committee of the Red Cross, surveying the enormous armies marshaled against each other, sent out a warning to all Red Cross societies:

> From today, the Red Cross is called to an intense labor of a kind never seen before. . . .
> The needs will be immense, but the International Committee is firmly convinced that
> the charitable zeal of all our societies will rise to the necessary devotion.[2]

But neither Ador nor anybody else imagined the extent to which the labor "of a kind never seen before" would exceed all expectations held by the political leaders and the humanitarians of Europe.

Everywhere in the world, Red Cross societies got ready to help. Mabel Boardman, who had replaced Clara Barton as head of the American Red Cross, chartered what the newspapers called a "Mercy Ship" to carry 170 doctors and nurses as well as huge quantities of medical supplies to Europe. Queens, duchesses and society ladies from France, Russia, Bulgaria, Italy, Great Britain and elsewhere formed or joined organizations to support their soldiers in the field. Thousands of volunteer women rushed to help, gladly receiving training in first aid.

The Killing Trenches

Sir Thomas Longmore, the English surgeon-general, had warned on several occasions during the early 1890s that the more powerful weapons of war, with their greater speed, range, blast and penetration, would reduce the ability of doctors to come to the help of the wounded:

> Everything thus tends to show that, while the number of sufferers urgently requiring help will be vastly increased in future wars, the means of affording them shelter and surgical attention will be pushed back to a greater distance than has ever before

been necessary. If a battle is fought on a very large scale, the number of wounded men most pitifully demanding aid will be so vast that obviously the arrangements made to meet the wants . . . will be quite inadequate to future needs.[3]

Sir Thomas' prediction came true. The sovereign states worked hard to expand their capacity to kill. World War I weapons made the rifles and cannon used at Solferino look like toys. New long-range artillery could reach those who thought they were safe in their trenches, headquarters or field hospitals. The new machine guns could shred bodies by the thousands. Mines and grenades finished off any who might be left. Three quarters of a million men on both sides were killed or wounded in the battle of Verdun alone.

The poison gas first used in April 1915 became the most feared new weapon of the war. Although forbidden by the 1907 Hague Conventions in which the nations that called themselves the "civilized world" had tried to outlaw those instruments of war that they regarded as inhumane, poison gas came into frequent and deadly use by both sides.

At least 10 million soldiers lost their lives in the war, destroying the flower of European youth. Nobody bothered to count the losses among civilians, which were a great deal higher. From the official standpoint, civilian war victims did not exist. And they certainly did not matter.[4]

The demands of the war, and the hostile attitudes engendered by the war, often overwhelmed the International Committee of the Red Cross or relegated it to the sidelines. Each army had its own military medical services, although some—such as the Russian—fell far short of what their forces needed. The national military medical services did not want any international volunteers to help their own wounded soldiers.

The national civilian Red Cross societies, like their military services, disdained ICRC support. They had become larger, more competent, much more ready and able to help, and just as nationalistic as their armed forces. They no longer saw themselves as neutral humanitarians, as Henry Dunant had planned and as they had all envisioned in the early decades of the Red Cross movement. Instead, they believed that they were there to help their own forces and no others. They campaigned for funds and for volunteers with blatantly chauvinistic appeals. They did not want neutrals around, especially because neutrals would help those whom they regarded as enemies.[5] Medical care had become part of war, not to be left to outsiders.

But Gustave Ador's ICRC found a new and vitally important calling which required exactly the neutrality that it had carefully nurtured over the years: to help prisoners of war. Although it could not do much to help the wounded and to enforce the laws of war, the International Committee could play an essential role in protecting prisoners of war and in making their existence at least a little easier.

The war produced prisoners at an unprecedented pace. After only the first few battles in France, the Germans had already captured several hundred thousand French soldiers and the French had captured many Germans. Under the provisions of the Hague Convention of 1907, the ICRC set up information offices to serve as a central clearinghouse for news about prisoners. The numbers staggered the imagination. By the end of the war, opposing armies held 7 million prisoners.

Ador wanted the ICRC to count all the prisoners and to try to keep track of them in order to let their families know their fates and to arrange for news and mail to flow. Red Cross offices in Geneva soon had stacks of file cabinets reaching to the ceilings of all their offices. Hundreds, then thousands, and finally a total of 120,000 volunteers tried to keep track of all the names to make sure that they could answer letters from anxious relatives about who might or might not have been found. Widely used names like Heinz Schmidt or Jean Martin jammed entire file cabinets, making it impossible to tell who was who. In a war in which the dead could hardly be counted and much less identified, a small hand-written card often served as the only means by which a family could know if a son, brother or father might still be alive. If a prisoner could be found, the International Committee would serve as an intermediary for exchange of mail.

The ICRC also tried to enforce the Hague Convention rules governing the conditions under which prisoners of war were to be held. Over 400 Red Cross delegates, all Swiss and all volunteers, visited camps across most of Europe all the way to Siberia to try to ensure at least the minimum standards. They inspected rooms, barracks, food, medical support and treatment.

The Germans at first handled prisoners of war brutally but improved their treatment during the war, although toward the end they began using prisoners as factory laborers. The British and Americans treated prisoners better, with some exceptions. Russian treatment remained abominable but not too different from conditions in Russia outside the camps. Prisoners could not expect to live better than natives. But the International Committee tried to ensure at least bearable treatment and inhabitable camps. As the war went on, that became more difficult, but the volunteers continued to make their visits, to speak with the prisoners whenever possible, to write their reports and to keep some hope alive for families.

The ICRC tried to do its work discreetly. It feared that too much attention would arouse a hostile reaction to its efforts to give fair and equal treatment to all prisoners. The principle of neutrality became less accepted as the war went on, but governments did recognize its value for certain purposes. They would let the Red Cross inspect their own prisoner facilities because it was the only way to get enemy facilities inspected as well. Nobody spoke of it more than necessary, and the Red Cross said virtually nothing about what it did.

Gustave Ador tried to stop the use of poison gas. His efforts became increasingly futile as the static nature of trench warfare made gas an ever more tempting weapon. Making a very rare Red Cross appeal, Ador on February 6, 1918, sent a message to the sovereigns, the heads of government and the generals of the warring parties to ask them to refrain from poison gas attacks. He said that he could no longer remain silent in the face of the "barbaric" nature of this weapon, which violated all the laws of war by scattering the "most atrocious" death across a battlefield. But his appeal elicited only unctuous replies from the Allies and from the Germans, all professing to favor a ban but only if they could be certain that their enemies would also respect it.

Civilians once again bore much of the brunt of the conflict. Because of the immobility of trench warfare, they rarely needed to fear armies coursing across their land, destroying their homes and barns and raping their women. But Germany and its allies began to feel the growing deprivations brought on by the allied blockade. The notion that an entire country constituted a "home front" had originated in medieval times but could not then be fully enforced. Even during the Napoleonic wars, when England tried to seal off the continent and Napoleon tried to isolate England, some trade had passed through the blockades. But the blockade of Germany proved highly effective. By 1917, many foods had disappeared from German tables and most medicines from German hospitals. The German and Austrian diet, while not at starvation levels, came perilously close to that.

The German counter-blockade, carried out largely by submarines, proved less effective. It constituted more of a nuisance than a strangulation. The blockade even proved to be a strategic disaster for Germany as German submarine attacks against American shipping ultimately helped to bring the United States into the war. The notorious German sinking of the steamboat *Lusitania,* which killed hundreds of civilians, raised war fever in the United States to an almost hysterical pitch and contributed to President Woodrow Wilson's later decision to declare war on Germany and the Central Powers.

Civilians close to the front, in Russia or in the occupied parts of France, Belgium and The Netherlands, suffered directly from the conflict. German forces drove them from their homes. Artillery or tank movements destroyed their property. Russia shipped hundreds of thousands of Germans from the Volga region, where they had lived for generations, to Siberia. Other states interned civilians, such as 20,000 Germans and Austrians in Britain or 6,000 French and 2,000 Belgians in Germany.

Once again the International Committee found that it could not help civilians no matter how it tried. The Red Cross agreements covered only soldiers and prisoners of war. With its mandate to help soldiers already threatened by the national Red Cross societies, the ICRC feared that it would lose its authority to help prisoners if it tried to extend its authority into new areas. The Western powers would have regarded any Red Cross efforts to feed German civilians as a hostile act. And the German navy would not have stopped submarine warfare in response to Red Cross appeals.

Frédéric Ferriere, one of the older veterans of the International Committee, persuaded the committee to let him keep track of displaced civilians so that people could at least find each other. He had cards on over 60,000 in his files by the end of the war. He did not, however, have any way to help them.

Ferriere complained bitterly about the callous treatment of civilians:

> We find ourselves obliged to admit that modern warfare is no longer a war be-
> tween armies but a struggle between nations. . . . War conducted this way is inhu-
> man, immoral, contrary to the law of nature and revolting to every human
> conscience.[6]

The British, French and Russian governments condemned the Ottoman Empire for attacks by Turkish troops against the Armenian civilian population of Anatolia, for the first time using the term "crime against humanity." But they could do nothing to stop the attacks.[7]

In the wrenching agony of unrestricted conflict, few were ready to help others and nobody would help those they did not need to help. They served their states as best they could. Beyond that, they tried to survive and to keep their families alive. But no states, no leaders and no organizations had the well-being of civilians on their agenda.

World War I showed the full power and glory of the nation-state in its unassailable sovereignty. The universal law of nature, as conceived by Greek, Roman and other philosophers, did not matter. The states of Europe ravaged an entire generation of their own young, wrecked their own land, ruined their own economies and in some cases collapsed their political systems. They had more force at their command than any organization in history and they used it to devastatingly destructive and self-destructive effect.

The people mutely accepted the decisions of their leaders and as long as humanly possible endured the suffering that those decisions imposed. Some questioned, but only a few. Soldiers remained in their trenches although they knew that the next artillery barrage or the next poison gas attack might kill them. They arose and they advanced out of the trenches, like lemmings, although they knew they would almost certainly be cut to ribbons by machine-gun fire. In the name of nation or cause, their acts defied all sense of self-preservation and all standards of humanity. When the war was over, they returned, gassed and shell-shocked, to civilian life, and, if they had lost the war, would be victimized again by the next group of extremist politicians. Human degradation triumphed as all states joined in a mad race toward annihilation.

The International Committee of the Red Cross, mankind's first effort at neutral humanitarian action, could not provide the solace Dunant had envisaged. But it could still claim a modest success because of the help it had given prisoners of war. It had been able to provide a clearinghouse for information and for the exchange of mail between prisoners and their families. ICRC delegates visiting prisoner-of-war or labor camps across Europe, North Africa, Russia and Asia had helped make conditions in those camps as tolerable as possible and had given the prisoners some level of human contact.

Dunant's concept of prompt medical help for troops had succeeded even if it had not been done by neutrals. And, ironically, even the national medical services wore the Red Cross emblem on their sleeves as a sign that they were engaged in humanitarian, not military, duties. Dunant had scored a real success, no matter how modest. But no humanitarian organization would claim or believe that it had been able to prevent the ghastly horror of the war.

The humanitarians had done what they could. As they were to learn time and time again, they could not pretend for even a moment that it had been enough.

After the Armistice—Repatriation and Relief

Henry Davison, the chairman of the War Council of the American Red Cross, thought that the war had opened the door for further Red Cross action. He thought that national Red Cross societies, and the Red Cross movement as a whole, should do more than help prisoners of war and wounded soldiers.

Davison expressed open contempt for the International Committee of the Red Cross, which he derided as a parochial Swiss organization. He proposed a real international Red Cross that would be composed of the leaders of the national Red Cross societies and that would mount an international effort to fight a wide range of global ills. In May 1919, he and others formed the League of Red Cross Societies, hoping to go well beyond the restricted role of the ICRC. The league established its headquarters in Geneva, promising to cooperate with the ICRC. It invited Gustav Ador to address its opening dinner in Geneva. The first secretary general of the league, a British aircraft manufacturer named Sir David Henderson, had been a hero of the Boer War.[8]

Davison's new league set the ambitious goal of attacking the social, medical and educational ills of the world. He wanted to address the countless problems that desperately needed attention after the end of the war and that were there for all to see.

Europe—and especially central and eastern Europe—had collapsed almost totally. Millions suffered from starvation, tuberculosis, typhus, influenza and cholera.
The bitter cold deepened the misery. Relief officials, nurses or national Red Cross
delegates told depressing stories about dozens and even hundreds of bodies lying in
fields, in ruined houses or in gullies all over central Europe. They reported children
frozen next to their almost naked mothers, as the mothers had taken off their own
clothes to try to keep the children alive.

The Austrian and Hungarian Red Cross societies reported that the children of
Vienna and Budapest were starving. The desperate situation in Russia dwarfed all
the others, with an estimated 25 million people dead from war, revolution, disease
and hunger. The victorious powers had not suffered as much but Davison reminded
them that they could take no genuine comfort in the pain of others.

Davison tried to get U.S. surplus military war rations released for civilian relief. He, Henderson and their colleagues called on national societies to provide
food, medicine or funds to help the desperate. But they got nowhere. British jour-
nals did not want to help the Bolsheviks remain in power in Moscow. Herbert
Hoover, the director of the American Relief Administration, had his own program,
which ultimately provided almost $1 billion in assistance in over 20 countries dur-
ing the 1920s.

Davison did not give up. On April 15, 1921, league representatives joined
Western governments, major charities, and 21 national Red Cross societies as well
as the ICRC in a major effort to gather necessary supplies and to devise a common
strategy to help overcome the desperate situation in Europe. But national societies
did not make the necessary commitments. The league could not energize the countries it claimed to represent. Even the American Red Cross held back, worried that
the almost limitless extent of Russian suffering rendered any effort futile. With
America and the West sinking into recession, they would not act.[9]

Only nature finally relieved the desperate humanitarian conditions on the European continent. The successful harvest of 1922 put an end to famine and misery a
full year and a half after the conference. The harvest helped more than governments
and national societies.

The prisoners of war posed a special problem. As many as 5 million men found the
gates to their camps suddenly thrown open but without any way for them to return
home or to survive until they did return. Some, like the 2 million Russian prisoners
in camps in Austria and Germany, were as near death from the effects of the blockade as the Germans and Austrians themselves. They had no clothes for the bitter
winter ahead. Many of them died on the way to Russia or to wherever they might
have tried to go. Most fell by the side of the road, to be abandoned and forgotten

among the countless anonymous corpses rotting all over Europe. Given its responsibilities for the prisoners of war while they had been in camps, the ICRC tried to help find routes and food for them, but the Western allies had little sympathy and few resources to offer to other than their own forces and returning prisoners.

The German and Austrian prisoners held in Russian camps fared even worse. Released by the new Soviet government of Vladimir Ilich Lenin, they had to make their way home through Russia's bitter cold and ruined countryside. They often found themselves trapped by the movements of the revolutionary and counterrevolutionary armies that roamed across Russia and Siberia and that had no patience for itinerant strangers. Few could even find a road to take them home, and most died whether they found one or not.

The League of Nations, which the allies established after the war, decided to help. On April 11, 1920, it appointed Fridtjof Nansen, a renowned Norwegian polar explorer and a dedicated humanitarian, to serve as a special commissioner to coordinate the repatriation of the remaining prisoners of war. Knowing the desperate situation of the prisoners, the league asked Nansen to act fast.

Nansen worked with the ICRC delegates who had visited prisoners during the war. They elaborated a coherent plan for relief and repatriation, which his office and the ICRC and others implemented as best they could. He also received some international aid. Within two years, by the spring of 1922, not a single prisoner remained in or near the camps and many had actually been repatriated. Nansen and the ICRC could draw some comfort from that humanitarian success.[10]

Ador and the ICRC could also draw some comfort from a new protocol they had drafted that prohibited "asphyxiating, poisonous or other gases and bacteriological methods of warfare," a protocol that was ready for ratification by June 1925. The ICRC and the League of Red Cross Societies also settled some of their jurisdictional disagreements, with the ICRC to concentrate on war while the league concentrated on peace. This agreement could help to give each form of humanitarian action a more definite focus.

Finally, the International Red Cross could rejoice in the signature of the Kellogg-Briand pact of 1928, in which the nations of the world renounced war and committed themselves to settle all disputes by peaceful means. It could also rejoice in 1929 about successful international negotiations on two new Geneva conventions, one to help the wounded on the battlefield to receive aid and the other to give greater assistance to prisoners of war. But the states of the world would still not agree to any Red Cross or other convention on aid to civilians. Nor could humanitarian impulses alter the ruinous course on which all the sovereign powers were to set the European continent.

Max Huber, the new president of the ICRC, announced as he took office in 1928 that "the Red Cross path [is] filled with grandeur and tribulation." He added that the age was "apocalyptic," a phrase he might often have occasion to remember during the 17 fateful years of his service.[11]

Fridtjof Nansen's Refugees

The victorious "Big Four," Premier Georges Clemenceau of France, Prime Minister David Lloyd George of Great Britain, Premier Vittorio Orlando of Italy and President Woodrow Wilson of the United States, set the basic tone of the postwar era.

When they convened at the Palace of Versailles on January 18, 1919 to devise a peace settlement for Europe, the four men had two alternatives: to act as vengefully as sovereign nation-states had acted during past centuries, provoking wars of retaliation and re-retaliation to the end of time; or to break the cycle of violence and hatred that had culminated in the deaths of tens of millions of soldiers and civilians.

The "Big Four" chose the former, although Wilson had earlier spoken as if he would choose the latter. The Versailles treaty signed on June 28, 1919, five years to the day after the assassination of Archduke Francis Ferdinand, set the terms for an armistice and not for a true peace of reconciliation based on humanitarian principles.

The "Big Four" redrew the map of Europe and of the world more than any victors had ever done, trying to establish a strategic situation that they could dominate in perpetuity:

- They dismembered the Austro-Hungarian Empire. They gave major parts of Austria to Italy or to new states in central Europe and the Balkans. They gave major portions of Hungary to Romania and Czechoslovakia.
- They created or re-created some states, such as Poland, Finland and the Baltics.
- Germany and Russia lost those parts of Poland that they had acquired in earlier partitions. In addition, Russia lost Finland and the Baltic states.
- Germany had to surrender some German-speaking areas of Prussia to Poland.
- The Ottoman Empire was totally dismembered, to be divided between half a dozen states—including Iraq—under British or French colonial domination, with Turkey left as a rump state.
- They accepted the decision of several Balkan peoples to join into a new Kingdom of the Serbs, Croats and Slovenes, which was later to become Yugoslavia.

The "Big Four" of Versailles thus added new humanitarian problems to those caused by the war. As the victors sometimes drew borders to follow ethnic lines and sometimes to follow their strategic or political ambitions, they forced entire populations to move and others to accept them. States and humanitarian agencies had to deal with mass flight in addition to the prisoners of war and the victims of famine.

Millions of people had to decide whether they would accept their new rulers or whether they would flee either to the newly shrunken entities that they considered their national homes or to areas where they would find asylum. The new rulers had to decide if they would accept or expel the people who had been living on the land they had just acquired. And the asylum states also had to decide whether they would accept those who wanted to flee to their control. Millions of Europeans found themselves on the move without knowing whether they would be welcome where they were going.

New concepts emerged out of this enormous movement of peoples, and especially the word "refugees." That term had first been applied to the Huguenots fleeing Louis XIV in the seventeenth century. Now it became a widely used word to identify whole populations in desperate flight from their old homes to what they hoped would be new ones.

The new refugee groups dwarfed all that had gone before. Many represented major political, religious or ethnic communities. A million Germans and 250,000 Hungarians had been expelled from the new states of Central and Eastern Europe. Many who had lived quietly and perhaps prosperously in the cosmopolitan kaleidoscope of the Austro-Hungarian or the Ottoman empires suddenly found themselves isolated minorities in one of the fiercely jingoistic successor nation-states.

In addition, 2 million Russians, Jews and Ukrainians fled or were expelled during successive revolutions in the Soviet Union and during the long resistance wars that followed. Within five years, one and a half million Greeks and Turks had been exchanged, and a million Armenians expelled from Turkey after the first major genocide of the twentieth century. Two million Poles sought repatriation from all over Europe. Hungarians fled Romania. Serbs fled Hungary. Refugees poured into Western Europe and, to a lesser degree, into the Middle East.[12] Although some special groups, like the Russian aristocracy or the continental Jews fleeing to England, could reestablish themselves through private means or could find support in older well-to-do communities, the overwhelming majority of refugees wandered uncertainly around Europe and the Middle East with nobody to help them.

The receiving countries, devastated by war, could not take care of the new arrivals. They could barely keep their own people alive and could not feed and shelter the helpless and destitute masses that now descended on them. They often denounced the refugees as "intruders" and tried to discourage and block their arrival. Only the United States had the space to accept large numbers but it began curtailing immigration soon after the war because the numbers and the desperate plight of the homeless overwhelmed even American resources.[13]

The new nation-states did not want to accept and assimilate foreigners. By their very nature, such states expected and demanded conformity of race, origin and often religion. Before World War I, Europeans had crossed borders without even needing passports. Virtually every major city held dozens of different communities. After the war, every European had to prove his or her identity countless times and had to establish his or her right to visit or live any place they might select. And relations between the different ethnic and religious communities became strained and embittered because in a nation-state only one nation could rule and others had to obey.

Europe resembled an endless panorama of peoples on the move, unsure of where they should go and where they might be admitted. New and old nation-states did not know whether to treat them as legitimate immigrants, illegal aliens or temporary visitors. National leaders did not even grasp the dimensions of the tragedy and the urgency of the needs.

The refugees shuffled on in confusion and disarray, searching for relatives, friends, fellow-nationals, churches or charitable institutions that could and would help. But those who did indeed try to help often found that their resources could not begin to match the needs. The refugee crisis risked becoming the greatest humanitarian tragedy of the postwar years, dwarfing even that of the prisoners of war.

The International Committee of the Red Cross tried to help. It convoked representatives of charitable organizations in Geneva in February 1921 to try to find an answer to the problem. But they found none. Totally overwhelmed, the ICRC then asked the League of Nations to appoint a commission that would guide and coordinate efforts to help the people in flight. A number of states joined in the appeal.

The League of Nations turned once again to Nansen, the man who had helped the prisoners of war. It gave him a totally new title, "High Commissioner on behalf of the League." The league asked Nansen most urgently to help the million Russian refugees, many of whom were near starvation. It further instructed him to determine the legal status of all refugees and to find a permanent solution, be it repatriation, integration into the countries where they had found asylum or resettlement to other countries where they might wish to go and might be welcome. The league expected Nansen's mission to be temporary, but the arrival of new groups of refugees—including Bulgarians, Greeks, Armenians and others—gave him what turned out to be an unending task.[14]

First of all, Nansen wanted to ensure that refugees would have some kind of legal protection so that they would not be forced back to almost certain death. He worked indefatigably, mediating between refugee groups and the countries where they found themselves. His personal prestige and unquestioned humanitarian commitment helped. Many governments in Europe granted his requests to let refugees remain in place even when they did not want those refugees.

Nansen achieved a major breakthrough when he persuaded the governments of the asylum countries to issue a new document to identify new arrivals and to give them a definite status. This document, which became known as the "Nansen Passport," literally became a lifesaver. For the first time in history, a refugee who could not have a passport would have a definite identity document and a recognized status. Nansen also worked with the International Labor Office to help refugees find jobs. He won one of the earliest Nobel peace prizes for his work.

Nansen followed the Red Cross model, insisting on strict neutrality. Although he often sympathized more with some groups of refugees than with others, and although he found some governments odious, he never took political positions in public. Instead, he worked with every government and with every other institution, insisting that his humanitarian mission kept him from making political statements or voicing preferences.

Nansen kept prodding the Western governments in the league to write formal international agreements that would define the status and the rights of refugees. Under his pressure and guidance, those governments reached agreements in 1922, 1924 and 1926 regarding the Russian and Armenian refugees. In 1928 they signed an accord providing special identity documents to these refugees as well as to several other groups.[15]

The stockmarket crash of 1929, followed by the worldwide depression, made Nansen's work harder. More and more states refused to accept refugees because they feared more unemployment and higher welfare rolls.

Nonetheless, the states of the League of Nations realized that they still needed to recognize refugees as legitimately needy whether they wanted to welcome them or not. After Nansen died in 1930, the League of Nations continued his work through the International Nansen Office for Refugees. But they still wanted the problem to go away. They instructed the Nansen Office to end its work no later than December 31, 1938.

Max Huber and the ICRC had not given up on another humanitarian aim, that of aid for civilians. And they received help from an unexpected quarter.

A new Japanese militarist regime wanted to look modern and respectable in the West by addressing humanitarian issues. Therefore, in October 1934, the Japanese Red Cross called an international conference of national Red Cross societies from 57 countries. Members of the Japanese royal family served as hosts and the Japanese Red Cross offered sumptuous facilities.

The assembled delegates had serious business to discuss, especially about help-ing civilians. They needed to come to some agreement. The International Commit-tee of the Red Cross and separate national Red Cross societies wanted to help civilians in conflict situations as they had helped wounded soldiers and prisoners of war. They stressed that this had nothing to do with the refugee crisis.

But the governments represented at the conference continued to assert that sovereign states had to have full control over their own people and that they alone should handle civilian needs. No outside organizations were to intervene. The meeting appeared deadlocked.

Huber still did not give up. And, finally, under great pressure from some na-tional societies as well as from the ICRC, the governments reluctantly agreed to let the Red Cross societies draft a document on helping civilians. The Tokyo conferees then even agreed on a draft convention that would authorize the Red Cross to offer some help, although only to two groups: civilians living in enemy territory and civilians living in occupied territory. That left governments fully free to act however they liked toward civilians at home.

Governments now had to agree formally to the convention drafted by the Red Cross delegates. The Swiss government tried to convene a formal international diplomatic conference to approve the "Tokyo Draft," as it had become known. But other governments, led by France, refused.[16] The Tokyo draft went nowhere and the hopes for agreement on help for civilians ended despite Red Cross efforts.

The Clouds Gather

Whatever hopes any Western leader might have had for an improvement of the hu-manitarian or political situation in Europe and the world could not survive four momentous events:

- Josef Stalin's seizure of power in the Soviet Union, leading to the murder or Siberian exile of tens of millions, including entire classes and ethnic groups such as the Kulaks and the Cossacks, as well as to an ever widening reign of terror.[17]
- Benito Mussolini's and the Italian Fascists' seizure of power in 1922, leading to increasingly aggressive policies abroad and a darkening dictatorship in Italy itself.
- The deep depression that hit Europe in two waves, the first coming after the American stock exchange crash in 1929–1930 and the second after the Eu-ropean banking collapse of 1931–1932.
- Adolf Hitler's January 1933 seizure of power in Germany, followed by a campaign of genocide against Jews and others as well as a revanchist and in-flammatory foreign policy.

Faced with these events, the League of Nations realized reluctantly that it had to prepare itself for wider humanitarian burdens including larger numbers of refugees. It appointed an American professor and journalist, James McDonald, as High Commissioner to succeed Nansen. It did not give him any funds, which came mainly from private agencies and foundations, but it did support him with the authority of the league. That, and a group of countries initially willing to accept refugees, enabled him to settle about 80,000 Jewish and other refugees in the British mandate of Palestine and elsewhere. But the refugee stream kept growing, especially after the Nazis promulgated the Nuremberg Decrees depriving Germany's Jewish citizens of their citizenship and of their right to vote.

The member states of the league did not want to accept the growing numbers of refugees. McDonald, finding no support, could not cope with the ever-worsening problem. Finally, on November 27, 1935, he resigned in anger and frustration, explaining his action in a letter that was widely publicized at the time:

> When domestic policies threaten the demoralization of human beings, considerations of diplomatic correctness must yield to those of common humanity. I should be recreant if I did not call attention to the actual situation, and plead that world opinion, acting through the League and its Member States and other countries, move to avert the existing and impending tragedies.[18]

McDonald's plea went unheeded. The league became ever more reluctant to deal with any humanitarian problems and least of all with refugees, even when they fled from brutal dictators such as Hitler, Stalin or Mussolini. The league also refused to intervene in Germany itself or to make any special appeal for Hitler to reverse his anti-Jewish decrees or for Stalin to stop his purges.

The members of the league and of the world continued to believe that a sovereign state had the sovereign right to treat its citizens as it wished and that others had no right to intervene or interfere. The league was no more ready to help civilians in peacetime than to help them in wartime. Governments faced economic and political crises at home and did not want even to think about humanitarian crises abroad.[19]

Despite this brutal reality, Nansen and McDonald and their offices had not worked entirely in vain. Neither had the states that supported them. While uncertainty, confusion and hesitation about humanitarian needs and rights deepened during the Great Depression and the 1930s as a whole, the interwar period brought forth some significant steps toward recognition and protection of refugees.

The states of the West had reached an understanding that refugees had a distinct status and were entitled to the legal protection that they could no longer get from their states of origin. They also agreed on what the French termed *non-refoulement*— that refugees should not be forced back, and that their physical needs would have to be met by some emergency relief. And they generally recognized that receiving countries had to devise a common or at least coordinated policy.

But the limits to refugee protection and care were even more plainly and painfully obvious. Would-be refugees did not get universal recognition and acceptance. Many of them, especially Jews trying to flee Germany or to find new homes after having fled, were turned back at European borders. Only a few states ratified agreements governing protection for refugees, and they did so with great reluctance.

Refugee acceptance and care had become the litmus test of humanitarian conscience for the states of the Western world. And most had failed that test, and failed it massively.

The American government fell as short of its own professed ideals as others did. It played only a very small role in helping the millions of refugees flooding Europe after World War I. Hobbled by isolationist sentiment and preoccupied with economic problems, Washington saw no reason to solve what most Americans saw as a European dilemma. The United States did not involve itself in League of Nations refugee relief operations spearheaded by Great Britain, France and especially the Scandinavian states.

The United States withdrew into itself even more after the onset of the Great Depression. The U.S. immigration laws of 1921 and 1924 had promulgated a quota system that already favored groups with an existing presence in the United States. That dramatically limited refugee entry because most refugees came from different areas than earlier immigrants. In addition, the United States would not accept persons who were "likely to become a public charge," immediately disqualifying most of the penniless refugees and especially so during and after the Depression. By the 1930s, immigration to the United States sank to the lowest peacetime levels in decades.

Americans regarded the motives of refugees, especially those who wanted to come to the United States, with deep suspicion. They feared that Soviet, Nazi or Fascist leaders would send refugees to conduct sabotage, subversion and propaganda. The U.S. government shifted the Immigration and Naturalization Service from the Labor Department to the Justice Department to permit closer surveillance of all applicants but especially of refugees.

President Franklin Roosevelt, the Department of State and many influential American groups had special reservations about admitting large numbers of Jews. The annual immigration quota of 23,370 for immigrants from Germany was not filled during most of the 1930s, with annual totals running between 4,000 and 10,000 (most of them Jewish). Under U.S. immigration laws, Roosevelt would have had to single out Jewish groups for special entry, which he was reluctant to do. He did, however, involve himself in special cases (such as Albert Einstein's and Sigmund Freud's). He also relaxed some consular requirements for documentation because many refugees did not have their papers. By 1939 and 1940, as the European crisis deepened, refugees filled almost all of the U.S. visa quota for entrants from Germany, but the Congress refused to permit refugees to come in above that quota.

When the Nazi annexation of Austria in March of 1938 provoked a new massive wave of refugees, Roosevelt became alarmed and called for an international forum on refugees. But the Western states at that forum, held in the French resort city of Evian-les-Bains, did not want to accept large numbers of Jews or of Romany Gypsies, whom Hitler had also selected for special persecution. They did agree to the formation of an Inter-Governmental Committee on Refugees (IGCR) but it could not break through the barriers that the Western states had established. Humanitarian needs of refugees might be growing rapidly, but the Western humanitarian conscience did not rise to meet them.

War Drums Across the World

Even as the delegates to the Tokyo conference were sipping mint tea and speaking politely, the real world seethed with hatred and war. Japan had launched an attack on China, invading Manchuria in the autumn of 1931 and establishing a base on the Asian mainland in an "independent" vassal state of Manchukuo in March 1932. The Japanese military fought by the most barbaric means, including biological warfare, with no deference to the humanitarian principles that Japan had so faithfully respected in 1905. Japan refused to ratify the 1929 Geneva convention governing the treatment of prisoners of war.

After capturing the city of Nanking in December, 1937, Japanese forces conducted an orgy of cruelty that became known as the "Rape of Nanking." They raped tens of thousands of girls and women between the ages of 9 and 75 and they killed at least 300,000 Chinese in the city. The brutality of the killings exceeded anything ever seen, with huge numbers of victims tortured, beheaded, drowned or shot at point-blank range. The Japanese then looted and burned the city.

The ICRC had sent one of its delegates, Sidney Brown, to investigate the reports of Japanese violations of the Geneva conventions in China. He returned to report that he had witnessed scenes even more horrifying than those that had shocked Henry Dunant at Solferino. He had seen rampant and needless butchery, including Chinese bayoneted in their beds or hacked to pieces by Japanese soldiers, left to die and to rot. He was able to persuade the Japanese Red Cross to help him at least to provide decent burials for some of the dead, but he could do little else.

Brown and the ICRC might have been shocked by Japanese behavior but they might have been even more shocked by the European and American response. With the West increasingly obsessed with its own problems, the states that had sparked the original laws of "civilized" wartime behavior now chose to ignore Japanese actions. The postwar humanitarian spirit had dissipated totally. Asia and China seemed far away. Japan could do as it wished. The ICRC had no authority to protect civilians, anyway. It could do no more than write and distribute reports. It could get no support for any action, and certainly none for pressure upon Japan to change its policies.

Mussolini attacked Ethiopia in October 1935, hitting closer to the European continent. The Ethiopian government asked the ICRC to help treat the wounded. In response, Sidney Brown left for Addis Ababa with a doctor and with tons of emergency medical supplies. Other national Red Cross societies, especially from Scandinavia and Great Britain, also sent help. They established hospitals as soon as possible several miles behind the front lines with large red crosses on their tents as provided in the Geneva conventions. They offered no help to the Italians, as the Italian Red Cross had told the ICRC that it could take care of its own.

Mussolini told the Italian army and air force not to respect the red crosses on the tents or on other equipment. The Italians even went so far as to make any red cross a "special target," as one delegate reported to Geneva. When Huber wrote directly to Mussolini to protest the violations of the Geneva conventions, he received only an oily reply asserting Italian respect for the conventions and accusing the Ethiopians of "terrible atrocities" against Italians.

But the ICRC faced another and even graver challenge to the Geneva conventions: poison gas. The Italian air force began dropping canisters of gas over Ethiopian forces and over civilian villages. An ICRC delegate could testify personally to the effect, feeling his hands burning after he had touched a bush that had been drenched with the gas. He wrote that "the Italian air force is dropping bombs and toxic gases without cease," creating "a veritable hell" and causing Ethiopians to die "like flies."[20]

Brown became increasingly alarmed about Italian behavior and in February, 1936, sent a remarkably prophetic telegram to Geneva:

> It is now very clear that this little colonial affair has become a war of extermination and that if we do not manage to have the Red Cross emblem respected by a country calling itself civilized we will never be able to do so later if we are ever faced by a war in Europe.[21]

Huber himself headed a delegation to meet with Mussolini in Rome to protest Italian behavior. Mussolini, whose troops were about to win the war, assured the delegates that Italy had not violated and would not violate humanitarian conventions.

Although the ICRC mission mentioned gas in passing, they did not make a major point of it and did not forcefully protest Italian behavior—after all, Italy had in 1928 ratified the 1925 protocol forbidding the use of gas. Huber came away feeling that he had made his point but many ICRC delegates believed that he had not spoken or acted forcefully enough.

The war in Ethiopia, won by Italy when the Emperor Haile Selassie fled Addis Ababa in the face of the advancing Italian army in May 1936, dramatically illustrated the dilemma that was to face the ICRC throughout the following decade. The Red Cross had been able to do some useful humanitarian work. It had gained some limited access and had helped some wounded soldiers even if its emblem had not been respected. This amounted to a success. In exchange, however, the ICRC had given up the right of protest. It had not been able to enforce the so-called laws of war. It had not issued public statements condemning the aggressors and the methods they used. It had preferred quiet diplomacy, which had not worked.

Not only the Red Cross had failed. The states of Europe and of the world had not acted either. They had not helped Ethiopia against Italy any more than they had helped China against Japan. All concentrated on their own problems and on their own immediate interests and needs. The Red Cross could not expect to achieve very much if nobody else helped.

Francisco Franco, then governor of the Spanish Canary Islands, on July 18, 1936, launched a civil war against the Spanish Republican government. Within weeks, the ICRC sent a delegate, Dr. Marcel Junod, to help the soldiers on both sides and, if possible, the civilian war victims. Junod quickly won the support of the Republican government but met with great mistrust from Franco and his forces.

The ICRC could at first do little to help the prisoners, a mixed group that included not only Spaniards on both sides but citizens—often volunteers—of the nations that helped each side: Germans, Portuguese and Italians helping Franco; British, French and some Russian and other volunteers helping the Republicans. The prisoners could not be easily exchanged, but information could be sent on who was alive and who was where.

The ICRC had some success arranging exchanges of civilians. For example, Arthur Koestler, the author, scheduled for execution by Franco's Nationalists, was exchanged for a woman. The Red Cross also arranged family reunification of children who had been caught on opposing sides from their parents because many had been away on summer vacation. As those exchanges succeeded, others followed.

But the conflict itself, being a civil war rather than an international conflict, included some vicious fighting against civilians. The Red Cross delegates could do little more than to visit both sides and persistently remind them of the laws of war.

They quoted the "Tokyo draft" for protecting civilians and appealed to both sides to end the ravages against innocent people. But every concession, even helping children threatened by bombings, had to be wrung from the opposing forces with the greatest effort.

Professor Louis Demoulis, writing in the ICRC *Review,* thought the battles of the Spanish Civil War portended the future. Like Sidney Brown before him, he warned of what was to come:

> The inhabitants of cities fleeing from fire or massacre, forced to leave their homes because of the devastating invasion of motorized troops; civilians . . . caught between two shifting tides of warring armies, swirling among and around military units . . . trying to find somewhere safe.[22]

The massive bombing of Guernica in northern Spain epitomized the horrors that the war visited upon civilians. Georges Graz, a Red Cross delegate, witnessed the city "still in flames" with "its houses collapsing one after the other."[23] But he could do nothing to stop the slaughter of innocents. All he could do was to help after the fact, establishing hospitals and trying to keep a lifeline open between those caught on opposing sides.

Finally, after three years, the war came to an end and the Red Cross delegates could return to Geneva with the sense that they had done as much as they could. They had been able to improve conditions at the margins. Especially, the ICRC had exchanged 5 million messages across the front lines, often offering the only point of contact and information for divided families. The delegates had visited more than 75,000 prisoners on both sides. Fifty different countries and Red Cross societies had provided aid. But they had not been able to prevent the excesses of the conflict.[24]

The crises of the 1930s showed that no Western government really cared about what happened to people elsewhere. Presidents and prime ministers might make speeches and launch protests but they would not act. And they would not grant to any humanitarian agency any authority to act.

Humanitarian organizations and humane considerations could not overcome this reality. Neither the League of Nations nor the Red Cross could do more than the states wanted them to do, which was nothing. After terrible wars and deep suffering, nothing fundamental had changed.

Ernest Hemingway had suggested in the title of his book about the Spanish Civil War, *For Whom the Bell Tolls,* that, as John Donne had written, "it tolls for thee." The ICRC and all humanitarians could have agreed. But the world did not see the advancing danger as Louis Demoulis and Sidney Brown had seen it. The humanitarian conscience had been left on the field along with the human dead.

Humanitarian NGOs Appear

More and more private citizens, and especially Americans, decided that they needed to help where governments would not. As one crisis after another shook the world, those citizens began organizing themselves into private groups that could and would act on their own. They came to be called non-governmental organizations (NGOs) or private voluntary organizations (PVOs) in order to distinguish them from governments and official organizations. They sometimes tried to coordinate their resources and their actions to have a greater effect.

Most of the humanitarian NGOs at first represented particular groups, often religious groups, who wanted to help like-minded people or co-religionists. They often expressed in concrete form the noblest religious or secular ideals. At first, after World War I, they concentrated on providing relief for those caught in famine or upheaval during the desperate postwar years in Europe. Later, as the Fascists came to power in Italy and the Nazis in Germany, they tried to help those who needed to escape from the new totalitarians or from impending war.

Many of the humanitarian NGOs began with very specific and limited purposes, unlike the Red Cross, which had an internationally mandated mission to help the victims of war. Many even began their work with very limited means before taking time to get formally organized. But many could operate internationally. And, over time, many of those that had started with specific goals widened those goals and especially the groups they tried to help.

Most of the major organizations established during and between the wars, and able to continue functioning during and after World War II, were American—although some of those had started elsewhere or had partners and branches elsewhere. The main ones included the following:

- The American Friends Service Committee, founded in 1917 to bring American Quaker ideals of peace to a warring world.
- The American Jewish Joint Distribution Committee, founded in 1914 to help Jews fleeing from Europe and especially to Palestine.
- Baptist World Aid, formed in 1905 to coordinate Baptist aid efforts.
- CARE (Cooperative Action for American Relief Everywhere), founded in 1945 to coordinate and bring relief through CARE packages and beyond.
- The Catholic Medical Mission Board, formed in 1928 to help provide medical supplies worldwide.
- The Christian Children's Fund, formed in 1938 to help children fleeing from the deepening European crisis.
- The Presiding Bishop's Fund for World Relief of the Episcopal Church of the USA, to coordinate Episcopalian relief.

- The Immigration and Refugee Services of America, founded in 1914 to help persons fleeing World War I to come to the United States.
- The International Rescue Committee, founded in 1933 at the suggestion of the physicist Albert Einstein and the humanist theologian Reinhold Niebuhr to help Jews and others fleeing from Hitler.
- The Lutheran Immigration and Refugee Service, founded in 1939 to help Lutherans fleeing from Hitler.
- The Near East Foundation, founded in 1915 to bring relief to those jeopardized by the collapse of the Ottoman Empire.
- The Oxford Committee for Famine Relief, later OXFAM, founded in 1942 to help European victims of World War II.
- Save the Children, founded in Great Britain in 1932 for children's relief after the devastation caused by World War I and its aftermath.
- The Tolstoy Foundation, founded in 1939 to help Russians and other Slavs fleeing from Stalin and from World War II.
- The Unitarian Universalist Service Committee, founded in 1939 to help those trying to escape from Nazi-occupied Europe.
- The Methodist Committee on Relief, founded in 1940 to bring aid to Europe and other devastated areas.
- The National Conference of Catholic Bishops Committee on Migration, founded in 1920 to help needy immigrants come to America.
- World Learning, founded in 1932 as the Experiment in International Living to encourage people-to-people contacts.
- World Relief, founded in 1944 to help the needy in the areas devastated by World War II.[25]

These NGOs could not solve the broader humanitarian problems that the ICRC and the national Red Cross societies could not solve, especially as they had limited mandates. But their very existence reflected the humanitarian conscience of private citizens even when governments did not act. They often sent their own members and staffers to do the actual work in humanitarian operations. Over time, they were to become the backbone of humanitarian care, with many of them committed to operations even as recent as those in Afghanistan or Iraq.

World War II

The Second World War reached the apex of what was to become the century of death. From the beginning, the opposing armies fought with every means at their command except for poison gas, which they avoided only because they feared it might be used in retaliation.

World War II affected the entire world even more than World War I. It touched every continent, most of the then independent states and dozens of colonies. Axis and Allied armies fought each other all over Europe and North Africa as well as over much of the Soviet Union. Japanese and Allied armies fought each other in China, Southeast Asia, Indonesia, the Philippines and countless islands across the Pacific. The navies fought across the Atlantic, Pacific and Mediterranean. German submarines sank allied shipping all over the northern and southern Atlantic and the Mediterranean.

No accurate statistics exist on the military or civilian dead because the scale of such conflicts as the war in Russia or China could not be measured. At least 20 million soldiers died. And, because of the ever-increasing range and power of weapons as well as the bombings and the extermination campaigns, civilian deaths must have come close to 50 million.

Max Huber's International Committee of the Red Cross could carry out even less of its mission than in World War I. It could not always help wounded soldiers or maintain contact between prisoners of war and their families. Neither Stalin nor the Japanese wartime prime minister Hideki Tojo permitted the ICRC to help prisoners of war or even to arrange an exchange of mail. Nor did they authorize any release of information about prisoners. And they would not accept or distribute relief packages that families sent to prisoners of war. Soldiers and their families remained for years without any news of each other and without knowing who might be dead or alive. And national Red Cross societies continued to insist that they would help only their own soldiers.

A British diplomat observed tartly that Japan broke every single humanitarian treaty that it had signed, including the convention on prisoners of war and the agreements governing the treatment of wounded in battle. A British prisoner whom the Japanese forced to help build the River Kwai road in Burma and Thailand observed that "death called to us from every direction." In the Bataan Death March, which killed 10,000 American and Filipino prisoners of war after the Japanese conquest of the Philippine Islands in 1942, as in every other campaign that followed, the Japanese military acted with unprecedented brutality. In China, the Japanese army conducted germ warfare experiments on Chinese prisoners. By the end of the war, more than a quarter of the prisoners in Japanese hands had died from ill treatment.[26]

The Germans and Austrians did at least abide by the rules governing mail and contacts for prisoners of war, so that the ICRC could function in the western areas of World War II if not in the eastern areas. They permitted the ICRC to have lists of prisoners and they allowed mail from and to the prisoners as well as relief packages of food and other necessities. As the ICRC kept up its work for the prisoners of war throughout the war, its 340 delegates made 11,170 camp visits to Axis and Allied prisoners.

National Red Cross societies collected packages and funneled them through the ICRC to Allied prisoners in German and Austrian camps, giving the prisoners at least some contact with home. The mail and package shipments even became quite substantial at times. And the Western Allies in turn offered proper treatment to German prisoners of war and to those of Germany's European allies.

But the help that the ICRC could provide for prisoners paled in comparison with the tragedies that it could not prevent in the treatment of civilians. Even more than in earlier wars, the states fighting in World War II targeted civilians. The Nazis conducted scorched earth campaigns, especially in Poland and the Soviet Union. They destroyed every village and town that they came upon, killing any civilians who had not been able to flee. The Soviets replied in kind once they invaded Germany and Austria. The Western allies acted with greater restraint in their military campaigns, especially as they were often operating in friendly territory such as France, but they also targeted civilians as necessary.

Prime Minister Winston Churchill observed: "We have a right, indeed are bound in duty, to abrogate for a space some of the conventions of the very laws we seek to consolidate and reaffirm."[27] He and other Allied leaders maintained total blockades against Austria, Germany, Italy and their allies throughout the war, knowing that any food that entered Germany would serve Hitler's war machine rather than civilian needs. The Allies rejected ICRC appeals to end the blockades, insisting that the damage they did to the Nazi war machine and to Axis morale counted for more than any suffering inflicted on civilians. The blockades actually did their worst damage after the war, as they remained in force even after the central European administrative and physical infrastructure had totally collapsed.

The civilian populations also suffered from bombing campaigns deliberately intended not only to destroy the enemy's war machine but also to break civilian morale. Hitler launched his "Battle of Britain" air raids against London and other British cities in 1940, killing tens of thousands and forcing Britons to spend many a night in air-raid shelters. Later he launched thousands of V–1 and V–2 rockets against British cities. The Western allies began their own bombing campaigns against Germany at about the same time as Hitler and intensified them throughout the war, culminating in the Anglo-American firebombing of Dresden that killed between 50,000 and 100,000 civilians. American "Flying Fortress" raids and the tactic of carpet bombing produced even more casualties than the Nazi bombings had. And the Americans finished the bombing campaigns by dropping atomic bombs on

Hiroshima and Nagasaki, aiming to kill as many civilians as possible in order to compel Japanese surrender.

The most horrible crime of World War II was the crime of genocide, practiced by the Nazis with the greatest bestiality against Jews although used as well against smaller numbers of other groups, such as Gypsies and homosexuals.

Although the camps into which the Nazis herded Jews and others continued to be called "concentration camps" as they had been called in the Boer War and since, many of the camps should really have been labeled "extermination camps." Hitler and his close associate Heinrich Himmler sent people into those camps to be killed by the most horrible means—including gassing and burning. Many were first compelled to work in slave labor contingents to help produce war materiel for the German armed forces, often dying from sheer exhaustion.

Altogether, a total of 11 million Jews, Gypsies, Catholics, political dissidents, Jehovah's Witnesses, homosexuals, mentally or physically handicapped people and other helpless souls whom the Nazis termed "marginals" died in Nazi camps before and during World War II.[28]

Hitler, Himmler and the Nazi apparatus first denied German Jews any rights of citizenship. Nazi goons then destroyed Jewish synagogues and shops in an orgy of violence on November 9, 1938, on a night called *Kristallnacht* because of the sounds of broken glass from the synagogue and shop windows. The *Nacht und Nebel* ("Night and Fog") decree of December 1941, led to the secret deportation of Jews to extermination camps in order to avoid any popular resistance to the deportations. In a conference held at the Wannsee lake in Berlin on January 20, 1942, Hitler approved the "Final Solution," to have the Reich and its conquered territories *Judenfrei* ("free of Jews").

The Nazis established such camps as Auschwitz in Poland to conduct that "solution," using those camps not only as slave labor centers but as places where Jews were herded into gas ovens for burning alive. Before the end of World War II, 6 million Jews had been killed in what has come to be called the "Holocaust."

Few Jews could escape. Some prominent Jewish scientists and intellectuals had been able to get to the West. But many others could not leave Germany because other countries would not accept them. Neither the United States nor Great Britain, where many Jews wanted to flee, would take more than a small number. Neighboring Switzerland could take even fewer because it could not send them on to other countries.

The Red Cross faced a searing dilemma. As the war continued, it began receiving reports of conditions in the extermination camps, of brutal treatment and of butchery. By the end of 1942, the ICRC—like Western Allied governments—knew that Hitler and the Nazis were systematically killing Jews and others. Many in the Red Cross itself argued that the ICRC should act.

The Red Cross could take two possible courses of action:

First, it could try to get into the extermination camps or the concentration camps to help the civilians who were there or at least to inspect the conditions under which the internees were held. It could try to improve camp conditions, to provide medical help, and to keep contact between persons inside and outside the camps.

Second, it could issue a public appeal for the Nazis to stop the imprisonment and murder of the Jews and others. It could reveal what it had learned about conditions in the camps and hope that Hitler would change his policies under the pressure of world opinion.

Huber and the International Committee of the Red Cross failed to act. In a crucial meeting on October 14, 1942, the ICRC considered a possible appeal to visit the camps or a public statement about Hitler's actions. But it chose to do neither. Huber and others decided that the Red Cross had no authority for such action. They also feared that offending the Nazis would mean suspension of the work they were mandated and able to do to help prisoners of war. Nor did they believe that anything they might have said would have restrained Hitler.

International rejection of the "Tokyo Draft" for ICRC help to civilians had shown that the states of the world did not want the Red Cross to intervene on behalf of civilians. Huber, ever cautious and legally minded, did not want to go beyond agreed ICRC tasks.

Thus, although the ICRC could help Jews toward the end of the war, as the camps were being emptied and abandoned and as some Nazi leaders may have wanted to improve their image, it did not issue a public appeal or try to get into the camps. The ICRC has been condemned for that failure, with a number of books denouncing the Red Cross and suggesting that some of its leaders may have harbored anti-Semitic feelings.[29]

After the war, the ICRC defended itself. It opened countless archives and gave a number of scholars access in order to justify its inaction. In a brief commentary on books that had denounced it for self-paralysis, the Red Cross stated that Huber and others had tried conscientiously to serve their humanitarian cause but had been afraid that they would lose their important claim to neutrality if they denounced the Nazis. They feared that Hitler would have retaliated by stopping the ICRC from helping prisoners of war.

The ICRC also pointed out, accurately and tellingly, that even the mighty Western Allies had not issued statements informing the world of what they knew and calling on Hitler and Himmler to stop. Nor had the Allies tried to bomb the extermination camps even when they knew where the camps were. Neither Roosevelt nor Churchill had acted to help to save the Jews or to try to destroy the camps, although they had as much information as the ICRC if not more.[30]

The American historian Michael Beschloss has revealed that Roosevelt himself waited for two years, from 1942 to 1944, before issuing any statement condemning Nazi killings of millions of Jews in the death camps. Some observers even believed that he mainly acted in 1944 because he wanted to be sure of winning the Jewish vote in New York during the upcoming election. Whatever may or may not be true, Roosevelt did finally issue a statement and he also established the War Refugee Board that played a role in helping Jews to leave Europe. But he still refused to give orders to bomb the extermination camps although he was pressed to do so. He argued that it might divert resources from bombing German military facilities and might thus delay Allied victory.[31]

The failure of the ICRC and others actually reflected 500 years of the international system more than a flaw in any single institution. Under the system's unalterable rules, no international organization could have any more power than the nation-states had deigned to give it. The ICRC could not help the Jews. Nor, for that matter, could it help the American prisoners in Japan or the German prisoners in the Soviet Union. Nor could it help the Jews who had been turned over to Hitler by German collaborators in France and other conquered states.

The states of the world had decided that they alone could make the rules, that they alone could choose when to obey or not to obey them, and that they alone could decide when to enforce or to ignore those rules. Even after overwhelming evidence of civilian suffering during World War I, the ruling states had still not yielded an ounce of authority for helping civilians to the oldest and most widely respected international humanitarian organization or, for that matter, to any other organization.

The states of the West could condemn Hitler's genocide after the war but they also bore some responsibility for his, for Tojo's and even for Stalin's murderous acts. They had failed to give the ICRC the authority to protect civilians, despite repeated appeals and efforts. During the war, they themselves failed to make any effort to protect civilians on either side.

In a system dominated by the sovereign states, Huber chose to play the role that he had been assigned and authorized. He did what he could, which was important. He did not try to do more, to the ICRC's eternal regret. Shameful as that might have been, it conformed to the spirit of the age. Huber had been given neither encouragement nor support to help civilians in China, Ethiopia or Spain, and he undoubtedly sensed that he would receive no support if he tried to help any civilians in World War II.

The system of sovereign states had revealed its murderous flaws. It had brought on a war. It had not made any efforts to stop the war or to attenuate its effects. It had not taken even the most basic steps to protect the lives of the innocent and of the helpless. And, ultimately, not only Germans and Japanese but others also were revealed to have played a role in dreadful crimes.

The state system had not only failed in the wars themselves. It had abandoned all humanitarian principles. Hitler killed six million Jews as well as other Germans and non-Germans, finally accounting for perhaps 20–30 million victims. Stalin and other communist leaders, whether in the Soviet Union, China or elsewhere, whose crimes have not been as carefully studied and documented, probably killed a total of 85–100 million. Later, others kept adding to the dreary record. Yet no Western government denounced or tried to stop any slaughter. The humanitarian conscience may have existed in common feelings but it did not affect how states would act. It could not protect victims of state inhumanity.[32]

Genocide became the defining crime of the twentieth century. One genocide followed another, some in the name of race, others in the name of war, ethnicity or ideology, and still others in the pursuit of sheer power. As the world was to learn, people kept killing each other by the tens of millions even as civilization allegedly scaled new heights. Genocide was also to become not only the worst but the most widely ignored crime. Those not directly affected usually preferred to look away.[33]

Numbers almost lost meaning when they reached such enormous proportions, but one could not and cannot forget that each represented a humanitarian as well as a personal and family tragedy.

Fifteen hundred years after the Visigoths destroyed Rome, eleven hundred years after Charlemagne tried to build a new universal empire, seven hundred years after St. Thomas Aquinas made the last effort to create a universal system of natural law, and six hundred years after the dawn of the sovereign nation-state, humanity faced a moment of reckoning.

If the system of fully sovereign states remained, and if governments continued to act with the same callous disregard for humanitarian principles and human life, the states would destroy not only each other but the entire human race and perhaps all life on Earth. At the midpoint of the century of death, the political leaders of the world faced a clear choice: either to change their ways or to have all the nations perish.

FOUR

STRENGTHENING HUMANITARIAN PROTECTION

GRAND-ADMIRAL KARL DÖNITZ, WHO BRIEFLY BECAME the German chief of state after Adolf Hitler's suicide, surrendered German forces to U.S. general Dwight Eisenhower on May 8, 1945. Earlier, he had tried frantically to get as many German troops as possible in position to surrender to Western rather than Soviet forces. Four months later, on September 2, 1945, U.S. general Douglas MacArthur accepted the surrender of Japanese forces.

As the Germans surveyed the suffering that they had caused and that they had endured, they said that they had reached *Die Stunde Null*, the "Zero Hour," the moment when time would start again for them. But the zero hour struck not only for Germans. The whole world had to start over.

The horrors that emerged after years of war sent shock waves across the world. The leaders and the public saw an even more grisly scene than at the end of World War I, with ruin and devastation everywhere. They could also see German and Japanese prisons and extermination camps. They learned of the Bataan Death March. They saw the evidence of Hitler's Holocaust against the Jews. They realized that German and Japanese behavior had violated all the humanitarian values that most men and women still regarded as part of their tradition and that had once been enshrined in human philosophy on all continents.

The human race had passed through a dark tunnel of butchery and destruction. The war had killed or maimed tens of millions of civilians and soldiers, wrecking lives and families without heed and without mercy.

World leaders, and especially the leaders of the victorious powers, drew back in awe and fear. They could not risk another such war or another such humanitarian disaster. The Allies could rejoice in their victory, but even they could not like what they saw when they looked at the behavior of the entire human race—including themselves. They decided that they needed a real peace this time, not only an armistice. This meant that they would have to look at the postwar arrangements and the peace treaties in a new and different way.

Humanitarian questions loomed large for the Americans and their allies. If they had shown more concern before the war for the fate of civilians in wartime, perhaps by supporting instead of opposing the "Tokyo Draft" that had tried to protect civilians (chapter 3), could they have offered at least some help to the helpless? Could they have made the Nazis, the Italians and the Japanese think twice? If they had permitted more immigration during the 1930s, if they had given more support to refugees, could they have kept Jews and others out of the gas chambers? Everybody felt uncomfortable as they thought about the answers to those questions.

Harry Truman, who became U.S. president upon Roosevelt's death on April 12, 1945, believed that he and others needed to chart a new course. The Americans could no longer try to hide behind the screen of isolationism. They had to become more involved. Also, they needed to show greater humanitarian compassion.

Truman and the new British prime minister, Clement Attlee, joined other Western leaders in wanting to find policies that would avert future wars. As part of that process, they also wanted to lay the foundations for a wider and more effective peace and to make the world more responsive to humanitarian principles and priorities.

Creating the United Nations

Truman set the new tone at the founding conference of the United Nations in San Francisco on April 25, 1945. He and others pledged a new start, with a new commitment to peace, international cooperation and plain decency. Truman's language echoed the early humanitarians:

> If we should pay mere lip service to the inspiring ideals and then later do violence to simple justice, we would draw down upon us the bitter wrath of generations yet unborn. . . . We must build a new world—a far better world—one in which the eternal dignity of man is respected.[1]

Truman and the Western allies chose to act in five humanitarian and related areas:

- Protecting refugees and displaced persons.
- Punishing war crimes.
- Promulgating a concept of human rights.

- Helping civilians in wartime.
- Keeping the peace.

Any visitor to Europe or Asia could immediately see the urgent humanitarian need to help the homeless and dispossessed. Even more millions than after World War I had been uprooted and did not know what to do, where to go or even how to start. As they wandered helplessly through the rubble of their homes and of their cities or villages, or as they found themselves in a strange and hostile land, they brought a new phrase into popular vocabulary, the "displaced persons," the "DPs."

The DPs had either been pushed from their homes or had chosen to leave because an alien government had taken over their land. The Soviets pushed out the Poles before them. The Poles in turn pushed out the Germans. Elsewhere, others pushed out others. Many simply fled the advancing Soviet forces. In even greater numbers than after 1918, those who had survived the war lacked the strength to pick up the pieces of their ruined cities and their shattered lives.

Europe had become a mass of rubble crisscrossed by endless lines of people on the move. The queues of European DPs sometimes stretched as long as 80 kilometers, or 50 miles. None had food, clothing for themselves or their families, or shelter.

To help bring war-torn areas back to life, President Roosevelt and the allies—including Stalin—had agreed to establish the United Nations Relief and Rehabilitation Administration (UNRRA). In Europe, the organization began by trying to help people to get home and then to give them whatever relief might be available. NGOs, like the Red Cross or CARE, also brought support.

James Carlin, a young American who had joined UNRRA after having been discharged from the U.S. Army, wrote later of his surprise that many Russians who had been prisoners of war in Germany did not want to return to the Soviet Union. Neither did Russian civilians. But UNRRA had to force them back because otherwise the Soviets would not repatriate the people under their control. Like others, Carlin felt uncomfortable with the decisions he was obliged to make. The British government, like the American, repatriated many Russians, sometimes at gunpoint. They learned only later—and too late—that many of those they had forced back had been killed on their return.[2]

Stalin's barbarity gradually made the Allies realize that many persons might have good reason not to return to areas occupied by Soviet forces. The Allies termed these persons "refugees" to distinguish them from the "displaced persons" who might actually want to go home. Trying to separate the two groups, they could count about 900,000 refugees and about 700,000 DPs, giving a total of more than one and a half million who needed urgent help and relocation.[3]

Sir Herbert Emerson, the Englishman who directed the Inter-Governmental Committee on Refugees that the Western allies had established at Evian-les-Bains in

1938, issued travel documents to the refugees and DPs so that they could at least be identified. The allies used the organization to break the logjam of persons wandering hopelessly around Europe. He also negotiated agreements with a number of European and Latin American countries to accept refugees.

Stalin insisted, however, that all Soviet citizens be returned. When the Allies wanted to put refugee protection and relocation under the aegis of the United Nations by creating the International Refugee Organization (IRO) in 1947, the U.N. General Assembly found itself embroiled in bitter debate about forced return. More hours during the first session of the United Nations General Assembly were devoted to refugee issues than to any other subject except international security. The Western allies could still establish the IRO, but only after a bitter fight.

The IRO grew from an emergency welfare agency helping European refugees into a worldwide network that not only took care of refugees but also tried to arrange for them to be settled either in Europe or on other continents. It handled protection, relief, resettlement and transport. At its peak, it had a staff of 3,000. It spent a total of over $400 million, a considerable amount in its time.[4]

The Western states believed after World War II, as after World War I, that the new refugee agency should be temporary. They still thought that refugees could be treated as a postwar phenomenon. They decided to close the IRO by July 1, 1950.[5]

Western governments and about 60 NGOs tried to help. Most aid came from the United States because the countries of Western Europe had little to offer. But western European states still had to grant refugees and DPs permission to stay until their future could be decided.[6] As the leaders of the West increasingly realized what happened to DPs returned to the Soviet Union, they stressed the basic right of the people to have a free choice. The U.N. General Assembly concluded that there should be no forced repatriation and that the refugee problem should be treated as "international in scope and nature."[7]

The world was changing dramatically even as the IRO was trying to complete its work. The Cold War, which had barely begun in 1947, started to dominate international politics by 1950 after the Berlin Blockade of 1948–49, the formation of the North Atlantic Treaty Organization (NATO) in 1949, the creation of two German states, the Chinese Communist victory under Mao Zedong and the North Korean invasion of South Korea in June 1950.

The IRO found itself at the center of many Cold War debates. It could repatriate only about 75,000 refugees to eastern Europe and the Soviet Union because others did not want to return. In contrast, almost 2 million wanted to come to the West. The IRO could resettle over a million in such Western countries as the United States, Australia, Israel, Canada and several Latin American states. But it could not find places for all of them, and more than half a million refugees had to remain in western Europe while awaiting resettlement.

Sir Arthur Rucker, the Deputy Director-General of the IRO, said that governments could not be expected "to continue their very heavy contributions indefinitely."[8] Many governments continued to want the refugee problem, like the refugees themselves, to go away.

But other voices spoke differently. The International Committee of the Red Cross and many other agencies, along with a number of European states, began calling for a new and more powerful international agency that would address all aspects of the refugee problem. With Stalin and his allies boycotting the discussions, the U.N. General Assembly on December 14, 1950, decided to establish the office of the United Nations High Commissioner for Refugees (UNHCR) for an initial period of three years from January 1, 1951.

Washington and the Western Europeans disagreed sharply about the length of the new High Commissioner's mandate. The Europeans would have preferred a much longer period. They also argued about the extent of the High Commissioner's powers and his ability to raise funds, with the Americans wanting to restrict both. Washington wanted the High Commissioner to do no more than arrange onward resettlement for refugees from Communism. The Europeans, who had the refugees living on their soil, wanted the High Commissioner to help them then and there.

The American government refused to help fund the High Commissioner's activities. Instead, it funded the Intergovernmental Committee for European Migration (ICEM), a new organization that it had established and that was limited to arranging travel. Because the Europeans had no resources for the High Commissioner, the Ford Foundation stepped in to provide funds.

The Western states also decided that they would need an international agreement to govern the status of refugees. They recognized that they had not offered enough haven to refugees during the 1930s. They met in Geneva in July 1951, and agreed on the United Nations Refugee Convention. While limited to refugees in Europe, the convention included a number of basic provisions that laid the foundation for later worldwide refugee protection and care.

First, the 1951 Refugee Convention gave a basic definition of a refugee as a person who:

> . . . owing to a well-founded fear of being persecuted for reasons of race, opinion, nationality, membership of a particular social group or political opinion, is outside the country of his nationality and is unable or, owing to such fear, is unwilling to avail himself of the protection of that country; or who, not having a nationality and being outside the country of his former habitual residence . . . is unable or, owing to such fear, is unwilling to return to it.[9]

Second, the Convention announced the guiding principle that was to govern the treatment of refugees:

> No Contracting State shall expel or return *("refouler")* a refugee in any manner whatsoever to the frontiers of territories where his life or freedom would be threatened on account of his race, religion, nationality, membership of a particular social group or political opinion.[10]

This prohibition against forcible return, the principle usually defined under the French term of *non-refoulement,* has remained at the heart of all refugee protection and care. It means that a refugee cannot legally be pushed back to the country from which he or she had fled. Those who drafted it had Stalin's Soviet Union clearly in mind, although they also remembered what had happened to those whom they had forced back into Nazi Germany.[11]

The new Refugee Convention marked a dramatic departure for humanitarian law and for the principles governing humanitarian action. It gave refugees a legitimate status as individuals, ultimately recognized by almost 150 states who adhered to the convention and its subsequent 1967 protocol. It also put states under obligation not to return refugees forcibly to a place where they would be under threat. These provisions contrasted with the rules and the practice before World War II. They also contrasted with earlier group determinations, under which refugees in certain groups or from certain states might be accepted but others excluded. Although the convention applied only to persons who had become refugees as a result of events taking place before January 1951, it gave refugees as individuals important rights that were linked to their personal fates and fears.

The United Nations also had to deal with another group of refugees, those created when the United Nations in 1947 divided the British mandate of Palestine between a Jewish and a Palestinian entity. About three quarters of a million Palestinians became refugees, either because they were forced to flee by the fighting or by Israeli forces or because they themselves decided to leave the area that had been designated as Israel. Many of those remained in camps while the rest either settled in cities or left the region.

The United Nations established the United Nations Relief and Works Agency for Palestine Refugees in the Near East (UNRWA) to help the refugees. The United Nations wanted the Palestinians helped separately from refugees in Europe because U.N. officials expected them to need more development aid than the European refugees. Washington and other Western capitals hoped that they would settle in neighboring Middle Eastern states. The Arab states also wanted the Palestinian refugees under a separate mandate because they wanted the refugees to be able to return to Palestine, whereas European refugees did not expect to return home.

Washington also took a different attitude toward funding refugee relief for the Middle East. Whereas the U.S. Congress at first refused to fund aid for European refugees, Washington became the main donor to UNRWA and to the Palestinian refugees while also being the principal supporter of Israel.

Punishing War Crimes

President Franklin Roosevelt and Prime Minister Winston Churchill had begun to make clear during the course of World War II that they would punish German and Japanese military and civilian officials who had committed war crimes. They established the United Nations War Crimes Commission to keep full records of war crimes committed by German and Japanese forces in order to prepare a postwar prosecution against the offenders.

The allies convened an international military tribunal at Nuremberg in Germany on October 18, 1945, with American, British, French and Soviet judges and prosecutors. With Hitler and Himmler already dead, the allies tried their 24 closest living followers including Rudolf Hess, Hitler's close adviser, and Hermann Göring, the head of the *Luftwaffe* (German Air Force).

The tribunal set forth three kinds of crimes:

- *Crimes Against Peace,* such as starting an aggressive war.
- *War Crimes,* actions that went beyond what might be regarded as the normal actions of fighting armies. These included such crimes as murder, torture, the deportation of civilians, the killing or ill treatment of prisoners of war, the killing of hostages and the wanton destruction of cities, towns and other places.
- *Crimes Against Humanity,* the broadest and newest category, intended especially to deal with the more brutal Nazi crimes against Jews and others. These included such crimes as murder, extermination, enslavement, deportation, other inhuman acts against the civilian population (for example, mass murder of hostages, mass extinction or destruction of a town in retaliation for resistance activities). They also included the persecution of innocent persons on religious, racial or political grounds.

The Nuremberg trials concluded on October 1, 1946, with 19 convictions. Although some Germans and others had first regarded the trials as "victors' justice," the fairness of the trials and the numbing recital of Nazi crimes brought home the validity of the sentences and legitimized the special character of war crimes and especially of crimes against humanity. They opened a new page in humanitarian law, especially because of the long recital of German crimes against civilians.

The German courts followed with further trials of known Nazis. They did it very differently from the war crimes trials that they had conducted after World War I, treating Nazi crimes far more harshly than they had treated war criminals after 1918.

The allies made sure that they established individual rather than collective guilt for war crimes. No defendant could claim that he had been ordered to conduct an illegal action and could not be held responsible. Instead, the Allies insisted that each and every defendant should have resisted an illegal order and would be personally liable if he had not done so. They thus placed on each separate official and officer the burden of responsibility for his actions.

The United States and its allies conducted similar trials in Japan under an international military tribunal that convened from May 3, 1946, until November 12, 1948. The court went so far as to convict Hideki Tojo, Japan's prime minister during most of the war. The allies also conducted separate war crimes trials in other Asian states. Afterward, Japanese authorities conducted further trials against Japanese offenders whom the allies had not prosecuted. But the Japanese trials never attracted the international attention of the Nuremberg trials.

President Truman voiced the opinion of many allied officials that the trials had "beaten a path" for the world to follow. They set a clear precedent for international prosecution of national officials who had violated laws and principles of humanity.

In an indirect sense, however, the trials had not set new rules but had harkened back to older rules, to the principles of natural law laid down by the Greek philosophers and medieval humanists. Those philosophers had argued that universal laws and principles had a higher standing than national laws because they represented commonly accepted standards of behavior. The terrible abuses committed in the name of national sovereignty had forced the international legal system to return to earlier principles.[12]

Mrs. Eleanor Roosevelt and Human Rights

Trygve Lie, the first Secretary-General of the United Nations, wanted more than war crimes trials. He wanted to begin to establish a body of law that would protect human rights internationally. So did Mrs. Eleanor Roosevelt, President Franklin Delano Roosevelt's widow, and Harry Truman himself. They proposed that the United Nations agree on a document that would guarantee universal human rights.

A number of non-governmental organizations strongly supported the idea, submitting far-reaching draft proposals for political freedoms and antidiscrimination rules. NGOs had already pushed successfully for human rights language in the

United Nations Charter. They followed up by exerting powerful pressure in favor of a universal document.[13]

Mrs. Roosevelt played the single most important role in helping to establish a U.N. Commission on Human Rights. She was chosen as chairman by acclamation. She became a principal drafter of the Universal Declaration. So did Charles Malik, the Lebanese delegate, who had been a scholar of natural law and an expert on the writings of St. Thomas Aquinas.

But a number of states, led by the Soviet Union, joined the drafting group only in order to water down the document. They also insisted that the document could only be a "declaration," with no legal standing, rather than a formal treaty. Even Washington hesitated, with the Department of State informing Mrs. Roosevelt that she would be "on safer ground" seeking a declaration than a formal convention that carried the force of law. The State Department feared that a formal treaty might not be able to muster the two-thirds majority of the U.S. Senate required to approve a treaty.

After two years of debate, the U.N. General Assembly on December 10, 1948, adopted the Universal Declaration of Human Rights with no negative votes and with only the Soviet delegate and the Soviet satellite states abstaining. It reflected a collective judgment that the world could not tolerate the kinds of brutalities that the Nazis and other dictators had practiced—and, in the case of Stalin, were still practicing.

Mrs. Roosevelt, who regarded the declaration as the culmination of her life's work, hailed its passage as a step in a new direction for the world. She said the declaration "may well become the international Magna Carta of all men everywhere" and termed its passage "a moment of achievement."

The declaration concentrated more on political, social and economic rights than on humanitarian rights. It did not duplicate the major provisions of the Red Cross conventions or of refugee law. Only articles 13 and 14, guaranteeing the right to leave a country and to "seek and enjoy in other countries asylum from persecution," protected rights normally defined as humanitarian. But it had a broad humanitarian purpose because it sheltered individuals from arbitrary state action. Some NGOs, therefore, have treated it as an element of international humanitarian law.[14]

At Last: A Convention for Civilians

The global reaction to the revelation of Nazi and Japanese war crimes led to a series of conventions that prescribed stricter rules than before about military and police conduct against civilians in wartime. These broke new ground, for the sovereign states had always resisted international rules governing their behavior toward civilians. They also helped the Red Cross.

The first new international convention came in December, 1948, when the U.N. General Assembly passed the Convention on the Prevention and Punishment of the Crime of Genocide. The convention, which came into force in January 1951, specifically prohibited the kinds of mass exterminations that the Nazis had conducted.

Next, the four General Conventions of 1949 further expanded the rules of war to give greater protection to victims of armed conflicts. The first three dealt with prisoners of war and the fourth with civilians.

The first three conventions—on the Wounded and Sick in Armed Forces in the Field, on Wounded, Sick and Shipwrecked Members of Armed Forces at Sea, and on the Treatment of Prisoners of War, expanded the protection of the 1929 Geneva conventions, notably for prisoners of war.

These conventions gave more specific guidance on treatment of soldiers and sailors, extending the rules which had been in force before World War II and which had not always been obeyed during the war itself. The United Nations had Japanese and Soviet treatment of the wounded and captured, and especially the Bataan Death March and the forced labor on the River Kwai road and on Siberian projects, very much in mind in passing these conventions.

The fourth convention, the one on civilians, was the only fully new one of the four. It gave the ICRC for the first time the powers that it did not receive in the 1929 conventions and that it had been denied when the "Tokyo Draft" of 1938 did not get the required number of approvals. It specifically authorized the Red Cross to protect civilians and to prevent abuse of civilians in situations of armed conflict.

The conventions also contained a common article stating some basic humanitarian principles that would apply in all circumstances, including in conflicts "not of an international character." But the conventions as a whole applied only in international conflicts between two or more states. They were expanded in the 1977 Additional Protocols, the second of which specifically covered non-international conflicts, although no existing state has actually acknowledged their application in such a situation. The convention against genocide went even further, having universal application at all times and not only in wartime.[15]

Peacekeeping Begins

President Truman and other world leaders also wanted to find ways to prevent tense situations from erupting into open war. To do that, they wanted to use U.N. forces to try to keep the peace in potential crises.

The Palestinian crisis offered the most immediate chance to try to define an important role for the new United Nations by using U.N. forces to keep the peace. Not only did it require a massive refugee support effort and the creation of UNRWA, but it also required a force to try to monitor a cease-fire between Israelis and Palestinians. No other organization could keep the peace, and the U.N. Security Council authorized such a force.

On May 29, 1948, the Security Council formally called upon Israeli and Palestinian forces to cease fire for four weeks. A U.N. mediator, Count Bernadotte, asked for 21 observers from 3 member states of the Truce Commission: Belgium, France and the United States. He also asked for five Swedish senior staff officers. Secretary-General Trygve Lie expanded the peacekeeping force by sending 51 security guards and President Truman sent auxiliary technical personnel to help in the operation. As the United Nations had no distinctive uniforms (with the blue beret and blue helmet not coming into use until 1956), all military observers wore U.N. armbands. Stalin wanted to send Soviet observers as well but the Security Council did not accept his offer because the Western states did not want the Soviet Union to play a role in the Middle East.

The observers served strictly as reporters, informing the Truce Commission of any violations of the cease-fire. They carried no weapons and had no authority to intervene directly if any fighting began. But the Security Council hoped that their very presence would exercise moral suasion and inhibit fighting.

After the temporary cease-fire had expired and fighting had resumed, the Security Council ordered an indefinite cease-fire as of July 18. Drawing on the experience of the earlier cease-fire, the Truce Commission asked for additional observers. Most were provided. Although Count Bernadotte was assassinated and fighting resumed, the new U.N. mediator, Ralph Bunche, was able to arrange a new cease-fire.

Israel also arranged general armistice agreements with several neighbors, giving the United Nations Truce Supervisory Organization (UNTSO) a wider role in supervising a truce not only between Israelis and Palestinians but also throughout the region. To help reduce the risks of war, demilitarized zones and mixed armistice commissions were established. UNTSO tried to maintain the peace by offering the parties to the conflict a neutral body that could investigate and examine complaints about cease-fire violations.

United Nations efforts to make a cease-fire function between Israel and the Palestinians as well as between Israel and its Arab neighbors came to nought, as war broke out repeatedly over the decades to come. But they marked an important effort to set a new and different course for an international organization.[16]

The creation of UNTSO marked a first step in what was to be a long road for the United Nations. Over time, the United Nations was called upon to establish more than 50 peacekeeping missions, with most of the missions proving more successful and shorter than UNTSO. Although the Cold War prevented the Security Council from reaching agreement on peacekeeping in many areas, the Soviet Union and the West agreed often enough to bring peacekeepers into a dozen different crises between 1948 and 1988. Even more followed after 1989, with the Soviet Union not exercising its veto as before.

Four of the peacekeeping operations that began during the Cold War remain in place, like the truce supervisory force in the Middle East, and may remain longer:

- The U.N. Military Observer Group in India and Pakistan (UNMOGIP), which supervises the demarcation line between Indian and Pakistani forces in Kashmir and has been in place since 1949.
- The U.N. Peacekeeping Force in Cyprus (UNFICYP), which supervises the demarcation line between the Cypriote Greek population and its forces on one side and the Cypriote Turkish population and Turkish forces on the other.
- The U.N. Disengagement Observer Force (UNDOF), also for the Middle East, which has provided a buffer between Israeli and Syrian forces along the Lebanese-Syrian border since the 1973 war.
- The U.N. Interim Force in Lebanon (UNIFIL), formed in 1978 because of continuing tensions in Lebanon and along the Israeli-Lebanese border. Like UNTSO and UNDOF, it remains in place because there has been no Middle East peace settlement.

Most of the peacekeeping missions launched during and after the Cold War have been brought to an end and the troops have gone home. They have served in Asia (e.g., West Irian and East Timor), Africa (e.g., Congo), and Central America (e.g., the Dominican Republic). Their presence often made a peaceful settlement possible because they could keep a situation stable while the parties had time to think and to negotiate.

After 1988 and the end of the Cold War, U.N. peacekeeping functions and missions multiplied, with another 30 added between 1988 and the new millennium. Although some of the new ones proved temporary, 13 full-fledged U.N. peacekeeping missions remained in place by early 2003. Adding to the older ones in the Middle East, Africa and Asia, the Security Council placed five new peacekeeping operations into Europe. It sent four of those to the former Yugoslavia (Chapters 8 and 9).[17]

Former U.N. Secretary-General Boutros Boutros-Ghali considered the peacekeeping function of the United Nations as central to the U.N. mission. He wrote in his 1992 report *An Agenda for Peace* that "peacekeeping can rightly be called the invention of the United Nations." Nothing like it had existed before, and Boutros-Ghali wrote that "it has brought a degree of stability to numerous areas of tension around the world."[18]

Peacekeeping gave the new United Nations a formal role in crisis areas that no international organization had ever had. The United Nations repeatedly tried to prevent a crisis from turning into a war, or—in many cases—tried to prevent it from turning into a war again. United Nations peacekeepers often did not appear on the scene until after the first round of fighting had ended inconclusively and both sides as well as the Security Council had decided that the time had come to try to stop further bloodshed.

Because of its efforts to prevent further fighting, peacekeeping often served a humanitarian purpose. It could keep the peace while humanitarian relief could be distributed and humanitarian principles applied. It became an expression of the humanitarian conscience, although some humanitarian agencies did not feel completely comfortable in working alongside military forces.

The Search for Reconciliation

President Truman and Secretary of State George Marshall also undertook actions designed to help the world recover from the destruction wrought by World War II. Marshall in June 1947, announced a program for relief and reconstruction in Europe that came to be known as the Marshall Plan. The program helped to rebuild Western Europe and generated a very different spirit from the vengeful mood that had prevailed after World War I. The victorious allies sought reconciliation and peace, not retaliation.

Truman himself launched several important aid programs during his inaugural address in January 1949, most notably the Point Four program to bring technical help to developing countries. Those proposals, together with the American commitment to the International Bank for Reconstruction and Development (now called the World Bank), tried to strike a different tone from the colonialist exploitation that had prevailed for over 300 years.

Although the steps that Truman and Marshall had taken, like the U.N. peacekeeping operations, might not be regarded as "humanitarian" in the traditional sense of the word, they had a humanitarian intent and effect. Ideally, they would help to prevent war and to reduce human suffering from war. They would also, by offering economic development, relieve the deprivation that might force people to choose war over peace.

Taken together, all these international agreements, and especially the U.N. agreements and U.N. operations, set a new and different course for Europe and the world as a whole. Having seen the horror of yet another global war and the immense suffering that it had caused, the victorious allies as well as a growing number of other states decided that they had to search for a new direction. They could no longer exploit their sovereignty to seek only victory and glory. They had to pay more attention to humanitarian matters.

Most of the new provisions served the long-neglected civilians who had been the main victims of war for centuries. Not only the new Fourth Geneva Conventions but many other accords and actions also aimed directly at the abuses that civilians had suffered. The Nuremberg and Tokyo war crimes trials concentrated on abuses against civilians, whether as groups or as individuals. So did the new rules designed to help refugees and the Universal Declaration of Human Rights. Civilians also stood to benefit from the new programs for economic aid.

The new rules had their limits. No declaration had as much legal power as a treaty or a formal convention. The war crimes trials had a powerful effect but everybody knew that other crimes had gone unpunished. Nonetheless, the states of the world had made real progress, at least on paper. They had taken a concrete step to punish perpetrators of humanitarian abuses. They had set new standards.

Although the rules of sovereignty remained in place and governments could still largely determine what could happen and what could not happen, U.N. officials, the ICRC, the NGOs and other humanitarians could hope for at least some restraint on state behavior. World War II had taught better lessons than World War I.

The late 1940s and early 1950s represented heady days for those who believed in the force of humanitarian law and humanitarian principles. They had few illusions. They knew from bitter experience that states would behave as brutally as possible and only as well as necessary. But they believed that the body of laws, conventions and declarations passed during that decade represented an important expression of the humanitarian conscience and an expansion of the humanitarian realm.

FIVE

HUMANITARIAN CARE GOES GLOBAL

PRESIDENT HARRY TRUMAN, MRS. ELEANOR ROOSEVELT and U.N. Secretary-General Trygve Lie had each helped to put a wider humanitarian system into place between 1945 and 1950. And they did not have to wait long to see it tested.

Truman and the Korean War

Kim Il Sung, the North Korean dictator, on June 25, 1950, ordered his forces to attack across the 38th parallel that had served as a temporary demarcation line between the North and South Korean armistice zones after the end of World War II. Two months earlier, in a secret meeting, Stalin had agreed to let Kim use force to unify the peninsula.

The North Korean forces quickly rolled over South Korean defenses and appeared poised to take over the entire country. But Truman, contrary to Stalin's apparent expectations, decided that the West should resist. The U.N. Security Council passed a resolution agreeing with Truman and directing American and other forces to oppose the North Korean invasion. Because Moscow was boycotting U.N. Security Council meetings at the time, it could not exercise its veto to block the resolution.

General Douglas MacArthur, appointed U.N. as well as U.S. commander, was able to draw a defensive perimeter of U.S. and South Korean forces to prevent the North Koreans from conquering all of Korea. He then conducted a major troop landing at Inchon, on the western side of the Korean peninsula, outflanking and routing the North Korean invaders. He drove them back toward the Yalu River, the border between North Korea and Mao Zedong's new Peoples Republic of China. At that point, Mao sent an army of several hundred thousand "volunteers" and in turn drove the U.N. forces back into South Korea. After more fighting, the two armies were able to hold and stabilize positions remarkably close to the original demarcation line at the 38th parallel.

Paul Ruegger, the President of the International Committee of the Red Cross, contacted all parties to the conflict within days of the beginning of the war to remind them of the Geneva conventions and to offer help. He appointed a delegate, Frédéric Bieri, to try to make sure that all sides observed the Geneva conventions, especially those on the treatment of prisoners of war, as well as the new Fourth Convention on civilians.

Syngman Rhee, the President of South Korea, replied to Ruegger that he and his soldiers would observe the Geneva conventions. But Kim Il Sung did not reply. United Nations forces captured over 100,000 North Korean soldiers, many of them trapped by MacArthur's Inchon landing, and accepted ICRC supervision. The North Korean and Chinese forces captured tens of thousands of American and South Korean soldiers trapped when they had advanced too close to the Yalu. But Kim Il Sung would not let ICRC delegates visit prisoners of war in North Korea.

The governments with forces in the U.N. command worried about their prisoners of war (POWs). They repeatedly demanded Red Cross access to the camps, especially once it became apparent that the North Koreans and Chinese used what became known as "brainwashing" to try to convert the POWs to Communism. They protested particularly sharply, and successfully, when the North Koreans suggested that they might try the POWs as "war criminals." But they could not prevent the North Koreans from conducting "reeducation" training and from offering "incentives" (such as adequate food rations) to any compliant American and other U.N. POWs.

In the meantime, conditions in the South Korean camps became overcrowded and inadequate by international standards. The Red Cross complained and the South Koreans promised to do better but had few resources. More troubling, Communist agitators tried to organize the POWs against their guards and against fellow prisoners who were less ideological. The North Korean POWs soon divided into Communist and anti-Communist factions struggling for control over the camps and over new arrivals. American and other U.N. troops had to stop murderous rioting and almost continuous fighting in the camps between North Korean factions.

Kim Il Sung issued many charges against U.N. conduct of the war. He, as well as some supposedly neutral observers, alleged that U.N. forces were using poison gas in violation of the laws of war. The Americans denied that charge, but had to admit almost 50 years later that U.S. forces had shot and killed innocent civilians in the confusing days following the original North Korean invasion. Nonetheless, the U.N. command and South Korean authorities tried hard to treat North Korean prisoners in accordance with humanitarian principles and with the new conventions.[1]

As both sides realized that they could not win the war and began armistice talks, the Chinese and North Koreans began to assert that all prisoners of war had to be "released and repatriated without delay." This demand, which paralleled the language of the Geneva conventions and which matched Stalin's postwar demand for the repatriation of all Soviet soldiers and refugees, put the U.N. forces before a quandary. The United Nations command did not want to repatriate Chinese and other POWs who wanted to stay in the West. But neither did it want to give up the right to insist on the full return of its own nationals.

The return of prisoners of war, basically a humanitarian matter, thus became the most sensitive political issue debated between the U.N. and Communist negotiators. It also proved the hardest to settle. It had enormous propaganda significance. Mao Zedong, like Kim Il Sung, would be deeply embarrassed to see many of his soldiers refuse to return. Dwight Eisenhower, who had become president in January of 1953 with a pledge to end the Korean War, did not want any American defections. He feared that "brainwashed" U.S. soldiers could be used for communist propaganda.

The negotiators could not resolve the problem until August 1953, when Mao Zedong and Kim Il Sung finally agreed to permit prisoners of war to have a choice. About 76,000 North Koreans went home. Another 23,000 preferred to go into the temporary custody of a Neutral Nation Repatriation Committee chaired by India before deciding where to go next.

Mao Zedong and Kim Il Sung released 13,000 prisoners, mainly South Korean but including 3,500 Americans and 1,300 other U.N. nationals (such as Australians and Turks). Some 16,000 were said to have died in captivity, a grimly high proportion which exceeded even the Japanese and Russian records in World War II.[2]

The war in Korea showed the limitations of the new conventions. The International Committee of the Red Cross could cite all the rules and regulations it wanted but it could still not get access to North Korean camps until the very end, as repatriations began. It could not prevail against those who rejected it and its functions. It could not even be pleased with the performance of the South Koreans, who had promised to adhere to the conventions but did not carry out all their provisions as punctiliously as the Red Cross would have liked.

Ruegger could still draw some comfort from things the ICRC had been able to do at the end of the war and from its ability to help repatriate prisoners. But the ICRC could not force its way past a closed door. In their first test, the new humanitarian conventions could still not compel Kim Il Sung and Mao Zedong to treat POWs as they should have been treated.

Eisenhower and the Hungarian Uprising

Josef Stalin died in 1953. Three years later, in February 1956, Nikita Khrushchev, who had become the head of the Soviet Communist Party (CPSU), made a secret speech at the twentieth CPSU congress denouncing Stalin. He listed some of Stalin's most heinous crimes, including mass murders and deportations. He condemned the way Stalin had suppressed independent Communist parties to establish his satellite regimes in Eastern Europe. He promised to put relations with those parties on a new footing.

Khrushchev's speech became widely known, reprinted in the West and circulated clandestinely throughout the Soviet Union and Eastern Europe. It sent shock waves through the ruling East European Communist parties as the people in the satellite states sensed a chance for more freedom.

Imre Nagy, the new Hungarian premier, introduced liberal reforms into Hungary in response to a demonstration by 300,000 people on the streets of Budapest. He also promised to withdraw Hungary from the Moscow-sponsored Warsaw Pact, a military alliance that Stalin had forced East European states to join in response to NATO.

After having initially accepted the new Hungarian government, Khrushchev changed his mind. On October 4, 1956, he sent a force of 200,000 Soviet troops and over 2,000 tanks into Budapest and across all of Hungary to suppress the new government. Many Hungarians chose to fight the Soviet army in Budapest and elsewhere. Over 3,000 Hungarians died in the resistance.

Soviet forces needed to concentrate on capturing Budapest and the center of Hungary, and thus could not also control the borders. Many Hungarians, afraid that they might be arrested and executed in a return to Stalinism, decided to flee to the West via Austria or Yugoslavia. Within days of the Soviet crackdown, tens of thousands were making their way across the border. The refugees brought their families. Some who could not flee sent their children to the West.

Gerrit Jan van Heuven Goedhart, the U.N. High Commissioner for Refugees, watched with deep concern. He knew that Austria, still desperately poor from World War II, could neither take care of refugees nor keep them. He got ready to help. When Austria appealed for immediate aid and asked him also to help refugees resettle in other countries, he agreed to do both. He sent Auguste Lindt, the man who was to be his successor, to coordinate the operation.

President Eisenhower reversed America's long-standing reluctance toward taking refugees. He announced that the United States would accept 5,000 refugees immediately. Other countries, including Australia, Canada, Chile, Denmark, France, New Zealand, Norway, Sweden and the United Kingdom, followed. The ICRC coordinated a vast relief operation in Austria itself.

Private NGOs helped. The International Rescue Committee (IRC), which had been originally founded to help Jews flee from Nazi Germany, despatched teams to help refugees find countries for resettlement. Leo Cherne and Angier Biddle Duke, chairman and president of the IRC, respectively, happened to be in Vienna at the beginning of the Soviet attack. They went into Budapest itself before the Soviet forces could seize full control of the city, bringing medicines that had been donated by American drug companies for Hungarians wounded by Soviet forces. A young American businessman, John Whitehead, who was later to be chairman of the IRC and who also happened to be in Vienna, drove into Hungary with supplies of radios so the Hungarians could find out how the world reported their struggle. Students from Oxford University drove from England to deliver relief supplies and to help rescue refugees.

Mrs. Roosevelt supported Eisenhower's appeal for Americans to help refugees and to provide them asylum in the United States. She also visited refugee camps in Austria, as did Vice President Richard Nixon.[3] The League of Red Cross Societies provided relief for Hungarian refugees who had gone to Yugoslavia. Other relief organizations, such as CARE, Church World Service and the British Voluntary Society for Aid to Hungarians, sent help.

James Carlin, who had become the director of the Vienna office of the Intergovernmental Committee for European Migration (ICEM), took charge of the travel arrangements for refugees. ICEM provided whatever papers could be arranged for persons who had fled without any documents. It also scheduled flights to countries of resettlement. By early December, more refugees were leaving Austria than arriving.[4]

Eisenhower came up against a peculiar dilemma, however. He and other Western leaders who wanted to help found that the Hungarians could not be termed refugees under any international agreement. Having wanted to avoid long-term refugee commitments during the postwar years, the United States and other Western governments had limited the refugee definition to a person who had become a refugee "due to events occurring before January 1, 1951." Washington had even insisted on that definition against the wishes of the Europeans because it did not want to help European refugees indefinitely. But in 1956 the U.S. Congress and American public opinion felt enormous sympathy for refugees fleeing from Soviet tanks. Moreover, Eisenhower himself wanted very much to help.

Lindt asked Paul Weis, legal adviser to the High Commissioner's office, to determine whether the refugee definition applied to the Hungarian exodus. On the surface, that seemed a hard case to argue. After all, the Hungarians had fled in 1956, five years after the old definition had expired. But Weis ruled that the events that had led to the exodus had occurred in 1947 and 1948, when Hungary had fallen under a Communist regime. They thus qualified under the old definition.

The U.N. General Assembly, which had the power to instruct the High Commissioner, agreed that the Hungarian refugees deserved support. Thus, the Hungarian exodus effectively extended the definition of a refugee well past the 1951 deadline.

Eisenhower's attitudes and policies gave the Hungarian refugees excellent resettlement chances. The first group left Vienna for the United States on November 21, 1956. By mid-1958, about 38,000 had resettled in America. Others went to many countries, including Australia (13,000), Canada (35,000), France (10,000), Switzerland (11,500), the United Kingdom (16,000), and West Germany (15,000), with smaller groups going to virtually every state in the Western world.

But Lindt did not want to work only with the states of the West. He wanted humanitarian assistance to be neutral and nonpolitical. When he learned that the new Hungarian government of Janos Kadar welcomed refugee repatriation and offered a limited amnesty to returnees, Lindt agreed to help those who freely wanted to go back. After several years, over 18,000 did return, accompanied by UNHCR officials to make sure the returnees were accepted and well treated. Lindt was the first United Nations High Commissioner for Refugees to work with East as well as West.[5]

The Hungarian refugee exodus totally changed the humanitarian landscape, especially for refugees but also for others. It put a human face on the Cold War and on the East–West crisis. Western governments had given refugees only minimal support, but they now provided whatever aid might be needed. They also continued to accept large numbers of refugees, in stark contrast to the 1930s or even the immediate postwar years.

Press reports and images in the new medium of television drew mass attention to the Hungarian resistance and exodus. Americans and Western Europeans could see heroic Hungarian civilians opposing Soviet tanks, showing that the Hungarian uprising was a gallant example of a small nation resisting a gargantuan invader. They could see families crossing into Austria and arriving destitute in the Vienna refugee camps. For the first time, the people of the West saw a humanitarian crisis as it happened.

With the Hungarian exodus, humanitarian relief and especially refugee support came of age. From a marginal activity linked to the immediate aftermath of war, it became a commonly accepted phenomenon. People everywhere understood that the Cold War could cause human suffering just as a hot war could, although perhaps in a different way. They wanted to help.

The refugee cause also appealed to Americans because they saw the Soviet oppression of Hungary as an example of the Communist aggression that they were committed to resist. Coming after the Soviet oppression of the Berlin uprising of June 17, 1953, it confirmed the image of civilians fleeing tanks and it provided a powerful motivation to help refugees survive and resettle in the West.

After 1956, Americans and others understood humanitarian aid in a new and different way from the interwar and postwar years. And they particularly sympathized with people in flight. Refugee protection, relief and resettlement became one of the most important elements of the expanding humanitarian movement. In particular, the Hungarian exodus established an international network of governments and NGOs ready to move refugees to a new life.

Congolese Independence

King Leopold II of Belgium, one of the most avaricious of the European conquerors of Africa, had seized the Congo as his personal possession during the second half of the nineteenth century. He had used Belgian forces to conquer the region in one of the harshest colonization campaigns on record, establishing the "Congo Free State" in 1885. He had exploited its vast mineral riches mercilessly. When ever-widening resistance among the Congolese made the Congo too costly to govern, he had turned it over to the Belgian state in 1905. Brussels continued to exploit the colony's mineral resources. It gave the people no political rights nor any access to education or to any form of advancement. The Congo suffered more than almost all other African colonies.

When the Congolese people watched the wave of decolonization elsewhere in Africa during the 1950s, they began demanding greater rights. The Belgian government, totally incapable of dealing with the popular demonstrations, decided to cut and run. After a minimum of political and economic preparation and no guidance in the principles of self-government, Brussels granted the Congo its independence on June 30, 1960, having first had the Belgian parliament pass a *Loi Fondamentale* to govern the newly independent state. The Congo had only 17 university graduates and no African doctors, lawyers or engineers.[6]

The Belgians also urgently arranged Congolese elections, which led to a Congolese parliament badly split between various factions. As a compromise, the parliament elected two rival leaders, Joseph Kasavubu and Patrice Lumumba, as president and prime minister, respectively. Belgium retained two major military bases at Kamina and Kitona and took over command of a Congolese security force, the *Force Publique.*

Dag Hammarskjöld, the U.N. Secretary-General who had succeeded Trygve Lie, appointed Ralph Bunche, the American Undersecretary-General of the United Nations for Special Political Affairs, to become his personal representative in the new state.

The situation soon began unraveling, especially as the Congo had no institutions even minimally prepared to function after independence. The Congolese troops of the *Force Publique* mutinied because of low wages. The Belgians remaining in the Congo feared for their lives. The Belgian ambassador urged Lumumba to ask for Belgian troops to help keep order, but Lumumba refused because he believed that it would return the country to colonial rule. Instead, he replaced the Belgian commander of the *Force Publique*. Nonetheless, Belgium ordered its troops to return to the Congo without Congolese permission in order to protect Belgian nationals. Heavy fighting broke out between Belgians and Congolese.

Moshe Tschombe, the provincial president of Katanga, the Congo's richest center for mineral exploration, exploitation and export, proclaimed Katanga's independence. The largest Belgian-owned mining company, the Union Minière du Haut-Katanga, supported and probably financed his bid for independence. Kasavubu and Lumumba asked for U.N. help to hold their country together.

The Organization of African Unity (OAU), the new African regional association, had decided at its very first meeting that the newly independent African states could not accept any secession. They realized that so many ethnic groups existed within each African state that many states could quickly unravel if each group claimed its independence. Any secession in any of the new African states thus raised alarms across the continent.

The members of the U.N. Security Council, therefore, unanimously approved the Congo's request to keep Katanga in the Congo state. To do that, the Security Council established a peacekeeping force for the Congo. In consultation with Hammarskjöld it issued a set of instructions that have over time remained general principles for U.N. peacekeeping operations in which the United Nations did not anticipate more armed conflict:

- The force would be a temporary security force deployed with the consent of the Congolese government.
- But the force would operate under U.N., not Congolese, orders.
- The United Nations would have free access to the area of operations of the force.
- The U.N. force would function separately and distinctly from the Congolese national army.
- The force would not become involved in internal conflicts, supporting one faction or group against another.
- Troops would not use force except in self-defense but could fire if fired upon.
- While the United Nations would decide its own force composition, it would take account of host government views.[7]

Under those guidelines, the Secretary-General put together a force composed at various times of troops from Ethiopia, Ghana, Guinea, India, Indonesia, Ireland, Malaysia, Morocco and Sweden. Initial units arrived in Leopoldville on July 15, 1960, less than 48 hours after the Security Council decision. Although the force began with about 8,000 soldiers, it peaked a year later at almost 20,000. The force became known by the acronym ONUC (Opération des Nations Unis au Congo—United Nations Operation in the Congo).

The United Nations force became the dominant element in the Congo for several years until its departure in 1964. Although pledged to distance itself from Congolese internal politics, it played a key role in virtually all important events and developments. It lost Moscow's support because Soviet leader Nikita Khrushchev regarded it as hostile to Lumumba, too activist and too pro-Western. The operation also cost the life of Secretary General Hammarskjöld in a plane crash while on his way to attend a meeting for possible reconciliation of various Congolese groups.

ONUC first had to remove the Belgian forces, as the Congolese government absolutely insisted. To do that, it had to establish a minimum of order throughout various cities and regions. It did so quickly, except in Katanga, although the Congolese government threatened to call in Soviet forces to help if ONUC did not move fast enough. Most Belgian forces had left by August 1960.

ONUC also tried to establish internal order, a harder task because of intense rivalries between various groups and regions in the country. As an independent force, ONUC could arrange cease-fires between warring armies and factions in various parts of the Congo. It thus helped to put an end for a time to widespread clashes. But it could not establish full stability over all the diverse regions of the country. That task remained unfinished even four years later, when ONUC left the Congo, and it remains unfinished to this day.

Although ONUC tried to distance itself from internal Congolese disputes, it found itself drawn in on several occasions. It had to help solve a year-long constitutional crisis when President Kasavubu and Prime Minister Lumumba quarreled and established rival governments and rival armies. ONUC arranged for cease-fires between those armies whenever possible. It tried to help civilians by delineating neutral zones and by arranging protected areas wherever it could. Finally, the Security Council gave ONUC authority to use force to end the violence, and it did intervene to stop rival army clashes on several occasions. It made the re-opening of parliament possible by forming protective cordons around the parliament building. But it could not stop the fighting completely. It could not even protect the life of Patrice Lumumba, who was caught by rival factions and transferred to Katanga where he was brutalized and murdered.

ONUC played a central role in ending the secession of Katanga in February 1963. This secession, aided and abetted by the Union Minière and other foreign mining interests as well as by large numbers of Belgian and other foreign mercenaries, violated the U.N. Security Council resolution that supported the territorial integrity of the Congo. For a long time, ONUC tried to use peaceful means to end the secession as it had no authority to use force except in self-defense.

After several efforts at reconciliation had failed in 1962, the Security Council ordered ONUC to end the secession by force. ONUC then began to round up mercenary troops and to move across Katanga to establish control. Some fighting ensued, leaving about 10 U.N. soldiers dead and 22 wounded, but the operation proceeded rapidly. Tschombe ended the Katanga secession, placing his forces under ONUC command and integrating his administration into the central Congo government.

At this point, ONUC took over many central functions, helping the Congo government to establish essential services nationwide, sending experts to help make a central currency market function and coordinating food and other aid for refugees and civilians. A United Nations civilian aid program gradually assumed these functions, helping to give the Congo the kind of infrastructure that Belgium had failed to provide before its departure. ONUC's basic mandate then no longer served a useful purpose. By June 30, 1964, it withdrew its forces, ended its operations and went out of existence.

The United Nations came of age in an operational sense through the ONUC engagement in the Congo. Although it had conducted earlier peacekeeping missions, the United Nations had never tried a mission on such a large scale. Nor had it ever launched one with such an ambitious agenda, trying to help to bring a major colony not only into independence but into some semblance of order. For several years, ONUC was the only structure that held the Congo together. Having some credibility with all sides most of the time, it also often served as an essential intermediary. In the process, the U.N. force carried out a wide range of military, civilian and diplomatic functions. Finally, it had to fight to hold the Congo together and to help to build a nation.

ONUC carried out a military mission but with a humanitarian purpose. It tried to prevent the loss of human life by maintaining peace. But it faced the problem that all peacekeeping missions were to face over time: what to do when the competing forces no longer wanted peace. It then had to fight to maintain the peace, going beyond a humanitarian task but still trying to reduce loss of life by building stable and lasting institutions.

ONUC was to have no successor in its peacekeeping mission for almost 30 years, until the end of the Cold War. Although it had achieved much of what it had set out to do, the states on the Security Council—and especially the Soviet

Union—questioned whether they wanted to yield that kind of responsibility to the United Nations again.

Civil War in Nigeria

Africa also offered the scene for the next humanitarian crisis, one that would further expand the role of humanitarian agencies but that would also raise further questions about that role.

The new state of Nigeria, which had emerged from the British colony of the same name, contained over 300 ethnic groups. One of the most important, the Ibos, lived largely in eastern Nigeria. Educated and entrepreneurial, largely Roman Catholic, they coexisted unhappily with the Muslim-dominated Hausa who controlled Nigerian politics from the north. As fighting spread between them, the Ibos retreated to their original homelands in the east. In the spring of 1967 they founded a newly independent state called Biafra under the leadership of Colonel Odumegwo Ojukwu. They hoped to attract recognition and support.

Because Biafra could not produce enough food to feed its people, Nigeria's military leader, General Yakubu Gowon, launched a systematic strategy of blockade and starvation. Within months, the Western press began carrying pictures of starving Ibo families, including children with distended bellies and bulging eyes, which won the overwhelming sympathy of Western public opinion, including the Catholic Church, as well as massive pledges of support for the Ibos. Many Western governments and agencies accused the Nigerian government of genocide.

Most Western and African governments supported the Nigerian central government because they continued to fear that a successful ethnic rebellion anywhere on the African continent could encourage similar uprisings. Although some African states recognized Biafra, most did not. France and China supported the rebellion but did not formally recognize Biafra. Britain, the Soviet Union and the United States supported Nigeria. But all Western states found their publics deeply disturbed by Nigeria's tactic of starvation. They wanted to end the famine, whether or not they favored an independent Biafra. A *Sunday Telegraph* correspondent wrote that "The agony of Biafra is an affront to the conscience of the civilized world."[8]

The International Committee of the Red Cross, conscious of its new mandate to help civilians, called on all parties to "respect urgent humanitarian measures." Nigeria's General Gowon and Biafra's Colonel Ojukwu both promised to respect the Geneva conventions and invited the ICRC to function freely. The Biafra war thus became the first real test of the new 1949 conventions. The war also became a test of the ICRC's ability to work in an African war. The ICRC hoped to succeed, especially as its delegate, George Hoffmann, had good relations with both leaders.

The ICRC went far beyond its traditional mandate to help soldiers and prisoners as it became the principal provider of civilian relief, especially to the Ibos. With Nigerian forces blockading Biafra's ports, the Red Cross chose to deliver the food by air. Because of its tradition of neutrality, it had to ask Nigeria for permission. General Gowon, anxious to cooperate with the international community, agreed, but he warned that planes carrying relief supplies would "fly at their own risk."

Food deliveries for Biafra became difficult and dangerous, especially because Colonel Ojukwu insisted that he would not accept any food that had been shipped through Nigeria. The aircraft had to fly at night, when they could not be easily seen, to reduce the risk of being shot down. They sometimes had to fly at the same time as aircraft smuggling arms and ammunition. This did not affect the flights at the beginning when the airlift could operate on a small scale but it became increasingly hazardous as Biafra needed ever-growing quantities of food. Fourteen Red Cross pilots and relief personnel died in the operation.[9]

Bernard Kouchner, a French doctor, gave up his work with the ICRC to found a new organization, Médecins sans Frontières, because he wanted to help Biafra without the constraints of Red Cross neutrality. Several private NGOs, including some Catholic relief agencies and Scandinavian Joint Church Aid, conducted their own relief operations with their own flights. Biafra attracted the most massive NGO assistance program since the European operations at the end of World War II. An official of UNICEF, the United Nations Children's Fund, noted that "we suddenly found that the world was full of competitive non-governmental organizations."[10]

Many problems, such as difficult flying weather or political shifts in Nigeria or Biafra, often interrupted relief operations. The flights could not end the starvation fully although they alleviated it. The Red Cross estimated that it had saved two and a half million potential victims of the war, which it regarded as a genuine humanitarian achievement. It also found that it had—unintentionally and reluctantly—practiced what some called "revolutionary humanitarianism," the use of relief on such a large scale that it could have a significant impact on the result of a conflict.

Although General Gowon supported the ICRC, many of his officers felt that they could end the war quickly if the relief flights stopped. They became increasingly irritated about the flights. Contrary to Kouchner, they believed that the ICRC had in fact abandoned neutrality and had leaned too much toward Biafra.

General Gowon grew particularly suspicious of ICRC delegate Auguste Lindt. He thought that Lindt wanted to become an intermediary between Nigeria and Biafra for political talks. Gowon would have none of that. He preferred a Red Cross that confined itself to delivering aid while leaving politics to African leaders. He believed that Lindt's efforts went beyond the ICRC mandate.

In July 1969, General Gowon put an end to the ICRC flights by threatening to shoot them down. He accused the Red Cross and other agencies of prolonging the war and thus causing rather than reducing suffering. He asserted that relief supplies supported the rebellion. He also complained that some of the NGOs made wild charges about Nigerian cruelty in order to get contributions for Biafra. The ICRC had no choice but to suspend relief operations although it could still engage in its traditional role of visiting prisoners of war and delivering messages between prisoners and their families.

The ICRC could regard its relief efforts in Biafra as a humanitarian achievement. It had been able to apply the 1949 Geneva conventions with some success, even if not perfectly. It had also carved out a new role for itself. For the first time in its history, it had conducted a truly massive relief effort for civilians in the midst of a conflict. Never before had so much foreign aid gone into such a limited area in wartime, although an estimated 600,000 Nigerians, Biafrans and others had still died.

But civilian relief followed different rules from those related to helping POWs, and the ICRC had paid for that. When the war ended with a Nigerian victory, General Gowon refused to permit the Red Cross or any other Western relief agencies to help the defeated Ibos.

The Biafra operation had brought relief operations fully into the modern era. It legitimized massive civilian relief in wartime as an addition to international humanitarian activities. Biafra had become a true media spectacle, intensely and closely reported by Western television and press, and the relief agencies became humanitarian stars.

The operations also, however, raised questions that neither the ICRC nor other humanitarian agencies could answer. Several of those questions had already arisen in the United Nations Congo operations, and they would arise again elsewhere:

- Had the humanitarian agencies and some of the governments that engaged in "revolutionary humanitarianism" really remained neutral as they had promised, actually supporting Biafran independence while claiming only to help the Ibo people?
- Or had the ICRC and other agencies been too neutral? Kouchner's resignation underlined this question but many others felt it as well.
- Most troubling, given the humanitarian motive of the ICRC and the NGOs, had aid prolonged the war and thus the longer-term suffering of the people by permitting Biafra to continue to fight instead of trying to negotiate a political solution?

The Red Cross debated these problems at length. So did all NGOs. None ever reached an answer that fully satisfied its own members and the outside world, perhaps because there was no answer.

In their heart of hearts, however, the agencies believed that they could not have acted differently. They had seen starving people and had chosen to help without regard to real or imaginary limits on their mandate. They had followed their humanitarian instincts. Many, like Kouchner, wished they had done more. At least, however, they had tried. And they had broken new ground for humanitarian action.

Worldwide Humanitarian Action

The Biafran war marked the end of the first phase of humanitarian action after 1950. During that phase, the United Nations as well as many governments and private agencies faced one humanitarian crisis after another as they tried to deal with the effects of decolonization and of the Cold War.

Humanitarians faced more crises than the seminal events described above. They helped floods of refugees from colonial wars in Tunisia, Algeria and elsewhere in Africa and Asia. A million Vietnamese fled from north to south after the division of Vietnam at the 17th parallel in the Geneva agreements of 1954. The break between East and West Pakistan, followed by the 1971 creation of Bangladesh as an independent state, might have led to a massive humanitarian tragedy. In each case the humanitarian movement helped to make practical solutions possible.

Virtually every crisis continued to produce questions about how the laws of war and humanitarian principles should be applied in anticolonial struggles and in the Cold War world. Was terror a legitimate expression of the fight for freedom? Should the rules governing the treatment of prisoners of war apply to members of revolutionary movements? Should persons fleeing colonial wars be treated as refugees if they might also have been fighters and might become fighters again?

As an absolute and unshakable matter of principle, the humanitarian agencies pledged to act differently from the way they had acted during the 1930s and during World War II. They insisted that they would apply the humanitarian conscience and humanitarian rules no matter how difficult the situation.

Even when they were confronted with governments that insisted on their sovereign right to act with brutality, the agencies tried to help people as best they could. This determination, more than any specific body of rules, became the lodestar of the new humanitarian world.

Sadruddin Aga Khan, the new U.N. High Commissioner for Refugees, often reminded the West that humanitarian crises and floods of refugees had become a global problem, not only a European one. Under his guidance, the United States and the West European governments agreed to the 1967 Protocol to the 1951 Refugee Convention. That protocol removed both the time and geographic limitations that the United Nations had written into the original convention, making it possible to help refugees who had originated outside Europe and who had fled events that occurred after 1951.

Julius Nyerere, the president of the newly independent state of Tanzania, made a similar argument before the Organization of African Unity. He warned that decolonization would lead to enormous humanitarian tragedies and that Africa had to prepare to deal with its own problems. In 1969, under his leadership, the OAU adopted its own Refugee Convention. It widened the definition of a refugee to include any person having to flee his or her home due to "external aggression, occupation, foreign domination or events seriously disturbing public order."

The new OAU refugee definition suited the colonial and postcolonial conditions of Africa. It legitimized humanitarian relief all over the continent. It also enabled Africans to help each other on a humanitarian basis without political implications.

By the early 1970s, a new and wider world of humanitarian action had begun to emerge. The humanitarian agencies could not challenge the sovereignty of governments but they could do much more than before to mitigate the effects of government policies, and at times they could find governments ready to help.

The leaders of the new world of humanitarianism did not hesitate to seize the new openings for humanitarian law and humanitarian action. They tried to go beyond the narrow limits of their charters. If Nikita Khrushchev decided to repress freedom in Hungary, international agencies could help those who fled. If the Nigerian government tried to starve out the rebellion in Biafra, the International Red Cross and other NGOs could try to bring in food. If the Congo collapsed, the United Nations and other organizations would try to act.

The new generation of humanitarian activists thus carried humanitarian principles further than they had ever been carried before. Some thought they did not do enough and others thought they did too much. One or another government usually complained. But the humanitarians believed that their noble purpose justified and legitimized what they did.

No single leader or group had planned this new humanitarian world, with its mixed record of accomplishments, perplexities and frustrations. They had not expected the humanitarian impact of the Cold War or of decolonization. But they had to deal with them in the context of their commitment.

Humanitarians also found that at least some of the sovereign states that had opposed humanitarian action in the past had changed their attitudes. Some Western governments might have done it for cynical reasons, sensing a chance to score some points in the worldwide struggle against communism. Or they might have done it because they still felt some lingering regret over the way they had behaved from 1914 to 1945.

Whatever the reason, the change in state attitudes opened new opportunities for humanitarian action. Of course, it also raised the risk that states would try to exploit their newfound humanitarian conscience for political gain. But they were at least helping and not hindering humanitarian work.

The humanitarians had a simple but important goal: to have humanitarian action finally expand as fast as humanitarian need.

They even dared to think that they might have a chance to reach that goal.

SIX

THE DECADE OF THE REFUGEE

HENRY KISSINGER, PRESIDENT RICHARD NIXON'S national security adviser, met in Paris on January 23, 1973, with Le Duc Tho, one of the senior Politburo members of the ruling North Vietnamese Communist Party. They had a brief discussion and then jointly initialed an agreement to end the American military role in the Vietnam War. Their agreement culminated three years of negotiation between them. They had first met in secret in February 1970, and had continued their talks off and on throughout many crises, including a massive North Vietnamese offensive in South Vietnam and a U.S. B–52 bombing of North Vietnam. They had finally reached agreement only after Nixon had been reelected.[1]

Kissinger and Le Duc Tho pledged that their governments would scrupulously implement the agreement, but they must both have had their reservations. The North Vietnamese leadership still wanted a united Vietnam under their own rule. The U.S. government still hoped that the South Vietnamese forces could resist the North Vietnamese military attacks that all knew would follow. Both Kissinger and Le Duc Tho expected the fight for South Vietnam and for control of Indochina to continue.

The peace agreement crumbled, as expected. In early 1975, the North Vietnamese army massively and openly invaded South Vietnam. South Vietnamese forces, ill-prepared for that kind of battle, could not resist without substantial American aid, which did not arrive. On April 29, 1975, U.S. helicopters evacuated the remnants of the South Vietnamese government and of the U.S. embassy staff, including U.S. Ambassador Graham Martin. The North Vietnamese front government for South Vietnam, the Provisional Revolutionary Government (PRG), took power in Saigon, which it renamed Ho Chi Minh City after the founder of the Vietnamese Communist Party who had led the Indochinese nationalist movement.[2]

Indochinese Refugees

South Vietnam's residents began to flee Vietnam in ever larger numbers as the North Vietnamese forces advanced. About 140,000 South Vietnamese, many of whom had worked with the Americans and the South Vietnamese authorities, left the country. They used commercial or U.S. military flights, passing through a Saigon airport processing center named "Dodge City." Some fled on small boats from many places on the Vietnamese coast to U.S. vessels waiting in international waters. Most came to the United States as refugees. Smaller numbers made their way to Hong Kong, Thailand, Malaysia, Singapore and the Philippines. Sadruddin Aga Khan, the U.N. High Commissioner for Refugees, hoped and believed that their flight might represent the last exodus caused by the long conflict and that the country could begin to recover from decades of war.[3]

Many American officials, including Martin, helped their Vietnamese friends and associates as well as Vietnamese government officials to leave the country. They also tried to bring out Vietnamese who might be slated for "reeducation" or worse. Two U.S. foreign service officers, Lionel Rosenblatt and Craig Johnstone, left their posts in the State Department temporarily to go to Saigon to bring out as many Vietnamese friends as they could. Kissinger gave them superior honor awards for their action.[4] Even a National Security Council staff member, Kenneth Quinn, traveled to Saigon for the same purpose. The State Department convened an emergency staff to help deal with the refugee crisis. A number of persons, such as Frank Wisner, Henry Cushing and Shep Lowman, began to establish what ultimately became a major office to manage and coordinate refugee care and resettlement.

Refugee flight did not stop after the fall of Saigon although it slowed for about two years. Many South Vietnamese still chose to leave whenever they could. A year after the North Vietnamese had conquered South Vietnam, they removed the PRG front regime and unified all of Vietnam as the Socialist Republic of Vietnam under direct control from Hanoi. They began a wide program of socialization. In particular, they expropriated most of the wholesale and retail distribution system, directly attacking the large ethnic Chinese community in South Vietnam which had been the backbone of the commercial economy.

By 1976, thousands were fleeing Vietnam. Many were ethnic Chinese. Over the years, more than a quarter million Chinese fled to China, and China accepted them as refugees and let them settle with some help from Poul Hartling, Sadruddin's successor as U.N. High Commissioner for Refugees.

But most refugees continued to be ethnic Vietnamese, such as teachers, professionals, farmers or others who did not want to be caught in the ever widening circles of arrest, expropriation, intimidation and "reeducation." Refugee numbers swelled dramatically during 1977 and 1978 when the Vietnamese government widened the "reeducation" program and long-term imprisonment of dissenters. A brutally conducted collectivization program drove even more Vietnamese to flee.

The U.S. government, including the U.S. Congress, did not at first want to accept or support refugees leaving Vietnam.[5] But Congressional leaders changed their minds as they learned more about the numbers and the desperate conditions of the refugees. Senators like Edward Kennedy and Alan Simpson, as well as House Members like Hamilton Fish, Jr., and Steven Solarz, worked hard to authorize and finance programs for the care and reception of refugees.

As the Vietnamese exodus exploded, the refugees stamped their image on the conscience of the world. They appeared on television screens everywhere. They became "the boat people," haggard, emaciated, bobbing precariously in frail and overcrowded craft on the choppy waters of the Gulf of Thailand or of the South China Sea. Even when they came in larger boats, they still drew sympathy because of their plight and the risk of pirates killing and robbing the men and raping the women.

Like the Hungarian refugees 20 years earlier, the boat people aroused deep sympathy and support, and that sympathy spilled over to help provide an understanding for other Indochinese refugees who were to follow in succeeding years. Even many persons who had opposed American involvement in Vietnam wanted to help refugees.[6]

The flow increased month by month, culminating in the flight of more than 50,000 during both May and June of 1979. Although several Southeast Asian countries initially pushed off many of the boat people, forcing the boats back even if it meant that the passengers drowned, more than 375,000 Vietnamese were living in makeshift camps across Southeast Asia and Hong Kong by July of 1979.

When more and more refugees also began to flee Cambodia (see below), the countries of Southeast Asia decided they had done all they could. Thailand in particular did not want to take any more refugees. The American ambassador, Morton Abramowitz, joined with Lionel Rosenblatt in trying to persuade them. But by the end of June, Thailand and four other members of the Association of Southeast Asian Nations (ASEAN) met to announce that they would not let any more refugees enter unless other states agreed to accept them in turn.

President Jimmy Carter decided to call an international conference in 1979 to coordinate the refugee policies of the United States and a number of Asian and European governments. At that conference, held in Geneva, U.S. Vice President Walter Mondale, other Western leaders and Asian leaders made mutually reinforcing commitments. The Southeast Asian states agreed to permit boat people and others to land and to remain, but only temporarily; the Western nations agreed that they would invite those refugees to resettle permanently in the West. Thailand announced that it would assign a senior army officer, Colonel Soonsiri Prasong, to run its refugee office.

Carter took the lead by announcing, even before the conference, that the United States would resettle up to 14,000 Indochinese refugees a month, or 168,000 a year. Australia, Canada, France and many others agreed to take substantial numbers. Japan, which regarded itself as a mono-ethnic society and did not want to resettle Vietnamese on its soil, agreed instead to pay up to one half of the cost of the asylum operation.

Poul Hartling and James Carlin, who had by then become the director of ICEM, agreed to work with interested governments to try to establish a new kind of global system for housing and moving Vietnamese refugees. Many NGOs signed on to the plan. By the following year, the number of refugees leaving Thailand exceeded the arrivals.

Because Vietnam needed to improve its relations with the West as its economy collapsed, the Vietnamese government agreed in 1979 to a special arrangement known as the Orderly Departure Program (ODP) to spare potential refugees—and especially relatives of persons already in the West—the hazards of flight. More than 125,000 persons were able to leave Vietnam for direct travel to resettlement countries between 1979 and 1987. But Vietnam would still not permit persons in "reeducation" programs, including many who had worked for Western embassies and would have been welcome in the West, to leave.

By the late 1980s, as the Cold War neared an end and as the Southeast Asian states and the Western world slowly drew back the welcome mat for Vietnamese refugees, the Vietnamese government agreed to permit some refugees to return if they had not been accepted for asylum. Although many refugees did not want to go back to Vietnam, UNHCR investigations indicated that the returnees were not persecuted. The Vietnamese also permitted about 18,000 children known as Amerasians, who had American fathers and Vietnamese mothers, to go to America so as to permit their fathers to fulfill a moral obligation. And the U.S. government finally persuaded the Vietnamese government in 1989 to let thousands of inmates of the "reeducation camps" come to the United States and to other resettlement states.

The arrangements made during the 1970s and 1980s by Western and Asian states made major humanitarian breakthroughs, as the Hungarian exodus had done 20 years earlier. They expanded the global system of refugee care and resettlement well beyond Europe and the United States.

The Cambodian dictator Pol Pot did his best during the 1970s to earn the title of "another Hitler." The North Vietnamese sent him to take control of Cambodia in the spring of 1975 while they were taking control of South Vietnam. His regime became known as the Khmer Rouge (Red Khmer) because of its especially intense ideological commitment to communism.

As the Khmer Rouge launched their well-equipped offensive in Cambodia, the U.S. Embassy staff evacuated the mission in Phnom Penh by helicopter on April 12, 1975. The Americans took some Cambodian political figures who chose to leave although a number of important leaders remained. The latter wanted to share the fate of their people. They also hoped to be able to construct a new Cambodia with the Khmer Rouge. That was not to be. The Khmer Rouge killed them all, often brutally. Pol Pot wanted no member of the old order to remain alive.[7]

Pol Pot had decided to create a radically different Cambodian society based on a mix of revolutionary leveling and traditional Cambodian rural existence. He ordered total evacuation of all cities, seized all property, abolished all rights and began a systematic campaign to eradicate every element of Cambodian society that he regarded as unacceptable to his new social order.

The Khmer Rouge killed more than 2 million of their fellow Cambodians during a brutal three-year rule, often burying or stacking skulls and bones in randomly placed mass graves or empty buildings. Even years later, farmers still suddenly come across masses of skulls and skeletons buried in caves or only a few feet underground.[8]

With hunger setting in all over Cambodia because of Khmer Rouge policies, prominent Americans came to the border to try to persuade the Khmer Rouge to accept food shipments. Such well-known humanitarian activists as Joan Baez, Leo Cherne, Robert DeVecchi and Bayard Rustin led the group. Liv Ullmann, the Swedish actress who was later to undertake many humanitarian missions, joined as well. Elie Wiesel, whose father had died in the Nazi camp at Buchenwald, recited a Jewish prayer for the dead and compared the extermination campaign of the Khmer Rouge to that of the Nazis. But the Khmer Rouge would neither accept the food nor let them enter.[9]

Hundreds of thousands of Cambodians tried to flee the Red Khmer terror by land. Most fled into Thailand or into the mountainous border region near Thailand. Tens of thousands even fled into Vietnam and perhaps 10,000 into Laos. The Khmer Rouge executed any that they caught in flight. Those who reached other countries told horrifying stories of the genocide they had barely escaped.

The Red Khmer increasingly defied even their Vietnamese patrons as they followed their own nationalist doctrines. They established collectivized labor camps on the Stalinist model. They also drew increasingly toward China. The Vietnamese government did not want a friend of China on its border. It invaded Cambodia and installed a more subservient government. At that point, the Khmer Rouge leaders and many of their followers fled to the Thai border, setting up special camps from which they kept up their fight against Vietnam and against the new Cambodian regime. By the beginning of 1979, more than 100,000 had fled to those camps. The Vietnamese army often expelled refugees like cattle down the steep hills along the border, sometimes forcing them across minefields.

Many Cambodians came into Thailand itself. Khao I Dang, the main camp for Cambodian refugees inside Thailand, became the largest single concentration of Cambodians in the world. It looked like a small city except for the red clay everywhere. It had large, evenly arranged homes and barracks teeming with refugees, international officials and dozens of voluntary agencies. The Thai government at first blocked their access until Washington made a firm commitment to resettle any Khmer who entered Thailand.

Colonel Prasong and other Thai officials feared that many refugees fleeing Cambodia were Khmer Rouge. He did not want them running military operations against Cambodia out of refugee camps. The Thai thus kept the Red Khmer on the Cambodian side of the border or in no man's land. Thailand did not receive them as refugees but called them "Khmer on the border." But Thailand did accept refugees who did not belong to the Red Khmer, provided they could resettle in the West.

Hartling did not want to support the border camps because he believed that those Cambodians qualified more as resistance fighters than as refugees. The International Committee of the Red Cross and the United Nations Children's Fund (UNICEF) took on the relief job there, finally turning it over to a new agency, the United Nations Border Relief Operation (UNBRO). Cambodians from Khao I Dang could hope to come to the West, but the people of the border camps remained in limbo.

It was only in 1991, 16 years after Pol Pot had taken over in Cambodia, that peace came to Cambodia and that refugees could return. Under an arrangement brokered by the United Nations, a special U.N. agency called the United Nations Transitional Authority in Cambodia (UNTAC) took over the administration of the country pending elections. Those elections, held in May of 1993, returned Prince Norodom Sihanouk to power in a capital that he had been forced to leave more than 20 years earlier.

Richard Solomon, the U.S. Assistant Secretary of State for East Asia, worked closely with UNHCR delegate Sergio Vieira de Mello to broker and then to implement the agreement. Solomon later wrote that the United Nations had achieved "a signal success in facilitating multilateral diplomacy and then competently managing a peace plan."[10]

The peace agreement also closed the humanitarian chapter for Cambodia. The U.N. High Commissioner for Refugees returned over 360,000 Khmer from Thailand to Cambodia in time to vote in the elections. Khao I Dang closed after 14 years as a combination holding camp and transit center. A quarter million Cambodians had passed through its gates, with about 150,000 going to the United States and the remainder to Western Europe, Scandinavia, Australia and elsewhere.[11]

Laos, the third state in Indochina, took a different course from Vietnam or Cambodia at the end of the Vietnam War in 1975. Laotian forces allied with North Vietnam seized power without any pitched battle or mass Vietnamese invasion. They established the Lao People's Democratic Republic. Many Laotians as well as ethnic Vietnamese, Chinese and Thai residents of Laos fled to Thailand. The largest single group, the Hmong highlanders, feared communist reprisals because they had supported the United States in the Indochina war.

Tens of thousands of Laotians became boat people of a different kind. They tried to paddle a large log as a boat for themselves and their families across the Mekong River into Thailand. The Mekong, which flows more than half a mile wide and very fast during the rainy season in the summer and fall, killed thousands when they capsized. Those who survived reached Thailand miles downstream from where they had started.

By the end of 1975, more than 50,000 Lao had fled, with most of them being the Hmong. After the 1979 Geneva conference, which opened the door for Laotian resettlement in the West, even more fled.

The Thai government discouraged Laotian refugees, especially the Hmong. It permitted no Western NGOs to operate in camps opened for Lao refugees. It opened camps for resettlement to the West only after several years and heavy American pressure. More Lao then came out, but never in the same numbers as Vietnamese or Cambodians. The new Lao regime did not follow the same brutal policies as the Vietnamese and the Khmer Rouge.[12]

The humanitarian resettlement of refugees from Indochina became the largest organized movement of people in modern times. By the end of the exodus in the 1990s, more than 3 million Indochinese had fled their homes and traveled to distant countries. There, they have usually made good citizens. More than two and a half million went to other continents, with well over one million going to the United States. More than a quarter million settled in China. Other large groups went to Australia, Canada and France, with smaller but still significant groups resettling in many other countries of Western Europe or Asia. Over half a million returned to Indochina as government policies changed.

The Indochinese refugees introduced two important new concepts to international humanitarian action. They formalized the notion of "temporary asylum," under which one country would accept refugees after another country had pledged to resettle them. They also formalized the principle of long-term humanitarian burden-sharing.

As opposed to the Hungarian refugee flow, which arose suddenly and subsided almost completely within weeks, the Indochina exodus lasted for 20 years, ebbing and flowing in almost direct response to the brutalities of the different Indochinese regimes and the hopes for a warm welcome in the resettlement countries. But, like the Hungarian refugee flow, it brought many new countries—especially those of Asia—into the global humanitarian system.

The refugee flow became a triumph of the humanitarian conscience. Not even the most optimistic humanitarian could have predicted such a worldwide system or expected it to function as well as it did or for as long as it did.

Allan Simmance, director of many refugee operations for High Commissioner Hartling, observed that the principle of burden-sharing offered about equal chances for common action and for shifting blame. It all depended on the humanitarian spirit of those involved. And for most of two decades, the humanitarian spirit held for the refugees from Indochina.[13]

African Refugees

African refugees played out a particularly poignant and painful humanitarian tragedy. The birth agonies of the Congo, like the Biafran struggle against Nigeria (chapter 5), had merely set the stage for what was to become a much more widespread series of disasters.

Several major forces contended in Africa between 1945 and 1990, generating one crisis after another:

- Nationalism became increasingly powerful, ultimately dominant across the entire continent. It fueled the anticolonial wars that expelled Western nations and whatever regimes they tried to leave behind. It spawned a new generation of political leaders and political parties that led the revolutions against Western colonialism and then governed the successor states.
- The East–West conflict added fuel to African crises, especially around the Horn of Africa and in several states in southern Africa. As the Soviet Union and the United States played out their confrontation through their African friends and client states, their conflicting interests and their overwhelming resources made volatile situations worse. Rival factions bristling with foreign weapons could force many Africans into exile.
- Ethnic and tribal divisions left many new states so divided that they suffered civil wars after independence. Because the borders left by the colonial regimes rarely conformed to natural or ethnic boundaries, most new African

states contained a bewildering mix of ethnic and religious traditions and competing tribal groups. These rival groups had played down their differences during the anticolonial struggle, but the differences came to the fore once the new states had become independent.[14]

An extraordinary sense of African brotherhood countered these contending forces. Africans describe this sense with genuine feeling because they see it as an important part of their history and also as part of their common experience in reaction to the white man. For Africans, as for many non-Westerners, systems of personal and communal relations matter more than the legal, financial and bureaucratic relationships of Western culture. Many African refugee streams move in extended families and communities rather than as individuals or political groups.

Refugees became a part of the African scene during the independence movement and the Cold War. Tens and sometimes hundreds of thousands fled during anticolonial wars in Algeria, Angola, Morocco, Mozambique, Guinea-Bissau, Namibia, Tunisia, Zambia and many others. They fled into a whole cluster of neighboring states.[15]

Soon thereafter came those fleeing the often violent process of nation-building in the newly independent states, such as the Ewe from Ghana, the Hutu and Tutsi from Rwanda and Burundi, the Lampa from Zambia and Asians from Uganda. Eritreans fled from Ethiopia into Sudan. A number of southern Sudanese ethnic and religious groups fled into Kenya. Smaller groups or individuals sought refuge from other African states as new regimes consolidated their power. By 1972, more than a million refugees had already taken flight from one African country to another.

As these groups fled, African leaders realized that the refugees could provoke war between the states they had left and those where they had found refuge. Countries of origin feared that refugees might use their asylum states as bases against their original home states. Asylum countries feared that countries of origin would attack them to pursue refugees.

Julius Nyerere, the president of Tanzania, urged African leaders to find a common policy toward refugees. At his suggestion, African leaders met in Addis Ababa in 1967 to define their own principles for refugee asylum. In particular, they agreed that persons who had fled violence and war should be recognized as refugees in addition to those who had fled persecution (chapter 5).

The African leaders also agreed that asylum was to be regarded as a humanitarian act toward people in need, not as a hostile act toward the country from which the refugees had fled. They agreed that countries of origin should respect that humanitarian act. Asylum countries in turn were to make sure that refugees did not engage in subversive activity or insurrection against their former state.

The African leaders thus laid down the principles that were later to find expression in the 1969 convention on refugees of the Organization for African Unity. And African states have, on the whole, respected the OAU convention and the status of refugees. With a few notable exceptions, they have not forced refugees back across their borders and most have treated refugees on a strictly humanitarian basis.

African refugees needed different humanitarian solutions from Indochinese refugees. Except for a few intellectuals and professionals, most had no connection with the outside world. Forced to flee, they assembled in camps but had no wish to move to the West for resettlement. They wanted to return home. Some asylum states permitted refugees to grow food on small plots of land, if they had enough land and enough water, but most could offer only space and time. The African camps became vast desert or jungle holding stations, often managed with the help of NGOs and supported by Western food and other relief. They kept refugee families alive until political changes at home permitted them to return.

Refugees in the Horn of Africa

Siad Barre, the president of Somalia, caused a major refugee crisis in late 1979. Encouraged by Soviet leader Leonid Brezhnev and the Soviet military, which was then providing military and economic aid for Somalia, he decided to conquer the Ogaden region, a part of Ethiopia that juts out into Somalia and that is largely peopled by ethnic Somalis. But Brezhnev, who saw Ethiopia as a potentially much more important African ally than Somalia, then switched loyalties and began supporting Ethiopia. With massive infusions of Soviet military aid, the Ethiopians began winning against Somalia.

Somali forces and their Ogaden allies with their livestock fled into Somalia, creating a wave of refugees. The U.S. government, anxious to help Siad Barre against a Soviet ally, decided to support the refugees. So did other Western states. With U.S. aid, Poul Hartling began a program to help the refugees. Because Somalia, a desperately poor country with barren soil and little water, could barely support even its own population, UNHCR and a number of NGOs had to provide massive aid. At one time, over one quarter of Somalia's income came in the form of international assistance, most of it food.

The Ethiopian president, H.M. Mengistu, then decided that Soviet aid gave him a chance to settle some old scores of his own. He tried to exert stricter control over ethnic Eritrean and Tigrayan minorities in the northern and western areas of Ethiopia. An estimated 500,000 Eritreans and Tigrayan ethnics fled into Sudan, another country too poor to take care of refugees.[16]

ICARA

As these and other crises erupted all over Africa during the 1970s and early 1980s, the total number of African refugees grew to 3 million. Few could hope for repatriation or for resettlement in the West. The refugees threatened to destroy the fragile economies of their host states, which were prepared to let them stay but could not support them.[17]

Hartling tried to deal with the crisis by joining with the OAU and the U.N. Secretary-General to call the International Conference on Assistance to Refugees in Africa (ICARA I) in Geneva in 1981. Western donor states announced pledges of $562 million in aid for African refugees, with Washington contributing half. Three years later, another conference (ICARA II) was held to promote development aid for African states whose hopes for economic progress had been dashed by floods of refugees.[18]

A visit to an African refugee camp quickly justified the concept of ICARA II by showing how refugee concentrations could destroy the economies of asylum countries. All vegetation for miles around a camp would disappear as refugees searched for firewood or as their remaining animals grazed. Local wells or streams often went dry in short order. Roads, worn down by relief trucks, lay rutted and destroyed. Even though refugee settlements may have had their own schools and clinics, often run and staffed by NGOs, those schools rarely went beyond the primary grades, and the clinics rarely offered more than the most basic medical care. For any additional services, refugees had to rely on local facilities, which were usually inadequate even for locals.

Donor states did not meet all pledges made at the ICARA conferences and the situation in the asylum states continued to deteriorate. In 1985, a devastating drought hit Africa and particularly the countries around the Horn of Africa. Hundreds of thousands of additional refugees streamed into Sudan from Ethiopia and Chad. Many, particularly children, died of starvation. An equally serious crisis arose in southern Africa, where an intensification of the Mozambique civil war after 1985 drove hundreds of thousands from Mozambique into the neighboring countries of Malawi, Zambia, Zimbabwe and even South Africa itself.[19]

In addition, tens of thousands of Angolans fled from an expansion of their civil war to find refuge in southeastern Zaire. Others fled into Zambia. Moreover, recurring crises between the Hutu and Tutsi tribes in Rwanda and Burundi led to almost continual upheaval in the part of central Africa known as the area of the Great Lakes.[20] Despite some successes in repatriating some groups as a few crises eased, Africa remained awash in refugees from the 1970s on, with other crises yet to follow in the 1990s.[21]

Afghan Refugees

Leonid Brezhnev saw Afghanistan as another opening for Soviet action. He wanted to have control over the country as a salient toward the Indian Ocean. As various Afghan factions fought internecine battles during the 1970s, Moscow tried to make sure that its friends kept the upper hand. When they failed to do so, Brezhnev sent in the Red Army at Christmas, 1979.

The Soviet invasion began a long and bitter battle that lasted ten years. The Red Army and its allies could control the main cities and roads but they could not hold the countryside. Instead, they met with continuous harassment and their forces faced attacks even in their own camps. They had begun a war but they could not win or end it.

Afghan refugees fled to escape the Soviet invasion and the war that followed. They also fled the anti-Muslim secular government installed by the Soviets. They became the largest single group of refugees in the world during the 1980s. Although almost a million repatriated after the Red Army withdrew in 1989, many again fled to escape the fundamentalist Taliban regime that seized control during the civil war after the Soviet departure. Like the Africans, and unlike the Indochinese, few of them wanted to resettle in the West. Only a few tens of thousands came to the United States or to Western Europe.

Afghans in Pakistan

By the end of 1979 about 400,000 Afghan refugees had reached Pakistan. That number continued to climb, sometimes at the rate of 3,000 per day, until they reached close to 3 million by 1982. As in many African countries, refugees in the camps were mainly farmers, nomads, artisans, small merchants and their families. Many of the middle and upper classes moved to cities in Pakistan or progressively moved to the West as they gave up hope of being able to return home soon.[22]

Impelled by the strong Islamic tradition mandating hospitality to asylum seekers, Pakistan gave the Afghan refugees a generous reception despite their high numbers. Moreover, most of the refugees, being Pashtuns, shared a similar ethnic, cultural, and religious background with most Pakistanis and especially with the inhabitants of the border provinces. They dominated large sections of Northwest Frontier Province and of Baluchistan by their sheer numbers.

Humanitarian relief agencies built water systems and provided kerosene and fuel-efficient stoves to help the Afghan refugees survive. Because tents offered little protection from the fierce winters, relief agencies and the refugees themselves brought in traditional building materials. Many camps had mud huts with gardens and some animals, and with walls high enough to hide women from outsiders' eyes.

They looked like Afghan villages. The refugees stressed traditional education because they hoped to return home, but Hartling and his successors as high commissioner insisted that Afghan girls receive a basic education.

Afghans in Iran

Large numbers of Afghans fled to Iran and many remained there for 20 years. They particularly settled in the eastern provinces of Khorasan, Kerman and Sistan-Baluchistan, and to a lesser extent throughout other sections of the country including Teheran itself. The Iranian government has estimated that as many as 1.9 million Afghan refugees may have lived in Iran at one time or another, but precise figures have been even more difficult than usual to get because Western agencies have not been active in Iran. Only about 200,000 Afghans have lived in camps. Most have lived in cities or small towns and have merged into the local population.

Afghans were welcomed in Iran as in Pakistan. In both instances, the refugees were largely of similar ethnic stock as the people of the border provinces. Many of the refugees in Iran were Shiite Muslims who fitted well into the population. The Islamic rules of hospitality applied. Moreover, it had been customary for about half a million Afghans to work in Iran even before 1979, and Afghans did not attract much notice there.[23]

With the defeat of the Taliban in the American retaliation for the September 11, 2001, attack on the New York World Trade Center and the Pentagon, some Afghans fled at first. Later, large numbers of refugees were able to return home. Their return appears in Chapter 12 below.

Refugees in the Americas

Refugees in the Americas have divided into two groups, from different geographical areas and having different humanitarian needs.

The first group has included the traditional Latin American and Hispanic refugees. These refugees have mainly come from urban, middle class, professional, political or intellectual backgrounds, and they have fled repressive regimes in Spain, Portugal or Latin America.

The second group, which exploded during the 1970s and 1980s but has since ebbed, has included Caribbean and Central American refugees fleeing from Fidel Castro's Cuba or fleeing various wars, revolutions or dictatorships in Central America or in Haiti. They include not only the same urban professionals as in South America but also many workers and farmers.

To help refugees in both groups, Latin American states negotiated a number of international agreements on refugees. They also brought together some of their earlier refugee agreements, such as the 1928 convention of Havana and the 1940 convention of Montevideo, in the two conventions of Caracas of 1954.[24] Those Latin American conventions, as distinct from the global conventions, draw a clear distinction between diplomatic and territorial asylum. The former covers asylum seekers who flee to a diplomatic mission, a war vessel or a military camp. The latter covers persons who flee to another country.

As more and more Latin American refugees fled from conflicts in Central America in the late 1970s and the 1980s, Latin American leaders decided to expand their definition of a refugee. They met at a colloquium at Cartagena, Colombia, in 1984, to formulate a declaration that tried to follow and even to widen the principles of the 1969 OAU convention.

The colloquium issued the Cartagena Declaration. It expanded the Latin American concept of a refugee, "bearing in mind as far as appropriate and in the light of the situation prevailing in the region, the precedent of the OAU Convention . . . and the doctrine employed in the reports of the Inter-American Commission on Human Rights."[25] It recommended that the refugee definition to be used in Latin America should include not only refugees covered by the 1951 Convention and the 1967 Protocol but also persons who had fled "because their lives, safety or freedom have been threatened by generalized violence, foreign aggression, internal conflicts, massive violation of human rights or other circumstances which have seriously disturbed public order." This definition went well beyond even the OAU convention because of its reference to violations of human rights.[26]

Caribbean refugees have posed particular problems for the U.S. government because most of them have wanted to come to the United States. American presidents have often changed policies, sometimes permitting and sometimes blocking refugees, more in response to American domestic pressures than to the specific needs of any groups of refugees. Virtually every major Caribbean refugee group has a strong political base in the United States, the Cuban refugees mainly in Florida and the Haitian refugees mainly in New York City.

Since 1958, when Fidel Castro came to power, about one and a half million Cubans have fled to the United States, where they have established "Little Havana" in Miami. But many have fled to Hispanic countries, including Mexico and some other Central American states as well as Spain. Those who fled were from virtually all social and economic strata. The professionals, intellectuals and political figures left first and other groups followed later.[27]

Many of the Cubans who came to the United States after the 1960s traveled under arrangements agreed between the United States and Cuba to spare them the risky sea voyage. Often, however, refugees have caused sharp arguments between the two countries. In 1980, President Jimmy Carter at first encouraged and then opposed a Cuban-sponsored boatlift to Florida from the Cuban port of Mariel.[28] He objected most strongly to several thousand social misfits and criminals who were included in the boatlift population of about 120,000. Subsequent efforts to arrange for a more orderly process for further Cuban emigration to the United States have generally worked. And American presidents as well as other Western and Latin American leaders have usually treated persons who fled Cuba as refugees not subject to forcible repatriation.

Haiti has generated the other major Caribbean diaspora, with about one million—at least 15 percent of Haiti's total population—living abroad. Most Haitian exiles have come to the United States. About half a million live in New York City, and more than 100,000 live in "Little Haiti" in Miami. Other large concentrations have moved to Montreal and the Bahamas.[29]

Jimmy Carter ordered the Coast Guard to intercept any boats from Haiti and return them and their passengers after inquiring about legitimate asylum seekers.[30] The U.S. government charged that Haitians were coming to the United States for jobs and not for asylum. Later U.S. presidents have generally followed Carter's lead, although Bill Clinton also tried to establish a democratic regime in Haiti.

The U.S. government has granted asylum to fewer than 10 percent of those Haitians who do reach the United States, by boat or otherwise. Many live illegally in various Haitian ghettos. The interception policy has been credited with reducing the flow of boats from Haiti to Florida, but some friends of the Haitians have asserted that the boat people do not get an adequate chance to claim asylum during the quick boat interception.[31]

By the late 1980s, refugees had scattered over much of Central America, mainly in Honduras, Nicaragua, Costa Rica and Mexico.[32] They aroused enormous political controversy, especially because they seemed to have become victims of the Cold War. Ronald Reagan wanted to support refugees from the Soviet-supported Sandinista regime in Nicaragua. Democrats, and especially American human rights groups, supported refugees from El Salvador. As the Cold War eased by the late 1980s, so did the plight of refugees in Central America and Latin America as a whole.

Many refugees from various states in the Americas have fled and continue to flee directly to the United States and in smaller numbers to Canada. Most have found jobs. They have then asked for asylum and appealed against deportation. American immigration authorities have treated them as illegal immigrants and tried to expel them. But American civil liberties organizations and churches have strongly supported the asylum seekers, even establishing a "sanctuary" movement for Central Americans. The U.S. Supreme Court in March 1987 decided that asylum applicants did not have to prove the likelihood of persecution but only that they had a "well-founded" fear in the words of the 1951 Refugee Convention and the U.S. Refugee Act of 1980.[33]

Refugees in Europe

The states of Western Europe have formed part of the core of the global refugee structure. After World Wars I and II, and especially during the Cold War, their publics felt stirrings of sympathy for the displaced persons who needed help. But the Western Europeans did not want to accept refugees on a continuing basis, only in response to specific emergencies.

During the Cold War, Eastern European refugees came into Western Europe mainly during crises, for the Eastern European regimes kept their borders sealed. The Hungarian uprising in 1956 had permitted massive refugee flight when border controls broke down for several weeks. In 1968, a number of Czechs had gone west after Soviet leader Leonid Brezhnev had suppressed the "Prague Spring," but they did not arouse the same emotions as the Hungarians had. When the Polish regime proclaimed martial law in December 1981, several tens of thousands fled, but not all of them sought refugee status and many later returned.[34]

Refugees continued to flee Eastern Europe during the latter years of the Cold War but in much smaller numbers. In 1985, for example, an estimated 1,000 fled Bulgaria, several thousand fled Czechoslovakia and Hungary, respectively, perhaps 15,000–20,000 fled Romania and several tens of thousands fled Poland. About 2,000 fled the Soviet Union itself.[35] Many left for the West as migrants, not as refugees, and did not formally declare themselves to be refugees. After the end of the Cold War, some have returned home. The U.N. High Commissioner for Refugees and the Director of the International Organization for Migration—which succeeded ICEM—helped settle new refugees and also helped repatriate them where necessary.[36] After the end of the Cold War, when many Russian Jews were permitted to emigrate, most went to Israel and the United States but a large community settled in Germany and especially in Berlin.

The Western European states, like the North American, offered resettlement to refugees from every corner of the world and not only to those from Eastern Europe. Several Western European countries had significant refugee populations. Around the end of the Cold War, France had close to 200,000; Great Britain, 150,000; and West Germany, another 150,000.[37] Some refugees were called "Jet People" because they came by jet aircraft from distant locations and had not been cleared for arrival or asylum in Western Europe, but the Europeans stopped or at least reduced that flow by threatening to fine airlines that permitted people without visas to board flights for Europe.

The 1980s became the decade of the refugee. The persecutions conducted by Communist regimes in East and West, and the absolute control those regimes had over their territory, forced many to flee. So, in Africa, did postcolonial crises and wars.

Any crisis of any kind produced refugees. They had no choice except to flee, and the West as well as others welcomed most of them.

During the decade of the 1980s, therefore, refugee flight, relief and resettlement became the largest single humanitarian task facing the world. Aid to refugees became almost synonymous with humanitarian care. The number of those covered by the 1951 Refugee Convention had reached between 10 and 12 million by 1980–1981 and the number continued to rise, albeit more slowly, throughout the decade. Some could, over time, move on; some could even go home; but many lived at least part of the decade in a state of grim uncertainty, in provisional arrangements such as camps, temporary settlements, hostels or other quarters that might have been put at their disposal on a temporary but not on a permanent basis.

By the end of the decade, the global refugee population included several major groups. Many of them had first sought refuge in the late 1970s and early 1980s, although the Palestinians had been in camps since the 1940s. The most massive flows had come from the states of Indochina, Africa and Central America as well as from Afghanistan.[38] Smaller groups existed seemingly everywhere.

From the visible emergency of flight, many refugees passed to the invisible emergency of stagnation. And the humanitarian work of the 1980s often remained in the same state, coping with the problems at hand but being unable to solve them until political conditions around the world had changed.

Humanitarians could do a great deal for refugees. They could welcome and support them and they could sometimes move them on to wherever they might wish to go. All too often, however, they could offer no lasting solutions for refugee problems until states solved the political crises that had caused the flight. In those cases, refugees could only wait and hope until they could move on to resettlement or until they could return home.

NGOs Go Global

By the end of the 1980s, the humanitarian NGO community had also exploded in number and in range of action. NGOs had become widely accepted as implementing partners for governments and for intergovernmental organizations such as UNHCR. They served as principal relief agencies in refugee camps and they also helped arrange resettlement for refugees in a number of Western countries. By 1990, they numbered in the thousands, although only several hundred could mount major operations on their own.

A lot of NGO work escaped notice. The woman in California or Iowa who would get up at 5 A.M. to meet a new refugee family coming to her town, and who would then drive that family to her church, to her doctors, to schools for the children and to various government offices, would hardly register on the statistics of a vast refugee resettlement program. But she, and the church or civic groups to which she and her family belonged, formed essential links in many vast intercontinental migrations. The entire world of refugee relief and resettlement could not function without NGOs and without the staff and the volunteers in those NGOs.

An NGO leader of long standing, Brian Neldner, the director of the Lutheran World Service, described the role of NGOs:

> The voluntary agencies have a specific and distinctive contribution to make: the humanitarian quality of their assistance, greater flexibility to deal with individuals and with groups; speedy reactions in new situations, be they large or small; diversity of competence which can be found in the range of the family of voluntary agencies; and a more personalized approach, especially in dealing with refugees as people and individuals.[39]

American relief agencies had begun putting their own volunteer stamp on the world shortly before and after World War II (see chapter 3). The American Congress, which did not want major U.S. government operations abroad, had encouraged NGOs to play a role by making tens of millions of dollars in food aid available for private groups to distribute abroad. The American public had contributed heartily to such groups, providing up to $50 million in funds for needy people in Europe as well as for resettlement of European refugees in the United States or Western Europe in the postwar years. Private funds had contributed twice as much as the U.S. government for relief.[40]

The United Nations helped international humanitarian NGOs to win recognition and status. Over 1,100 NGOs attended the charter session of the United Nations at San Francisco in 1945 in order to make their views known and to get U.N. recognition. Article 71 of the charter of the United Nations Economic and Social Council (ECOSOC) gave NGOs consultant status. It also permitted them to attend ECOSOC meetings.[41]

The NGOs became more and more of a global phenomenon. Although most of the big ones had their roots in the United States or in Great Britain, a growing number had other national roots. Many of those also operated internationally during the 1980s and have continued to do so. Many are members of the International Council of Voluntary Agencies (ICVA):

- Europe, for example, has ACCION International, Médecins du Monde, Médecins sans Frontières, the Diakonisches Werk of the German Evangelical Church, the Danish, Norwegian and Swedish Refugee Councils, the Dutch Relief and Rehabilitation Agency, Save the Children, the International Committee of the Red Cross and countless others.

- Africa has Africare, Africa Humanitarian Action, African Refugee Foundation, All-Africa Conference of Churches, Association Beninoise, the Forum of African Voluntary Organizations, the South African National NGO Coalition and the Sudanese Women General Union, etc.
- The Islamic world has brought forth the Aga Khan Foundation, the Islamic African Relief Agency, the International Islamic Relief Organization, the Islamic Relief Agency, many agencies associated with Afghan relief and resettlement including the Afghan NGOs Coordinating Bureau and countless Red Crescent societies, etc.
- Latin America has Accion Para Refugiados de El Salvador and the Federacion de Organismos de Nicaragua as well as many agencies in South America, etc.
- The Asian subcontinent has the National NGO Council of Sri Lanka, the Rural Development Foundation of Pakistan, many Pakistani NGOs helping and teaching Afghan refugees and the Voluntary Health Association of India, etc.
- Others include the Amel Association of Lebanon, AUSTCARE, the Australian Council for Overseas Aid, the Canadian Council for Refugees, the Chinese Refugees' Relief Association, Mission Armenia and the Soka Gakkai of Japan, etc.

This listing, by no means complete, reflects the scope and flexibility of the voluntary community. One or another humanitarian NGO functions virtually everywhere, on every continent and in every country. They are usually there by the dozen.[42] When a crisis erupts in their country and often when one erupts elsewhere, they volunteer to help. They may be compensated for their services, but they bring far more in commitment and dedication than they could possibly be paid to do.

In particular, the NGOs bring highly motivated staff. Many join right out of high school or college. They want to help. They will accept conditions that others could not tolerate. They can live in tents without air conditioning. They do not need showers every day. They will climb mountains in the snow. They will deliver food to the sick and the dying. They do not run away when they see a scorpion or a roach. They do not worry as much about their next promotion as about the people they are sent to help.

But the NGOs also bring experience. The leaders of major NGOs have spent more time in humanitarian crises than most military officers have spent in combat. They know what to expect. They know how to run an operation. They know what to do and—perhaps more important—what to avoid. They know how to account for funds. Some, like the ICRC, bring diplomatic skills, perhaps honed in the face of a gun pointed at their heads. They face complaints that their offices and homes take up a lot of houses in a relief area and that their ubiquitous Land Rovers become too conspicuous (and widely coveted), but they also know what they are doing.

The NGOs usually bring funds to the table. They organize widespread campaigns in their churches, synagogues, mosques, temples and communities, especially in the United States. Because of a global outpouring of support, they can sometimes have more funds for an operation than the American and other governments. They are paid for their services when they act as program implementers for a government, for the High Commissioner for Refugees or for other international organizations, but they do not rely only on such payments. On a total basis, they may bring as much as $5 billion a year to the various operations in which they play a role.[43]

Most important, the NGOs express the humanitarian conscience and bring a humanitarian spirit. They do not have the kinds of political agendas that governments may have even in a humanitarian operation. Some NGOs, like Human Rights Watch or Lawyers for Human Rights, may have a political as well as a humanitarian agenda. But most NGOs involved in humanitarian operations want mainly to do good. They genuinely want to help people who need help. That quality adds immensely to a humanitarian operation because it gives the victims of tragedy a real sense that somebody wants to provide for them and their families.

In the total picture of humanitarian work, NGOs have represented an essential element for operations and a valuable reminder that humanitarian care is about people more than about policy. They add human and moral energy, and they offer the clearest expression of the humanitarian conscience.

Generosity, Strategy and Stability

Mikhail Gorbachev, the President of the Soviet Union, understood by the later 1980s that the Soviet Union had reached the limit of its strength. It could not continue to fight its war in Afghanistan and to keep supplying and supporting the many satellite and dependent regimes that it had built all over Eastern Europe and the world as a whole. He made it clear that he would accept changes in those regimes.

The Eastern Europeans sensed that their time had come. They began to challenge the Communist parties openly and consistently. As one after another Eastern European government gave its people a greater voice at home and a greater right to travel abroad, Soviet authority faded. Finally, on November 9, 1989, the East Berliners broke through the Berlin Wall. The stark symbol of East–West division buckled under the pressure of people wanting to leave. The Cold War ended with the collapse of the Wall.

George Bush, the new U.S. President, negotiated with Gorbachev to reestablish a united Germany. The hollow regimes of Eastern Europe crumbled. Within two years, the Soviet Union itself ceased to exist. Russia remained a great power but no longer an empire with world-wide reach and global ambition. The Baltic states, the Ukraine, White Russia, Georgia, Kazakhstan, Uzbekistan, Turkmenistan and all the other states of what had been called "Soviet Central Asia" became independent.

The West had won a global victory of historic proportions in the Cold War. It had won that victory without having to fight another world war although such a conflict seemed imminent at times.

Humanitarian care shared a signal role in that victory. Humanitarians played no favorites and followed a neutral policy. But Western recognition and support of the humanitarian conscience helped the West to win. By supporting refugees the West helped to undermine the legitimacy of the regimes from which refugees had fled. By obeying as well as enforcing the laws of war the West reminded the world that all states had to act in accordance with higher principles. And the West won friends and influence by offering economic aid to its friends and by honoring humanitarian principles. World opinion admired and supported those who followed ideals of natural law and humanism.

Dedication to the humanitarian conscience became the bed-fellow of Western strategy. This made many humanitarians uncomfortable because they believed that they served a humanist, not a political, purpose. It also made strategists uncomfortable because they often regarded humanitarians as irresponsible do-gooders who gladly got in the way of important national business.

Yet a shadow level of cooperation evolved, one that was acknowledged by none of the participants even as it became very real.

In the short run, the two worlds remained largely apart, although peacekeeping forces could advance humanitarian action by making it easier for humanitarians to function in the midst of a potential or real conflict. Humanitarians did their work and strategists pursued their plans. They did not coordinate with each other and they often did not trust each other.

In the long run, however, they supported each other. Humanitarian care, which corresponded to the humanist spirit of the great philosophers, had a powerful appeal—an appeal enhanced by being above politics. States that supported it were more in tune with basic human feelings than others. Humanitarian action could help advance the interests of the West. The two levels of action needed to remain distinct from each other for the sake of both, but they could support each other indirectly.

Humanitarian care thus served many purposes, directly or indirectly. Generosity could join with strategy in setting a standard of humanitarian conduct and political tolerance. Instead of acting like the traditionally brutal nation-states, the Western states spoke to the great principles that lay at the foundation of the human and the humanitarian conscience. By helping people they served their own purposes. Often, they helped to bring stability into desperate people's lives and into their politics. This reflected their own interests, yet they were also thanked for it.

Some national governments thought more in strategic and political terms than others. The U.S. government saw a definite advantage in showing that refugees fled from communism to come to the West. But other governments, such as the Scandinavians, followed humanitarian principles without having global political objectives. So did many countries of the developing world. So did the humanitarian NGOs. They gave voice to the humanitarian conscience because of a common spirit that had come from the distant past.

The international agencies, beginning with the United Nations itself, tried to keep their independence and their neutrality in fulfilling their humanitarian mandates even during the East–West confrontation. Otherwise, they would have been destroyed. But their very neutrality helped the West in a humanitarian mission.

Western humanitarian policy merged with the humanist traditions of Greece, Rome, China, India and the Muslim and other worlds. It showed that the West, not the Communist states, remained true to those humanist traditions. At one after another conference as well as in private meetings, people from all over the world expressed their appreciation of the Western humanitarian message even when they did not agree with many Western policies. Intentionally or not, the charitable policies of the West coincided with Western interests. And the West helped to find support for itself by serving the humanitarian conscience for others.

The ambiguity of the mixed objectives contained the seeds of disagreement and frustration for both humanitarians and governments, but the pressures of the Cold War had reconciled their purposes. With the end of the Cold War, however, those questions would have to be addressed again and in a different form.

SEVEN

BRAVE NEW WORLD

PRESIDENT GEORGE BUSH MIGHT HAVE HOPED that the end of the Cold War would lead to a world of peace and progress. But that was not to be. While Bush and Mikhail Gorbachev were still negotiating about Germany and Eastern Europe, President Saddam Hussein of Iraq invaded Kuwait in August 1990, provoking the United States and the United Nations into a massive campaign—called the Gulf War—to drive out the Iraqi forces. By January 1991, the forces of the American-led coalition had freed Kuwait and entered Iraq itself. The invasion, the allied reaction and the aftermath brought on a major humanitarian crisis.

George Bush, the Gulf War and the New World Order

Saddam's invasion forced hundreds of thousands to flee from Kuwait to Iran, Jordan, Saudi Arabia and elsewhere. Most of them were expatriate laborers working in Kuwaiti oilfields and service industries. Smaller numbers of Iraqi Shiite Muslim groups opposed to Saddam who had sought refuge in Kuwait also had to flee. The refugee agencies, from UNHCR to the NGOs, tried to take care of them. The displaced could not be described as refugees in the traditional sense. Some feared persecution, like earlier refugees, but others left Kuwait mainly because they had lost their jobs or perhaps risked losing them.[1] Most wanted to come back once Saddam's forces had been pushed out of Kuwait.

Saddam used his remaining units to beat back a Shiite revolt after the international coalition forces had expelled his forces from Kuwait and had destroyed parts of the Iraqi army. He forced about 200,000 refugees into Iran. Other smaller groups also fled to Iran. Counting Afghan refugees in Iran as well as earlier refugees from Saddam's rule, Iran briefly became the country with the world's largest refugee population. It asked Mrs. Sadako Ogata, who had just been appointed U.N. High Commissioner for Refugees, to provide help for the new groups. She agreed, setting up camps and running relief programs.

The Kurds of northern Iraq, living in Kirkuk, Mosul and near the Turkish border, posed a more thorny problem for ethnic and political reasons. They made up the most bitter opposition group to Saddam. He had consistently persecuted them. Bush saw them as allies and encouraged them to revolt against the Iraqi ruler. But the revolt failed. Iraqi forces defeated the Kurds and drove them north. When the Kurds tried to flee into Turkey, the Turkish army refused to let them cross the border. They found themselves caught in the bitter cold of the mountainous no-man's-land between the Turkish and Iraqi armies.

Bush believed that the United States had an obligation to help the Kurds. But he could not persuade the Turkish government to let them enter because Ankara feared that the Kurds would try to carve out a separate state in eastern Turkey. With the Kurds trapped in Iraq, Bush turned to the United Nations Security Council. It passed a resolution demanding that Iraq "allow immediate access by international humanitarian organizations to all those in need of assistance."

Bush justified the U.N. resolution as a humanitarian act:

> Some might argue that this decision is an intervention in the internal affairs of Iraq, but I think the humanitarian concern, the refugee concern, is so overwhelming that there will be a lot of understanding about this.[2]

Bush asked Mrs. Ogata to provide relief for the Kurds. Sadruddin Aga Khan, the former U.N. High Commissioner for Refugees who had been appointed as U.N. Secretary General Javier Perez de Cuellar's Executive Delegate for Iraq, negotiated an agreement under which Saddam Hussein permitted humanitarian agencies to operate in Iraq.

Bush also wanted to protect the Kurds militarily. Even as American troops were pulling out of southern Iraq, they and their British and French allies carved out a northern Iraq security zone for the Kurds in "Operation Provide Comfort." They also offered initial relief and protection for the Kurds because UNHCR at first had no staff or resources in the area. They protected the area by making it part of the northern Iraq "no-fly" zone over which they would not permit Iraqi aircraft to operate. Mrs. Ogata, with help from American and other forces, was then able to bring in relief supplies to help the Kurds survive in their new security zone.

Mrs. Ogata had accepted a new kind of responsibility for herself and for UNHCR by agreeing to help the Kurds. Some of her staff objected, for the Kurds qualified as "refugees" even less than some of the groups that had left Kuwait to avoid the Iraqi invasion. The Kurds had not fled to another country, as the 1951 Refugee Convention had stipulated. Instead, they had remained in Iraq. Many had even joined in a military campaign against Iraq and might have more properly been put under Red Cross care as a defeated army. But Mrs. Ogata felt that she had no choice except to help where she found an obvious need and a ready supporter.

As a number of analysts tried to define this new category of humanitarian relief, they called the Kurds "Internally Displaced Persons," or IDPs, instead of "refugees." Forced to leave their traditional homes by war or Iraqi suppression, they had fled to another part of Iraq beyond the reach of Saddam Hussein. Mrs. Ogata had helped them because they needed help and because the major states supporting UNHCR had asked her to do it. Over time, various groups of IDPs were to become a new and massive element among the displaced.[3]

Operation Provide Comfort had also broken new ground in another direction. Because the American and allied military forces had begun the relief effort for the Kurds before U.N. agencies could arrive, the international refugee agencies and refugee NGOs had to cooperate closely with the military for the first time in post-war history. It was not to be the last.

President Bush hailed the end of the Gulf War and the success of U.S. forces and of others who had helped in the operation. He said that their actions marked a "new world order" in which all states would work together to keep the peace and to punish those who broke it.

The Humanitarian Array

If Henry Dunant had given free rein to his wildest ambitions, he could still not have imagined the vast number of organizations, laws and resources that the world had committed to humanitarian action during the closing years of the Cold War. They exceeded anything that had ever been conceived by the original founders of the International Committee of the Red Cross, the League of Nations or the United Nations.

The humanitarian array had many parts by 1990. Each had a specific task and carried out an essential part of the total humanitarian mission although many of them also had other things to do as well. Each supported the total humanitarian effort although the agencies often competed with each other for money, staff and publicity. Together, the major international humanitarian governmental and non-governmental organizations had operations that cost several billion dollars a year by the end of the Cold War.

The East–West confrontation and the tragedies it created had brought forth a prodigious international outpouring of support for victims. It had called many of the new organizations and new responsibilities into being. But some, especially in Africa and Asia, would have existed even without the Cold War because they served a wider purpose. Two international organizations, the U.N. High Commissioner for Refugees and the International Organization for Migration (the successor to ICEM), had begun their existence on short-term charters because governments did not expect or want them to continue their work very long. But they had found permanent and even expanding roles as the world needed them.

Six organizations stood at the center of the new array, having done the main humanitarian work during the Cold War and being ready to turn their attention to whatever humanitarian missions might follow:

- The United Nations itself
- The U.N. High Commissioner for Refugees (UNHCR)
- The World Food Program (WFP)
- The United Nations Children Fund (UNICEF)
- The International Committee of the Red Cross (ICRC)
- The International Organization for Migration (IOM)

The United Nations Itself

By the end of the Cold War, the United Nations had become the global center of humanitarian operations. It had been forced to give up its original mission of keeping the peace across the world because the five permanent members of the Security Council could use their veto to block any action or resolution that they disliked. It had concentrated much of its effort on humanitarian action. In those areas, it had played a major and important role. United Nations agencies and United Nations officials served in virtually every humanitarian crisis in the world during the Cold War, and they were clearly ready to do more. And U.N. peace-keeping operations had helped to ease many crises and had probably prevented others from flaring into full-scale war.

The United Nations High Commissioner for Refugees

UNHCR had become the best-known humanitarian agency because of the many persons forced to flee from Communist states or from various conflicts either around the periphery of the Soviet and Communist orbit (as in Afghanistan) or in areas where Communist and Western interests clashed (as in the Horn of Africa and in Central America). Its annual expenditures fluctuated wildly, depending on the number of refugees at any given moment, but had reached over $550 million by 1990.[4] It had originally expected to concentrate on giving legal protection to refugees in Europe, but had expanded around the world and had in the process become a major relief agency, often even the lead agency in humanitarian relief operations that went well beyond refugee care and protection.

The World Food Program

WFP served as the food aid arm of the United Nations system. Most of its work concentrated on the developing world. It also helped other agencies, such as UNHCR, by providing food support for refugees. Its reports around the turn of the decade showed an annual budget of about $1.3 billion.

The United Nations Children's Fund

UNICEF at the end of the Cold War was running programs at an average level of $800 million per year. It had served primarily as a development agency, concentrating on children's needs in the developing world and especially in Africa, Latin America and Asia, but it became increasingly engaged in humanitarian relief. UNICEF took particular pride that a quarter of its budget came from private contributions, especially from sales of its Christmas cards all over the world.[5]

The International Committee of the Red Cross

The ICRC had a 1990 operating budget of 441 million Swiss Francs, about $300 million. Over one third of that went to Africa, with another third divided between Asia and the Middle East. It concentrated mainly on relief but also continued to stress its traditional functions: medical help, protection, tracing missing soldiers as well as civilians and the dissemination of international humanitarian law. It also visited prisoners and political detainees and it helped to arrange the exchange of prisoners of war between Iran and Iraq.

The International Organization for Migration

The end of the Cold War enabled IOM to send more refugees home, even to former Communist countries, and to move more of them into resettlement countries. Over time, some former members of the Soviet bloc joined the IOM Council, raising hopes for more orderly international migration instead of the sudden mass flows of refugees. James Purcell, director of IOM, reported that IOM had moved 227,000 refugees and regular migrants during 1990.[6] But he warned that operations might get more complex, with crises like the Gulf War potentially triggering huge flows of people.

Funding and Coordination of Humanitarian Aid

Government funding for these programs came mainly from the West and from Japan, although some of the oil-exporting states in the Middle East as well as smaller countries also contributed. The United States remained the major single contributor, but the European Union actually exceeded U.S. funding levels if one counted the funding levels of separate European donors together with the amounts contributed by the European Union Humanitarian Office, ECHO. The Scandinavian states, such as Norway and Denmark, contributed the most per capita, with some of the smaller European states such as The Netherlands also contributing heavily per capita. Some of the Western European contributions, such as agricultural commodities, were overvalued because the Europeans valued them at their own subsidized price levels. Nonetheless, they constituted a significant part of the food relief offered in humanitarian crises.[7]

The main Western donors of humanitarian aid, and especially the American government, wondered whether this vast architecture functioned as efficiently as possible. They wanted to see more interagency coordination to improve humanitarian services, to lower costs and to make it easier for them to see how their money was being spent.

But Western donor attitudes often fluctuated during any single crisis. When a humanitarian emergency hit, whether in the form of widespread starvation or war, and especially if it attracted media attention, donors wanted immediate action and did not care how much it cost. After the emergency had continued for some time or had subsided, donors began to count their money more carefully. They did not always pay the sums they had pledged. Each donor tended to prefer some kinds of activities over others, with Washington more ready to fund refugees from the Soviet bloc and the Europeans more ready to send food aid to Africa.

After the Gulf War, with streams of refugees and non-refugees going in all directions and with urgent needs across a large area, the major donors intensified their pressure for better coordination of humanitarian programs. They would have preferred to deal with one humanitarian budget instead of with six or more. They also found that they had to go over the same consultations separately with every agency because the United Nations secretariat had no coordinating staff.

But coordination of humanitarian actions suffered from four handicaps:

- The major agencies had different areas of responsibility and could not work together on every program, with some not even belonging to the U.N. system;

- The Western states wanted U.N. coordination but did not want such U.N. members as Russia and China to help decide on humanitarian operations even after the Cold War;
- Finely honed bureaucratic instincts also worked against coordination. The senior heads of U.N. agencies—all equally ranked as Undersecretary-General of the United Nations—did not want to have anybody else making decisions on matters for which they felt competent and responsible;
- The developing states feared that the West would use "coordination" as an excuse to cut their development aid or to redirect it into other strictly humanitarian channels.

Secretary-General Javier Perez de Cuellar and some major donors still wanted better coordination. After long deliberation, the U.N. General Assembly in December 1991 passed a resolution establishing a new Department of Humanitarian Affairs (DHA) to coordinate humanitarian assistance. It also created an Inter-Agency Standing Committee (IASC) to serve as a coordinating mechanism for about 15 member and observer agencies and to eliminate duplication or to fill gaps between the responsibilities of different agencies. The DHA office later became the Office for the Coordination of Humanitarian Affairs (OCHA), receiving $75 million to coordinate humanitarian and natural disaster relief.[8]

With that step, the United Nations hoped to bring the vast effort of humanitarian assistance under coordination. In reality, the major agencies have largely continued to control their own budgets and operations because donors want to know exactly where their funds are going and how they will be spent. But OCHA has still served its purpose, although it has itself been accused of having become excessively bureaucratic and of duplicating others' work.

As these United Nations and other agencies took over humanitarian work, Western states surrendered some of their operational sovereignty. They still reserved the final decisions for themselves because they provided the authorization and the funds, but they permitted the agencies to undertake major responsibilities. This helped to give the Western programs legitimacy. Although much of the humanitarian response helped refugees who opposed communism, the presence of international agencies made it a humanitarian and not a national cause. Therefore, America and its allies gained from the presence and the role of the United Nations.

The Security Council and "An Agenda for Peace"

President George Bush represented the United States at the U.N. Security Council on January 31, 1992, when the Security Council had its first meeting ever at the level of chiefs of state and government. President Boris Yeltsin represented the Russian

Federation; President François Mitterrand, France; Prime Minister John Major, the United Kingdom; and Premier Li Peng, China. The states that held the veto power in the Security Council sent their most senior political figures for the first time in almost 50 years. It was also to be the last time as of this writing.

With the end of the East–West confrontation that had often paralyzed the U.N. Security Council, the major powers could begin giving the United Nations greater authority then they had given it during the Cold War. The United Nations experienced some heady moments when the world leaders stressed "the importance of strengthening and improving" the United Nations. They particularly applauded U.N. humanitarian and peacekeeping activities.

The leaders also asked Boutros Boutros-Ghali, who had just become U.N. Secretary-General, to prepare a report giving "his analysis and recommendations" on ways to strengthen the capacity of the United Nations for preventive diplomacy, for peacemaking and for peacekeeping.

This request contained a trap, for it asked the Secretary-General to put flesh on the bones of an old concept of the United Nations as a real force in world affairs. It could be misinterpreted as a sign that the states might be ready to turn over some of their sovereign authority to the United Nations.

By asking Boutros-Ghali for recommendations about "peace-making," the Security Council members were even asking him how the United Nations could use force. This went well beyond anything that the sovereign nation-states had asked the United Nations to do for decades. It seemed to put aside the rage that Moscow, for example, had felt about Dag Hammarsköld's handling of the Congo crisis, as well as the irritation that all Security Council members had at times voiced about the United Nations or about U.N. actions.

Boutros-Ghali took the bait. He welcomed the task, which he regarded as a sign of the new authority that the United Nations would be able to exercise. At the beginning of his report, which he entitled *An Agenda for Peace,* he wrote that the end of the Cold War had given the United Nations a "second chance" to function as it had originally been intended and that the nations of the world must not squander that chance.[9]

Boutros-Ghali wrote that preventing war remained the most important task for the United Nations and for all states, but he warned that prevention did not always seem to work. As requested by the Security Council, he also addressed issues of peacemaking, peacekeeping and, in a section he added himself, peacebuilding after conflict.

Boutros-Ghali pointed out that the United Nations remained bound by the principles of national sovereignty. States still had to consent to any U.N. action, humanitarian or otherwise, to be taken within their borders. But he added that: "The time of absolute and exclusive sovereignty . . . has passed; its theory was never matched by reality." Leaders would have "to find a balance between the needs of good internal governance and the requirements of an ever more inter-dependent world."[10] He then added the following strong words:

> At a time when nations and peoples increasingly are looking to the United Nations for assistance in keeping the peace—and holding it responsible when this cannot be so—fundamental decisions must be taken to enhance the capacity of the Orga-nization in this innovative and productive exercise of its function.[11]

Noting the increase in peacekeeping operations after the end of the Cold War, Boutros-Ghali asked states to let him know what forces they would make available for U.N. operations when called upon. He also asked for states to make "stand-by arrangements" under which they would keep certain levels of troops available on call for service with the United Nations "as the needs of new operations arise." States should also make equipment available to be stockpiled for use by such forces, and should establish and finance a revolving fund that the Secretary-General could call upon to finance such operations.[12]

Recognizing that funds for such forces would exceed regular U.N. budgets, Boutros-Ghali proposed that national defense budgets should be called upon to contribute to U.N. peace-keeping, for only those budgets had enough money for such projects.

He added that such forces, when serving under the U.N. flag, should be "under the command of the Secretary-General."

Major governments, and especially the five permanent members of the Security Council, did not accept the proposals for standby military forces or for U.N. com-mand authority. But they did show a wish for stronger U.N. action to solve or to avoid crises with potential humanitarian effects. The United Nations would hence-forth be expected to do more.

Actually, the United Nations had already been asked to do more. Whereas the U.N. Security Council had only agreed on 13 peacekeeping operations during the three decades between 1948 and 1978, and on none whatsoever between 1978 and 1988, it had added another 10 in the three years between 1988 and 1991. Some went into battlefields left over from the Cold War, such as Afghanistan, Angola, Central America and Cambodia. Some operated only briefly. For example, the U.N. Good Offices Mission in Afghanistan and Pakistan (UNGOMAP) could observe the departure of Soviet forces relatively quickly; the U.N. Angola Verification Mis-sion I (UNAVEM I) could observe the withdrawal of Cuban forces from Angola equally fast; and the U.N. Observer Group in Central America (ONUCA) could quickly help implement the ceasefire and cessation of mutual interference in several Central American states. Other missions, like the implementation and supervision of election plans in Angola (UNAVEM II) or in El Salvador (UNOSAL) took longer, but they began quickly after the end of the Cold War.[13] Each of these operations directly or indirectly supported one or another humanitarian effort. And more were to come during the 1990s.

The humanitarian array stood strong and confident at the end of the Cold War. Bolstered by massive expenditures on a scale that nobody could have imagined in 1945, with many major and many smaller organizations operating around the world and around the clock, and with the prospect of more important missions in the future, the world appeared ready to help solve lingering humanitarian and other problems that no state and no international organization had been able to solve or even to address for years.

Humanitarian action, working through its complex of agencies and resources, was expected to play a major role in this brave new world. It was little wonder that Boutros-Ghali concluded his report with the following hope:

> The United Nations was created with a great and courageous vision. Now is the time, for its nations and peoples, and the men and women who serve it, to seize the moment for the sake of the future.[14]

Boutros-Ghali's proposals had gone very far, sketching out bold ideas for a major U.N. role in bringing true peace and humanitarianism to the world of the future.

It remained for Boutros-Ghali and for others to learn how the sovereign states would react to his agenda and to the many new problems that would confront them after the Cold War.

EIGHT

YUGOSLAVIA EXPLODES

WARREN ZIMMERMANN, THE FIRST AMERICAN AMBASSADOR to Yugoslavia after the end of the Cold War, knew at the time of his appointment that he would have to define a new policy. He called on his old friend, Lawrence Eagleburger, who had earlier been ambassador in Belgrade and who had become Deputy Secretary of State in 1989 under President George Bush.

The two agreed that Zimmermann would deliver the message that American policy toward Yugoslavia had changed. He would make clear that the West no longer needed a united Yugoslavia. Washington would no longer treat Yugoslavia as a "protected and sometimes pampered child." It had new priorities, such as international human rights. Henceforth, Washington would oppose Yugoslav unity maintained by force.

When Zimmermann arrived in Belgrade on March 9, 1989, he especially criticized the president of Serbia, Slobodan Milosevic, for ignoring human rights. In doing so, Zimmermann said that he was making a "course correction" in American policy.[1]

Yugoslavia faced a particular crisis in Kosovo, a province sacred to the Serbs although they had become only a minority part of the population. For years, Kosovo Albanians had suffered under Serb domination. They had set up a shadow provincial government that provided many services to the Albanian ethnic population. They had adopted a policy of passive resistance and believed that they would prevail over time. But a new force, the Kosovo Liberation Army (KLA), did not want to wait. The KLA had launched a terrorist campaign of killing Serbian police and bureaucrats. Milosevic had reacted by suppressing human rights even more. The Albanians believed that the U.S. Ambassador's remarks supported their cause.

Zimmermann may indeed have perceived his comments as merely a "course correction," but the Yugoslavs interpreted them as signs of a radically new policy. They understood that America would henceforth support independence for the separate peoples of Yugoslavia and especially for Kosovo Albanians. With no Soviet ships threatening to patrol the Adriatic and the Mediterranean from Yugoslav ports, a united Yugoslavia had lost its strategic value for America and NATO.

The Life and Death of Yugoslavia

Many ethnic groups in Yugoslavia wanted to secede, for the country had a long history of ethnic tensions. Different tribes, nations and religions had arrived there over the millennia: Slavic, Caucasian, Roman Catholic, Orthodox, Muslim and Romany. They coexisted uneasily, mainly because they could better resist real or potential outside pressures and not because they particularly wanted to be together.

Each major group had one or another separate homeland, such as the Slovenes in Slovenia, the Serbs in most of Serbia or the Croatians in most of Croatia. But in other areas, such as Bosnia, Macedonia or Kosovo, no single group formed a dominant majority across an entire province or state. They mingled, often living in adjoining small villages nestled within deep valleys or in separate ghettos within a city. They might live and work close together and they might have good personal relations and might even intermarry, but they retained their pride in separate ethnicity. All lived on constant guard. Cycles of rivalry, war or assassinations succeeded each other in endless waves.

The young learned from the old who was friend and especially who was foe, passing hatreds along from one generation to the next. All learned of the harm that others had done to them over the centuries. They did not learn of any harm they might have done to others, each preferring its self-pitying, self-justifying and self-perpetuating version of history. Outsiders, whether Turks, Austrians or Nazis, could—and did—exploit these rivalries for their own purposes. The Balkans became the nuptial grounds for countless marriages of convenience.

The Balkans thus always faced the interaction between their own jumbled mixture of peoples and the predatory circling of outsiders. Six outside states—Austria, Germany, Russia, Turkey, Italy and Great Britain—had taken the most advantage of this over the years, using one Balkan people against another with ceaseless killing and ever-reinforced grievances. Now America had also become a player.

Balkan tensions had lit the spark that ignited World War I when a young Bosnian of Serb ethnicity, Gavrilo Princip, assassinated the Austrian Archduke Francis Ferdinand in Sarajevo on June 28, 1914 (chapter 3). Austria, suspecting that Serbia lay behind the assassination, had demanded the right for its forces and police to conduct their own investigation throughout Serbia. The Serbs, as expected, rejected that demand. Austria then attacked Serbia, Russia defended Serbia, and World Wars I and II followed.

As World War I ended and as both the Austrian and Ottoman empires collapsed, the great powers of Europe saw a chance to grab the remains at the peace conference to be convened at Versailles and other European cities. Premier Vittorio Emanuele Orlando of Italy led the push into the Balkans, wanting the Adriatic coast and parts of Slovenia and Croatia. His forces occupied the Croatian city of Fiume in November 1918, a week after the World War I armistice. Great Britain and France seized most of their loot from the remnants of the Ottoman Empire in the Middle East and did not have matching territorial ambitions in the Balkans, although they did want influence there.[2]

The Balkan peoples, and especially the Serbs, Croats and Slovenes, decided to counter those foreign ambitions by organizing their territories into a new "Kingdom of the Serbs, Croats, and Slovenes" on December 1, 1918, even before the peace conference had opened. They wanted to resist the imperialism of the great powers, although it meant having to live together.[3]

Many Muslims in Bosnia-Herzegovina as well as other peoples in Macedonia, Montenegro and Kosovo did not want to be included in the same kingdom with the Serbs and Croats, but they had little choice. Some ethnic resistance continued for years as the new kingdom entered upon an uneasy existence. But it held together, even as a multiethnic entity, because the people feared outside threats even more than internal tensions.[4]

When an upsurge in ethnic rivalries threatened to doom the new kingdom in 1929, King Alexander I assumed full powers and tried to govern as a dictator so as to end the squabbling. He gave the state a new name, Yugoslavia ("Land of the Southern Slavs"). But a Macedonian nationalist then assassinated Alexander on a visit to France.

Adolf Hitler ordered the German *Wehrmacht* to invade Yugoslavia on April 6, 1941, after the Yugoslavs had beaten back a Mussolini invasion. The pro-German Croatians welcomed the Nazis and joined them in killing campaigns against Serbs. But the Nazis could not defeat Serb-led partisans. The guerrilla leader, Josef Broz Tito, finally proved victorious and he formed the postwar Yugoslav government in March 1945.

Tito promulgated a new constitution that divided Yugoslavia into six separate entities, which he called "republics": Serbia, Croatia, Slovenia, Bosnia-Herzegovina, Montenegro and Macedonia. Serbia included within itself the "autonomous region" of Kosovo-Mitrovica with a large Albanian minority. Each republic could have its separate language but no separate sovereign authority. Tito, half Slovene and half Croat, became the communist dictator.

Tito broke from Josef Stalin's satellite system on June 28, 1948. He remained neutral between East and West but with good contacts to the West throughout the Cold War. Bordered on the east by massive Soviet forces, the peoples of Yugoslavia felt that they could not show internal dissent without risking their independence. They remained together, bound by expediency if not by conviction. Tito kept all ethnic groups under tight and often brutal control. He occasionally altered the status of one or another area, notably granting Kosovo a larger measure of autonomy within Serbia in 1974.

During most of the Cold War, the Western states accepted and even supported Tito's Yugoslavia, although they recognized that his dictatorial methods violated the human rights of separate ethnic groups as well as Western principles of democratic rule. They dared not lose control over the ports on the Adriatic coast to the Soviet fleet. But, after the rise of Mikhail Gorbachev in Moscow during the mid-1980s, Western and especially American priorities shifted.

American-dominated international institutions read Gorbachev's policies as an invitation to increase pressures on Yugoslavia. The International Monetary Fund (IMF) insisted that Belgrade repay large loans made during the 1970s to ease the effects of the "oil shock" price rises. The IMF demanded that Prime Minister Ante Markovic introduce severe domestic austerity to pay the debt. Markovic tried to comply, but the resulting austerity made the two most prosperous Yugoslav "republics," Slovenia and Croatia, think they could do better on their own. Even such poorer areas as Kosovo and Macedonia wanted to be freed of Belgrade-imposed austerity.[5] Terrorist attacks on Serb properties and officials, especially police, rose in Kosovo.

Slobodan Milosevic, then a rising Serbian political figure, used the deepening tension in Kosovo to political advantage. He went to Kosovo in 1987, to the hallowed "Field of the Blackbirds" where a Serbian army in 1389 had fought fiercely against an Ottoman invasion and had left a legacy of honor despite its defeat. He made a fiery speech in which he shouted to the assembled Serbs: "No one should be allowed to beat you!"[6] Rallying to his fervent nationalism, the Serbian parliament elected him president of Serbia in May 1989. From that position, he became president of Yugoslavia.

Ambassador Zimmermann had a deep personal interest in one message that he kept delivering in Yugoslavia. Having been Washington's ambassador to the Conference of Security and Cooperation in Europe (CSCE) and valuing the human rights principles of the CSCE, he used every occasion to press for greater human rights in Yugoslavia and especially in Kosovo.[7]

In a multiethnic federation like Yugoslavia, however, and especially in such peripheral regions as Slovenia, Macedonia and Kosovo, human rights meant national rights: Yugoslavs of every ethnic group interpreted any talk of human rights and freedom to mean freedom *outside* Yugoslavia, not freedom *inside* Yugoslavia. Although the U.S. government, especially Secretary of State James Baker, stressed continued American commitment to Yugoslav unity, the separate peoples of Yugoslavia heard what they wanted to hear.

Zimmermann's role carried particular irony. As an expert on Yugoslavia who knew all too well what a bloodletting any secession would provoke, he had a personal commitment to the unity of Yugoslavia. Yet his comments on human rights fed the fire, whether he wished it or not.

Eagleburger paid a visit to Yugoslavia that may also have contributed to separatist sentiment. At a dinner in Zimmermann's residence to which the ambassador had invited every ethnic resistance leader, Eagleburger said that the United States would have "no choice but to live with" the dissolution of Yugoslavia, although he did not advocate it. Zimmermann observed that the Slovenes perceived that remark as a "green light" to push secession.[8] Other groups probably interpreted it the same way, as they could have been expected to interpret a meeting by the U.S. Deputy Secretary of State with opposition figures known to favor independence or at least greater autonomy.

Milosevic himself regarded Zimmermann's remarks and actions as a threat to Yugoslav unity and to Serbia's position as the leading republic within the confederation. He did not receive Zimmermann for the first nine months of the ambassador's presence in Belgrade. But he also exploited Zimmermann's comments. Nothing could better serve to rally the extreme nationalist Serbs to Milosevic's political ambitions than to have them see that Milosevic was resisting foreign pressure for Yugoslavia's dissolution.

Zimmermann's human rights comments helped to shape the Yugoslav political dialogue. Milan Kucan, the Communist party leader in Slovenia, began speaking up in support of human rights in Kosovo, showing that Yugoslav politicians themselves saw a clear link between human rights and separatist rights from republic to republic. Otherwise, Kucan would have had little reason to speak of Kosovo.[9]

As Yugoslavia began to dissolve, old patterns began to emerge again. Western states began to help their favorites to secede from the federation. The separate Yugoslav groups, wanting aid and international support, happily cooperated. And Washington officials began to see the risks more clearly. An American National Intelligence Council study warned in 1990 that Yugoslavia would break up and that the process would be bloody.[10]

Austria, Germany and Italy supported independence for Slovenia and Croatia. Those two Yugoslav republics had been part of the Austro-Hungarian Empire before World War I and shared the Roman Catholic religious beliefs of those three Western European states. Slovenia's Alpine economy meshed closely with Austria's and Italy's. Austria began opening bank affiliates there. And the newly united German government wanted to please its own domestic Croatian as well as Catholic constituencies.[11]

To legitimize their planned declarations of independence, Slovenian and Croatian political leaders scheduled elections during the spring of 1990. The newly elected Slovenian government then declared complete independence and sovereignty in July. Its new foreign minister, Dimitrij Rupel, declared: "Yugoslavia no longer exists."[12]

The new Croatian parliament followed suit, declaring "political and economic sovereignty" for Croatia. But this declaration aroused far more controversy because Croatia contained large Serbian minorities in the Krajina region and also in the Eastern Slavonia border area near Serbia. If Croats had rights within Serbian-dominated Yugoslavia, did Serbs have rights within Croatia? Milosevic played on Serb fears, promising to help them against the Croats.

The predictable reactions followed. On July 26, 1990, the leader of a principal Krajina Serb party announced that: "In the event that Croatia secedes, the Serbs in Croatia have a right to decide in a referendum with whom and on whose territory they will live."[13] If Croatia could become independent of Serbia, could the Serbs in the Krajina and Eastern Slavonia regions of Croatia become independent of Croatia? How far could ethnic secession go?

The attitudes of the outside powers became more obvious and potentially more damaging. Germany supported Croatian national rights and independence but expressed no concern about the rights of Serbs living in Croatia. Russia voiced support for Serbia, its historic ally with which it shared the Eastern Orthodox religion. Washington sympathized with Kosovo Albanians but not with Kosovo Serbs. As foreign governments weighed in selectively, each pushing for its own favorites, the nightmare of ethnic warfare loomed ever larger.

On July 2, 1990, the Albanian members of the Kosovo state assembly followed the Slovenes and Croats, although without first holding an election. They declared the political autonomy of Kosovo as an independent unit of equal status in the Yugoslav federal system.[14]

The Western states and their allies had thus reversed the 1918 decision of the Yugoslav peoples to form their own united state in order to avoid outside exploitation and division. With no outside state threatening to annex one or another Yugoslav republic, as Austria had annexed Croatia before World War I and as Italy had tried to annex Fiume during World War I, a number of Yugoslav peoples were ready to split the federation. But the Serbs, who had dominated the federation, were not ready. In particular, Milosevic was not ready to let Serbs living in other parts of Yugoslavia be ruled by one of the newly independent regimes.

Bosnia, the third of the major Yugoslav states, faced the most sensitive problems. Being a truly multiethnic state, it would confront the gravest difficulties if Yugoslavia broke into separate ethnic entities. Bosnian elections held in 1990 gave no clear guidance for the future, as the results ran completely along ethnic lines: the Muslim party, led by Alija Izetbegovic, won 33 per cent; the Bosnian Serb party won 29 per cent; and the Bosnian Croat party won 18 per cent. Unlike Slovenia or Croatia, Bosnia had no mandate for independence as an ethnic state. It did not even have a mandate for a majority government. But the Bosnians feared being left in a rump Yugoslavia dominated by a powerful Serb majority without Slovenia and Croatia to balance the Serbs. Slovene and Croat independence threatened Bosnia almost as much as it threatened Serbia.[15]

Ethnic war came ever closer. Slovenia and Croatia began to lobby for official recognition from friendly states in the West. They found a ready welcome. Austria secretly printed currency for an independent Slovenia. The United States supported the independence movements by intensifying its criticism of the Yugoslav government under Milosevic.

Milosevic planned for war. He had decided to make sure that all Serbs could live under a Serbian government and would not be forced to live under any other ethnic group. As soon as Slovenia and Croatia formally announced their independence, on June 25, 1991, Milosevic ordered the Serbian-controlled Yugoslav People's Army (YPA) to attack the new governments.

Serbia's war with Slovenia lasted only ten days, largely because the lack of a Serbian minority in Slovenia made the war pointless. Milosevic needed no part of Slovenia for a Serb state.

But the war in Croatia widened, involving not only the YPA but the Serb population in Krajina and Eastern Slavonia. As it continued for months, it caused thousands of dead and tens of thousands of refugees as well as mass destruction. The familiar humanitarian agencies, the International Committee of the Red Cross (ICRC) and the U.N. High Commissioner for Refugees (UNHCR) came in to help the sick and the wounded and to provide relief. The U.N. Secretary-General, Javier Perez de Cuellar, asked Mrs. Sadako Ogata to have UNHCR protect civilians in the war zone. He also asked her to provide food and other relief for them. UNHCR, originally established to help refugees, again had to care for internally displaced persons (IDPs) in the middle of a war as it had done for the Kurds after the Gulf War (chapter 7).

In October 1991, Perez de Cuellar appointed the former U.S. Secretary of State, Cyrus Vance, as a special envoy for Yugoslavia. He wanted Vance to help the various states and ethnic groups in Yugoslavia to reach some agreements. He particularly asked Vance to try to find a peaceful solution in Croatia. Vance achieved a breakthrough, being able to arrange a cease-fire in January 1992, by persuading the Croatian government to offer respect for Serb minority rights in the Krajina and Eastern Slavonia. This did not fully satisfy Franjo Tudjman, the president of Croatia, who wanted to expand Croatia without giving rights to others, but the Serb forces were winning at the time. Tudjman, like Milosevic, wanted his own national state with all Croats under one government.

As Yugoslavia disintegrated, no ethnic group wanted to become a minority in anybody else's state. Each wanted to become a majority in its own state, either by redrawing the boundary lines, by expelling other groups or by becoming dominant over them. And every minority wanted to devise a state in which it could become a majority.

As Vladimir Gligorov, the Yugoslav political theorist, said: "Why should I be a minority in your state when you can be a minority in mine?"[16]

Every Yugoslav ethnic group saw a new prospect: national sovereignty; a separate territorial state; perhaps separate membership in the European Union and the United Nations. And, if Yugoslavia was to be dissolved, each group had to move fast to get—or to increase—its share, either by drawing the right borders or by expelling the wrong people. One or the other had to give.

The human rights of one group contravened the human rights of another. A group that had suffered oppression now had a chance to become the oppressor. And the oppressors could be expelled or excluded by a new map. Not even the wisdom of Solomon could decide where justice might lie.

The European Union (EU—formerly the European Community—EC) wanted to play the principal role in Yugoslavia. Jacques Delors, then president of the EU Commission, thought that this could become a defining moment for the Europeans. He is reported to have said: "We do not intervene in American affairs; we trust America will not intervene in European affairs." Luxembourg's foreign minister, holding the presidency of the European Union at the time, said that Yugoslavia represented the "Hour of Europe," as the Europeans anticipated the important role that they would be able to play.[17]

Because of that European attitude, and because U.S. President George Bush did not want to be accused of becoming "the policeman of the world" after the American victory over Iraq in the Gulf War, Washington did not try to play the leading role. Baker commented acidly that "we don't have a dog in that fight."[18] But when he called on Milosevic in June 1991, he made it very clear that the United States would choose democracy over unity if it came to such a choice. He thus privately reinforced Zimmermann's and Eagleburger's warning that the United States would favor independence for the Yugoslav peoples who chose it.[19]

The Europeans obviously believed that they could keep control over events and could say what they liked. On March 13, 1991, before the Slovenian and Croatian declarations of independence, the European Parliament—led by Germany and Austria—had passed a resolution supporting the human rights of the separate Yugoslav peoples. It declared that "the constituent republics and autonomous provinces of Yugoslavia must have the right freely to determine their own future in a peaceful and democratic manner and on the basis of recognized international and internal borders."[20] The European Parliament had never made any statement guaranteeing that such distinct groups as the Bretons, Scots, Catalans or Basques could determine their future freely within France, Great Britain or Spain. But the parliamentarians proved more generous toward the ethnic groups of Yugoslavia, which was not a member of the European Union, than toward their own separate ethnic groups.

Brussels thus encouraged separate ethnic groups in Yugoslavia to go forward on separate paths. The European Union helped dismantle Yugoslavia. And, like Washington, it did not apparently weigh the humanitarian consequences.

The German Foreign Minister, Hans-Dietrich Genscher, took the most dramatic step. He decided that Germany would recognize both Slovenia and Croatia as fully independent and sovereign states. He also decided to persuade the entire membership of the European Union to recognize the two new states.

Many prestigious international personalities and others tried to persuade Genscher to hold off, especially on his plans to recognize Croatia. They asked Genscher not to act until some protection for the Serb community within Croatia had been agreed. They also warned that any step toward recognition of Croatia would provoke violence in Bosnia, where the Serbs and Croats would immediately try to get into the front row to be recognized as rulers. Alija Izetbegovic, the leader of the Bosnian Muslims, himself appealed to Genscher on behalf of the peoples of Bosnia-Herzegovina, warning Genscher that recognition of Croatia would lead to war in Bosnia-Herzegovina.[21]

Vance tried to dissuade Genscher. So did the incoming U.N. Secretary General, Boutros Boutros-Ghali, as well as Lord Peter Carrington, whom the EU had appointed special envoy to Yugoslavia. Eagleburger, by then fully aware of the forces that had been unleashed, also appealed to Genscher.[22] They all warned that recognition would jeopardize all efforts to stabilize the ethnic situation in Yugoslavia, with Carrington predicting that it would be the "death knell" for talks between various factions.[23] Vance wanted to offer recognition only to those states that had first guaranteed the rights of all minorities.

Genscher chose to ignore all those appeals. On December 15 and 16, 1991, Genscher and German Chancellor Helmut Kohl himself pressed the members of the European Union to recognize both Slovenia and Croatia within the month. Genscher then did not even wait for common European action. Instead, he proclaimed Germany's unilateral recognition of both states on December 23, 1991.[24]

Cyrus Vance, bitterly angry at what he regarded as an irresponsible act against the advice of senior United Nations and EU envoys, called the subsequent hostilities "Genscher's War."[25] One observer noted that it plunged Bosnia "into the abyss."[26]

The West had created a perverse incentive, encouraging every group in Yugoslavia to establish new realities in its own favor by force. Any state could now expect international recognition if it proclaimed its independence. It would then be recognized for whatever territory and people it controlled. Minority rights did not matter. The humanitarians were expected to take care of that.

Vance's cease-fire in Croatia, which took effect in early 1992, had indeed already brought in the humanitarians. He had arranged for a United Nations Protective Force (UNPROFOR), a new contingent of about 14,000 "blue helmets," to enter Croatia. UNPROFOR was to supervise demilitarization of disputed areas and to permit UNHCR and other agencies to distribute relief supplies throughout those areas in order to avert a humanitarian disaster in the midst of a rapidly exploding conflict.

UNPROFOR's arrival gave U.N. military contingents a direct humanitarian role that they had not had before. They had to protect civilians and also to protect those who were trying to help the civilians. Some NGOs felt distinctly uncomfortable about that arrangement. They had always believed that humanitarian aid had a civilian and neutral role and that military contingents were, by their very nature, political. They accepted the peacekeepers only because those peacekeepers themselves promised neutrality. And peacekeepers became a fully accepted part of the humanitarian response to disaster, ultimately serving in many different crises around the world.

Milosevic, War and Intervention

While Vance and UNPROFOR had helped to stop the Croatian civil war, they could not prevent war in Bosnia. Presidents Slobodan Milosevic of Serbia and Franjo Tudjman of Croatia immediately recognized the possibilities inherent in the new international recognition practice. Early in 1991, with the prospect of European Union recognition in the air, they had met secretly and had tentatively agreed to partition Bosnia between Serbia and Croatia. They had also agreed to compel the necessary population transfers to make the partition effective.[27] But they had never sealed the deal because they could not decide on the terms for partition or on the boundary lines. Nonetheless, their talks showed that they would try to create realities that they might then expect the West to recognize, and each set about to get the borders he wanted.

That kind of thinking turned Wilsonian principles upside down. It promoted conquest instead of human rights. Worse, it encouraged what came to be known as "ethnic cleansing." The group that could expel others from the largest possible area could expect to win recognition as fully sovereign over whatever "state" that it had "cleansed."

Bosnia became the setting for the most traumatic Yugoslav battles to date. The Muslim, Serb and Croatian communities had intermingled there most closely over the centuries. Croats lived generally in much of northwestern Bosnia, closer to the Dalmatian coast. Serbs lived for the most part in the north and northeast, near the border to Serbia and the Serb populations of Croatia. Muslims lived throughout much of the center, especially within and around the old capital city of Sarajevo. Bosnians, generally urban, concentrated in Sarajevo and in smaller cities and towns. Serbs and Croats, mainly farmers, lived more in villages and in the countryside.

After Tudjman and Milosevic had decided to annex parts of Bosnia in order to expand their ethnic bases and states, mutual tolerance among the three communities in Bosnia could not continue. War followed. Tudjman tried to expand Croat parts of Bosnia and annex them into Croatia. Milosevic, even more ambitious, wanted to expand the Serb-populated parts of Bosnia and merge them into a "greater Serbia." That state would incorporate every Serb part of the former Yugoslavia as well as any areas from which Serbs could expel others. Before it ended, the civil war had killed 200,000 and forced 4 million from their homes.[28]

The horrors of the communal war in Bosnia exceeded the imagination as neighbor fought neighbor and friend fought friend. Organized troop units and separate individuals used every conceivable weapon to exterminate each other in every imaginable and unimaginable way. The Western Europeans and Americans found themselves paralyzed by the intensity and brutality of the conflict. They could do little to stop the killing and chose not to do even what they could.

Bosnian Croats, with support from Croatia itself, attacked toward the southeast to drive Serbs and Muslims out of the center of Bosnia. The Croats launched an especially brutal campaign against the old medieval city of Mostar. They literally razed much of the city and destroyed the old city bridge, one of the greatest examples of Ottoman architecture, which had often symbolized Yugoslavia in tourist posters. They began a systematic campaign of "ethnic cleansing" in the area bordering on Croatia, massacring Muslim civilians in their home villages.[29]

Milosevic had two particularly ruthless vassals to direct his campaign: Radovan Karadzic, the political leader of the Serbs in Bosnia, and Ratko Mladic, the Bosnian Serb military commander.[30] The Serbs under their command more than matched the Croats in brutality, killing them and Muslims freely in order to carve out their own ethnic area. The Muslims retaliated in kind, but were badly outnumbered and outgunned. Lord David Owen, former British Foreign Secretary, whom the European

Union had appointed as envoy for Yugoslavia to succeed Lord Carrington, recalled the extermination campaigns in Cambodia during the 1970s (chapter 6) and labeled Bosnia the "killing fields," as the world had earlier labeled Cambodia.[31] By then, Washington had already withdrawn Zimmermann as ambassador in protest against Milosevic's behavior.

Vance and Owen tried to stop the fighting by devising what became known as the Vance-Owen Peace Plan, an arrangement that divided Bosnia into ten separate areas along ethnic lines for administrative purposes while keeping the country under joint sovereignty. Under the plan, conceived as a type of federal solution, each of the Bosnian groups was to receive a measure of authority over three areas where they already predominated while all three parties would share a tenth area for the capital Sarajevo and for a central administration.

Vance and Owen had no illusions that their plan offered a perfect solution. But they believed that a freeze on internal borders would remove the incentive for each party to expel others in order to widen its own area. It might at least stop the killing. The European states supported the plan as "the only game in town." Milosevic accepted it. Izetbegovic also welcomed it although he did not say so in public because Milosevic might then have opposed it.

When Bill Clinton became U.S. President in January 1993, he vetoed the Vance-Owen plan. He and the new Secretary of State, Warren Christopher, did not see the Bosnian conflict as a civil war but as a case of Serb aggression against Bosnia. They wanted to repel the Serbs from Bosnia and thought that the Vance-Owen plan gave too much land to the Bosnian Serbs. They wanted instead to arm the Bosnian Muslims to try to help them win the war, although Russian Foreign Minister Andrei Kozyrev warned them that this would provoke a wider Balkan conflict. Clinton also disliked sending U.S. forces to help enforce the plan. Christopher said "we do not like the maps."[32]

Thus, just as Genscher had helped foment the war in Bosnia by recognizing Slovenia and Croatia, Clinton helped perpetuate the war by rejecting the Vance-Owen Plan. But Clinton did not carry out the other part of his policy. He did not commit U.S. forces to help the Bosnian Muslims or to enforce some other plan. Nor did he arm the Muslims enough to expel the Serbs and Croats, if they could indeed have done so. Like other outsiders, Clinton and Christopher made the situation worse instead of better. They blocked what might have worked but had nothing to put in its place.

Nonetheless, Clinton and European leaders realized that they had to do something to prevent total elimination of Bosnian areas. The Europeans especially feared that masses of Bosnian and other refugees would flood into Western Europe, as they were beginning to do. After several more rounds of fighting, the Western leaders formed a new consultative committee called the "Contact Group" to try to stop the fighting.

Christopher invited the Russian, British, French and German foreign ministers who were members of the Contact Group to meet in Washington. On May 23, 1993, they issued what they called the Washington Declaration. It offered no political solution and pronounced no set boundaries. It did, however, decree "safe areas" in and around several Bosnian Muslim towns surrounded by Serbs, including Sarajevo itself and Srebrenica and Gorazde. This move, by totally abandoning the Vance-Owen Plan and reopening the boundary lines, also reopened incentives for each party to widen its area of control.

The Contact Group also expanded UNPROFOR into Bosnia from Croatia but did not give it the level of forces that Boutros-Ghali wanted. He said that he needed at least 34,000 troops to protect the Bosnians, to secure relief supplies, and to shelter the "safe areas." The Western members of the Security Council gave him 7,000, but only 2,000 immediately, and also rejected his request for heavy arms. UNPROFOR did not rise near requested levels until three years later and it never received the heavy weapons that the United Nations had recommended. During the entire Bosnian conflict, it remained inadequately staffed and inadequately armed.

The Europeans wanted to introduce the concept of the "safe areas" because they could tell Bosnian Muslims to go to the safe areas instead of becoming refugees in Western Europe. Although many asylum seekers did slip into Western Europe, the Europeans generally tried to block them. They insisted that they did so to prevent Milosevic from doing his "ethnic cleansing," not because they wanted to keep out refugees. They also used UNPROFOR to stop Bosnians from fleeing Sarajevo or other towns attacked by the Bosnian Serbs. One observer remarked bitterly that the Western states who refused to give entry to potential victims of Hitler's Holocaust might have used a parallel argument that they wanted to avoid contributing to Hitler's "ethnic cleansing" of Jews.[33]

Milosevic recognized that the Washington Declaration would help those who could help themselves. He had been pressing the Bosnian Serbs to accept the Vance-Owen Plan and had even been prepared to permit some Serbs in Croatia to live under Croatian sovereignty. But he now changed his mind. The war in Bosnia, which had appeared to be easing, resumed with full ferocity. And the "safe areas" became particular targets.[34]

With the war re-energized, the Serbs, Muslims and Croats fought each other everywhere, often where there were no clear fronts but where they wanted to move their own ethnic boundaries forward. And Bosnian Serb forces under Karadzic and Mladic reached new heights of bestiality. They brought Sarajevo itself under siege from their headquarters in the city of Pale lying in the hills above Sarajevo. They rained artillery fire from those hills into the city. They destroyed much of the center of the old city, including a treasured library built in the days of the Ottomans. Serb sharpshooters in the hills above the city could target individual Sarajevo citizens walking or driving along one of the main avenues. The avenue came to be known as "sniper alley." The Serbs also machine-gunned Bosnians trying to flee the city.

As the war intensified, some governments worried about the safety of UN-PROFOR itself. That force had been intended to keep a peace but not to join in a war. It had neither the training, the equipment nor the stomach for a real fight. The European states that had soldiers in the force became genuinely alarmed over their safety. They talked of general withdrawal and asked NATO to help protect UN-PROFOR as it withdrew. Clinton agreed in principle to send as many as 20,000–25,000 U.S. soldiers to help shield a withdrawal. But Clinton wanted to use air strikes to punish Serb forces, whereas the Europeans feared that the Serbs would retaliate against their UNPROFOR troops. The disagreement brought NATO into a major crisis.[35] It also meant that the "safe areas," allegedly under the protection of UNPROFOR, became highly vulnerable.

Many UNPROFOR units did pull out because the situation had become too dangerous for them. Even the International Red Cross did so at one point after one of its delegates was killed. But agencies like the World Food Program and UNICEF stayed in order to provide humanitarian relief, and UNHCR remained as lead agency.

The humanitarian operations in Bosnia set new standards for operations in the midst of a war. As in Croatia, the High Commissioner for Refugees provided protection and relief not only for refugees but for the millions of IDPs. They may have had no claim to protection or relief under any international agreements but secretaries-general Perez de Cuellar and later Boutros-Ghali asked Mrs. Ogata to help because no other agency had the experience of combining protection and relief and because it had become painfully clear that an understaffed UNPROFOR could provide neither.

Nothing fell into the well-known categories of the Cold War. Ogata had to protect IDPs from murderous attacks in a war zone, not—as UNHCR had done previously—from governments that might want to send them home. She had to provide relief in beleaguered towns and villages as well as in snowy mountains and valleys, not in designated and organized refugee camps. And she, as well as the U.N. and NGO relief workers, had to provide that relief in the face of constant threat and frequent harassment.

One relief convoy commander recorded 90 checkpoints at which his convoy was stopped on only one delivery mission. Local Serb military commanders often held up food bound for Bosnian areas in order to seize some for their own troops. Countless food items also suffered spoilage, sabotage and pilferage. Nothing that happened could be described as neat and orderly, with every form of expediency and pragmatism used in the desperate humanitarian effort to get relief supplies to those who needed them.

The humanitarian agencies set new records almost every day. UNHCR ran the longest air supply operation in history, from July 2, 1992, until January 9, 1996, a four-year airlift that brought over 160,000 tons of food to Sarajevo and brought out over 1,100 civilians who needed medical care. During those years, UNHCR and other agencies coordinated a massive effort that delivered over 950,000 tons of humanitarian relief supplies all over Bosnia, much of it food provided by the World Food Program. By 1995, the agencies were helping almost three million Bosnians, as big an operation as UNHCR had run for Afghanistan or Sudan.[36]

The United Nations agencies literally kept Bosnia alive. At one point, over 3,000 humanitarian workers from over 250 agencies and NGOs cooperated in the effort, with all of them carrying UNHCR identification cards that they hoped the Serbs would respect. The governments of Denmark, Norway, Sweden, Great Britain, Germany and Russia participated in the convoy teams, with another 15 governments joining in the Sarajevo airlift. UNHCR airlift operations also included airdrops to beleaguered cities and "safe areas." Over 50 civilians involved in the UNHCR-led operations lost their lives, as did 117 UNPROFOR soldiers. Hundreds of humanitarian civilians and military personnel suffered injuries.

In addition, the relief agencies tried to help Bosnians who wanted to escape from their towns and villages because of Serb death threats. As tens of thousands fled into neighboring areas, relief workers tried to help them and others although they were ill empowered and equipped to do so. Ogata, UNHCR, IOM and the ICRC also evacuated Bosnians when necessary despite the criticism that they were facilitating "ethnic cleansing."

For almost three years, Western governments could not make any decisions that would end the war or stop the attacks conducted by Karadzic and Mladic and masterminded by Milosevic. The Western governments made firm pronouncements but did not back them up with the necessary national or international force. They could agree on only one action: relief. And they then expected the humanitarians to carry out the mandated relief operations in the midst of war. As one UNHCR delegate, François Fouinat, said, U.N. humanitarian operations "have been transformed into the only manifestation of international political will."[37]

The Western governments did decide to deploy UNPROFOR around the Sarajevo airport as well as at other key points in Bosnia. This enabled the airlift to proceed and also helped to make relief possible. But it did not provide security throughout the country, leaving the humanitarians to fend for themselves. Only in 1995, when Western governments had boosted UNPROFOR to 30,000 throughout Bosnia, could the troops deploy around much of Bosnia, and then they did not venture into all the areas where the agencies distributed relief.

UNHCR and the ICRC thus found themselves compelled to act not only as humanitarians but as wartime observers. They could watch the process of "ethnic cleansing" although they could not prevent it. All too often, they alone could tell the international press and the United Nations itself what was happening where. It became a humanitarian role in Bosnia to record the grim truth even if one could not prevent it. This often subjected United Nations staff to Serb threats.

Western humanitarian agencies trying to help Sarajevo survive accomplished one of the most remarkable feats of relief in the history of humanitarian operations. The International Rescue Committee reestablished a functioning water supply for the city by airlifting a water purification system that could be installed in a long vehicular tunnel where it was safe from Serb artillery bombardment. The late Fred Cuny supervised the installation. George Soros, an international financier, paid for it. Cuny made sure that the pieces of equipment were precisely measured, with clearances smaller than an inch, to fit into the tunnel and into C–130 cargo planes. He arranged for the planes to land and take off so quickly that Serb mortar and artillery fire could not zero in on them. When they had finished, Sarajevo again had a water supply.[38]

As the humanitarian effort continued, the "safe areas" turned into the greatest danger zones. The humanitarian agencies could usually get relief shipments into the beleaguered areas by truck convoys or, where necessary, air drops, even though the numbers kept rising as masses of refugees fled into the "safe areas." But the humanitarians could not end the blockades around those areas nor the attacks against them. The Serbs learned that they could halt relief convoys with impunity and could exact tolls in the form of food for their own troops. They also learned that they could keep the areas under threat by shelling and other forms of harassment.

In February 1994, an artillery shell killed 68 persons and wounded another 200 on the marketplace in Sarajevo. The major Western states threatened air strikes and were able to use the threat to impose several cease-fires. Those cease-fires did not end the war but did reduce the number of victims for a time. The Contact Group also agreed on the allocation of Bosnian land in any peace arrangement: 51 per cent to be divided between the Bosnian Muslims and Croats, with 49 per cent to go to the Bosnian Serbs.[39] But they offered no specifics on the boundary lines and they had no way to enforce any lines they might propose.

Karadzic and Mladic continued their attacks despite several cease-fires. Another shelling in 1995 killed 11 persons in Sarajevo and left hundreds badly wounded. Although the West could not clearly identify where the shells had originated, suspicion logically fell on the Bosnian Serbs. When the Serbs took several other provocative steps, NATO launched limited air strikes. In return, the Serbs threatened to arrest U.N. peacekeepers. Great Britain and France, fear-

ing the risk to their forces, persuaded the U.N. Security Council to stop order-
ing air strikes.

Jacques Delors and the new united Europe had failed in Yugoslavia after choosing it
as the first test of their ability to act. Five years after Slovenia's and Croatia's thrust
for independence, with German, Italian, Austrian and general European encouragement, Yugoslavia lay in tatters. Bosnia, the most multiethnic state, had suffered
three years of brutal civil war. Although the Europeans wanted to take the lead in
solving the Yugoslav problem, they had reached no consensus about what to do.
Nor had any individual European leader advanced any plan that promised to lead to
a solution or that suggested any readiness to enforce a true peace.

The United Nations had fared a little better because of its humanitarian work,
for years the only effective international action in the former Yugoslavia. But it had
achieved little else. Boutros-Ghali had appointed a seasoned American negotiator,
Cyrus Vance, but neither the Secretary-General nor Vance could persuade even
Washington to carry out Vance's recommendations. And UNPROFOR, which had
been established in February 1992, "to create conditions of peace and security" in
Croatia and later in Bosnia, had never received enough support from the members
of the U.N. Security Council and had become a liability instead of an asset.

Washington could offer no solution, either. It had vetoed the Vance-Owen
Peace Plan but had nothing to put in its place. It had, in fact, contributed to the
"winner-take-all" mentality of the struggle for Bosnia by refusing to negotiate a distribution of land and people. Like the Europeans, therefore, it had encouraged
killing rather than peace. Baker could say that the United States had "no dog in that
fight" but both Bush and Clinton had suffered major losses in prestige.

Yugoslavia had been broken up in the name of the noblest human rights principles. But the selective application of those principles had led to a humanitarian
disaster. They had fomented massive killing instead of inspiring reconciliation.

And the worst was yet to come.

Srebrenica

Karadzic and Mladic in early 1995 intensified the pace of their attacks on the small
Bosnian Muslim town of Srebrenica, a refugee-swollen enclave in Serb-dominated
territory east of Sarajevo. The town had been declared one of the UNPROFOR-
protected "safe areas," but every Western state shrank in horror at the thought of actually using force to keep it safe. The UNPROFOR contingent for Srebrenica
consisted mainly of troops from The Netherlands, increasingly fearful for their own
lives as Serb attacks multiplied.[40]

Joris Voorhoeve, the Dutch Defense Minister, did not believe that the Serbs wanted to take Srebrenica despite the growing pressures against the enclave. Because the Serbs attacked intermittently and at different points, he assumed they did not mean to carry out a full-scale assault but were mainly shelling to harass the town as a prelude to some partition agreement. He did not realize that General Mladic had calculated his tactics very precisely.

Karadzic and Mladic wanted Voorhoeve to react exactly as he did. They made their attacks appear random, uncoordinated and unplanned. They had learned that they could avoid air strikes if they stopped their shooting and shelling just before an air strike could be ordered and launched. They also knew that UNPROFOR did not like to run a military operation during negotiations because the West did not want to risk jeopardizing diplomacy. Therefore, the Serbs usually coordinated their attacks with negotiating sessions.

The Dutch peacekeepers in Srebrenica operated under a Western-sponsored U.N. Security Council resolution that instructed them "to deter attacks against the safe areas" and "to monitor the cease-fire" in addition to "participating in the delivery of humanitarian relief to the population." But the Western Security Council members had also authorized an internal UNPROFOR directive that made "the security of U.N. personnel" its top priority, more important than "the execution of the mandate." Force should be used only "as a last resort."[41]

To add to the inhibitions caused by these instructions, the Dutch had to try to obey two independent command systems:

- The first system, the official one, ran through the Balkan U.N. headquarters under the command of several officers nominally serving the United Nations, British Lieutenant-General Rupert Smith and French Lieutenant General Bernard Janvier. The U.N. command worked closely with regional and continental NATO commands. But the special representative whom Boutros-Ghali had appointed for the Balkans, Sasushi Akashi, did not want to use force. This combination of Western and Japanese voices made for confusion and stalemate. Nobody felt responsible for Srebrenica itself.
- The second and unofficial command system ran through national military and diplomatic channels. With the troops being Dutch, they obeyed Dutch instructions more than those coming from U.N. or NATO commands. Any U.N. order had to be approved by the Dutch government, and the Dutch could veto any U.N. plans or strike proposals. That second channel added even more inhibitions than the first. It made the U.N. system a façade for Dutch commands.

Voorhoeve could—and did—regularly countermand U.N. instructions. For example, the Dutch Ambassador to NATO rejected as "dangerous" and "counter-productive" a U.S. proposal for NATO air strikes at an early stage of the attacks against Srebrenica. The Dutch feared for the safety of Dutch soldiers more than for the lives of the Bosnians.

The UNPROFOR system imposed a double and sometimes triple veto, paralyzing United Nations, UNPROFOR and NATO actions. Any international or national commander at any level could delay or block any order to act. So could the cautious civilian, Akashi. He announced in public that the United Nations would return to "traditional peacekeeping principles," a remark that Mladic must have welcomed because it signaled that Akashi did not want the United Nations to fight.[42]

Mladic intensified his assault on July 6, 1995. But he still operated differently at separate points of the perimeter. His troops shelled at some places. At others, they merely approached the Dutch forces and quietly asked them to surrender. They promised early return to Holland for those who accepted the offer. Dutch soldiers actually did surrender at some spots; at others, they retreated. They did not hold their positions. The Bosnian soldiers and civilians in the enclave, deeply alarmed, tried to block the Dutch retreat. The civilians grew increasingly panicky.

The U.N. command did finally decide to launch retaliatory airstrikes after intensified Serb shelling made it impossible for the Dutch to continue to believe that they were not under attack. But NATO could not assemble the aircraft quickly enough because the rules of engagement did not permit bombers or fighterbombers to enter Serb airspace without escort aircraft to suppress any potential Serb air defense. NATO did not want to risk its planes any more than its soldiers.

The French UNPROFOR commander Janvier hesitated even after the aircraft had been pulled together and were ready to launch, He asked for the forces to be kept on alert but not to launch until he had asked the Dutch government for its views. Voorhoeve agreed to the strikes. But Janvier hesitated further. He decided to wait until the following day because it was getting dark.

Voorhoeve then also had second thoughts. He and senior Dutch defense officials agreed that "the security of our people must be paramount." They decided to send a Dutch general to consult with Janvier.

Mladic thereupon gave the Dutch forces in Srebrenica an ultimatum to evacuate Srebrenica within 48 hours. The Serbs shelled the enclave to back up their words. But they timed their actions to respond to NATO air activity. When NATO planes with possible instructions to bomb appeared on Serb radar, Serb attacks ceased. Once the Serb radar showed the planes returning to base, the Serbs resumed their attacks. In total confusion and uncertainty about their mission, only two NATO aircraft finally dropped any bombs at all—and harmlessly.

At this point, Mladic moved. He threatened to kill his Dutch prisoners and to shell refugees if NATO did not stop the attacks immediately. When this message reached The Hague, Voorhoeve immediately called the NATO air operations center.

There, the surprised liaison officer heard the Dutch Defense Minister shouting "Stop! Stop! Stop!" at the top of his lungs into the telephone. UNPROFOR commanders accepted that instruction, informal or not, and NATO launched no further air attacks.

General Mladic could proceed unhindered as the Dutch forces in Srebrenica opened cease-fire negotiations that gave the Serbs free access to the "safe area." Several years later, rumors surfaced that Janvier, with the consent of the French government, had negotiated the safe departure of the Dutch forces in return for his willingness to delay and suspend airstrikes against Serb positions near Srebrenica.[43]

Mladic used the next several days to carry out further phases of his plan. First, his forces separated the Bosnian Muslim men from the women and children, herding them into separate trucks. The Serbs said that they would screen the Bosnian men for "war criminals" but it became increasingly clear that they would kill the men whether they had committed "war crimes" or not.

To make sure that the Dutch forces would not help the Bosnians, Mladic's commanders told the Dutch that they would not be harmed if they cooperated. But the Serbs warned that they would attack any Dutch soldiers who resisted. Mladic himself summoned the local Dutch commander, Lieutenant-Colonel Ton Karremans, to warn him that Serb artillery would decimate the Dutch if there were any more air strikes and if they resisted. Karremans, helplessly intimidated, accepted the ultimatum. The Dutch did nothing to stop Serb killing of the Bosnian Muslims.

Individual Dutch soldiers, appalled at those instructions, tried to help Bosnians. Some tried to follow Bosnians as the Serbs removed them from Srebrenica. But the Dutch did not have enough soldiers to follow every bus and truck. Moreover, the Serbs—who had total control of the situation—sometimes confiscated Dutch jeeps at gunpoint and forced the soldiers to walk back to their bases.

By July 12, a week after Mladic had begun his direct assault on Srebrenica, the deportation had ended. But a grimmer process followed, as the Serbs began systematically killing the men whom they had separated from their families. The Dutch could see groups of Bosnian Muslims being taken into buildings or behind walls. The Dutch could hear shots. They could then watch Serb soldiers walk away without the Bosnians.

Mladic would reiterate that the Serbs were looking for "war criminals." They would pull men and boys forcibly from their relatives. A Bosnian woman told Human Rights Watch:

> By that night, the people who hadn't been transported yet became hysterical and frightened. We began to hear talk about corpses being discovered in the area. . . .
> By Thursday morning, women were wailing and crying because many of their hus-

bands and/or sons had been taken away . . . for one reason or another, but had not been brought back.[44]

Rumors of murdered Muslims abounded. The Serbs tried not to let the Dutch or other outsiders watch. But one Dutch lieutenant, Eelco Koster, saw groups of Bosnian men dead on the ground and he took the identity papers lying around. Another Dutchman actually saw Muslims being murdered.

Voorhoeve and the Dutch did nothing, however. When Bosnians who were being taken away asked Dutch soldiers what would happen, the Dutch did not answer even when they knew all too well. They did not try to interfere with Serb actions. By July 13, Srebrenica had been "ethnically cleansed."

Voorhoeve mainly wanted to get Dutch soldiers out alive. He asked the new German Foreign Minister, Klaus Kinkel, to persuade the Russian Foreign Minister, Andrei Kozyrev, to use Russia's influence with the Serbs to let the Dutch leave safely. Mladic graciously permitted them to do so. By July 21, the Dutch had pulled out of Bosnia and out of the "safe area."

Anxious to get out safely, the Dutch did not try to take any of their Bosnian employees even when the employees begged to join them. The Dutch did not want any complications to prevent or delay their own evacuation. Many of those employees disappeared and have not been seen since.

In contrast, Mrs. Ogata and relief NGOs put their local Bosnian employees on their evacuation lists and were able to remove them from Srebrenica and from Mladic's impending revenge. As an ultimate touch of irony, civilian U.N. agencies and NGOs did more to protect Bosnian Muslims than NATO soldiers had done in their designated "safe area."

Dutch NATO soldiers had violated one of the most basic tenets of peacekeeping, neutrality. By succumbing to Serb pressure, the Dutch had endorsed the Serb campaign to exterminate the Bosnians. Neutrality required impartiality. They had not held to that. Instead, they had joined the Serbs.

The Dutch had also taken back the absolute sovereignty that many states had yielded to the United Nations and its agencies during the Cold War in order to legitimize their support for humanitarian operations. The Dutch Defense Ministry took back command of Dutch forces from U.N. and NATO commanders, although the Dutch still labeled their forces international peace-keepers. And the Dutch acted primarily to protect their forces, not to carry out international humanitarian assignments. Srebrenica had become a turning point in many ways, none of them based on the humanitarian conscience.

The humanitarian agencies did not emulate the Dutch. Mrs. Ogata, commenting on her cooperation with UNPROFOR in Yugoslavia, insisted that "it is essential for the humanitarian organizations to maintain the strictly non-political, neutral and impartial nature of their mandates." She wrote that humanitarian agencies had found it possible to cooperate with peacekeepers in many areas, but only on nonpolitical terms.[45]

The Serbs accelerated their work after the Dutch had left. As witnesses later testified, the Serbs escorted large groups of Muslims to various farms or forests and systematically murdered them. In one case, they herded hundreds into a dark warehouse and then fired at random into the warehouse. Most died but a few managed to escape to tell the tale. In one case, a U–2 spy plane photographic record showed Serb soldiers escorting large numbers of Muslims and later, on another pass over the same site, showed mass graves. Outsiders who managed to get near the execution sites reported the ground covered with blood.

Nobody, including perhaps General Mladic himself, knows with any certainly how many were killed under the general's orders. At one site, the Serbs reportedly killed about 1,200 men. At another, near the town of Potocari, the Red Cross reported that 1,700 men had been removed and never recovered. The ICRC had the names of 6,546 missing from Srebrenica, almost all men. None have been found.

The final death toll, on the basis of ICRC and other estimates, may have run as low as 6,500 or as high as 11,000. On that scale, it could legitimately be labeled an act of genocide. Shamefully, the dead were supposedly being sheltered by UNPROFOR troops, by the threat of NATO retaliation and under a U.N. Security Council mandate agreed upon by the United States, Great Britain, France and others.

After the fall of Srebrenica, the impotence of U.N. Security Council member states and of the NATO peacekeepers reeked to high heaven. Fifty years after Hitler's defeat, Europe had experienced yet another overt act of genocide, this one in the presence of an international force instructed to prevent it.

Mladic confidently predicted that, "by the autumn, we'll take . . . Sarajevo and we'll finish the war."[46]

Milosevic and the Serbs established themselves as the principal villains of the Yugoslav drama by their bloody assault on Srebrenica. Milosevic might say, correctly, that others had also sinned against his people, but nothing had reached the same level of barbarism as the murders committed by the Bosnian Serbs under Milosevic's instructions and Mladic's orders.

The Dutch government published a report absolving its soldiers of wrongdoing, asserting that they did not know and could not have known what would happen to the Bosnian Muslims whom they abandoned. Several years later, however, in April 2000, when the International War Crimes Tribunal at The Hague began hearing charges against Bosnian Serb General Momcilo Krajisnik, who had helped to lead the assault on Srebrenica, a fuller account emerged.

In that tribunal, which the Security Council, ironically, had established just before the assault on Srebrenica, Dutch soldiers called on to help prepare the case testified that they had seen the Serbs kill Bosnian Muslims even in the presence of the U.N. "peacekeeping" force. The Dutch soldiers concurred when one Bosnian witness described how Serb soldiers had lined up and shot columns of Muslim civilians and had led away their wives and children to an unknown destination. In the process, the Dutch soldiers gave the lie to their own government's investigative report and revealed the coverup.[47] The Dutch could only argue that their small force could do nothing against General Mladic and his troops.

To set the record straight, the Dutch government conducted another investigation, which blamed the government itself for the failure of its forces to defend Srebrenica. The investigation led to the resignation of Prime Minister Wim Kok and his government in April 2002, seven years after the event. But the investigation also revealed a number of problems in the management of the operation itself, including the confusing command structure and the lack of proper training and of adequate intelligence facilities.[48]

But long before these investigations, the stain of acquiescence to Mladic's attack on Srebrenica sullied the entire West, including the United States, NATO and the members of the Security Council. All understood that they needed to act more forcefully. French President Jacques Chirac proposed a firm stand at Gorazde, another threatened "safe area." NATO agreed that it would defend other "safe areas" by air strikes. Clinton announced U.S. support for an air campaign. Nonetheless, he would not accept any Western responsibility for the failure of the West to act at Srebrenica. Much to Boutros-Ghali's irritation, Clinton blamed it on the United Nations, which had actually been bypassed by all the crucial commands.

The killings at Srebrenica did galvanize the West, no matter whom Western leaders blamed. When Karadzic and Mladic launched another mortar assault on Sarajevo on August 28, killing a number of innocent civilians, even the most reluctant governments in the West felt compelled to react. NATO began a swift and—by the standards hitherto applied in Yugoslavia—massive bombing campaign against Bosnian Serb concentrations in the Sarajevo area. Kofi Annan, then Undersecretary-General of the United Nations for Peacekeeping, called the American Assistant Secretary of State for European Affairs, Richard Holbrooke, to make clear that no U.N. official would be authorized to veto air strikes. Annan and Boutros-Ghali wanted to avoid any possible delays in the Western reaction.[49]

Franco Tudjman of Croatia took advantage of the new anti-Serb mood to solve his own most pressing problem. He began an "ethnic cleansing" operation of his own, expelling Serbs from Krajina as well as Eastern Slavonia. Although the U.N.

Security Council approved some resolutions criticizing his actions and telling him to stop, he could act as he wanted in the wake of the widespread international condemnation of Serbia. American officials, including Holbrooke, even encouraged Tudjman and urged him to get as much land as possible before the new internal boundaries of Bosnia were fixed. Holbrooke told Tudjman: "Don't waste these last days" before a cease-fire.[50]

Muslim forces also rallied against the Serbs, reconquering lost territory and reversing the impressions of inevitable Bosnian Serb victory that had been permitted to grow. Suddenly, the Serbs began to lose what they had won before.

Milosevic, faced by Western bombing and by Croat and Bosnian assaults, recognized that he needed to negotiate. Holbrooke, who had decided to host and to chair the negotiations himself, chose a U.S. Air Force base at Dayton, Ohio, as the place to talk. Europe had failed and the Americans would now take over.

Holbrooke at Dayton

Richard Holbrooke, as chairman of the Dayton talks, drove them relentlessly. He finished them within the planned three weeks, between November 1 and 21, 1995. He found Milosevic surprisingly helpful, ready to abandon and even deride his Bosnian Serb friends Karadzic and Mladic—whom he officially represented. He found Tudjman difficult but finally cooperative. He found Izetbegovic unpredictable, ready at the end to delay (but not to block) signing the agreement over points that Holbrooke regarded as insignificant.[51]

The other Western delegates at Dayton, Jacques Blot of France, Wolfgang Ischinger of Germany, Pauline Neville-Jones of Great Britain and Igor Ivanov of Russia, cooperated and often added useful elements although they did not find Holbrooke's impatient and often abrasive behavior easy to accept.[52] The EU representative, Carl Bildt, who would become the senior international official in Bosnia, worked closely with Holbrooke.

All the Western delegations agreed that they wanted two results: a cease-fire and an agreement that Bosnia should remain a multiethnic state. The Dayton accord provided for both of those.

The various foreign and Yugoslav parties at Dayton also agreed that the Bosnian-Croat federation would control 51 per cent of Bosnia's land and the Bosnian Serbs would control 49 per cent. The exact area assigned to each side became one of the most vexing issues at Dayton but was finally settled through Milosevic's personal intervention against the Bosnian Serbs. This delineation finally removed the incentive for different ethnic groups to expand their areas of control. It thus put an end to "ethnic cleansing" as Vance had tried to do with his map four years earlier.

The states represented at Dayton wanted to create a real chance at peace. They therefore agreed on a five-part international political and humanitarian operation to put Bosnia back on its feet and to take care of those who had suffered in the war:

- A "High Representative" would coordinate the international operation in conjunction with the Bosnian government and would report to a "Peace Implementation Council" of states to make sure the Dayton accords were carried out.
- A special United Nations office, called the United Nations Mission in Bosnia-Herzegovina (UNMIBH), was charged with coordinating the work of all U.N. agencies in Bosnia and also with training a multiethnic Bosnian police force and bringing about the rule of law. The police training function closed at the end of 2002, with its mandate accomplished, and the European Union Police Mission assumed the responsibility for police training.
- An international military force, first called the Implementation Force (IFOR) and then the Stabilization Force (SFOR), was assigned to give military backing to the plan. Originally containing 60,000 troops, it had declined to less than 15,000 by the year 2003.
- A mission of the Organization for Security and Cooperation in Europe (OSCE) was to encourage stable political development.
- An office of the U.N. High Commissioner for Refugees would act as lead agency for continued humanitarian aid to Bosnia and encourage the return of refugees. About a dozen U.N. agencies continued to function, including UNDP, UNICEF and WFP. The World Bank also remained to help with the Bosnian development program.

But the Bosnian Serb and the Bosnia-Croat structures could not be completely merged. Each was given its own government and prime minister. They were to handle mainly domestic matters but those matters could obviously loom large at times.

European and American negotiators at Dayton did not find agreement easy. The Europeans resented American leadership and occasionally bridled at Holbrooke's hard-charging manner although they recognized it as perhaps the only way to force agreement. They had to concede that he sometimes protected points that they might have been prepared to yield, but they still did not like to be negotiating a European and Balkan deal at a U.S. base in Ohio and under American leadership. In his memoirs, Holbrooke returned the compliment, complaining that the Europeans wasted time on trivial procedural and prestige matters and that they could not reach quick agreement even on matters that were in their common interest. The French insisted that the Dayton agreement be signed in Paris, a point that Holbrooke conceded to keep Europe engaged.[53]

Holbrooke played his own power games. Washington insisted on an "exit strategy," placing an unrealistic one-year limit on the presence of U.S. forces.[54] The original deadline for U.S. withdrawal, 1996 (an American election year), has long since been ignored although all international forces have declined in number.

The Americans had their internal disagreements as well, mainly because the U.S. military feared the "mission creep" that had destroyed their operation in Somalia (chapter 10). They wanted to know exactly what they were to do, and what they were not to do, before they committed themselves.

The humanitarian mission in Bosnia has scored many successes over the years since Dayton. The economy has stabilized and life has returned to a semblance of normality. Reconstruction of Sarajevo and of other major cities has gone on apace. The European Union has built hundreds of schools and health centers as well as water and sewer projects all over Bosnia. It is also playing ever greater roles in the military supervisory force and may assume responsibility for it.

Many states joined. For example, the international police training force had contingents from over 50 states, with the largest contingents coming from Germany, France, Jordan, the United States, India and Pakistan.

Many refugees have returned to Bosnia. Although the exact number is hard to calculate because many have returned informally, the number of returnees is certainly over 500,000. Of those, about 200,000 returned under a special International Organization for Migration program in which they received some help to reestablish themselves.[55]

The humanitarian agencies have fulfilled their obligations under the Dayton agreement. In addition, many organizations also worked to bring Bosnia back to normal life and to try to overcome the effects of the war. During 2002 and 2003 small signs appeared that the three communities were more disposed to live and work together than they had been during the 1990s. These signs included an increase in 2001 and 2002 to over 100,000 "minority returns"—Bosnians returning to areas dominated by other ethnic groups.[56]

But some major Dayton provisions remain unfulfilled as of this writing and may remain unfulfilled for some time. There is still no single Bosnian armed force. As of 2003, there were three (Serb, Croat and Muslim). And there is as yet no fully united political structure. Despite some elections, no such united structure could emerge quickly.

Refugee repatriations have also sent warning signals. Many of the refugees returning to areas dominated by other ethnic groups consisted of older people, often farmers or retirees, who wanted to return to reclaim their land or their houses. Even then, groups of returnees were sometimes blocked from returning. Efforts to rebuild Muslim mosques in areas controlled by Serbs were also blocked, with the Serb population physically attacking international administrators or forces trying to escort Muslim returnees or to rebuild mosques.[57]

The Dayton accords could not reverse the most important long-term loss for Bosnia, the loss of its professional class. Many young Bosnians have not returned but have remained in Western Europe. Many Bosnian lawyers, doctors, scientists and administrators have decided to remain in the West. They had gone there in the early 1990s, having seen the handwriting on the wall for Yugoslavia. They have found jobs, homes, schools and communities. Although the International Organization for Migration and other organizations have returned some professionals to Bosnia under special programs to encourage such returns, many such professionals remain in Western Europe.[58]

To punish the crimes committed during the wars of the former Yugoslavia, the U.N. Security Council had established a United Nations tribunal in The Hague in 1993, the first international war crimes court since Nuremberg. The United States had threatened to stop aid to Yugoslavia if the Yugoslav and Serb governments did not turn over potential war criminals to the court. Partly as a result of that pressure, Zoran Djinjic, the former Prime Minister of the Serbian Republic that is part of Yugoslavia, turned over Slobodan Milosevic to the court in 2001 and turned over the former Serbian President, Milan Milutinovic, in January 2003. A former Bosnian Serb leader, Biljana Plavsic, surrendered to the court in 2002 and was convicted and sentenced.

Milosevic has not cooperated with the court. He has conducted his own defense, refusing to follow normal court rules and procedures while haranguing and denouncing witnesses. His failing health may make it impossible to complete the lengthy trial plans for his war crimes not only in Bosnia but also in Kosovo. Although the prosecutors have mounted a body of increasingly damaging evidence against him, he has become something of a folk hero again in Serbia for his resistance to the court. The Serbs, whose long sense of victimhood has been reinforced by the actions of the court, complained that neither the leaders of other Yugoslav republics nor Kosovo Albanian terrorists have been called to account as Serb leaders have been, although some non-Serbs have at last been called in 2003.

Much to the irritation of many Europeans and Americans, neither Radovan Karadzic nor Ratko Mladic has as of this writing been brought to trial in The Hague although they were widely regarded as the worst of the mass murderers. Serbs in Bosnia and in Serbia itself continue to shelter them, sometimes even permitting them to walk and dine in Belgrade without alerting an international patrol that might arrest them. The war crimes trials thus remain an item of unfinished and controversial business.[59]

The Dayton accords played a vital role in bringing peace to the former Yugoslavia despite their slow and still incomplete implementation. They offered an example of what diplomacy could achieve, opening the door to possible reconciliation over time. They ended the war in Bosnia. They did not yield a perfect peace nor total reconciliation, but that could not have been arranged at the time. They did stop the killing. Bosnia has been stable although still tense. It is entering the Council of Europe. Neither of the three major ethnic groups now sees any advantage in trying to begin another conflict. Holbrooke achieved a major success.

But Holbrooke's success could not conceal that Western policy in Bosnia, as in other parts of Yugoslavia, had been a disaster from the humanitarian standpoint. After having helped to provoke the civil war, the West had permitted a genocide that it could have prevented and had let tens of thousands of innocent civilians die. In the first major ethnic conflict of what President George Bush had termed the "new world order," it had suffered a disgrace that no shifting of responsibility by war crimes trials or by blaming the United Nations can erase. All Western participants insisted that they would never repeat the experience. But they still found themselves unprepared for the next major Balkan crisis in Kosovo (chapter 9).

Klein in Eastern Slavonia

Few people had heard of Eastern Slavonia, a part of Croatia populated largely by ethnic Serbs, before the disintegration of Yugoslavia began. In contrast to Bosnia, it served as a model for humanitarian action in crisis situations.[60]

Being the part of Croatia closest to Serbia and with a Serbian ethnic majority, Eastern Slavonia became an area of intense competition. Serb forces seized it when they advanced in 1991. Croat forces threatened to win it back during their advance in 1995.

As Croat forces advanced and as Serbs fled eastward, the Western states that had first welcomed Croat advances began to question the Croats' own version of "ethnic cleansing." If the Croats tried to kill or expel the Serbs of Eastern Slavonia, where Serbs were in a majority, they might well provoke a Serb counterattack and the Balkans would be plunged into another conflict. Clinton and other Western leaders wanted to prevent that. They wanted to have Eastern Slavonia returned to Croatia but they wanted it to remain ethnically Serb.

The American Ambassador to Croatia, Peter Galbraith, and a U.N. mediator, Thorvald Stoltenberg of Norway, agreed on a formula for what they termed a "Transitional Administrator," an office and a person who could supervise a peaceful transition of Eastern Slavonia back to Croatia. They hoped that this would transfer the land back to Croatia while giving the Serb population enough confidence to remain.

Like other Balkan problems, Eastern Slavonia became part of the agenda for the Dayton conference. Tudjman wanted to use the meeting to get Eastern Slavonia back but Holbrooke insisted that Tudjman agree to a lengthy, peaceful transition. Tudjman, who wanted to improve his own relations with the West, accepted that condition. Milosevic was prepared to agree but he wanted protection for the Serbs who would be a majority in Eastern Slavonia but a minority in Croatia. He had to be sure that the Serb population could stay.[61]

Tudjman and Milosevic argued fiercely about the length of the transition between Serb and Croatian control. Tudjman wanted only one year. Milosevic wanted three years. After a long stalemate, they accepted a formula proposed by Warren Christopher for one year subject to extension for a second year if any party asked for it. Milosevic, unhappy about being responsible for turning any Serbs over to Croatia, insisted that the local Serb leaders also had to agree. They did, and the so-called "Basic Agreement" was signed in Erdut in Croatia on November 12, 1995.

Once the transition of Eastern Slavonia had been agreed, it quickly became clear that no organization wanted to manage it. The major powers, having suffered so many embarrassments in the Balkans, wanted to dump the problem on the United Nations. They spoke of an "international force" for Eastern Slavonia but really meant a United Nations force.

Secretary-General Boutros-Ghali bridled. He resented that Clinton and other Western leaders had blamed the United Nations for their own failures in Somalia (chapter 10) and in Bosnia. He wanted no more undeserved ridicule. He would not accept any more mandates that he was not in a position to enforce. If the United Nations was to handle Eastern Slavonia, he wanted an achievable and enforceable mandate and a U.S. share in the responsibility. He wanted to have a success, not another listing in the Washington blame game.

Boutros-Ghali later wrote that: "Again it appeared that the United States wanted to avoid putting its own soldiers in harm's way by pushing inadequately armed or mandated U.N. troops out in front." He added that any force would have to be strong enough to achieve its mission, and he suggested that NATO should perhaps undertake it.[62] He thought that Washington would give NATO the kind of support it had not given the United Nations.

When Clinton and other Western leaders insisted that the United Nations should take the responsibility, Boutros-Ghali reiterated that he would do it only if he had a real force and a real mandate. His military adviser proposed a mechanized division of two brigades with full logistics, altogether about 11,300 troops.[63] Boutros-Ghali also wanted the force to have a strong peace enforcement mandate under Chapter VII of the United Nations Charter (the chapter that deals with "threats to the peace") and not the Srebrenica-style weak peacekeeping mandate under Chapter VI ("pacific settlement of disputes").

Tudjman himself also wanted solid guarantees that the transfer would actually happen and wanted American forces to supervise the transition of Eastern Slavonia. When Clinton refused to send forces, Tudjman insisted that the Transitional Administrator at least had to be an American general. Like Boutros-Ghali, he wanted to force the Americans to accept responsibility.

Under pressure from Tudjman and Boutros-Ghali, Washington offered Jacques Klein, a career American diplomat and a reserve U.S. Air Force officer with the rank of Major General. When Clinton told Tudjman that he would send Klein, Tudjman agreed.[64]

Klein almost rejected Clinton's assignment. He did not want to be stuck with an impossible mission. Before taking it on, he met with Milosevic and Tudjman to be sure that they would both support a transitional administration. He agreed with Boutros-Ghali that he would need a "robust" force. The senior Security Council members decided that they would not finance a force of more than 5,000, and France, Great Britain and the United States announced that they would not send troops. But Klein decided that 5,000 would be sufficient because the Security Council had at least given him the firm Chapter VII mandate he wanted. His operation would be different from that of the Dutch at Srebrenica.[65]

Klein was able to get armored Belgian and Russian units that had already served in the Balkans. By keeping the Russians, he had a channel to Serbia through its traditional allies. He made a Belgian general his force commander to solidify a NATO connection. He made a Russian general the second in command. In addition, he had battalions from Jordan and Pakistan and a Ukrainian helicopter squadron. Although the force was not large, it had at its disposal over 70 tanks as well as attack helicopters. Smaller specialized contingents from half a dozen other states, such as Argentina, the Czech Republic, Slovakia, Indonesia and Poland also came to help. Klein's United Nations Transitional Administration for Eastern Slavonia (UNTAES), was the largest and most powerful United Nations force assembled in the Balkans to date, although it was to cover an area much smaller than any of the earlier forces.

Klein chose an early moment to make it clear that he wanted his mission to be taken seriously. When a group of Serb paramilitary called the "Scorpions" seized an important oil field and denied entry to UNTAES, Klein ordered the Jordanian battalion, supported by assault helicopters and other armored forces, to take the oil field. They did so by surrounding the field with armor and flying over it with assault helicopters carrying weapons on the ready. They then offered the "Scorpions" immediate safe passage to Serbia, which the intimidated "Scorpions" accepted.

Klein also showed UNTAES authority to the Croats. When some Croat irregular militia began to harass local civilians, he sent a powerful force to disarm them. He then returned the militia to Croat authorities and asked the Croats to keep their paramilitary forces under control.

But Klein and the United Nations faced bitterly suspicious Serbs, who saw their lives and property threatened by the Croats. He had to persuade those Serbs to stay and to be the "minority in somebody else's state" that no Balkan people had wanted to become.

This task became a daily exercise for UNTAES at all levels. Klein and his senior staff attended services in Serb Orthodox churches as well as Croat Catholic churches. They walked the streets to be seen as a presence and to make it plain that they watched the behavior of the victorious Croats as well as that of the dejected Serbs. UNTAES civil affairs officers spoke at town meetings. They brought seeds and fertilizer for the farmers and fuel for the police cars. They coordinated with pharmaceutical companies to deliver multivitamin pills for the undernourished children of the area. They arranged mail exchanges across an area known as "no-man's-land." They called together conferences of Serb and Croat doctors, lawyers and teachers to discuss common problems as well as details of transition arrangements.

UNTAES sponsored a weekly market in "no-man's-land" in order to bring the people together at a common site. It produced the first true mingling of the Serb and Croat populations in years. And UNTAES sponsored a newspaper printed in both Serb Cyrillic and Croat Latin script as well as radio broadcasts that told their listeners what UNTAES was doing and how they could take advantage of any UNTAES-sponsored services. To relieve the anguish of Croats whose family members had been the victims of earlier ethnic cleansing by Serb forces, UNTAES arranged for proper identification and proper burial of the dead and for investigations of war crimes and human rights violations.

The international and local NGOs proved equally active. They brought medical supplies for Serb as well as Croat families and they helped provide for children in need. They arranged sports events. The ICRC helped with postal services and searched for lost family members on both sides to help them meet again. Slowly, indeed very slowly, the two communities began to develop contacts.

Most Serbs chose to remain in Eastern Slavonia although the area had again become part of Croatia. Most were farmers whose families had lived in the same small villages for 400 years or more. They did not want to move if they were given a decent chance to produce and live in peace. UNTAES moved to protect them and to give them that chance. Most important, Klein insisted on a multiethnic police force in Serb areas, giving the Serbs an assurance that at least some of the police represented them and would protect them.

Klein and UNTAES had one very specific and major political task in their mandate, to organize elections for local government and for the upper house of parliament by April 13, 1997. They faced enormous reluctance by the Serb population. Many Serbs did not believe in elections. Others, who had fled to Eastern Slavonia from other parts of Croatia, hated the Croats and did not want to join in political processes of any kind in a Croat state. They wanted no Croat documentation and were in some cases even afraid to register.

Klein argued forcefully that the Serbs could not change the reality that they were now in an independent Croatia but that they should at least use the elections to try to make their views known and to support their friends rather than to let the Croats select all the delegates. UNTAES encouraged the Serbs to get their documents, to register, to organize for their candidates and to vote. It had a measure of success, with Serbs registering and voting in large numbers and getting some representation although, due to their relatively small numbers in Croatia, not very much.

On January 15, 1998, UNTAES ended its work, two years to the day after it began. The Transitional Administrator transferred Eastern Slavonia to Croatian authority on that day. Although OSCE monitors remained in place and aid programs continued, the United Nations mandate ended as did the exercise of U.N. authority over Eastern Slavonia.

The work done by UNTAES has remained valid. Most Serb farmers have stayed in Eastern Slavonia. And Croats have been able to return without generating too much friction with the Serbs. Although Croat authorities have not always treated Serbs fairly, the Serb population that remained has been able to live and to work in peace. The United Nations carried out its mandate although it lost one soldier. UNTAES even caught an indicted war criminal for trial.[66]

The United Nations could not control what was to happen after its departure. But the situation has remained better than it would have been without UNTAES and without the United Nations role. Tudjman, anxious to have Croatia join the European Union, has avoided the kinds of incidents that could make EU officials question his commitment to peace and stability. Klein and the UNTAES forces and administrators showed that a multiethnic society could function in the Balkans despite the horrors of history. They also gave Boutros-Ghali the success that the Secretary-General had wanted.

As Klein left, he offered some advice for other humanitarian missions of the same kind:

- There must be a real and precise mandate;
- Equally important, a credible force;
- Enough resources firmly committed;
- Clear and enforced rules of engagement;

- A combined political and military command;
- A single and united, not divided, chain of command;
- A commitment to confidence building;
- A good public information program.[67]

Klein's advice rang true. It had worked for him. It might also work for others. Like Holbrooke, he had been able to salvage something from the ruins of the former Yugoslavia. But others were not able to do that, especially in Kosovo where the entire Yugoslav upheaval had begun.

NINE

"HUMANITARIAN WAR" OVER KOSOVO

SLOBODAN MILOSEVIC HAD A FIXATION ABOUT KOSOVO, a relatively small part of Serbia and Yugoslavia but an important cog in Balkan history. Kosovo represented hallowed ground for him and for many Serbs.

The Serb defeat at the "battle of the blackbirds" of 1389 had become, paradoxically, the supreme moment in Serb history. The Serbs might have lost the battle but they had stood alone to oppose the Muslim advance into Europe and into the Christian world. No Serb leader, neither Milosevic nor any other, could let that land go without a fight. All the raw emotions, deep-seated historical resentments and tribal animosities aroused by the conflicts within Yugoslavia came together in Kosovo.

And yet, even as they insisted that Kosovo was theirs, the Serbs had lost the silent war, the population contest. Over five centuries, and especially during the twentieth century, ethnic Serbs had been emigrating from the province. The Nazis and their Yugoslav sympathizers, who favored Albanians over Serbs, had killed many Kosovo Serbs during World War II. Ethnic Albanians had come in to replace them. Moreover, the Albanians had a higher birthrate and larger families. By 1990, when the Cold War ended and Yugoslavia began to break apart, the Serbs constituted at most 15 per cent of the population of Kosovo. They resented their minority status bitterly. They still wanted to control the province even as they had lost it. They were claiming land that had been taken from them by demography, not by force.

The Kosovo Albanians, knowing that they were in the majority, wanted more self-government even after Tito had granted them autonomy in 1974. Many of them did not want independence from Yugoslavia. They understood the world around them and knew that a small landlocked state surrounded by potential enemies had few prospects for success. Nor did most of them want to join with other ethnic Albanians in Albania, Montenegro and Macedonia to form a "greater Albania." They knew it would spark fratricidal wars and they did not want to be ruled from the Albanian capital of Tirana. But they wanted to become a separate republic within Yugoslavia, like Slovenia or Croatia, with considerable power to govern themselves.

Serbs, on the other hand, opposed even the autonomy that Tito had granted, although they could not reverse it while Tito lived. They saw Kosovo as a part of Yugoslavia even as the Spanish see Catalonia as a part of Spain, perhaps different but certainly not separate or separable.

Kosovo therefore remained racked with tension and occasional violence during the 1980s and early 1990s. Frequent incidents between the two communities exacerbated mutual hatred, especially as the aggrieved party in each incident swore revenge and often sought it. The Kosovo Albanians complained that the Serbs violated their human rights; the Kosovo Serbs complained that the Albanians violated theirs.

As Serb resentment and hatred grew, Slobodan Milosevic—then only a relatively obscure Communist politician in Belgrade—decided to use it for his own purposes. On April 24, 1987, he went to Kosovo to attend a meeting at which Serbs planned to vent their grievances against Albanians.

After he had heard from enraged and frustrated Serbs both inside and outside the meeting hall, Milosevic shouted to them: "No one should be allowed to beat you!" This single sentence, as one Kosovo Serb leader later said, "enthroned Milosevic as a Czar."[1] It made him a hero to all Serbs, in Kosovo and beyond.

Milosevic went further. Inside the hall, he said to the assembled Serbs:

> This is your country. These are your houses, your fields and gardens, your memories. . . . You should stay here, both for your ancestors and your descendants. . . . Yugoslavia does not exist without Kosovo! Yugoslavia would disintegrate without Kosovo! Yugoslavia and Serbia are not going to give up Kosovo![2]

Milosevic's speech could not change reality, but it made him the unquestioned idol of the Kosovo Serbs and the Serbian nationalists. He used the fervor that it aroused to promote himself to chief of the Serbian Communist Party and, beyond, to President of Serbia and later President of what remained of Yugoslavia. And he used his positions and Serbian rage to pass laws that in 1989 stripped Kosovo of its autonomy.

Ibrahim Rugova, whom the Kosovo Albanians had chosen to be their leader as the head of the Democratic League of Kosovo (DLK), could not have been more different. He followed a policy of quiet and passive resistance modeled on the ideals of the Indian leader Mahatma Ghandi.

Rugova believed that the Kosovo Albanians would win self-government over time by showing that they could administer Kosovo. He also expected some support from the West, perhaps as part of a general settlement on the Balkans that would follow the end of the Cold War. He established a shadow administration, which functioned as the real government of Kosovo, with a parallel system of schools that taught the truth about Kosovo history. The Kosovo Albanians ignored the Yugoslav administrators and ran the province largely on their own.

On May 24, 1992, the Kosovo Albanians held elections for their own president and for a parliament. Rugova and the DLK won overwhelmingly without much Serb interference. But the shadow government and parliament had to meet either in secret or in the West because the Serb police continued to prevent them from meeting openly. For a time the government made its headquarters in Bad Godesberg, near the former West German capital of Bonn. It received strong financial support from the Albanian diaspora community in Germany, Austria, Switzerland and elsewhere in Europe.

Rugova believed that the shadow administration would give the Kosovo Albanians the satisfaction of autonomy because they were running their own province. Most Kosovo Albanians agreed with him. Until 1991, when they saw that Slovenia and Croatia had gained independence, many had not envisaged independence for Kosovo. After that, however, some of them began endorsing independence. They reflected this in a secret referendum, which the DLK organized on September 22, 1991, but they still accepted what they regarded as unavoidable delays.

Despite Rugova's effort to coexist with Serbia, tension and spontaneous violence continued in Kosovo. The Serb army and Serb police forces exercised their power demonstrably and brutally, fomenting ever more resentment. Milosevic, who faced more immediate problems in Slovenia, Croatia and Bosnia, did not concentrate on Kosovo, but he remained determined to keep control over the area. He saw all the problems as linked.

President George Bush had other things than Kosovo on his mind after losing the election to Bill Clinton in November 1992. Nonetheless, he specifically warned Milosevic on December 23, 1992, that the United States would respond to any Serb use of military force in Kosovo. That message, which became known as the "Christmas warning," had actually been drafted by Lawrence Eagleburger, who had become U.S. Secretary of State in the waning months of the Bush administration. It stated that: "In the event of conflict in Kosovo caused by Serbian action, the United States will be prepared to employ military force against Serbians in Kosovo and in Serbia proper."[3]

Clinton initially repeated the "Christmas warning" but he later allowed it to lapse after conducting a wider policy review toward the Balkans. And the warning again showed separate Western policies toward the former Yugoslavia: Russia still leaned toward Serbia; Germany and Austria still leaned toward Slovenia and Croatia; and Washington increasingly leaned toward Kosovo.

The agreements that Milosevic reached with the West at Dayton and elsewhere, as well as his accords with Slovenia, Croatia and Bosnia, changed the Kosovo equation. They showed, as Rugova had expected, that the international community would play a role in the Balkans and that it would support separatist movements. They also showed, however, that Rugova had been wrong to predict that Kosovo would be freed, or would at least regain its autonomy, as part of a general Balkan settlement. At Dayton and elsewhere, nobody spoke of Kosovo.

Thus a new Kosovo organization that had been formed in 1993 began to look for new solutions. The Kosovo Liberation Army (KLA) argued that Rugova's policies had failed and that passive resistance would never succeed because the West would help only those who fought for their independence and who were then attacked by Milosevic.

Hashim Thaci, who directed the KLA, pursued a terrorist strategy: to kill or wound Serb administrators and especially Serb policemen. The KLA began such attacks on a small scale by 1993 in order to provoke Serb retaliation. By 1996, the KLA had gained enough confidence in its strategy and its tactics to begin a major campaign of terror.[4]

Rugova and the DLK had tried peace. Now Thaci and the KLA would try terror.

Rambouillet

Between 1996 and 1998, a war of terror and counter-terror raged in Kosovo. The KLA, which grew ever larger as it drew more recruits and more funding from Albanians living in Western Europe and the United States, increasingly attacked Serb installations throughout all of Kosovo. Its leaders began to step out of the shadows and to show themselves in public in Kosovo and elsewhere.

Madeleine Albright, the new U.S. Secretary of State, began paying more attention to the war by 1998. She appointed Richard Holbrooke to serve again as negotiator in Yugoslavia, and he launched a round of shuttle diplomacy that led to meetings between Rugova and Milosevic as well as between Rugova and Clinton. But the talks led to no results and actually damaged Rugova's position because he appeared to be talking while his people were bleeding.

The struggle in Kosovo continued relentlessly and predictably in a classic pattern, which had prevailed in countless liberation wars for decades: carefully calculated KLA attacks against Serb police, installations or residents; savage Serb retaliation, often killing or wounding civilians in large numbers; at the end, more bitterness, less chance for reconciliation, more recruits for the KLA and even the beginnings of "liberated areas" primitively administered by the KLA. The Serbs might have appeared to be winning the war by all outward signs but they could not end the resistance.

Milosevic in February 1998 decided to launch a concerted military and police campaign against KLA fighters and KLA areas throughout Kosovo. As the conflict widened, so did the plight of innocent Kosovars. By the end of 1998, as many as 300,000 Kosovo Albanians had fled their homes, with over 100,000 leaving for neighboring Albania and Macedonia.

Many Serbs also fled Kosovo. They had seen that Milosevic had been unable or unwilling to save the Krajina Serbs from being expelled by Croats. Many believed that Milosevic would not be able to help them either, for the Albanian majority had begun to show its rule over Kosovo ever more openly. The Albanians, and especially the KLA, had no regard for Kosovo's Serbs, even for those who might have lived there for generations and who had befriended their Albanian neighbors. As the war intensified, the human suffering deepened.[5]

Western and Eastern governments alike began to worry that the war could spin out of control. NATO members, and especially the Americans, also began to worry about the popular and political reaction at home as more and more gruesome pictures appeared in the press and on CNN. Those images convinced Western governments that they had to act quickly and to act against the Serbs.

Theoretically, the West could not intervene in Kosovo without U.N. Security Council approval—which would be subject to an almost certain Russian or Chinese veto. But the Western states decided that they needed to act even without the council. President Jacques Chirac of France argued that "the humanitarian situation constitutes a ground that can justify an exception to the rule" that states could only act after a Security Council vote.[6] Albright in particular insisted that NATO should not wait for the United Nations.

Igor Ivanov, the Russian Foreign Minister, offered NATO the opening it wanted. He told the Western members of the Contact Group that Russia would have to veto a Security Council resolution but that it would "just make a lot of noise" if NATO acted on its own.[7] Moscow even accepted a September 1998 Security Council resolution demanding an end to Serb operations and the return of refugees. And it agreed to permit the Organization for Security and Cooperation in Europe (OSCE) to establish the Kosovo Verification Mission (KVM) in Pristina to monitor the conduct of the war and especially Serb actions.

Holbrooke persuaded Milosevic to accept a cease-fire in Kosovo in October 1998. But the KLA advanced and continued killing police officers as the Serb forces withdrew to their barracks. The Serbs then resumed their attacks on Albanian villages.

After several particularly ugly atrocities, including a Serb massacre of 45 ethnic Albanian men, women and children, another cease-fire was arranged. And OSCE monitors thought they might be able to do more to bring about a longer cease-fire. But by then the Western governments, and especially the U.S. Secretary of State, had decided that they wanted a comprehensive political settlement. To do so, they needed to get the Serb and Albanian leaders together and to press them to agree.[8]

On February 6, 1999, the members of the Contact Group met at the French government conference center at Rambouillet castle with Serb and Albanian delegations. The negotiating conditions posed problems. The Serbs and Albanians would not meet or talk with each other directly but only through Contact Group members acting as intermediaries. The Albanian delegation included both Rugova and Thaci, despite their intense dislike for each other. But Milosevic did not lead the Serb delegation, which meant that no real decisions could be made on the spot. The one-week deadline set by the Contact Group proved to be wildly unrealistic.

The Western delegations, supported by the Russians, tried to negotiate a settlement. But they soon realized that the Serbs and Albanians would not reach agreement quickly, if at all. Milosevic told Holbrooke that he agreed to four conditions that some U.S. officials regarded as important and promising: NATO could have air access over Kosovo to survey the situation; 2,000 unarmed civilian monitors could enter Kosovo; the Kosovars who had been driven from their homes could return; and a political process could begin. But the Albanians did not agree to those terms. And American officials remained uncertain how any agreement might be carried out in practice.[9]

For its part, the United States—led by Mrs. Albright—wanted more than Milosevic's four points. Albright insisted that NATO should have the right to station forces and equipment all over Yugoslavia, not only in Kosovo. She set the following terms:

> NATO personnel shall enjoy, together with their vehicles, vessels, aircraft and equipment, free and unrestricted passage and unimpeded access throughout the Federal Republic of Yugoslavia for bivouac, maneuver, or operations . . . [and the] sole authority to establish rules and procedures governing the command and control of the airspace over Kosovo as well as within a 25-kilometer Mutual Safety Zone.[10]

The Rambouillet draft proposals also included the provision that all Yugoslav forces except border guards be withdrawn after 180 days and that there should be a referendum in Kosovo within three years to decide whether Kosovo should become independent of Yugoslavia.[11]

The Western delegations knew that Milosevic would not accept either of these proposals. Any expert on the history of Yugoslavia knew that the formula for total freedom of movement for NATO forces throughout Yugoslavia directly recalled the ultimatum that the Austro-Hungarian Empire had presented to Serbia in 1914 after the assassination of Archduke Francis Ferdinand. No Yugoslav leader, least of all Milosevic, could be expected to accept such an ultimatum. Nor could Milosevic agree to a referendum on Kosovo independence, whether in three years or at any time.[12]

Secretary Albright had another objective, as she told her staff: "Getting rid of Milosevic is my highest personal priority. . . . I want him gone before I am gone." The Western parties at Rambouillet, and especially the U.S. delegation, did not want an agreement. They wanted war, and were ready for it.[13]

Albright and the Americans took a leading role in the negotiations. She personally supported the Albanian cause and especially leaned toward the KLA. She dealt more with Thaci than with Rugova although Rugova had wider support among the Albanians and although Thaci was following a policy of terrorism.

Albright used private talks with the KLA leader to persuade him to accept the Western proposals that dominated the draft. She stressed the prospect for a referendum on Kosovo's independence. She also made clear that NATO would bomb Serbia if the Kosovo delegation accepted the Contact Group proposal and Milosevic rejected it. She thus made it obvious to Thaci that his acceptance of the Rambouillet proposals would lead to war by NATO against the Serbs.

Albright's assistant, James Rubin, went so far as to tell the press that "we cannot put the full amount of pressure [on the Serbs] if we don't get an agreement from the Kosovar Albanians." He added that "in order to move toward military action, it has to be clear that the Serbs are responsible." Albright wrote Thaci privately that, no matter what language might be agreed at Rambouillet, the United States would make certain that Kosovo would hold a referendum on its future status within three years.[14]

Thaci hesitated despite Albright's and Rubin's promises. He returned to Kosovo to consult with other KLA leaders. When he returned to Rambouillet after that consultation, he was ready to sign. Because Rugova had already agreed, the Kosovo Albanians now supported the Rambouillet outcome and thus opened the way for the military action that Albright and Rubin had promised.

Thaci's agreement may have surprised Milosevic, who had told the Contact Group that he accepted its political proposals but whose delegates to the conference had often remained silent. When the Albanians accepted Albright's proposals, the Serb delegation would not sign. It proposed a last-minute alternative draft for an agreement, but that draft did not meet Albright's conditions—including the plans for NATO freedom of movement and for a referendum.

With war on the horizon, Holbrooke took one more trip to Belgrade to warn Milosevic that NATO would bomb Serbia if he did not sign the Rambouillet agreement. Holbrooke warned that NATO would bomb intensely, and for a long time.

Philosophically, almost stoically, Milosevic made clear that he understood: "You will bomb us."

Milosevic's foreign minister, Zivadin Jovanovic, denounced the Rambouillet process itself. He claimed that Rambouillet was "all about geopolitics, not about human or minority rights." He said that NATO wanted to expand to southeastern Europe for strategic reasons and that it had made its plans to attack Yugoslavia before the conference had even opened. But he added that "Yugoslavia has never capitulated in all her history."[15]

Rambouillet had the predictable outcome. Albright turned to the logic of force. The French, who believed that no settlement could possibly have been reached under the NATO ultimatum and with Albright obviously on Thaci's side, called it "Madeleine's war." And Albright thought that it would be over quickly, saying "I think this is . . . achievable within a relatively short period of time."[16]

Like other wars, the Kosovo conflict held surprises for all participants. The West, and especially Secretary Albright, had expected Milosevic to yield after a few days. Basing their expectations on the Serb decision to go to Dayton after only a few days of bombing in 1995, they thought Milosevic would again yield quickly. Americans thought that: "Bosnia had proved Milosevic to be a bully coward; if we hit him hard, he would fold."[17] Milosevic may in turn have made a similar miscalculation, expecting the bombing to stop quickly. He may have based his expectations on NATO leaks.[18]

American and other NATO officials and staffers had predicted confidently to each other and to the press that Milosevic would surrender and they could stop bombing. They did not prepare themselves, their military, their publics or the United Nations for anything longer. Worst of all, they did not prepare President Clinton.[19]

General Clark Bombs Serbia

As Holbrooke had warned Milosevic, NATO bombing began on March 24, 1999, giving the Balkans the dubious honor of sparking the last as well as the first major European conflict of the twentieth century. But the bombing did not end quickly. To everybody's surprise, especially that of the Americans, it was to last for 78 days, until June 9, 1999.

President Clinton called the bombing "the first humanitarian war." This seemed like an oxymoron. War had never been regarded as a humanitarian act, although it could have been seen as having a humanitarian purpose in the battle against Hitler or Tojo. In fact, NATO had begun bombing for political and not humanitarian reasons. A NATO staff report to British Prime Minister Tony Blair and to German Chancellor Gerhard Schröder said that the alliance had begun the bombing to preserve its credibility. NATO celebrated its fiftieth anniversary in 1999 and could not neglect—or lose—a conflict on its own border. Having issued countless threats, it had to act. But the NATO paper warned that "there are never military solutions to difficult political problems."[20]

Serb actions held another surprise for most American officials, and an especially brutal one. The Serb army and militia poured into Kosovo within days of the bombing's start, in a move that was widely seen as prepared or at least planned in advance but that only the NATO military commander, General Wesley Clark, had foreseen. Serb forces fanned out across much of Kosovo, driving the Albanians from their homes, sometimes killing them and often leaving the homes looted and burning. They emptied the cities and left whole villages and farming communities in ruins. Within days, masses of refugees were fleeing, streaming out of Kosovo into Macedonia, Montenegro or Albania itself. Those ethnic Albanians who did not leave Kosovo often went into hiding in the hills and woods, foraging for food and surviving as best they could.

The NATO bombing was mainly directed against Serbia proper. It did not try to stop Serb forces attacking Kosovo. By the time it had ended, almost half a million Albanian Kosovars had fled to Albania, about a quarter million to Macedonia, and about 75,000 to Montenegro. Almost 100,000 were taken by air to Western European countries as well as to Australia, Canada and the United States in order to relieve the pressure on Macedonia. Several hundred thousand had hidden within Kosovo itself.[21]

Mrs. Sadako Ogata, the U.N. High Commissioner for Refugees, found herself in a bitter argument with Western governments, and especially the United States, about her inability to help the massive numbers of Albanian refugees immediately. Clinton and Albright, frustrated that the war continued longer than expected and that refugees were not swiftly received by UNHCR tents and relief supplies, complained that Ogata and her office had not readied themselves properly for mass flight. American officials charged that Ogata and UNHCR had failed their humanitarian duties.

Ogata replied tartly. She said that no Western government had warned her that such a massive flight was anticipated and that NATO had not even let her know of a report allegedly received by the German government about a supposed Serb plan to expel ethnic Albanians from Kosovo. She also retorted that, when she had asked for additional contingency funds shortly before the bombing began in order to be able to help refugees, NATO officials had told her that the bombing would last for only a few days and that they expected few new refugees. She wrote that "UNHCR received no advance warning from any government or other source."[22] She also reminded the U.S. government that it kept asking UNHCR to take on ever larger tasks in the Balkans at precisely the moment when Washington and other donor capitals would not fully fund her budget.

Once again, the supposed Western expertise on the Balkans had been thrown into question. The Western states had obviously failed to prepare themselves, the United Nations or the humanitarian agencies for the humanitarian aspects of this "humanitarian war." Clinton and Albright had expected a short war, with Milosevic conceding quickly. A senior State Department source, asked if the Department had been surprised by the scale of the exodus, replied: "Quite a bit!" The Macedonian government also complicated refugee relief by not permitting refugees to relocate deeper into Macedonia; it feared that a massive Albanian presence would intensify Albanian demands for a larger role in Macedonian government—as indeed emerged later. Nonetheless, once the initial problems had been solved, UNHCR and other agencies had been able to take care of all refugees, whether in the Balkans or by sending them to Western Europe.[23]

Milosevic and Serb forces acted with widespread brutality throughout Kosovo. They did not match Karadzic and Mladic by repeating the Srebrenica massacre, but they engaged in repeated wanton acts of cruelty. The Western media may have exaggerated the scope of that cruelty and of Serb actions. For example, a report of 10,000 Kosovo Albanians massacred by Serb forces proved to be exaggerated. But the refugees who reached the border told of being expelled from their homes in the middle of the night, of firebombings, of villages set aflame and of men gunned down in front of their families. Many Kosovo Albanians left even without being directly threatened, believing that they should get out before the Serbs killed them and their families.

The NATO spokesman in Brussels, Jamie Shea, warned that "we are on the brink of a major humanitarian disaster," and NATO commander General Wesley Clark charged that Milosevic was trying to accomplish an ethnic reengineering of Kosovo.[24]

NATO did nothing to stop the humanitarian tragedy on the ground. NATO aircraft, under orders to avoid the risk of anti-aircraft fire, remained largely above 15,000–25,000 feet and could not intervene in any military actions on the ground. They could hit most of their targets in Serbia accurately by using precision weapons, such as laser-guided bombs and rockets, but they could not prevent Serb intimidation and terror against the local population in Kosovo without flying low enough to risk being hit by anti-aircraft fire. They could not stop "ethnic cleansing" because they did not attack the forces doing it. Although they had begun their bombing campaign over Kosovo to drive Serb forces back into Serbia, they actually damaged very little Serb equipment in Kosovo.

General Clark wanted to use low-flying U.S. Apache helicopters to attack Serb troops in Kosovo, arguing that they could stop "ethnic cleansing." But Clinton feared losing Apache aircraft and pilots to Serb ground fire and suffering casualties. The Secretary of Defense, William Cohen, shared those fears. Clark never received

U.S. authorization to use the aircraft, although the U.S. government did send them to Albania and although NATO officials—including Secretary-General Javier Solana—wanted to use them.[25]

Clinton and other NATO leaders did not want their publics to face large numbers of casualties. They had promised not to send ground forces into Kosovo even as they began the bombing campaign. This removed any threat of a Western invasion that might have stopped "ethnic cleansing."

Clark quickly learned that in Kosovo, as in earlier humanitarian operations in the Balkans (chapter 8), each military commander would receive two and perhaps more sets of orders. First, through NATO channels; second, from their national command authorities and through their own national channels. Clark later wrote that NATO commanders, "like puppets," had to respond to at least two and sometimes more strings. He often ordered aircraft from NATO states to carry out certain bombing runs only to learn later that they had not followed his orders but the orders of their national commands to run different missions or none. Even the U.S. government did not respect Clark as a NATO commander but treated him as a U.S. officer subject to American instructions. He could not follow his own instincts to try to protect Kosovo civilians.[26]

But the air campaign began taking a toll within Serbia itself. Having quickly destroyed many of the major military installations on its original target list, NATO began attacking civilian facilities, including bridges, electric utilities, and broadcasting stations. It termed them "dual-use facilities" because they might be used for military as well as civilian purposes (i.e., tanks had to use bridges to cross rivers, etc.).

NATO targeting caused serious humanitarian damage. Attacks on utilities and bridges aimed directly at the civilian economy. Attacks on power stations could paralyze hospitals. Attacks on convoys killed civilians. About 60 per cent of the targets could be described as "dual use," having civilian as well as military purposes, but many had only or mainly civilian functions.

As one observer wrote, NATO had ventured into a "legal grey zone," potentially violating the international conventions protecting civilians. But by then NATO could not afford to lose the war, so NATO decided to attack even civilian targets. NATO argued later that Milosevic aimed his campaign at civilians even more than NATO did, although some observers thought that this did not represent a strongly moral position.[27]

The war over Kosovo became a new kind of military confrontation. The opposing forces fought on different horizontal planes: one fought above 15,000 feet; the other fought on the ground. Neither force fought the other directly. Instead, both concentrated their attacks on civilians:

- Serb forces on the ground in Kosovo expelled ethnic Albanian civilians while occasionally skirmishing against the KLA.
- NATO forces in the air punished Serb civilians for the policies of Slobodan Milosevic.
- The Serbs could not engage NATO in the sky, and NATO did not want to engage the Serbs on the ground. The KLA, a guerrilla hit-and-run force, could not defeat or even resist the Serb army. The Serbs could not defeat or even resist NATO air attacks.

Clinton's "first humanitarian war in history" largely became a war against civilians, thus ranking among the least humanitarian. Each side hoped that the suffering it caused the opponents' civilians would force the opponents to end the war.

The war thus often seemed oddly reminiscent of medieval military campaigns, with both sides concentrating their attacks on civilians, except that medieval armies did at least engage in battle from time to time. NATO and the Serbs never did.

The war also took the world back to World War II, the last time civilians were deliberately targeted by all sides. NATO forces and Milosevic attacked civilians more than each other. Humanitarian law had been set back by 50 years.

By the end of May, both Milosevic and the NATO leaders began to realize that they could not continue as they had been doing.

Milosevic's ethnic cleansing of Kosovo had strengthened NATO's determination to defeat him and had generated widespread public support for the NATO bombing. It had fomented such hostility in Kosovo that Belgrade could never hope to rule the province again.

NATO had not done much better. It had failed to help the civilians of Kosovo during the first phase of the war. While NATO had destroyed a great many important installations in Serbia, Milosevic remained in power and Serb forces had been able to kill and expel Albanians for almost two months.

NATO leaders had another option, the ground war that Clinton and others had vowed they would not conduct. British Prime Minister Tony Blair had wanted to keep the possibility open from the beginning. He now began to argue for it again. General Clark recommended that NATO at least prepare for it. If Serbia could outlast the bombing, only a ground invasion could end the war on favorable terms. NATO defense ministers even met secretly to make plans for such an invasion. Clark warned them that they would have to plan urgently and to begin an operation by early fall unless they wanted to fight a mountain war during the bitter Balkan winter.

Clinton and most other NATO leaders did not want to send an army into the Balkans, a harsh environment in which an entrenched enemy could kill thousands of soldiers. NATO had trained and equipped itself to fight Soviet armies on the open plains of northern Europe. The American military firmly opposed fighting a ground war in Kosovo or Serbia.

NATO thus needed to end a conflict that it did not want to lose or to escalate. Clinton feared the casualties, which journalists called the "body bags," even more than he feared losses among the Apache aircraft. Casualties would become a political issue. And the allegedly humanitarian cause of the war did not seem worth the prospective loss of American lives. Albright or somebody would have to find a way to end the war before it escalated or before the United States emerged humiliated.[28] A senior U.S. Army officer told General Clark, "We don't do mountains."[29]

Milosevic also wanted to end the war. His forces had not suffered from the bombing. In three months of bombing, NATO aircraft had destroyed only 14 tanks and a few armored vehicles. The Serb army remained in fighting shape as did many of its facilities. Milosevic did not, therefore, fear an American ground invasion. The Serbs had repelled invaders from Turks to Germans many times and they could make an American campaign very costly.[30]

But Milosevic did fear a continuation and an expansion of the bombing of Yugoslav civilian targets. It could force Yugoslav cities to face the winter without electricity, heat or water. And it could crush the morale of the people, already traumatized by the bombing they had endured to date. Just as the Yugoslav ground campaign had threatened to wreck Kosovo, the American air campaign threatened to wreck Serbia.[31] Allied air forces commander Lieutenant General Michael Short, perhaps not realizing that under the laws of war he was supposed to be targeting military rather than civilian installations, threatened more intense bombing of civilians by warning the Serbs:

> I suggest you go outside, get in your car and ride around the city of Belgrade. Remember it the way it is today. If you force me to go to war against you, Belgrade will never look that way again—never in your lifetime or in your children's lifetime.[32]

Russian President Boris Yeltsin faced a particular dilemma. Russia and Serbia had been close friends over the centuries. He knew that many Russian political and military officials and officers felt angry about sitting idly by while NATO operated freely in the Balkans. He feared that they would react sharply to a NATO ground force in the area. Yeltsin might face a coup if Russia did not help Serbia.

Thus, as the prospect of an expanded war in the Balkans came closer, all parties to the conflict began to look for ways to avoid it—not for humanitarian but for domestic political reasons.

Yeltsin took an important step. He appointed Viktor Chernomyrdin, a former Russian premier who had good contacts in the West, as his special envoy for

Kosovo. Chernomyrdin contacted Clinton to explore diplomatic options. Clinton, reluctant to become a "war president," showed interest. So did the Deputy Secretary of State responsible for Russian contacts, Strobe Talbott.

NATO leaders decided to reach agreement with Milosevic. To do that, they dropped the issues that had doomed the Rambouillet conference and forced a war. They gave up their demand that NATO troops be able to move freely across all of Yugoslavia. Instead, they asked for a NATO presence in Kosovo itself. Even more important, they abandoned the demand for a Kosovo independence referendum in three years. Instead, NATO agreed to continued Yugoslav sovereignty over Kosovo. NATO also offered to disarm the KLA, an offer it had not made at Rambouillet when it was allied with the KLA. But it would not yield in its demand that all Serb forces had to leave Kosovo except for some specific sites.

NATO claimed to have won the war, but it offered Milosevic much better conditions to end the war than it had offered him at Rambouillet. In fact, Milosevic might well have accepted at Rambouillet the terms that he was offered six months later, especially because NATO accepted Yugoslav sovereignty over Kosovo. But at Rambouillet NATO—and especially the Americans—had wanted to help the KLA. Now the KLA no longer mattered.

Thaci and the KLA were left high and dry. At Rambouillet, the Americans and especially Secretary Albright had asked Thaci to accept terms that they knew Milosevic would reject. He had done that. Now Thaci would have to swallow terms that Milosevic would accept. He had no choice. Clinton and NATO would not send a ground army to enforce the terms that Mrs. Albright had set at Rambouillet.

Russia and the West turned to the United Nations, as they usually did when they needed a neutral party to find a solution to their problems. Secretary-General Kofi Annan, also anxious to end the conflict, proposed a U.N. envoy to negotiate a settlement. He suggested Martti Ahtisaari, President of Finland and a widely respected international humanitarian figure whom the Europeans, Americans and Russians trusted.

After a meeting of the Group of Eight (G–8) foreign ministers in Germany, Talbott and Chernomyrdin negotiated terms for a cease-fire and for the departure of Serb forces from Kosovo. Milosevic also conducted a secret negotiation with NATO and Moscow through a Swedish-born London businessman, Peter Castenfelt, who had close ties to Moscow.

Berlin became the site for some official and unofficial contacts, as both sides trusted the Germans. Castenfelt arranged a visit to Belgrade to meet with Milosevic at a time when NATO did not want to negotiate formally with the Serbian leader.[33] But he first discussed the prospect with a German foreign affairs consultant, Karl Kaiser, and then with Chancellor Gerhard Schröder's foreign policy adviser Michael Steiner and Foreign Office State Secretary Wolfgang Ischinger. Ischinger wanted to get negotiations going because Germany feared an East–West crisis over Kosovo. Castenfelt worked with the Russian government and the Germans in seeking the formula that Milosevic would accept.

Clinton took the negotiations out of Secretary Albright's hands and turned them over to Talbott because he wanted a fast agreement with Yeltsin and Milosevic. Recalling the negotiations in his memoirs, Talbott did not even mention that Washington had abandoned Albright's conditions. He thus conveyed the false impression that the West had gained its original purposes and that Milosevic had surrendered.[34] In reality, diplomacy had achieved what bombing had not.

Schröder believed that he was promoting American, European and Russian interests as well as German interests by helping to arrange a peace.[35] He was also reaching a solution that offered an opening for humanitarian action to repair the damage of the war.

At that point, the machinery for humanitarian relief within Kosovo swung into action. The major Western states and Russia, with promised support from Japan, agreed on a United Nations administration for Kosovo with several elements very much like those that had taken over the responsibility for Bosnia:

- The main responsibility fell upon the United Nations itself through the U.N. Mission in Kosovo (UNMIK), to be headed by Bernard Kouchner. As he had for long directed Médecins sans Frontières, he understood humanitarian operations. He was later succeeded by two other Europeans, Hans Haekerup (a Dane) and Michael Steiner, who had been foreign affairs advisor to Chancellor Schröder.

- An international security Kosovo Force (KFOR) took over military duties. Because of Milosevic's objections, it was not a direct NATO force although NATO members provided most of its soldiers. KFOR at first contained elements from France, Germany, Italy, the United Kingdom and the United States, with each having a separate zone in Kosovo. Later, Russian forces also joined, but they were not given a zone of their own because of Western fears that such a zone would be only a first step to the partition of Kosovo with the Russian zone to become a part of Serbia. NATO instead agreed to assign Russian forces to several other sectors in Kosovo (for example, in the American and German sectors). Smaller contingents from 40 nations joined KFOR within months, making it even less of a NATO force and more of an international United Nations contingent despite its NATO membership. Although KFOR was nominally a military command and most of its duties consisted of security functions, its members also performed such humanitarian tasks as protecting Serb churches and houses in Albanian ethnic areas and protecting Albanian churches and houses in Serb areas. With the KLA nominally disarmed in September 1999, and with the Yugoslav army withdrawn, KFOR remained the only official military force in Kosovo.

- An OSCE office, also directed by a European, was charged with bringing democracy to Kosovo through civil service reform, instructions in the rule of law and directing elections.
- A European Union office supervised economic reconstruction and development of the area.
- A humanitarian reconstruction and relief effort, called the "humanitarian pillar," was coordinated by the U.N. High Commissioner for Refugees and directed by a senior UNHCR official, Dennis McNamara. It included most major U.N. agencies and dozens of NGOs.[36]

The humanitarian process of reconstruction, like other processes, has moved slowly but has made progress. Although ethnic Albanians refugees returned quickly, they had to receive not only food and medicine but such building materials as wood, bricks, plastic sheeting and plumbing materials. The exact costs of reconstruction have not been determined because of the many agencies involved but they have been well over $1 billion.

Most ethnic Serbs fled with the Serb forces and remain as refugees in Serbia. Few have returned to the predominantly ethnic Albanian areas, although a large number have returned to the northeast corner of Kosovo near Mitrovica, which has a Serb majority. As in Bosnia, those that have returned to Albanian ethnic areas are often older farmers who want to reclaim their land, while younger families do not plan to return. About 50,000 Romany gypsies who fled have also been slow to return.

Europe is assuming growing responsibility for security as well as for economic development, with the European Union scheduled to assume command of KFOR and the European Bank for Reconstruction and Development helping to finance development.

Ibrahim Rugova and his Democratic League of Kosovo easily won a 2001 election to form a provincial assembly and ultimately a government. The KLA received only a minority of the votes. Rugova called for Kosovo independence but many Kosovars remain uncertain whether they could sustain themselves economically as an independent state. Many analysts recommend partition, with the northeast corner becoming part of Serbia, but the UNMIK administrators have opposed such a partition as a failure of their goal to establish a multiethnic state.

The "humanitarian war" in Kosovo was a humanitarian tragedy. It was also an unnecessary war, causing enormous hardship and lasting damage for little purpose. The West had helped to cause it, as it had the wars in Croatia and in Bosnia. The

West will never know whether an agreement for greater autonomy could have been made because the negotiating process at Rambouillet excluded such an agreement. But, as one analyst has written, it could have been termed a "perfect failure."[37]

The war would eventually drive Milosevic from office by persuading the Serbs to turn against him. It also accomplished what may have been its principal purpose, to gain "credibility" for NATO.[38] But the West, and particularly the United States, may well have violated the laws of war by deliberately bombing civilian targets. Thus the humanitarian price inside and outside Kosovo was high, both during the war and after.[39] It will remain high for some time to come.

A New Reticence over Macedonia

President George W. Bush had a chance to show within a month after his inauguration that he would not be sucked into the Balkans like his predecessor. It involved the Former Yugoslav Republic of Macedonia (FYROM), the name that had been given to the Macedonian part of Yugoslavia when it had declared its independence from Yugoslavia in 1991.

When a new terrorist force, called the "National Liberation Army" (NLA), emerged in Macedonia in February 2001, Bush did not support it as President Clinton and Secretary Albright had supported the KLA in Kosovo. The NLA launched multiple guerrilla attacks and terrorist bombings in Macedonia, one of the former Yugoslav states that had appeared relatively stable. The NLA asserted that Macedonia had not sufficiently recognized the rights of its Albanian minority although two ethnic Albanian parties held seats in the Macedonian government headed by President Boris Trajkovski and by Prime Minister Ljuaco Georgieuski.

The very existence of the NLA showed that the peacekeepers in Kosovo had not thoroughly patrolled their sectors. For the NLA would not have been able to plan and direct its operations without having been able to operate freely in the German and American sectors of Kosovo, which bordered on Macedonia. With German and U.S. peacekeeping forces strictly instructed to avoid engagements that might lead to casualties, the peacekeepers had not patrolled energetically enough to prevent ethnic Albanians from using Kosovo as a base against Macedonia.

NLA operations expanded throughout the spring. By May and June, the guerrillas began to occupy villages and small towns in the border area and even near Skopje, the Macedonian capital only 30 miles from the Kosovo border. The Macedonian government retaliated, attacking the villages as well as the surrounding hills with shells and air strikes in the usual counter-terror pattern. They did not kill the rebels but forced close to 100,000 villagers and farmers to seek refuge in Kosovo. Some of the aid organizations working in Macedonia warned of another "humanitarian tragedy."[40]

By 2001, however, the West had tired of Balkan wars and divisions. Neither Bush nor other NATO leaders wanted yet another one. They feared that a conflict in Macedonia would unhinge the entire Balkan balance. Instead of encouraging either side, they tried to arrange a political solution. Javier Solana, special EU envoy for foreign and security matters, became a frequent visitor to Skopje to urge President Trajkovski to form a government with more ethnic Albanian groups and to give greater political rights to the Albanian minority (perhaps a quarter to a third of Macedonia's population). Trajkovski made moves in that direction.

Bush and his Secretary of State, Colin Powell, pushed for a political solution. They used their contacts with Albanian organizations to arrange a dialogue. Robert Frowick of the OSCE persuaded Albanian groups to negotiate a settlement. American envoys also arranged for some trapped Albanian insurgents to be safely evacuated to Kosovo, a move that sparked widespread anger and even riots in Skopje because many Macedonians felt it saved Albanians they had hoped to destroy. They feared that the United States would favor radical Albanian groups over moderates in Macedonia as it had favored the KLA over Rugova in Kosovo.[41]

Lord Robertson, the Secretary-General of NATO, took a different tack. He criticized the NLA for terrorism and for trying to destroy a democratic government. He supported Solana's efforts to encourage a political solution to the clash and he joined Powell in making clear that the West did not want to send more troops to the region.

Under diplomatic pressure from NATO and the European Union, the leaders of the Macedonian and Albanian ethnic communities reached what became known as the "Framework Agreement" on August 13, 2001. Its main points included a more decentralized government, greater minority rights and the amendment of some discriminatory passages in the constitution. Elections held on September 15 increased the odds for a successful ethnic coexistence although many political issues remained.[42]

NATO put a mission of about 750 soldiers into Macedonia. Bush offered American logistics and technical intelligence support but made clear that he did not want another Bosnia or Kosovo on his hands. He wanted European and other diplomats to be more in the lead than Americans had been through much of the 1990s.[43]

The quick political solution and the combined pressure from NATO and the European Union as well as from all major Western governments averted a potential humanitarian disaster although there had been brief flows of refugees and although some reconstruction was still required. The European Union had taken over command of the peacekeeping operation by 2003. Macedonia had become a model for international diplomatic action designed to avert conflict.

Humanitarian Action in the Balkans

As the decade of the 1990s passed into history, Western leaders could not feel pleased about what had happened in the Balkans. The former Yugoslavia had passed through a humanitarian disaster. Western leaders, including "experts" on the area, had encouraged secession of separate Yugoslav republics and peoples without considering the potential humanitarian consequences. As the cumulative horrors had unfolded, the West had failed to react in time or with adequate means.

The Balkan peoples had played out their historic antagonisms and their historic roles in the most bestial manner possible, and many Balkan leaders and politicians had fully earned punishment by the International Criminal Court. But nobody in high office within the Western states could or should feel smug about such punishment. The Western leaders did not try to stop the Balkan extremists or to channel their antagonisms into diplomatic channels. Only a few Western personalities, like Cyrus Vance and Lord Owen, had tried to foster reconciliation, and their proposals had been blocked by American and European outsiders even more than by Balkan leaders.

The only bright spots, in Eastern Slavonia and Macedonia, had emerged toward the end of the crises in Croatia and Kosovo, when everybody had become exhausted and Western leaders had learned caution. But by then the humanitarian tragedy had been played out to its bitter and often deadly end.

For humanitarian organizations, the Balkan crises represented an unprecedented challenge. The humanitarian response required five closely coordinated processes, often almost as demanding as the wars and rebellions going on all around:

- To feed and care for refugees, displaced persons and normal residents in one or another Balkan state, republic or province, almost always in the middle of a war.
- To feed and care for those who had managed to escape to neighboring states or republics, such as Macedonia, Albania or Serbia itself, and to arrange for their legal protection so that they would not be sent back to a war zone.
- To help those who returned to the crisis areas after the fighting had ebbed, often providing food and care while also helping them to rebuild their houses and their lives.
- As required, to move persons and families either to other parts of the Balkans, to Western Europe, to the United States, to Australia or elsewhere, and then to move some of them back again.
- In many areas, and especially in Bosnia, Croatia and Kosovo, to work closely with peacekeeping forces of different nationalities and different command structures.

Throughout all this, the international and non-governmental humanitarian agencies had to work with the United Nations administration itself; with other agencies of different backgrounds and often different nationalities; and with local administrators. They increasingly worked in conjunction with the European Union, which took charge of police functions in Bosnia and of the overall mission in Macedonia. Unfortunately, the humanitarians also had to suffer dozens of casualties.

Often international agencies had to withdraw their European or American staff when the risks became too great. This left the humanitarian work in the hands of local administrators, who worked with enormous dedication and more success than others might have dared to expect.

The Yugoslav crisis also brought into play a renewed and expanded commitment of international peacekeepers under U.N. or other auspices. They—and especially the Dutch—played an abysmal role in Srebrenica. But other peacekeepers later performed vital functions in helping to solve crises in Bosnia, Kosovo, Eastern Slavonia and Macedonia. Through its performance in Yugoslavia, more than anywhere else, peacekeeping became an accepted and even an expected part of the humanitarian mix.

The end of the Cold War thus compelled the humanitarian conscience to carry out its service in much more complex and demanding ways than had ever been imagined before. The humanitarian agencies and those who worked for them had to function simultaneously as protectors, administrators, diplomats, logisticians, doctors, nurses and care-givers. Agencies often abandoned the specialized mandates of their traditional roles and helped wherever they could in whatever ways they could.

International humanitarian care came of age in the pressure-cooker of the Balkans. From the early days of the Red Cross through the feeding and refugee operations of the world wars and the Cold War, the humanitarian world had become a massive structure of its own. In the Balkans, it performed in ways that nobody had earlier imagined and that some even found it difficult to reconcile with their concept of humanitarianism.

Faced with a massive crisis and with unprecedented needs, the humanitarians had done what needed to be done. They had probably done it as well as it could have been done.

And yet the humanitarian conscience had no voice in the events that caused the suffering. It could only help after one or another catastrophe had already happened. Those who had caused the catastrophe even felt free to complain about the United Nations or about various agencies if the humanitarians did not help as quickly or as perfectly as national governments—which helped to cause the emergency—thought they should.

The world of the 1990s thus often drove the most dedicated humanitarians to deep frustration even as it forced them to expand their horizons almost every day. And yet, no matter what happened, they continued to try. They believed, rightly, that nobody else would do what they could do, and so they did what they had to do as best they could do it. In desperate situations, they often made the difference between life and death.

TEN

TRAGEDIES IN SOMALIA, RWANDA AND TIMOR

JONATHAN HOWE, ROMEO DALLAIRE AND SERGIO VIEIRA DE MELLO came from three different countries: the United States, Canada and Brazil. They had different careers, two in the military and one in the United Nations. Each had been very successful. And each had to face a profound humanitarian crisis around the end of the twentieth century. Each followed different policies, not necessarily of their own choosing. Their results differed dramatically.

Howe directed a peacekeeping mission in Somalia; Dallaire directed one in Rwanda; Vieira de Mello directed one in East Timor. Their actions, the actions of others and what happened to each mission, reflected the global uncertainty about how—and how not—to cope with humanitarian tragedy after the Cold War. They raised more questions than they answered, especially because two of the three failed openly and tragically.

Howe Faces Anarchy in Somalia

Jonathan Howe in 1993 assumed command of a U.N. peacekeeping mission in the eastern African nation of Somalia, a state that had about as complex an ethnic composition as any state in the world. It suffered from an extreme mix of clans and warlords that few Somalis and no foreigner could hope to understand. That mix had evolved over centuries of internecine struggles at least as intense as in the Balkans. British and Italian colonial rule had roiled the mix even further.

Somalia became independent in 1960 through a merger of two colonies, British Somaliland in the northwest and Italian Somalia in the southeast. An attempt to develop a multi-party democracy failed because the tradition of multiple clan rivalries made a national government by any single group unacceptable to others. On October 21, 1969, Mohammed Siad Barre seized power in a military coup. He governed the country until January, 1991, when he fled to Kenya. He allied himself closely with the Soviet Union for his first five years and then allied himself equally closely with the United States. His regime featured brutality at home, occasional—and unsuccessful—adventurism abroad and sky-high levels of corruption.[1]

During the colonial era, various European powers had split the Somali people into the two Somali states and into parts of separate colonies in Djibouti, Kenya and Ethiopia. Siad Barre wanted to unite all of them under his rule. He particularly had his eye on the Ogaden desert, where hundreds of thousands of Somalis lived but which the British had given to Ethiopia. In 1979, sensing Ethiopian weakness and urged on by his Soviet friends, Barre decided to invade. But the Soviets reversed alliances and helped Ethiopia after the war began. Ethiopian forces thereupon rallied with the help of Cuban "volunteers" and enormous Soviet arms deliveries. They expelled not only the Somali army but also hundreds of thousands of ethnic Somalis who had been living in the Ogaden region and who became refugees.

Refugee camps in Somalia became one of the largest elements of the global refugee crisis during the late 1970s and the 1980s. The U.N. High Commissioner for Refugees, Poul Hartling, provided tens of millions of dollars of aid to Somalia every year, for the Somali refugees had become genuine humanitarian victims even if the war that had caused their suffering had been started by a government claiming to represent them. Various Western governments, and especially the United States, funded the refugee programs.

After Siad Barre's flight in 1991, Somalia entered a time of deepening anarchy. Two leaders, Ali Mahdi and Mohammed Aideed, became very powerful. They sometimes fought and sometimes cooperated. Lawlessness spread as the fighting spread and as rival gangs stole whatever they could. Food markets came to a halt. Farmers could produce very little and merchants could not get food to market. Rival factions used food mainly to bargain against each other. They also seized stores of international humanitarian aid to sell or to hold for greater profit. Food often rotted even as Somalis starved to death a few hundred yards away.

Andrew Natsios, the Director of the Office of Foreign Disaster Assistance of the U.S. Agency for International Development (AID), and Frank Wisner, the State Department's Undersecretary for International Security Affairs, wanted to help. The Pentagon and the White House had serious reservations because they had the Gulf War on their hands. But many members of Congress, moved by CNN images of starving families, began to demand action. The new U.N. Secretary-General, Boutros Boutros-Ghali, favored U.N. intervention.[2]

President George Bush decided that the United States would have to act. In August 1992, under pressure from the media, human rights groups, NGOs and the U.S. Congress, he supported Boutros-Ghali's call for major food shipments to be protected by U.N. monitors and security guards. Bush ordered the U.S. Central Command, responsible for U.S. military operations in the Middle East, to operate an airlift.

The U.N. Security Council in April 1992 had already authorized the U.N. Operation in Somalia (UNOSOM I) to try to deliver food to the starving. Mohammed Sahnoun, director of UNOSOM I, asked the president of CARE, Philip Johnston, to devise and implement an action plan for humanitarian relief, which Johnston did. CARE and others distributed some food to ease the immediate crisis.

But UNOSOM I could not provide enough security for food distribution. A few hundred Pakistani forces could not hold back the tough Somali gangs. The peacekeepers themselves became victims of robberies and murders. Sahnoun, getting no support from the West, resigned in disgust. By the end of 1992, an estimated half a million Somalis had died of starvation and internecine fighting. Something needed to be done.

General Colin Powell, the Chairman of the U.S. Joint Chiefs of Staff, recognized that a humanitarian operation needed U.S. military support to have any chance of success. He and President Bush approved sending U.S. military forces to help protect the food deliveries. The Security Council thereupon launched a stronger operation in Somalia by the name of United Nations Interim Task Force (UNITAF). Eighteen countries, including Australia, Belgium, Botswana, Canada, France, Morocco, Nigeria, Saudi Arabia, Tunisia, United Emirates and Zimbabwe, joined UNITAF. American forces would take a lead role for the six months remaining in President Bush's term, but the White House would not agree to have them join UNITAF because they would not serve under U.N. command.

UNITAF proved a striking humanitarian success during its brief existence from December 1992 to May 1993. The food saved hundreds of thousands of lives. Other commodities also moved freely. Even more encouraging, farmers began growing crops again, confident that they would not be punished for it and also confident that the food could reach markets. Mogadishu became safe for the first time in years.

Robert Oakley, a former U.S. Ambassador to Somalia who had been asked to lead the civilian side of the operation, was able to neutralize the opposition of the warlords by sagacious maneuvering among the various factions. The warlords, including Mahdi and Aideed, even began to cooperate a little. Oakley's diplomacy and the mass deployment of thousands of U.S. forces in the worst areas, as well as the vigorous patrolling and security services of the other forces, brought some stability.

The handover from Bush to Clinton appeared to work smoothly. Bush visited U.S. forces in Somalia on New Year's Eve 1993, to wish them well. Clinton said he would support a follow-up U.N. operation, to be named UNOSOM II. The American military promised to leave about 4,000 special operations troops, including some U.S. Marines and a helicopter Quick Reaction Force, to support UNOSOM II, but most U.S. forces withdrew.

On March 26, 1993, the U.N. Security Council approved UNOSOM II as the successor of UNOSOM I and of UNITAF. Because many Security Council members, including the United States, feared some kind of trouble and perhaps Somali resistance, the operation became the first U.N. peacekeeping operation launched under the authority of Chapter VII of the Charter. That chapter, labeled "Action with Respect to Threats to the Peace, Breaches of the Peace, and Acts of Aggression," permits a stronger military force and firmer action than the normal peacekeeping provisions under Chapter VI, which is labeled "Pacific Settlement of Disputes."

Madeleine Albright, the U.S. Ambassador to the United Nations, gave UNOSOM II a highly ambitious task, saying that the resolution meant "an unprecedented enterprise aimed at nothing less that the restoration of an entire country," a mission that went well beyond the humanitarian purpose of UNOSOM I.[3]

Clinton sent Admiral Jonathan Howe to command UNOSOM II when Boutros-Ghali, anxious to ensure continued U.S. involvement in Somalia, asked Washington to name a commander. As Howe had been Deputy National Security Adviser for President Bush, this appeared to offer continuity in all directions. Oakley, considering that his work was done, left Somalia.

But UNOSOM II, and especially Admiral Howe, ran into early trouble with Mohammed Aideed. The powerful clan leader formed a deep suspicion of Howe when the latter opposed a political conference called by Aideed and instead supported another conference run by rival clans who were less powerful but were happy to bask in U.N. support. Howe, in turn, believed that Aideed could never be satisfied with power-sharing and compromise but would have to be cut down to size.

Howe decided to inspect Aideed's weapons stores, an act that Aideed saw as a sign of hostile intent. Trouble erupted quickly. On June 4, Pakistani soldiers sent to inspect the weapons unexpectedly found themselves trapped by an angry mob of armed Aideed supporters. Although the U.S. Quick Reaction Force and Italian armored units were able to extricate the Pakistanis, 24 had been killed and scores injured. Many of the dead were mutilated and subjected to vicious and degrading treatment, such as being dragged through the streets.

Howe reacted angrily. At U.S. urging, the U.N. Security Council passed a resolution authorizing "all necessary measures" against those who had been responsible for the attacks on the Pakistanis and other U.N. peacekeepers. The resolution specifically named Aideed's United Somali Congress, thus labeling him as the enemy of the United Nations. The United States was among those urging strong action, citing the risk to other peacekeeping operations worldwide if Aideed went unpunished.[4]

As the tensions between Howe and Aideed rose, several European states decided that they did not want to be under U.S. and U.N. control. They pulled their forces back under their own national command, as they had earlier done in the Balkans. The French, noting that Admiral Howe had established direct links to the U.S. Central Command, established their own link to Paris. They then pulled out of Mogadishu although UNOSOM II had ordered them to stay. The Italians remained in Mogadishu but, after suffering casualties, largely dissociated themselves from the increasingly American-directed operations against Aideed.

UNOSOM II, under Howe's direction, attacked Aideed's enclave in south Mogadishu on June 17. Moroccan peacekeepers suffered heavy casualties. Howe then issued a warrant for Aideed's arrest with a $25,000 reward, ending any hope for dialogue. Aideed, under pressure from some of his own followers to leave Somalia, asked former U.S. President Jimmy Carter to conduct an inquiry into the confrontation of June 4, but Carter declined, although he reported the request to President Clinton.

On July 12, the American Quick Reaction Force under U.S. command (with agreement from the White House) raided Aideed's compound to capture weapons and documents. They hoped to capture Aideed himself. But they suffered from poor intelligence, perhaps provided by Somali rivals of Aideed. The 16 missiles that American helicopters pumped into the compound succeeded mainly in killing tribal elders allegedly discussing the possibilities for reconciliation. A mob of angry Somalis killed four journalists who came to report what had happened. Somali opinion swung dramatically behind Aideed as many Somalis decided that the United Nations and especially the United States had a domineering colonial mentality.

The American confrontation with Aideed became the focus of Somali life. Howe had concluded that he would reshape Somali politics and rebuild the Somali body politic by eliminating Aideed and his gang. Having made a successful career in the U.S. Navy prior to his service in the Bush White House and in Somalia, he believed that he could solve the Somali political problem by military means. Although he had a U.N. mandate, he conducted all his military actions primarily through U.S. forces and in contact with the U.S. chain of command.

Somalis paid a high humanitarian price for the confrontation between the Americans and Aideed. As the battle for Mogadishu drew attention and resources, humanitarian operations in the capital and its surroundings virtually stopped. Many Western NGOs, blaming the United States and the United Nations for the confrontation and for the collapse of the humanitarian mission, curtailed their operations and left Mogadishu for Nairobi to get out of the line of fire.

The American Task Force Ranger, commanded by U.S. Major General William Garrison, undertook more raids and arrested more Somalis allegedly connected with

Aideed. But the confrontation boosted Aideed's credentials among most Somalis. As U.S. and U.N. raids ravaged his compound and surrounding areas in south Mogadishu, more Somalis from the countryside joined Aideed's forces. Many Westerners and Somalis criticized Howe's use of helicopter gunships against civilian targets. A series of battles in early September killed or wounded hundreds of Somalis as well as dozens of Pakistani, Nigerian and Italian peacekeepers.

Secretary of State Warren Christopher and others in Washington began to harbor doubts about the operation. But they did not call it off. Washington even helped to sponsor a U.N. Security Council resolution vowing to continue the battle. Boutros-Ghali, who despised Aideed and Aideed's clan, agreed with that. The U.S. military, which had taken effective control of operations in Somalia as other national contingents had drawn back, remained engaged.

On October 3, 1993, Mogadishu exploded. American Ranger forces under General Garrison's command conducted a surprise helicopter raid in downtown Mogadishu, hoping to capture Aideed. They captured several of his staff as well as other Somalis.

But American forces had underestimated the fighting capacity and the growing sophistication of Somali forces. Using rifle grenades and automatic weapons, the Somalis shot down two Blackhawk helicopters. As American Ranger and Delta Force reinforcements joined the fray against a growing number of Somalis, it became a major confrontation that covered several blocks with hand-to-hand fighting.

The Somalis won the battle. They captured an American Warrant Officer, Michael Durant. They also dragged the body of a dead U.S. soldier through the streets of Mogadishu, an event filmed by American television reporters. Hundreds of Somalis died but those casualties had less media impact in the United States than the loss of 18 U.S. soldiers and the wounding of 78 others.[5]

Clinton reversed course. After a meeting with senior U.S. officials and military, he decided on an American withdrawal from Somalia by March 31, 1994. He notified Boutros-Ghali, who unhappily accepted the decision. Clinton said that it had been a mistake for U.S. forces to "personalize the conflict." He ordered Howe to cease operations, and Howe returned to the United States. Clinton then reappointed Oakley as special envoy and asked him to meet with Somalis to bring out the captured warrant officer and to move toward a political solution.

Clinton and the United States did not accept responsibility for the debacle, although Admiral Howe and U.S. forces had been in charge of Somalia policy and tactics for months. Instead, Clinton, as usual, made a major point of blaming the United Nations. He said that the United Nations had become involved in nation-building, which had not been its task. Boutros-Ghali had certainly urged action against Aideed, but Clinton blamed the United Nations even for tactical decisions made by the American military.

Clinton's action saddled the United Nations with a responsibility for reckless bungling that it did not deserve. It also persuaded the U.S. administration and Congress to avoid future commitments to U.N. operations, a legacy that weakened U.N. effectiveness at a time after the Cold War when American support could have helped both the United Nations and the United States.

Clinton did authorize U.S. forces to remain in Somalia for another six months. He assured the Congress that U.S. forces would henceforth be under official U.S. command—as they had indeed been all along—and that they would limit their activities to support of U.N. humanitarian operations, not military actions.

Oakley returned to Somalia several times over the next several months. On his first trip he brought General Anthony Zinni, the commander of the U.S. Central Command, to show that his mission also reflected the views of the Pentagon. He spoke to a variety of Somali factions and argued that they should settle their differences among themselves without outside help. Although he did not try to meet with Aideed, he insisted to Aideed's office that he wanted the release of American Warrant Officer Durant as well as of a captured Nigerian soldier in time for Durant to leave Mogadishu with Oakley. He threatened that the U.S. military would inflict major damage on south Mogadishu if the prisoners were not released. Oakley's threat worked.

Oakley then traveled to the capitals of several African countries that had supported the United Nations operation, urging them to find "an African solution to African problems." He also briefed members of Congress and others on this new policy. The Congress passed a law that no funds could be spent on U.S. forces in Somalia after March 31. And the U.N. Security Council passed a resolution cutting back the military effort in Somalia and leaving it to the Somalis to solve their own problems. Nonetheless, some military contingents, such as those from Botswana, Egypt, India, Malaysia, Morocco, Pakistan and Zimbabwe, remained because they felt that they still had a humanitarian job to do.[6]

UNOSOM II finally closed before the end of 1994. The remaining peacekeepers withdrew. Although the United Nations had eased the famine of 1992, Somalia did not stabilize. Some NGOs remained, trying to continue some relief programs. The disputes among the Somali factions grew so severe over the next few years that the country split into three parts, with northern Somalia becoming a separate entity and the south dividing among two principal groups. Hundreds of thousands of Somalis fled to neighboring states, including Kenya and Ethiopia. The United Nations could take care of their humanitarian needs as refugees but had very limited success encouraging them to return.

Somalia had brutally shown the limits of intervention, making it painfully clear that outsiders could not build a political architecture for any state by force, even under the guise of humanitarian action. The United Nations, the United States and the NGOs had certainly relieved a humanitarian disaster in 1992. But they had then gone astray. The U.S. government, and particularly the U.S. command, swore that they would never repeat what they termed the "mission creep" of the Somalia operation. This mantra became a guiding principle whenever any American president faced a humanitarian crisis or a peacekeeping operation. It meant that every president has had to think twice before sending U.S. forces into humanitarian operations that appear risky.

But Americans had absorbed the wrong "lesson of Somalia," like the cat that had once sat on a hot stove and then never sat on any stove again. The American failure in Somalia, and the heavy number of casualties, resulted from a misguided effort to change a charitable humanitarian mission welcomed by the Somali people into a domineering political mission resented by the Somali people. America had changed from friend to foe. It then left Somalia to its fate, although some international humanitarian operations continued in order to help the Somali people to survive.

Admiral Howe's pursuit of Aideed, like the U.S. Ranger attack on Aideed's headquarters, served no humanitarian purpose and certainly showed no sign of the humanitarian conscience. Unfortunately, however, it hampered American readiness to play the kind of humanitarian role it could have played in later operations. The tragedy of Rwanda showed the effect of that misjudgment.

Dallaire Faces Genocide in Rwanda

General Romeo Dallaire faced a different problem in Rwanda from Admiral Howe's in Somalia. He did not have to deliver food to a starving people but had to try to keep the peace in a cauldron of ethnic and tribal animosity. He had a United Nations mandate, as did Jonathan Howe. But Howe's mandate let him act as he wished, whereas Dallaire's mandate prevented him from acting as he wished. Dallaire did not want to reshape Rwandan politics; he merely wanted to save people from genocide.[7] But Howe's failure in Somalia cast a shadow over Dallaire's efforts.

To a tourist or other casual visitor, Rwanda does not look like a likely spot for a humanitarian calamity. Once known as "the pearl of Africa," the little mountain country sits virtually at the center of the continent, near beautiful lakes and near the deep triple canopy jungle habitat of some of Africa's beloved mountain gorillas. But it has one of the highest population densities in Africa and its people have long been desperately poor.

Rwanda's two principal groups, the Hutu and the Tutsi, often lived together in apparent harmony. Legend has it that the Tutsis may have arrived from the north, perhaps from around Ethiopia. They tend to be slimmer and taller than the Hutus, but anthropologists generally regard them as being of the same broad ethnic stock. The Tutsis practice cattle herding while the Hutus pursue subsistence farming. The Tutsis have long exercised domination over the Hutus, although the Hutus outnumber them by a large margin.

When Germany's imperial chancellor, Prince Otto von Bismarck, organized the Berlin Conference in order to divide Africa between the European great powers during the latter nineteenth century, the conference participants allotted Rwanda and its neighbor Burundi to the new German empire in Africa. But the Germans did little with their new possession. They then lost it to Belgian trusteeship in the general division of German, Austro-Hungarian and Turkish territories among the victors of World War I.

Belgian colonial administrators stressed and apparently exacerbated the differences between Tutsis and Hutus, favoring Tutsis for the few posts that they deigned to grant to native peoples in their administration. In 1933, the Belgians issued cards identifying most of the population as Tutsi or Hutu. This made both groups more conscious of the distinctions between them, helping to stimulate resentment among the Hutus.[8]

By the late 1950s and early 1960s, Hutu resentment had reached the point of action; Hutus pushed the Tutsis aside and discriminated against them—sometimes with Belgian support. Many Tutsis fled to neighboring countries. After Rwanda's independence, the Hutus, in December 1962, began a campaign of killing against Tutsis. Although the exact numbers of victims never became known, they certainly ranged into the tens of thousands. A quarter million Tutsis fled into exile, mainly into Uganda. Lord Bertrand Russell, the British philosopher, said that it was the most horrible and systematic extermination of a people since Hitler's campaign against Jews.[9]

Juvenal Habyarimana, the new President of Rwanda, in 1973 launched a brutal dictatorship that again marginalized the Tutsi population. He conducted persistent killing campaigns against them although he did not treat Hutus much better.

Tutsis who had fled to Uganda during the 1970s began organizing for revenge. They received international relief through the U.N. High Commissioner for Refugees, but they still found themselves subject to discrimination in Uganda and wanted to go home. Yoweri Museveni, who became ruler of Uganda in 1986, decided to help them. With his encouragement, they formed the Rwanda Patriotic Front (RPF) and in 1990 launched an invasion which failed.

Paul Kagame, a young Tutsi who had played a prominent part in Museveni's rise to power in Uganda, at that point took over leadership of the exiled Tutsis and of the RPF. Kagame, having fled Rwanda as a child, had gone to the United States and had taken a military training course at the U.S. Army Command and General Staff College at Fort Leavenworth, Kansas. He reorganized the RPF and made it an effective if small fighting force.

President François Mitterrand of France began taking an interest in Rwanda. Wanting to nurture a strong francophone presence across the middle of Africa, Mitterrand saw the invasion from anglophone Uganda as a threat. He decided to support Habyarimana militarily. France sold large quantities of weapons to Habyarimana and his army. So did Egypt, under the authority of its francophone foreign minister at the time, Boutros Boutros-Ghali, who was later to become U.N. Secretary-General. The weaponry sold to Rwanda included thousands of machetes, heavy two-foot-long slashing knives that made ideal weapons not against armed soldiers but against unarmed civilians. French credits gave tiny Rwanda one of the largest arsenals in Africa.

Habyarimana also used French funds to increase the size of Rwanda's army from 5,000 to 28,000 and to begin building a special militia force of 30,000 called the Presidential Guard. He carried out periodic killings of Tutsis between 1990 and 1994, including a one-time massacre of about 7,000 in 1992. He formed close links with President Mobutu of Zaire to Rwanda's west in order to counter Tutsi links with Uganda to the north. He organized a secret society, the Akazu, to begin planning for the extinction of all Tutsis.

Johan Swinnen, the Belgian ambassador to Rwanda, warned Brussels about these trends. He cited a Rwanda Defense Ministry document that described the Tutsi as the "principal enemy." A French journalist, writing in *Libération* in February 1993, warned of "death squads" intended to exterminate the Tutsi.[10]

Kagame and the RPF began to advance across northern Rwanda, establishing a military presence. And Washington began to express its own concern about the worsening human rights situation. The State Department Assistant Secretary for African Affairs, Herman Cohen, visited the Rwanda capital Kigali to urge negotiations between the different factions and particularly between Habyarimana and the RPF.

Willi Claes, the Belgian Foreign Minister, fretted about the reports from his ambassador. He pressed for negotiations between the Rwandan groups. So did Salim Ahmed Salim, the secretary-general of the Organization for African Unity (OAU). Under such international pressure, the various Rwandan groups negotiated for a full year in Arusha, Tanzania. They finished their talks in August 1993, agreeing on a democratic transition regime in Rwanda and on the integration of the Rwandan army and Kagame's RPF—which had launched another offensive during the talks.

Kagame's offensive may have given him a bigger voice in the negotiations but it had also alarmed the extreme Hutu groups. They prepared themselves ever more for an extermination campaign against the Tutsis. Mitterrand, worried that his ally Habyarimana might be driven from the scene, sent two companies of French troops to Rwanda. By then, the Hutu-Tutsi confrontation had taken on a distinctly international flavor. As in the Balkans and Somalia, outside parties began to play a prominent role.

Many observers doubted that Habyarimana and the Hutu extremist groups would give up power as readily as the Arusha agreement required. Human rights organizations expressed alarm about the deepening crisis in the country and especially about the continued killing of Tutsis. A special envoy for the U.N. Commission on Human Rights, Bacre Waly Ndiaye, who visited Rwanda in April 1993, wrote that the Tutsis were being subjected to a campaign of genocide. He cited carefully prepared massacres and anti-Tutsi propaganda.

General Dallaire arrived in Rwanda at this highly sensitive point as the head of a peacekeeping mission authorized by the U.N. Security Council. Members of the council had disagreed about the mission. The U.S. Ambassador, Madeleine Albright, had many reservations about any mission because of its potential cost and because of the Somalia debacle. She also questioned the value of peacekeeping in general. But France supported a Rwanda mission, as did Boutros-Ghali, who had become U.N. Secretary-General in January of 1992 and who still sided with the Hutus. In a carefully drafted compromise, the council decided on October 5, 1993, to send the mission but to give it only very limited resources and a very limited mandate.

Once he had been selected to lead the mission, Dallaire went to Rwanda and returned to recommend that his mission should have more than 5,000 troops. He received less than half that number. Few states volunteered any forces, and he finally had only 400 from Belgium, 940 from Bangladesh, and 800 from Ghana. His United Nations Assistance Mission in Rwanda (UNAMIR) offered a weak foundation for peace in a perilously divided country.

The members of the Security Council severely limited the mandate for the peacekeepers. Under the Arusha agreement, the peacekeepers were to have the power to assure security throughout Rwanda and, if necessary, to confiscate weapons to help keep the peace. Under the Security Council resolution, they were to assure security only for the capital Kigali and they had no authority to seize weapons. They were to perform their mission under Chapter VI of the U.N. Charter, which meant that they should expect to have the cooperation of the local parties.[11] Nobody could seriously have expected that. Both Kofi Annan, the Undersecretary-General for Peacekeeping, and Boutros-Ghali himself had recommended a more vigorous mandate.

The members of the Security Council thus sent out a U.N. mission with inadequate personnel, inadequate means and inadequate authority. The peacekeepers lacked ammunition, barbed wire, sandbags and even writing paper. They had to borrow petty cash from another U.N. agency. They also had no trained intelligence capability and had to function blind. Yet they were sent into a potentially explosive situation with emotions running murderously high on all sides.

Dallaire later wrote: "You sort of wonder . . . when you look back at the whole thing, whether or not we were set up . . . whether or not the U.N. and myself fell into something that was beyond our ability to manage."[12]

Shortly after Dallaire arrived in Kigali, a mysterious informant, obviously well placed within the government, came to warn Colonel Luc Marchal, the Belgian commander of UNAMIR's Kigali operation, that the Hutu extremists planned to exterminate the Tutsis. The informant, going under the code name of "Jean-Pierre," told Marchal that the extremist groups joined under the name of "Hutu Power" had trained thousands of militia to kill Tutsis. He had himself been instructed to draw up target lists of Tutsis living in Kigali. The militia had been trained to kill up to 1,000 civilians every twenty minutes.

"Jean-Pierre" added that President Habyarimana had lost control over the Hutu extremists. Hutu Power might provoke incidents to engage UNAMIR forces in order to kill peacekeepers. The Security Council would then withdraw UNAMIR, as it had withdrawn UNOSOM II from Somalia, and the killers could do their work.

Dallaire, deeply alarmed, sent a coded telegram on January 11, 1994, alerting U.N. headquarters to the information. He wrote that he regarded it as sufficiently serious to make an effort to locate a weapons site and to confiscate the weapons. That would make clear that UNAMIR would act to prevent mass killing.

United Nations headquarters reacted cautiously. Annan feared a trap. He did not even reply directly to Dallaire but instead cabled Jacques-Roger Booh-Booh, Boutros-Ghali's representative in Kigali, that UNAMIR should not act until it had received "clear guidance" from headquarters. When Booh-Booh replied that he had full confidence in "Jean-Pierre" and his information, Annan cabled the instruction that UNAMIR was to do nothing and especially nothing that might lead to the use of force. Arms seizures were "beyond the mandate."[13]

Annan instructed Dallaire and Booh-Booh to call on the American, Belgian and French ambassadors for advice and also to pass the information to Habyarimana to get his reaction. The ambassadors promised to report to their capitals. Habyarimana denied any knowledge and promised to investigate. Booh-Booh later reported to the United Nations that the Hutu Power groups had ordered accelerated distribution of weapons, exactly the contrary of what U.N. headquarters in New York had hoped to achieve. Boutros-Ghali nonetheless vetoed a suggestion from Belgian ambassador Swinnen that UNAMIR have the authority to seize the weapons being freely distributed around Kigali and Rwanda.

The NGO Human Rights Watch echoed warnings about the situation, publishing a report that "It is impossible to exaggerate the danger . . . in light of the widespread and horrifying abuses committed by Hutu civilian crowds and party militia armed primarily with machetes and spears."[14] But that report, although public, fell on the same deaf ears as others.

Willi Claes, appalled at the weak instructions under which Dallaire and UNAMIR were trying to operate in Kigali, asked for firmer action to seize weapons and disarm the militia. But Boutros-Ghali replied that his hands were tied: neither Washington nor London wanted to change the mandate and were actually threatening to pull UNAMIR out of Rwanda if the situation deteriorated. Washington still had Mogadishu on its mind.

Dallaire tried to keep peace and order even with his weak mandate. He sent out as many patrols as he could staff and he tried to stop or at least contain the increasingly violent demonstrations against the Tutsis as well as the murderous assaults on civilians. But he had few resources and was continually hamstrung by instructions from New York. Neither the members of the Security Council—who were preoccupied with the Balkan crisis—nor Boutros-Ghali were ready to take firm steps to protect civilians in Rwanda.

With President Bill Clinton wanting to show that the United States would not be drawn into any more distant conflicts involving the United Nations, Albright voted to restrict the UNAMIR term to four months and reiterated the threat to withdraw UNAMIR if the situation did not improve. Only the Nigerian Security Council delegate wanted a firmer mandate and stronger action.[15]

On April 6, President Habyarimana was assassinated as he was returning to Kigali from a Tanzania conference at which he had finally pledged to form the interim democratic government promised in the Arusha agreement. The cause and the circumstances remain obscure to this day, although suspicion has long pointed in the direction of the Hutu Power extremists who did not want a compromise.

Habyarimana, who normally did not travel at night, had flown back from Dar-es-Salaam in his own aircraft maintained by a special French team. As his plane, which also carried the president of Burundi, approached Kigali airport, the airport runway lights suddenly fell dark. When the plane circled to attempt another landing, two ground-to-air missiles streaked toward it. One hit the plane, destroying it totally.

Within less than an hour, the Presidential Guard and the Hutu Power militia set up roadblocks to begin surveying the movement of people and especially of Tutsis. UNAMIR officials reported that firing also began almost immediately all around the city, and that people were driving around with guns and machetes. Dallaire's deputy wrote that "things happened very quickly, as if they had been rehearsed."[16] The militia and Presidential Guard used the roadblocks to check identity cards and pulled those identified as Tutsis out of their cars to kill them. They claimed that Habyarimana had been killed in a Tutsi plot.

The Rwandan Prime Minister, a moderate Hutu woman named Agathe Uwilingiyimana, wanted to address the nation. Dallaire tried to send an escort to bring her to the radio station past the roadblocks but one of the senior Hutu Power leaders advised against it, labeling her as untrustworthy. When UNAMIR nonetheless sent an escort to her house, the peacekeepers discovered that the Presidential Guard and the government militia had already surrounded it so that UNAMIR could not enter. Later, when the militia began attacking the house, she fled over the back fence with her husband and five children.

The Prime Minister and her family found temporary refuge at the United Nations Volunteers (UNV) compound. Dallaire called New York and said that he wanted to protect her. Iqbal Riza, Annan's Assistant Secretary-General, told Dallaire that UNAMIR was not to fire unless directly fired upon.[17]

Before the end of the next day, the militia had murdered the prime minister and her husband, although a UNV civilian employee managed to rescue the children. The militia were also killing other opposition politicians, with UNAMIR unable to protect them because of roadblocks and because the peacekeepers were—as Marchal explained to a journalist—a "minority on the ground."[18] UNAMIR could do nothing.

Dallaire could not even protect his own forces. Belgian peacekeepers sent to shield the Prime Minister's house were disarmed by the militia and taken to the Kigali military barracks. They could not inform their own headquarters what had happened to them because they had no radios. By the time Dallaire and UNAMIR could get to the military camp, all he saw of his troops was a pile of eleven dead Belgian soldiers. He bribed some local Rwandans to clean the bodies and had to wait for two days before he could get them to his headquarters.

After the bodies of the Belgian soldiers were returned to Belgium, public and political opinion demanded scapegoats. The Belgian government tried to court-martial their military commander Luc Marchal for failure to protect the men, but it was patently obvious that he had neither the means nor the authority. One of the

Belgians explained: "My perception of classic U.N. operations has been that the U.N. does not fight."[19]

The killing of the Belgian peacekeepers sent tremors throughout all Western capitals with staff in Rwanda. No political leader wanted to have to explain why he or she left people in such a dangerous situation. Virtually every Western government sent special flights and armed teams to get their nationals out of Rwanda within days.

The Americans went out first. A U.S. colonel who was visiting Kigali to design an evacuation plan immediately organized a convoy and had the Americans out by April 9.

Others did not wait much longer. Belgium, France and Italy quickly sent troops to take out their nationals. Foreign Minister Claes, as he withdrew the Belgian component of UNAMIR, urged the U.N. secretariat to instruct Dallaire to evacuate all other peacekeepers as well so that the Belgian departure would not be too obvious. But the Tunisian and Bangladesh peacekeepers volunteered to remain.

As in Srebrenica, evacuation teams sent in by Western states had instructions to rescue only their own people, not any Rwandan Tutsis who might have worked for their embassies or voluntary agencies. Tutsis who had worked for foreign embassies or for U.N. agencies were often shot on the spot as the foreigners withdrew.

Mitterrand sent a military contingent on April 9, taking control of the Kigali airport and of the road to the French embassy. They flew out all French citizens as well as some Hutu politicians friendly to France. This included a number of Hutu Power figures who feared for their lives because RPF forces under Kagame were beginning to move toward Kigali. But France took no Tutsis out.

The only foreigners who remained in Kigali were the United Nations peacekeepers and the international staff of the International Committee of the Red Cross (ICRC) as well as some Médecins Sans Frontières (MSF) doctors who chose to stay and to work in the ICRC hospital. The Red Cross Chief Delegate, Philippe Gaillard, refused to contemplate leaving Rwanda as long as the ICRC hospital remained one of the few places of refuge in Kigali. He and his staff went out every morning to look for any wounded, bringing them to the hospital by noon before the Hutu soldiers became so drunk that all movement was risky.

Dallaire and others began seeing evidence of vast-scale killings even as these evacuations proceeded. At Gikondo, a parish at the center of Kigali, they found a church in which about 500 Tutsis had sought refuge. The priests had tried to conduct a service but had been interrupted by soldiers of the Presidential Guard and militia bearing rifles and machetes. A witness remembered:

The militia began slashing away.... They were hacking at arms, legs, genitals, breasts, faces and necks. There was total panic. Some people were dragged outside and beaten to death. The killing lasted about two hours and then the killers walked slowly among the bodies, looting them and finishing off the wounded.[20]

Similar massacres occurred everywhere in Kigali. The militia even rampaged through hospitals, seeking out Tutsis and killing them. The city morgue could not handle the bodies, which had to be stacked outside. Gaillard estimated that 10,000 had been butchered within a few days. Many had been horribly mutilated. The killers also killed the children to eliminate future as well as present Tutsis. Western journalists who had come to see what had happened at Gikondo reported it as a genocide.

Boutros-Ghali wanted Dallaire to close the U.N. mission and withdraw the peace-keepers. He first tried to get others to instruct Dallaire to leave. When that did not succeed, Boutros-Ghali himself called from Bonn (he was traveling around Europe during most of the Rwanda crisis). But Dallaire preempted him by telling him immediately that UNAMIR could not leave and that a reinforcement of the U.N. mission could stop the genocide before it grew worse and expanded across the entire country.

Dallaire believed that the United Nations, instead of retreating in the face of the genocide in Kigali, should reinforce its staff quickly. He saw the events in Kigali as confirmation of the warning that "Jean-Pierre" had given UNAMIR, and he believed that the Hutu Power militia and Presidential Guard would begin killing Tutsis throughout all of Rwanda if UNAMIR did not make an immediate show of force.

Dallaire made his recommendation firmly to U.N. headquarters. He saw a window of perhaps a week or two during which a strong reinforcement of peace-keepers would halt the genocide in its tracks. He asked for a one-time assignment of 5,000 troops with equipment. He requested more arms and ammunition for the forces he already had in order to intimidate the Hutu Power militia. He believed that Chapter VI of the U.N. Charter contained the authority to stop crimes against humanity.

But neither the Western members of the Security Council nor Boutros-Ghali nor Annan wanted to send more forces to Rwanda or to strengthen those already there. American Senator Robert Dole, the Republican leader in the U.S. Senate, told CBS's *Face the Nation* that: "I don't think we have any national interest there" and "I hope we don't get involved there."[21]

The Nigerian ambassador called for Security Council action, but the American and British ambassadors made clear that they would neither send their own forces nor support a resolution reinforcing UNAMIR and giving it a mandate to stop the genocide.

Ambassador Albright and several members of the council believed that the council should seriously consider withdrawing the entire contingent. Even after Boutros-Ghali reversed his earlier position and recommended reinforcement of UNAMIR, the Western ambassadors refused to support it. The Nigerian ambassador, virtually isolated, warned that the members of the Security Council would become the "laughing stock" of the world.[22]

Although ever more reports of killings in and around Kigali began to appear in the international press, Clinton and Albright continued to insist that the Security Council could consider only one resolution, the total withdrawal of UNAMIR. Although no more Americans were at risk, Washington did not want the mission to stay. Albright, in a phrase eerily reminiscent of Dutch statements regarding Srebrenica, argued that the primary purpose of UNAMIR was the safety of its own personnel. After the Rwandan ambassador to the United Nations, a Hutu loyalist, relayed this information to Kigali, the Hutu government decided to push ahead with "pacification" outside Kigali.[23]

President Clinton even objected to using the term "genocide" to describe the mass killings in Rwanda, for under the Convention on the Prevention and Punishment of the Crime of Genocide, voted by the U.N. General Assembly on December 9, 1948, the United States would have been compelled to take steps to prevent and punish such a crime. After the *New York Times* reported on April 23 that "what looks very much like genocide has been taking place in Rwanda," State Department spokeswoman Christine Shelley said on April 28: "The use of the term genocide has a very precise legal meaning. . . . Before we use that term, we have to know as much as possible about the facts of the situation."[24]

Clinton did not want to be pushed into any commitment to stop the genocide, even as more and more NGOs—including Human Rights Watch and Oxfam—warned that genocide was indeed happening. When the Czech ambassador to the Security Council said the same thing, British and American diplomats quietly told him that such inflammatory language was not helpful.[25]

African states, more courageous and closer to the situation than the Western governments, volunteered troops to fight with UNAMIR. Ghana, Ethiopia, Senegal, Nigeria, Zimbabwe and Zambia offered to send either companies or entire battalions. But they needed armored vehicles and other equipment to move quickly in an insecure situation, and no Western state would volunteer equipment any more than personnel.

Two U.S. senators on the Foreign Relations Committee, Paul Simon and James Jeffords, contacted the United Nations and even called Dallaire himself to learn what could be done. On May 13, they sent Clinton a letter urging him to ask the Security Council to approve sending troops to Rwanda to stop the slaughter. Clinton replied one month later, reviewing the efforts his administration had made to bring about a cease-fire, to help refugees and to impose an arms embargo. He wrote nothing about stopping the genocide.[26]

Dallaire complained later about the "inexcusable apathy by the sovereign states that made up the U.N. that is completely beyond comprehension and moral acceptability." He added bitterly that "The people of Rwanda were forgotten."[27] He praised some of the smaller states that tried to help "out of the media limelight" and that "shamed the world." But he remained bitter toward the major Western powers and especially the United States, accusing them of procrastination, bickering and cynical pursuit of their own selfish interests. He termed U.S. actions "a paradox that does not suit a global power."[28]

But Dallaire could do little more than complain. He could certainly do nothing to stop the widening arc of genocide as the Hutu Power militia fanned out across all of Rwanda except the RPF areas. The Hutu killed individual Tutsis as well as entire families and communities. When the Tutsis sought refuge in churches or in any kind of assembly area, the Hutus would turn machine guns on them before finishing them off with machetes. They frequently disfigured the victims and they routinely killed women and children so as to eliminate the Tutsi race. Gaillard's Red Cross hospital worked full-time but could not begin to help all those who needed attention. Without adequate transportation and security, he could do nothing for those outside the immediate Kigali area.

Paul Kagame exploded in a meeting he had with Dallaire at the end of April after the RPF had reached Kigali. Unaware that Dallaire had resisted U.N. instructions to evacuate and had violated specific orders to reduce his forces, the Tutsi leader complained that the "peacekeepers" had done nothing. He said that he and the RPF army would now themselves protect the Tutsis for they were the only ones who would act. Separately, he said that he had "developed contempt for those people in the world who claim to stand for values of moral authority."[29]

Although the Hutu Power militia and the Rwandan army outnumbered Kagame's forces, the RPF proved to be the more efficient and better-led fighting force. Within weeks, it conquered Kigali, forcing the Hutu Power militia to flee, and began expanding across all of Rwanda and pushing the Hutu armies toward the southwest. Kagame could not stop the genocide immediately, for the Hutus killed Tutsis even as they retreated, but he drove the Hutus away from the killing fields. Unfortunately, his forces also killed many Hutus, including some who had not joined in the genocide. By June, Hutu forces had been pushed from one temporary capital after another. They had been forced to retreat to Lake Kivu in the southwest and to several long-term strongholds.

François Mitterrand chose this moment to intervene to protect his Hutu allies facing military disaster, after not trying to protect the victims of genocide. On June 14, two months after the assassination of Habyarimana and the beginning of the genocide campaign, Mitterrand announced that France was sending troops to Rwanda to protect the country's people from extermination. He added that the massacres had to be stopped immediately. Boutros-Ghali voiced enthusiastic approval. The U.N. Security Council endorsed the action reluctantly, with several members preferring that French forces join UNAMIR instead of conducting a separate operation. But, as expected, Mitterrand kept French forces under French command independent of Dallaire.

The French intervention, labeled *Opération Turquoise,* ostensibly served as a peacekeeping mission but mainly protected Hutu extremists who were fleeing from the RPF. About 5,000 French troops established a perimeter that covered the southwestern part of Rwanda. They held it for 60 days and refused to permit any RPF forces to enter. They thus permitted many Hutu killers to remain at large and to continue killing in that area. The French also assisted elements of the Hutu Power organization to flee into Zaire.[30]

But the French could not protect Hutus all over the country. Hundreds of thousands of Hutus fled abroad. About 500,000 fled into Tanzania. Even more, ultimately estimated at well over a million, fled toward the Goma region in eastern Zaire. Most of the Hutu killing squads also went to Goma. So did many of the Hutus who had been protected by France but who dared not return to their Rwandan homes after French forces withdrew. Many innocent Hutus might not have wanted to leave Rwanda but the Hutu militia forced them to leave as well.

Ironically, at that point the United Nations suddenly got to work. For the Hutus did not enter the Goma area as killers but as refugees. Unlike the Tutsis, who had perhaps counted on the Security Council to protect them, they counted on Mrs. Ogata, the U.N. High Commissioner for Refugees, to take care of them whether she wanted to do so or not. With no facilities or food in eastern Zaire to take care of the sudden arrivals, UNHCR had to establish facilities to house the visitors. Within weeks, hundreds of thousands of Hutus had arrived in Zaire and found themselves sheltered and fed in refugee camps.

But the refugee camps presented very dangerous problems. They held two different groups of Hutus. One group, the Hutu Power "refugees," had blood on their hands. They could not return to Rwanda except by force. They wanted to keep their movement organized and wanted to recruit others to join them. The other group had fled because they wanted to get away from the war zone but they had not participated in the genocide. They hoped to go home as soon as possible. Many of them tried to leave at night to get away from "Hutu Power" control. But they found that they were not welcome in Rwanda, with the RPF killing many Hutu who returned.

The camps seethed with tension. "Hutu Power" commanders tried to seize control. They carried out stoning and summary executions of innocent refugees in order to force more Hutus to join their militia. They also began to control the food supplies and the housing arrangements for the same purpose. Desperate refugees could not go home because they feared the RPF and they could not stay in the camps because they feared "Hutu Power."

The resulting confusion generated tensions between Ogata and several major NGOs. Médecins sans Frontières and the International Rescue Committee as well as other agencies refused to work in what threatened to become a militia training camp. UNHCR had to try to keep control, which sometimes proved impossible. But the United Nations would not give Ogata the forces needed to make the camps safe for real refugees. Thus the camps remained in turmoil, with clandestine paramilitary training in some areas and terrified refugees doing the best they could to survive. They did not want to stay but they could not go home in the face of RPF threats.

Kagame and the RPF took matters into their own hands in 1995. Having taken full control of Rwanda, they moved against the refugee camps in the Goma area. They concentrated on attacking the underground Hutu leadership of the camps. But they also scattered other refugees, with some of them disappearing to their deaths in the jungles of the Congo and others trying to return to an uncertain fate in Rwanda. Many Hutus who had not joined in the genocide ended in Rwandan prisons next to those who had. The prisons themselves, run by Tutsis, became dangerously crowded terror sites of their own.

Western NGOs resented some of the steps taken by the RPF and worried that a number of refugees were being forced to go back to Rwanda or to flee into the Congo although they might have felt safer in the camps. The NGOs also told Mrs. Ogata that she should not have permitted the RPF to force Hutus to go home, but she had no more control over events than other U.N. officials. The Security Council still did not put adequate security into the camps.[31]

Kagame joined forces with Laurent Kabila, a long-standing enemy of Zaire president Joseph Mobutu. The Tutsis wanted to end Zaire's support of the Hutu camps, and Kabila wanted to lead a civil war against Mobutu. By 1997, they had overthrown Mobutu, whose regime had been hollow for years because most Zairians, including many of Mobutu's military, would not support him and much less fight for him. They renamed Zaire the "Congo Peoples' Democratic Republic."

The war soon involved every state that bordered on the Congo with some supporting the new regime and some the old. The government in Kinshasa lost control over much of the country. With civil war as well as international conflict raging all around Laurent Kabila, he himself did not last long. He was killed by unknown assassins and was succeeded by his son, Joseph Kabila. In the meantime, international aid agencies tried to meet the food needs of the desperate Congolese people caught in the civil war and the collapse of the Congo's political and economic system.

The crisis in the Congo reflected not only the problems of the Congo itself, but showed how a refugee flow could unbalance the domestic politics of a neighboring state. The Hutus coming into what was then Zaire had an impact on Congo relations with Uganda, Zimbabwe, Angola, Burundi and Rwanda itself. Their presence could not be absorbed, as most other refugee movements had been absorbed, because they constituted a fighting army with a distinct mission of revenge against a neighboring state. And the Tutsis under Kagame changed allegiances in the Congo when it became clear that the Congo government would not disarm the Hutus. By the turn of the millennium the Congo had fallen apart and its mineral resources were steadily plundered by armies from neighboring states and by private mining companies. Dallaire must have reflected bitterly that the Security Council's failure to give him peacekeeping reinforcements destabilized the entire center of Africa.

The genocide in Rwanda left many wounds. Many African governments continued to harbor a deep resentment toward the states of the Security Council, especially when they observed the huge effort that Western governments had made to stop Milosevic in Kosovo. They thought Africans had been treated as second-class citizens and spoke bitterly of a "double standard."

Kofi Annan—who had succeeded Boutros-Ghali as Secretary-General in 1997—tried to deal with these complaints. He ordered an independent inquiry to look more deeply into what had happened. He instructed the inquiry to spare nobody, including himself.

The inquiry concluded that the UNAMIR mission had been badly planned, badly conceived, badly instructed and badly supported. A larger force (as originally proposed by Dallaire), properly instructed and with adequate resources, could have prevented the genocide. The inquiry also concluded that the mandate should have been updated as the situation changed, as had been recommended by Dallaire. Although the inquiry politely spared the members of the Security Council, it recalled that the United States had presented a number of proposals that had weakened the mandate just when it should have been reinforced. It also pointed out that the U.N. secretariat had not handled Dallaire's warnings properly and had not always made the Security Council aware of the gravity of the situation as he saw it. It chided Boutros-Ghali for not having made a stronger case for reinforcement of the mission.[32]

The independent inquiry agreed with others who had complained that the states that contributed U.N. forces took over command of their own troops at crucial moments, just when the United Nations most needed to act with unity and conviction. This paralleled complaints made in the Balkans, Somalia and elsewhere. The inquiry noted that the practice contributed to disarray and demoralization within UNAMIR, for the commander lost control over his troops when he most needed them. It concluded that any future U.N. operations had to preserve unity of command and control.

Most important, the independent inquiry reiterated at several points that U.N. member states, and especially the permanent members of the Security Council, did not act with conviction or courage. They did not want to send their own forces and yet did not want to support the forces that were there or that African states offered. They lacked the political will to stop the genocide because they lacked a strategic interest in Rwandan stability.

This stinging rebuke cleared the air but left open whether anything would really change.

The sovereign members of the U.N. Security Council turned the concept of humanitarian aid on its head in the Rwandan crises. They refused to provide the protection against Hutu murderers that the Tutsis needed. France protected Hutu killers as they fled to the Congo and then dumped them on the U.N. High Commissioner for Refugees. The U.N. system began assistance to all the Hutu refugees and had to include the Hutu murderers Mitterrand had sheltered. Then the United Nations had no forces to stop the Hutu Power people from trying to gain control over all the Hutus in the camps. Finally, Kagame and the Tutsi RPF cleaned out the camps and turned on the Congo regime itself. And the governments of the Security Council sat by and watched it all without trying to arrest the process at any point.

The international community did try to help to ease the pain in Rwanda by establishing an international criminal court in Tanzania to punish those who had instigated and committed the genocide. But the process moved painstakingly slowly, and by 2003 had not even begun to proceed against the principals. The Rwandans decided to use their own traditional justice system called "Gacaca" to punish perpetrators and to try to put the genocide behind them.

Under the leadership of South African President Thabo Mbeki, Congo political leaders reached agreement in December 2002 to settle their long civil war and to arrange for a government of national unity within four years. It remained to be seen, however, whether the agreement would hold and whether it would mean that the wealth of the Congo would go to its own people so that they could stop relying on international humanitarian aid.[33]

In June 2003, appalled by the continuing civil war in northeastern Congo, the U.N. Security Council agreed to send a stronger peacekeeping force, headed by French troops. They are to try to stabilize the area, although French commanders say that they plan to concentrate on the city of Bunia, where there has been particularly heavy fighting. Peacekeepers from Bangladesh may later follow the French.[34] There is some irony in the French decision to go into northeastern Congo, for the crisis in the region might never have occurred if President François Mitterrand and the French government had decided to prevent the genocide in Rwanda almost ten years earlier. Nothing better shows the ghastly humanitarian effects of Western political failures.

Vieira de Mello Faces Nation-Building in East Timor

Sergio Vieira de Mello, like Howe and Dallaire, had to handle a humanitarian crisis of baffling complexity. He also became, by accident more than by design, the first viceroy appointed by the United Nations to take charge of an entire state.

That state, East Timor, seemed a land apart, both geographically and politically. It made up the eastern half of a large island on the eastern end of the Indonesian archipelago close to Australia. Green and subtropical, it seemed remote from the strife of the world. The population, relatively uniform, shared a common Melanesian culture overlaid with Catholicism which it had inherited from centuries of Portuguese colonialism.

The Portuguese government decided in 1974 to grant East Timor its independence under the Leftist Revolutionary Front for an Independent East Timor (Fretilin) which had been leading the anticolonial struggle. But independence lasted little more than one year.[35]

The Indonesian government, which governed West Timor, invaded East Timor in December 1975 and annexed it in July of the following year. Western leaders, including President Gerald Ford and Secretary of State Henry Kissinger, did not contest the annexation because they wanted to support the anti-Communist Indonesian government of General Suharto. But—with the exception of neighboring Australia—Western states did not officially recognize East Timor as a part of Indonesia. The people of East Timor continued to resist the Indonesian conquest.

Indonesian sovereignty kept the Timorese in a form of serfdom. The Indonesians imposed a virtual economic depression with a poverty rate twice as high as in Indonesia itself. They permitted Timorese to become clerks or policemen but reserved professional, officer and government positions for themselves. They repressed the continuing nationalist protests brutally, killing 200,000 people—out of a total estimated population of one million—and sealing East Timor off from the outside world.[36]

Indonesia could not continue its occupation after the end of the Cold War and after its colonial rule drew widening attention and rebuke. Resistance leaders Jose-Ramos Horta and Roman Catholic Bishop Carlos Ximenes Belo won the Nobel Peace Prize in 1996, calling worldwide attention to their cause. When the Indonesian economy collapsed in 1998, forcing major economic retrenchment, the Indonesian government began to wonder about the wisdom of keeping up its expensive rule over East Timor. When General Suharto was forced to resign in May of that year, the new Indonesian president, B.J. Habibie, decided that Indonesia would have to end its annexation of East Timor.

In coordination with Portugal, Indonesia agreed to a United Nations–organized "popular consultation" to determine whether the people of East Timor wanted greater autonomy or full independence. The U.N. Security Council in June of 1999 established the U.N. Advisory Mission for East Timor (UNAMET) to conduct the referendum and to oversee the subsequent transition to independence or autonomy. Although Indonesia supported the referendum and many analysts predicted that the election would go smoothly, persistent rumors suggested that the Indonesian army would oppose East Timor independence violently.

More than 98 per cent of the people of East Timor voted on August 30, 1999, in an astonishing show of determination. More than three quarters of them voted for independence over autonomy. UNAMET certified the results.

All hell broke loose at that point in East Timor. The Indonesian army and the local Indonesian militia went on a rampage. They systematically looted and burned virtually every house in the capital Dili and in every city, town or village. They killed or raped any occupants who had not fled in terror. Although they did not engage in the systematic genocide that the Hutus had conducted in Rwanda or the Red Khmer in Cambodia, they killed thousands and perhaps tens of thousands of Timorese. The exact number may never be known. They destroyed every piece of property they could find, from cattle and chickens to furniture, books, telephones and bicycles. Brynjar Nymo, a United Nations spokesman, commented that "the principal weapon was gasoline."[37] An estimated 500,000 East Timorese fled the towns, with about half hiding in the hills or the jungle and the others escaping to the relative security of West Timor. Army and militia units also dragged or forced thousands of others into Indonesia, apparently planning to use them for a possible reinvasion force against East Timor.

Portugal and Australia demanded urgent Security Council intervention, with Australia volunteering to lead a multinational force and to form the principal component. A chastised Habibie told Secretary-General Annan that Indonesia would accept such a force. On September 15, the Security Council passed a resolution noting the "worsening humanitarian situation in East Timor" and authorizing the International Force for East Timor (INTERFET).

Five days later, with Australia in the lead, INTERFET began to deploy in East Timor and within 32 days had secured the entire territory. The Australians, having learned some lessons from earlier peacekeeping efforts, went in with full force. They tolerated no resistance in any form.

On October 19, the Indonesian People's Consultative Assembly recognized the independence of the territory. A week later, the Security Council established the

U.N. Transitional Administration for East Timor (UNTAET) to guide the territory toward full independence. The United Nations in effect took over East Timor, assuming that kind of responsibility for the first time in its history.[38]

The members of the U.N. Security Council and Kofi Annan asked U.N. High Commissioner for Refugees Sadako Ogata to provide shelter and relief for the displaced persons in East Timor as well as for those who had fled to West Timor. Dozens of international voluntary agencies helped on both sides of the border.

Outsiders at first entered the refugee camps in West Timor at the risk of their lives. Elements of the Indonesian army and particularly of the militia wanted to use the camps as bases from which to attack or harass the new East Timor government (as the Hutu had tried to do in Goma in the Congo). They permitted relief supplies for the refugees to enter the camps but they resisted the arrival of the High Commissioner's staff. They wanted to control the camps and particularly wanted to force refugees to help them to retake East Timor. They resisted efforts to repatriate refugees as individuals and groups on their own. Any persons associated with the United Nations and especially with UNHCR needed armed escort to enter the camps. The militia killed three UNHCR staffers in cold blood (chapter 1). Mrs. Ogata protested bitterly to the Indonesian government.

Because of Indonesian interference, the High Commissioner could only begin to organize the return of refugees very slowly throughout 2000, using the International Organization for Migration (IOM) to help. Refugees at first returned mainly by boat, beginning at the rate of a few hundred per week and then picking up pace as the repatriation became better organized and as some could return over land. It was only in the second half of 2000 that significant numbers could return from the camps, and even then they had to be careful not to arouse militia anger. Those who had joined in the looting and killings did not dare to return until the United Nations had arranged a system of justice (see below).[39]

Annan had by then appointed Sergio Vieira de Mello, a highly regarded senior United Nations career official, to go to Dili and to take personal charge of governing and rebuilding the country. Being Brazilian, Vieira de Mello spoke fluent Portuguese, the language of educated East Timorese.

Annan understood the risks that the United Nations was taking when it agreed to take charge of East Timor. He knew that many governments, including the American and the Australian, would carefully and skeptically judge how the United Nations assumed sovereignty and control over any area for the first time in its history. He also knew that many U.N. member states would be very ready to criticize any failure. He gave Vieira de Mello authority to ask for whomever he wanted, and they put together what one commentator termed "an A-team" of the international bureaucracy.[40]

Hans Strohmeyer, a German legal scholar who served as counsel to UNTAET, described East Timor as an "empty shell."[41] He himself had to build a new legal and judicial system without existing laws, legal precedents, law books or trained legal personnel. Others had to found a banking system and a currency (at first, U.S. dollars) so that people could be paid and markets could function. The United Nations had to establish a fiscal and tax system, a civil service, hospitals and clinics, a school system and transportation infrastructure in a land without functioning automobiles. The only vehicles were the ubiquitous U.N. and NGO Land Rovers. And all this had to be done with persons who might be willing to work but who had never been expected, trained or even permitted to hold any administrative or other function. The training of an entire administration became a totally new type of humanitarian response for the United Nations.

De Mello knew that the United Nations would have to assure security to a shell-shocked people and he gave a high priority to the peacekeeping force. About 4,500 Australians formed the backbone of a multinational contingent of 8,000 that occupied and stabilized East Timor with help from almost 2,000 international police. The police and military included members from such other Asian states as Bangladesh, China, Japan, Malaysia, Nepal, New Zealand, Pakistan, Singapore, South Korea, Sri Lanka and Thailand. Thailand contributed the deputy force commander and 1,500 troops. Malaysia contributed priceless experience in more than a dozen international peacekeeping operations all over the world. Others from beyond Asia also joined, including Russians. The United States, reluctant to send fighting forces, provided logistics support.[42]

The INTERFET force met with little resistance. Being large, powerful and determined, it intimidated any militia commanders who might have wanted and dared to try to keep the territory under Indonesian control. Like Jacques Klein's force in Eastern Slavonia, INTERFET troops made a point of acting firmly enough at the beginning so that they would not be challenged again.

De Mello initially established an international (not a national) sovereignty, administration and economy. Only the international civil servants had any recognized positions and had the money to buy food or goods of any kind. Other residents had to wait until they could get some of it as it flowed through the economy or until aid had spread throughout the population. Few could find jobs at first, and even fewer had been trained for them. Over time, international relief supplies began pouring in. Later, development aid arrived as well.

Several United Nations agencies, including the World Food Program and UNICEF, helped bring in relief supplies. The U.N. High Commissioner for Refugees and the International Organization for Migration continued to bring back refugees and to reintegrate them into society while also providing relief and aid to rebuild housing.

One man who had served as head of UNTAET's Office of District Administration later complained that the U.N. bureaucracy was not moving quickly enough to give authority to the people of East Timor and to include them in the administration of the territory. He denounced what he termed "The UN's Kingdom of East Timor," asserting that it gave the people of East Timor no true responsibility and kept them in a state of servitude.[43] Vieira de Mello subsequently introduced a policy of greater "Timorization" to bring more local persons into the administration, especially as district officers. He also arranged for early elections to begin the political processes needed for self-government in East Timor.

To help promote reconciliation, the United Nations established a Reception, Truth and Reconciliation Commission after the widest possible consultation with all elements of East Timorese society. It formulated procedures by which militia members who had not been accused of grave crimes could return to their communities after undergoing whatever those communities would regard as suitable punishment. With the people of East Timor being surprisingly generous toward those who had attacked them and burned their property, reconciliation proved faster and more successful than it had been in Kosovo, Bosnia or Rwanda.[44]

The Indonesian government in 2001 did try a number of senior military and militia officers for crimes against humanity in connection with the murders, rapes and looting conducted after the East Timor vote for independence. A number of international human rights groups criticized the trials, complaining that the most guilty senior officers were not even being brought to trial because the government did not dare to offend the army. The human rights groups would have preferred an international tribunal like those for the former Yugoslavia and for Rwanda. But both Indonesia and many U.N. officials wanted to avoid such a trial because they wanted rapid reconciliation.[45]

Vieira de Mello and the INTERFET forces slowly began to establish a measure of security throughout the territory. But even though they were able to forestall major challenges to their authority, some of the remaining militia who infiltrated from West Timor throughout 2000 were able to kill or wound members of the international force as well as civilians. INTERFET had to conduct continuous operations in the border region to assure security. To get East Timorese soldiers and police to take over the functions of the international force, the United Nations created an East Timor Defense Force (ETDF) as well as a civilian police force.

UNTAET and INTERFET for several years had to do all the things that a central government would have done elsewhere, as well as many things that would have been done by local administrators or even by the private sector anywhere else. This included getting the port of Dili back to work, rebuilding and repairing government buildings and establishing a national archive system to help keep administrative and personal records for the new citizens of East Timor.

The United Nations engaged in nation-building in East Timor. Vieira de Mello had to build that nation fast enough to satisfy the aspirations of the East Timorese people and yet meticulously enough so that the United Nations or others would not have to do it all over again later.

On August 30, 2001, East Timor held elections for a constituent assembly. Once again, over 90 per cent of the electorate voted, with Fretilin emerging victorious as it had in 1975. Several of the earlier nationalist figures, such as José Ramos Horta, joined the transitional government. Mari Alkatari became Chief Minister, operating still within the overall authority of UNTAET and Vieira de Mello.

The work of setting up the new government proceeded apace under INTER-FET protection. Vieira de Mello continued to recruit civil servants, bringing the total to the planned 10,000 level by 2001. He also brought the ETDF to about half of its planned 1,500 level. As the number of incidents along the border with West Timor continued to decline, the United Nations administration believed that such a force provided adequate security and that the new state could afford it over the long run. To make certain that East Timor would be respected until its forces became fully functional, the United Nations planned to keep a peacekeeping force of about 5,000 as long as needed and even after independence day.

Kofi Annan nonetheless reported to the Security Council that the United Nations did not envisage a permanent role in East Timor. He did not want all the effort that the United Nations had made to be lost after independence by pulling out too quickly. But neither did he want the dominant U.N. presence to last too long, wanting instead to move as soon as possible toward what he termed a "normal development assistance" relationship. He wrote that the peacekeeping force would continue downsizing over a period of two years, starting from independence day. He also wrote that even the other essential functions that the U.N. administration would have to continue to perform would slowly be reduced until East Timor would be substantially on its own.[46]

Despite delays, Annan and Vieira de Mello insisted that they would stick to the agreed schedule for East Timor's independence. On April 14, 2002, East Timor voted for its first president. By a significant majority, the East Timorese chose a former guerrilla leader, Xanana Gusmao. Barely a month later, the donors held their last conference before independence, pledging the resources to get East Timor started on its own.

Finally, on May 20, 2002, East Timor became independent, as its people had voted in August 1999. And the United Nations could count its role in East Timor as a success despite the many problems. For once, the United Nations did not have to play the scapegoat.

Vieira De Mello himself left East Timor in the summer of 2002 and in September became U.N. High Commissioner for Human Rights.

The international humanitarian operation in East Timor succeeded for the same reasons as the one in Eastern Slavonia (chapter 8):

- A real and precise mandate.
- A true commitment, seriously intended.
- A full compliment of U.N. agencies and NGOs.
- Adequate funding and relief supplies.
- A peacekeeping force ready to keep the peace.
- Fully integrated command authority.

Perhaps most important, the sovereign governments acted with an eye to the humanitarian aspect of a problem in order to help solve it. They joined with the humanitarian conscience of the people of East Timor and of the many agencies trying to help. They worked with Vieira de Mello to establish a framework that respected the humanitarian as well as the political element of the crisis. They looked for a humanitarian as well as a political solution, and they found both. One could not help but wonder how Somalia and Rwanda as well as other places might have turned out if the same thinking had been applied there.

ELEVEN

THE LOST DECADE AND
THE NEW MILLENNIUM

PRESIDENT BILL CLINTON AND AMERICA AS A WHOLE rejoiced as the new millennium dawned in 2000, to great celebrations in Washington and elsewhere. One self-congratulatory speech followed another as fireworks lit up the skies.

Around the world, but especially in the West, billions celebrated. And the citizens of the West could indeed look forward to a safe future. Much of Europe, most of the Americas and many parts of Asia had been at peace for five decades.

But humanitarians could not join in the glory or in the rejoicing. They had distinctly mixed emotions. Their work had advanced throughout the century but had suffered all too many setbacks during the 1990s. Even though they had been able to help in many disastrous situations during that decade, they believed that at least some of those disasters could have been avoided.

The century of death ended as it had begun, in widespread tension and conflict. And the Western states that had appeared ready to surrender some of their sovereignty for the sake of humanitarian action during the Cold War had again begun to think and act in primarily national terms.

The decade had produced a paradox. Humanitarian aid had expanded into new areas, including major peacekeeping operations in the Balkans. Organizations like the European Union (EU), the North Atlantic Treaty Organization (NATO) and the Organization for Security and Cooperation in Europe (OSCE) had joined in peacekeeping. A number of U.N. organizations had run major new relief programs for refugees and other victims of war and violence.

Moreover, the sovereign states had remained ready to support whatever humanitarian response might be necessary. Ironically, although they often generated or exacerbated crises, Western governments also funded humanitarian operations to try to overcome those crises. They largely met humanitarian funding requirements although they often complained about improper management or did not provide as much money as the humanitarians needed. Money also grew much tighter after the turn of the millennium.

Yet the West as a whole seemed to have lost its devotion to the humanitarian conscience after the Cold War. European states did not protect potential and real victims of war as they had between 1950 and 1990. And the United States reacted inconsistently to humanitarian needs. Failures outnumbered successes.

That was not what the humanitarians had expected. President George Bush had spoken of a "new world order" at the beginning of the decade. Many people all around the world had hoped to see—and perhaps to help shape—a time of greater justice, peace and freedom. They had hoped that men, women and children would not die in political and military crises. But they were to be bitterly disappointed. They saw violent confrontations and pointless battles all around them.

President Clinton and other Western leaders had failed to keep the peace even within Western-dominated territories such as the Balkans or Africa, the lands where the West supposedly had some control or influence. More innocent people died in the Western parts of the world during the last decade of the old century than had died there during the entire 40 years of the Cold War. Africa suffered a major genocide. The Middle East continued to boil. And Asian problems, like the confrontation over Kashmir, continued to erupt. People were dying needlessly. Something had gone terribly wrong.

There could be no excuses. Western leaders, claiming to be the originators of humanitarian care, could no longer explain away their failures by saying that they could not act against a nuclear power like the Soviet Union and its allies or satellites. They could no longer blame human suffering on Communist rulers.

Mikhail Gorbachev, the former President of the Soviet Union, criticized Clinton in March 2002. He told an interviewer that Clinton had been a "novice" who "is guilty for the fact that the United States has wasted those ten years at the end of the Cold War . . . and missed out on opportunities to develop a new world order."[1]

But Clinton had not been the only one to fail. Other Western leaders and officials had also ignored humanitarian ideals. American and German officials had helped to precipitate Balkan wars and crises. Dutch soldiers had failed to prevent a slaughter in a "safe area" they had been chosen to protect. American, Belgian, French and other troops had failed to protect innocent Rwandans although they had been amply warned, and an American officer had provoked a fatal crisis in Somalia.

Some stories had a happy ending. The Dayton peace agreement and the Kosovo settlement seemed to be working, as did the multinational structures put into place to carry them out. Multiethnic coexistence had resumed in Eastern

Slavonia. East Timor was on its way to peace and independence. Many refugees as well as prisoners had been kept alive. Some had even been able to go home. And many international peacekeeping operations were helping to save human lives all over the world, as states did turn to the United Nations in a number of places after all else had failed. As Secretary-General Kofi Annan commented afterwards, "we never start it but we often have to finish it up."[2]

But the humanitarians also realized something more profound: humanitarian problems would not go away. Between 1914 and 1990, humanitarians might have been able to believe that their work might come to an end after the world wars and the Cold War. During the 1990s, however, they realized that their work might well go on into the indefinite future.

Time after time, humanitarians had been called in to keep people alive during crises or to help repair the damage that crises had caused. Humanitarians were busier than ever but also more frustrated.

Humanitarians also had to realize that their work would become harder rather than easier. The nature of humanitarian action, like the types of humanitarian work, had changed. The West and its humanitarian agencies no longer had to overcome the effects of Soviet and Communist brutality at home or adventurism abroad. Crises did not erupt mainly along the borders of the Soviet system or in areas where Communist forces or allies might try to challenge a Western position. Instead, crises could erupt anywhere.

The nature of the crises had also changed. Communist states had generally exercised tight control within their borders. No rebellion could succeed. Opponents of the Communist regimes had to flee and become refugees. They could be protected and taken care of as such. Over time, most would return home or move on. And humanitarian relief could identify specific problems and help to solve them, as during the wars of decolonization.

In the new world, however, humanitarians faced much more dangerous and also unsolvable crises. Governments could not really control the countries they claimed to govern. Nor could they always keep the peace. They could not contain crises at home. They could not prevent civil wars. Sometimes a state collapsed, as in Afghanistan, Somalia, Sudan, Rwanda, the Congo or Yugoslavia. Journalists and others called them "failed states."

People in those states often needed help merely to survive. They would not or could not flee to safer areas. Instead, they remained within the nominal boundaries of the collapsing state, as they had in Bosnia. Then they were described as internally displaced persons instead of as refugees, although they may have had similar needs. The arrangements made to help refugees did not fully work for them.

Relief workers all too often found themselves in the middle of war and genocide. They were sent into Iraq in 1991 to help Kurds who were in full rebellion.

They were sent into Bosnia in 1994 to save lives in a civil war that peacekeepers were not authorized to stop. And they were sent into the Congo in 1996 although the Security Council would not protect the safety of the Goma camps. They sometimes had national forces to protect them but all too often those forces pulled out while the humanitarians stayed. Annan observed scathingly that the humanitarians served as "palliatives" when states did not want to solve a problem.[3]

Humanitarian workers all too often faced seemingly endless problems resulting from apparently endless dislocations. Earlier crises, like Nigeria, Hungary or Indochina, might have lasted months or even years, but a humanitarian agency could foresee an end. The new crises seemed to have no fixed end, or certainly not one that could be easily foreseen.

Humanitarians faced a conceptual dilemma. They realized that the plans and organizational structures they had devised to meet the humanitarian crises of the Cold War had not functioned properly during the 1990s. New ideas and new forms of organization might have to come. But what were those ideas? And what could the humanitarian agencies do while they were waiting? And what kinds of persons would be needed to solve the new dilemmas?

The lost decade had left some bitter memories and some lessons for the future. At the beginning of the new millennium, humanitarians needed a new agenda. They needed to look at themselves to see if they could even meet the new needs. And they needed first of all to look at the kinds of crises that awaited them.

The Humanitarian Agenda: Crises in Waiting

Most baffling for the humanitarians, new crises kept arising even as old ones remained unsolved.

The "failed states" presented the worst dilemmas, especially because nobody wanted to deal with them. Americans and Europeans did not help Afghanistan during the 1990s, even before the fundamentalist Muslim movement of the Taliban had taken over the country. During the entire decade of the 1990s, humanitarian agencies in Afghanistan did not get more than half the funds they wanted and needed from American, European and Japanese donors, although the aid agencies repeatedly pleaded for more funds.[4]

Neither did Americans and Europeans help Sudan or Somalia or other "failed states" mired in civil wars and chaos. Humanitarian agencies, and especially NGOs, continued to work in those states during the decade. They tried to provide food and to meet basic medical needs. But they never received more than the minimum resources they needed. Western leaders had other problems closer to home, such as the Balkans, and they saw no reason to worry about "failed states" on distant continents.

The future looks no more promising than the past, for the list of potential humanitarian crises seems unending.

Many civil wars and other conflicts arise out of ethnic problems. When England, France, Portugal and other Western colonial states retreated from their empires, they left new state governments in the hands of groups that had led the fight for independence but that did not represent all the people of the state. These new states had British or French-style unitary governments that might be termed "mini-empires," for one ethnic group tried to rule over several and sometimes many others by controlling the army, the police force, the trade ministry, the customs service and other levers of power. Usually, but not always, the African ethnic groups along the coast ruled over dispossessed and resentful inland Muslim ethnic groups.[5]

All too often, the West did not pay much attention to the risk of ethnic strife. Instead, the Western governments, investors or traders dealt with the powers that Western colonialists had left in place and that were ready to grant mineral and agricultural concessions, but were incompetent and ruinously corrupt. Finally, different tribes or ethnic and religious groups would rebel. And the country would become a humanitarian tragedy as civil war erupted.

The Organization for African Unity, under the leadership of President Julius Nyerere of Tanzania, had decided during the 1960s that African states should not change their borders, so the frustrated ethnic groups had no hope for their share of power and wealth. Over time, many rebelled.

President Jacques Chirac, Mitterrand's successor, faced a classic example of that problem in the Ivory Coast during 2002 and 2003. The Muslim ethnic groups to the north of the country had long resented dictatorial rule from the southern ethnic groups around the capital, Abidjan. They launched a major armed rebellion in the summer and fall of 2002. Chirac sent almost 3,000 French troops to protect French nationals and to defeat the rebellion. But the French troops found themselves intervening in a civil war that they could not win. They were able to negotiate a power-sharing settlement in the spring of 2003, but nobody could be sure that the settlement would hold. A lot depended on the readiness of the southern ethnic groups to relinquish not only power but income from mineral concessions and cocoa exports.

Separate rebellions broke out in other African states. Various groups in Liberia and Sierra Leone fought for power and for control over part of the diamond trade. In Sudan, the Muslim north ruled the state and the black tribes of southern Sudan fought for independence. The Congo increasingly became a mass of small private warlord states, each making separate mineral deals with Western concerns that paid off the warlords and exported the minerals without asking—or paying—the central government in Kinshasa. The state finally collapsed between 1998 and 2002 when the Tutsi armies allied themselves with Congolese factions to win control of the government (chapter 10).

Asian states suffer from the same problem. Muslim minorities in a number of southern Philippine islands oppose the central government, sometimes by force of arms. Indonesia has dozens of different tribal and national groups increasingly demanding either independence or a share of power. The Indonesian government has had to grant autonomy to rebellious groups in the small state of Aceh who no longer want to be ruled from Djakarta. In Sri Lanka, the sizable Tamil minority has fought for decades to gain a separate and independent state.

The new mini-empires cannot last any more than the old empires and yet they try to do just that. The established rulers will not share power with others until forced to do so, and in particular do not want to share royalties for their mineral exports.

As wars and other crises rack those states, many people must flee their homes. Sometime they flee the country, becoming refugees. Sometimes they remain within the theoretical boundaries of their state as internally displaced persons (IDPs). But no solutions now seem possible for either. The numbers of refugees around the world barely declined during the 1990s, from about 16,700,000 refugees in 1990 to 14,900,000 in 2001. And the number of IDPs, hardly worth counting in 1990, had risen to 22 million by 2002.[6]

Even states that do not suffer from ethnic divisions face crippling problems. Many find themselves falling behind economically. Their people suffer from AIDS, malnutrition, inability to export to the protectionist West, and bad government. They want a better life but see no way to get it. They rail against what they perceive as the inequities of the global system, with some peoples being wealthy and at peace while they suffer from poverty, injustice and hunger.

To complete the picture, older problems also remain to be settled. The Middle East dispute over Israel and Palestine has lasted for over 80 years without a solution. In Kashmir, India and Pakistan have not solved a problem that first arose in 1946, with India unwilling to hold a referendum in Kashmir and Pakistan unwilling to yield without that.

Every one of these problems presents real or potential humanitarian crises. With countless weapons of mass destruction potentially loose in the world, each could explode into an unprecedented calamity. And every one of them will probably require either new or continuing humanitarian help, most probably organized through the United Nations.

The Humanitarian Agenda: Better Structures

Secretary-General Kofi Annan has often expressed his concern about the risk of humanitarian crises. He also believes that the United Nations should try to improve its ability to deal with those crises. And he believes that the system for humanitarian care needs improving if it is to handle whatever might come next. If humanitarian crises did not end with the Cold War, and if the new millennium comes up with new problems, humanitarian agencies need to find new solutions. They also need to prepare themselves for the long haul and for more dangerous situations.

Lakhdar Brahimi's Report

The new dimensions of international peacekeeping have presented the United Nations with some of its most baffling problems. Whereas peacekeeping missions had been sent only rarely during the Cold War years, they have burgeoned since. As Annan pointed out in late 1999, 36 peacekeeping missions had been created in ten years since 1988, when the peacekeepers had won the Nobel Peace Prize. Over 750,000 military and police personnel from 118 different countries had served on peacekeeping missions since 1949, and 1,500 had been killed in service.[7]

Peacekeeping had also grown in complexity. Whereas peacekeepers during the Cold War had mainly been asked to supervise military truce arrangements, during the 1990s they were instructed, among other things, to support the growth of civil society, to supervise elections, to train police and other legal institutions, to maintain "safe areas" and to monitor the introduction of human rights. At the same time, they worked closely with humanitarian relief agencies, sometimes protecting relief workers and almost always coordinating to make sure that neither got in the way of the other. Peacekeeping, as directed during the 1990s, had become part of the humanitarian response in what had become known as "complex emergencies." A number of states, such as Canada and Ireland, had established special training facilities in peacekeeping techniques for their forces.

The U.S. government has raised objections to international peacekeeping operations to protest against the risk that American peacekeepers might be subject to frivolous war crimes accusations in the International Criminal Court. It initially refused to vote for renewal of the Bosnian multinational force in June 2002. But other states have objected to the U.S. position, arguing that it makes no sense to throw out the baby with the bath. If Americans worry about the risk of lawsuits, then Americans should not be peacekeepers. But the system as a whole must continue. As of this writing, the United States has accepted that position and peacekeeping operations are continuing across the world, but the subject is not closed.[8]

Annan believes that the United Nations should manage its own share of any peacekeeping operation better than before. In early 2000, he asked Lakhdar Brahimi, a widely respected former foreign minister of Algeria, to conduct a study on the subject. Brahimi presented his report on August 23, 2000, in time for it to be considered and approved in principle by the "Millennium Summit" of the United Nations that fall.[9]

Brahimi and his panel minced no words. In a 50-page document remarkably candid by the cautious standards of the United Nations, Brahimi made clear that the United Nations itself, the Security Council and the international community as a whole had failed to use peacekeeping effectively to protect and preserve human lives and humanitarian principles in crisis situations.

Brahimi warned that force, while an essential element of peacekeeping, could not be relied on to do it all: "Force alone cannot create peace; it can only create the space in which peace can be built." But, if force had to be used, it should be "robust" and it should have rules of engagement that would not permit peacekeepers to stand idly by while one party to a peace agreement was "clearly and incontrovertibly" violating the terms of the agreement. The United Nations urgently needed to make "significant changes" in its own culture. It had to move more quickly and to react more decisively. Undoubtedly reflecting on the murders committed in Rwanda and Srebrenica, Brahimi wrote that the vaunted U.N. principle of neutrality should not allow a peace force to be neutral toward massive attacks against humanitarian principles. United Nations peacekeepers who witnessed violence against civilians "should be presumed to be authorized to stop it" even if their mandate did not specifically tell them to act.

Brahimi reserved his most critical comments for the member states of the United Nations, especially the members of the Security Council. He said that they should stop passing toughly worded Security Council resolutions in order to sound decisive at home if they did not intend to make those resolutions effective. Recalling Rwanda and the Balkans, he warned that states should not pass resolutions that called for troop levels that they had no intention of reaching or of funding.

In a thinly veiled slap at the United States, which always blamed the United Nations for its own failings, Brahimi added that member states needed "to summon the political will to support the United Nations politically, financially and operationally to enable the United Nations to be truly credible as a force for peace." Member states could not instruct the Secretary-General to do a job, then fail to support him when he was trying to do it and later blame him if things went wrong. He noted that the United Nations had actually carried out a number of successful peacekeeping missions since its founding but that it was never given credit for those achievements but only blamed for any failures.

Brahimi recalled that 87 member states had pledged 147,900 military personnel for U.N. operations but that most of those—especially from the developed world—were usually not available when actually called upon. All too often, during the last few years, the impoverished states of the developing world provided most of the soldiers available for U.N. missions, reversing the ratio that had prevailed during the first 50 years of the United Nations.

Brahimi and his panel made a series of specific recommendations to improve U.N. operations in preventing war, in keeping the peace and, if necessary, in making peace:

- The United Nations should be able to deploy a peacekeeping force within 30 days at the most after the Security Council has passed a resolution (or 90 days in a "complex" operation).
- To do this, member states should offer standby forces and equipment that would be available on short notice for U.N. missions, and that would have trained together at brigade level (of several thousand soldiers) in order to be effective immediately.
- The U.N. should have an "on-call" list of about 100 experienced and well-qualified military officers to be available on seven days' notice to serve as part of a start-up team. Parallel "on-call" lists should be made for civilian police, judicial and penal experts, as well as human rights specialists, in order to permit the United Nations to field teams of experts in civil society as well as military forces.
- The Secretary-General should develop a global logistics support strategy that would include stockpiled equipment, standing contracts and "start-up kits" to be kept at the U.N. logistics facility at Brindisi in Italy.
- The Secretary-General should have the resources to staff adequate support offices for peacekeeping operations. Noting that U.N. supporting staff never came close to matching that of any normal national military operation, Brahimi wrote that lack of adequate support had caused some of the failures of the operations in Rwanda and elsewhere.
- The Secretary-General should be authorized to commit up to $50 million in funds even before a Security Council resolution once it becomes clear that an operation is likely.
- The United Nations should develop an independent intelligence capacity so that it could prepare for the kinds of crises it would need to confront.
- The Secretariat must tell the Security Council what it needs to hear, not what it may want to hear.

Brahimi stressed several times that the U.N. Charter gave member states the responsibility for maintaining peace and security. The Secretary-General could not act without the states' support.

NGO Evaluation

Without the Cold War to justify humanitarianism at any cost, the governments that fund humanitarian operations have increasingly wanted to make sure they are getting value for money. They want the agencies to be using the best possible practices and especially want aid to go to the people who need it instead of to corrupt officials. NGOs share that wish.

John Borton, a British relief planner, began to systematize various evaluation efforts during the 1990s. While working at the Overseas Development Institute (ODI) in London, he and others looked for a mechanism to evaluate humanitarian aid programs. In 1997, they founded the Active Learning Network for Accountability and Performance in Humanitarian Assistance (ALNAP) to systematize the effort.[10]

ALNAP's board of directors represents funding and operating institutions, including U.N. agencies, donors, the International Red Cross and Red Crescent movement, NGOs and academics. Under their direction, ALNAP has begun sending field teams to evaluate humanitarian aid operations for efficient and effective aid delivery.[11] ALNAP has thus become a useful place for agencies to discuss common problems and to concentrate on learning and accountability. It publishes reports on its evaluations and helps to formulate and implement a code of conduct for relief agencies.

By 2001, ALNAP had prepared 288 separate reports. While evaluations and recommendations are not as widely used as they should be, their very existence has helped set standards for agencies to follow. They have helped to introduce and to advance a concept of humanitarian accountability and have, in the process, defined standards for good practice. In addition, some governments—like the American— have arranged periodic evaluations of NGO performance in such humanitarian operations as Kosovo, but not as systematically as ALNAP.

The reports have generally given good marks to the humanitarian agencies, concluding that those agencies have worked efficiently and effectively to provide protection and immediate medical and food relief in crisis situations. The agencies have helped people to survive, the fundamental goal of humanitarian action.[12] Despite the dangers posed in fluid situations like Bosnia, Kosovo and Rwanda, a remarkable number of volunteers have been ready to help even in the most difficult and risky situations.

Recognition

As crises deepened and multiplied, the humanitarian agencies and their staff even began to get some recognition for the unending and often dangerous work they performed.

The Nobel Prize

Humanitarian agencies received the Nobel Peace Prize a number of times. Kofi Annan and the United Nations system as a whole won the prize in 2001. The United Nations High Commissioner for Refugees and the International Committee of the Red Cross had each received it twice before then. And a well-known NGO, Médecins sans Frontières, also won it.

The Hilton Prize

In special recognition of humanitarian NGOs, the Conrad N. Hilton Foundation, founded and endowed by the American hotel magnate, started the annual $1 million Conrad N. Hilton Humanitarian Prize in 1996. Several NGOs, including the International Rescue Committee, have won the prize. In 2002, the prize went to St. Christopher's Hospice in London. Hundreds of other NGOs have been nominated.

Training Programs

As humanitarian work promised to continue, it became recognized ever more widely as a profession and as a subject for specialization. Georgetown University in Washington offers a Master of Arts degree program in migration and refugee studies. The Fletcher School of Law and Diplomacy and other centers at Tufts University in Boston offer a Master of Arts degree program in humanitarian assistance. The Hauser Center at the John F. Kennedy School of Harvard University offers similar degrees, as does Oxford University in England. Most of the students working in those programs have worked in field operations for at least several years before even being accepted for the programs.

More and more students at American, European, Asian and African universities plan to work at one or another NGO after graduation. They want to have the experience of helping people all over the world, some as a career and others for at least several years. As they have entered this world, it has become more professional and more widely respected. They have brought the same dedication as the older generation of humanitarians. They have also brought the organizational and operational skills of modern management training. The modern NGO is a very different organization from that of only 20 years ago.

As the new millennium dawns, humanitarian care can draw on a wide range of organizations and methods to carry out its agenda and to do it better than in the past. It does not come cheap. The 2003 "Consolidated Inter-Agency Appeal" issued by the U.N. Office for the Coordination for Humanitarian Affairs showed that the U.N. agencies principally committed to humanitarian care needed a total of over $5 billion for 2002, with almost the same amount needed for 2003.[13]

Peacekeeping in particular can be expensive. The U.S. General Accounting Office, basing itself on U.N. data, concluded that the total cost had amounted to almost $20 billion over the ten years from 1992 to 2001. The amounts had peaked in 1994 and 1995 near $3.5 billion because of the Balkan crisis and again in 1999 at $2.3 billion because of the Kosovo crisis. Operations in Afghanistan and Iraq will drive them higher yet. But, like other humanitarian costs, both the financial and humanitarian costs of peacekeeping remain lower than those of war.[14]

Dennis Jett, an American expert who testified before the U.S. House Committee on International Relations, said that he saw no other option for the United States than cooperation in U.N. operations. He said that U.S. forces would not want to take on the missions that the United Nations would be prepared to take on. And he rejected the other alternative, which was to do nothing. Thus, he concluded, U.N. operations "may be the only option available."[15]

But the United States, like other contributing states, cut back on its support for humanitarian and other operations. Ruud Lubbers, the new U.N. High Commissioner for Refugees, told his executive committee in September 2002 that contributions to UNHCR were running at 10 percent less than refugee and IDP needs even after he had already made significant cutbacks in UNHCR programs.[16] The United States, Western Europe and Japan all spoke of cutting back on their humanitarian contributions across the board.

Even as all this has been happening, humanitarian problems have not waited for the West and for the humanitarians to get around to them. Major parts of the world boiled with pain, sorrow and anger even while American and other Western leaders and publics celebrated the millennium.

Like the French monarchs and aristocrats on the eve of the Revolution of 1789, Western leaders had little understanding of what lay ahead, for them and for others. The new millennium would soon show them their mistake, and would show it in the most barbaric way.

TWELVE

SEPTEMBER 11, OSAMA BIN LADEN AND AFGHANISTAN

ON THE MORNING OF SEPTEMBER 11, 2001, terrorists commandeered four passenger jets that had taken off from Boston, Washington and Newark airports. They flew three of the jets into well-known buildings: the two World Trade Center towers in New York City and the Pentagon in Washington. The towers collapsed, but the Pentagon could be rebuilt. The fourth jet crashed in southern Pennsylvania. Its terrorist crew had perhaps intended to crash it into the White House but courageous passengers had prevented that. Altogether, the terrorists had killed over 3,000 persons of 90 different nationalities, the vast majority of them Americans.

The pilots who flew into the buildings had all served al Qaeda. That organization, established by Osama bin Laden, a Saudi multi-millionaire who had become a terrorist mastermind and organizer, had become a network of terrorists sworn to attack the United States and the West.

Bin Laden had found Afghanistan a congenial base for his operations, including attacks against the destroyer U.S.S. *Cole* and two U.S. embassies in Africa. He lived at various places in Afghanistan and had major training bases and storage sites there.

Afghanistan and the Taliban

According to Afghan legend, Allah made Afghanistan after he had made the rest of the world: "He saw that there was a lot of rubbish left over, bits and pieces and things that did not fit anywhere else. He collected them all together and threw them down to the earth. That was Afghanistan."[1] This phrase contains more than a germ of truth, for Afghanistan holds many different topographies, from burning desert to impenetrable mountains. It also has a wide-ranging mix of tribes and factions. The largest, the Pashtun tribe, makes up about 40 percent of the population. Two northern tribes, the Tajiks and the Uzbeks, account for perhaps 25 and 8 percent, respectively. A tribe of Shiite Muslims, the Hazara, are about 20 percent. Many smaller groups make up the rest. They all mistrust and oppose each other, usually uniting only when they have a common enemy and then fighting that enemy with deadly ferocity. But they do not have the mutual hatred that some Balkan groups, such as the Serbs and the Croats, have for each other. They can cooperate when necessary and want to remain within the same state.[2]

Many world leaders have tried to control Afghanistan because of its strategic location at the central point of the south Asian arc. Alexander of Macedonia, Tamurlane of Persia, Genghis Khan of Mongolia, Queen Victoria of England and Leonid Brezhnev of the Soviet Union tried to conquer it. All failed.

Sir Henry Mortimer Durand, a British nineteenth century colonial official, in 1881 drew the international boundary between Afghanistan and British India, the "Durand Line." But England hardly had a glorious record in Afghanistan, having been badly beaten in two nineteenth century wars and again in 1919. The Afghans have never formally accepted the Durand Line because it cut the land of the Pashtun tribes in half, but the Pashtuns were neither then nor since in a position to challenge the border openly. Thus Afghanistan remained as it is today, originally a nineteenth century buffer between England and Russia and now a twenty-first century buffer between many other states as well. It has never been colonized and was a member of the League of Nations and of the United Nations. It signed a treaty of friendship with the United States in 1936.

Brezhnev's Soviet troops invaded Afghanistan on December 24, 1979. When the Mujaheddin fought against the Soviets, President Ronald Reagan sent funds, small arms and Stinger missiles to shoot down Soviet jet fighters and helicopters. After ten years and the loss of an estimated 1.5 million Afghan lives, Soviet forces withdrew in 1989. In barely more than a century, the Afghans had beaten off two of the world's great powers. But the Soviet invasion and Afghan resistance had left the land in ruins and had forced millions to flee either to Pakistan or to Iran. In 1989, Afghanistan desperately needed help.

The country sank deeper and deeper into chaos and misery as various tribal groups, having won the war, took to quarreling among themselves. Finally, in 1992, northern Afghan forces that combined Tajik tribal units under Ahmad Shah Masud and Uzbek tribal units under General Rashid Dostum captured Kabul and installed a new president, Burhanuddin Rabbani.[3] The Pashtuns reacted in shock. They resented having the northern forces in control of the capital. They could not expel them but could get close enough to Kabul to shell the capital and leave it in ruins. Civil war roiled the entire country.

The Taliban, the "students of Islam," arose out of this chaos in 1994. Originally young and idealistic, they had a religious fanaticism and political absolutism that provoked resistance, which they subdued with savage determination. Many had come from Pakistan and from Arab states of the Middle East and North Africa, having originally been drawn to Afghanistan to fight Moscow. Others had become orphaned by the war and saw fighting and brutality as normal elements of existence. Tightly organized and led by a Pashtun, Mullah Mohammed Omar, the Taliban rallied many of the Pashtuns and launched a campaign of conquest across Afghanistan. Omar sent his forces ever closer to Kabul, swooping down on the city and taking it on September 26, 1996.

Omar then seized the former Soviet puppet president, Najibullah, and had him castrated and killed after being dragged behind a Jeep for several trips around the presidential palace. He and other Afghans hated Najibullah because he had directed the Soviet-era Afghan secret police which had tortured and killed countless Afghans. The Taliban also killed Najibullah's brother and hanged the two men on a traffic control post outside the palace, where all of Kabul could see how the Taliban treated its opponents. Only the International Committee of the Red Cross helped him, taking his body from the Taliban and returning it to his home city where he could be buried among his tribesmen. The Taliban kept going, conquering the northern capital, Mazar-e-Sharif, in August 1998.

The Taliban also began a campaign to enforce the strictest kind of Islamic law against Afghan and other women under their control. They ordered women to stop working, to remain in their houses and to avoid all contact with men outside their immediate family. They also ordered women to wear clothing that covered them from head to toe. And Taliban policies brought the Afghan economy to a standstill, except for subsistence farming and poppy production for heroin exports.

The U.S. government under President Bill Clinton at first had some sympathy for the Taliban because of the Taliban's opposition to Iran—which Washington then saw as the major threat in the Muslin world. So did the Pakistani government under Prime Minister Benazir Bhutto, although she must have been offended by the Taliban's contempt for the rights of women. But the U.S. government paid little attention to Afghanistan during most of the 1990s. Secretary of State Warren Christopher was said not to have mentioned Afghanistan during his entire tenure from 1993 to 1997. He ignored Egyptian and Algerian pleas to re-engage the United States in Afghanistan to curtail the Taliban, who threatened moderate Arab states as well as the West.[4]

Under Clinton, the United States gave virtually no help except for basic humanitarian aid to the Afghan people themselves. And the lack of American interest meant that the United Nations and its major agencies had few resources to support the Afghan people. After the vast military assistance operations of the 1980s collapsed, very little official U.S. economic aid came to help rebuild the country. Many Afghans reacted with bitter disappointment that the United States turned its attention away from them once they were no longer useful in the fight against communism. This bitterness came back to haunt the Americans.

Nonetheless, humanitarian NGOs kept up enough aid to feed the Afghan people. The International Committee of the Red Cross and a number of international NGOs played a role. So did Pakistani and Iranian NGOs as well as Afghan NGOs. Most Western NGOs relied on their local staff for distribution of supplies, keeping only small Western staffs. The level of aid sufficed to keep up relief programs at subsistence levels for a few returning refugees and for the desperately poor Afghan people, buffeted by drought as well as war.

The World Food Program estimated that 5.5 million Afghans depended on foreign food relief because of the war, the drought and the Taliban.[5] Most refugees in Pakistan and Iran—not to mention those who had gone to the West—could not return to Afghanistan because there was nothing there for them. The official West thus abandoned the country to its worst elements, the Taliban.

The Taliban policy against women, bitterly opposed by American feminist groups, turned the United States firmly against Afghanistan. Secretary of State Madeleine Albright used a visit to Pakistan in November 1997 to denounce the Taliban: "We are opposed to the Taliban because of their opposition to human rights and their despicable treatment of women and children." Emma Bonino, the European Union Commissioner for Humanitarian Affairs, had echoed similar sentiments after a visit to Kabul in September.[6]

U.N. Secretary-General Kofi Annan appointed Lakhdar Brahimi, the former Foreign Minister of Algeria, as a special envoy to mediate between Iran and Afghanistan when war seemed likely between the two states. Brahimi found the Taliban totally uncooperative and could persuade them to ease tensions with Iran only after he had met personally with Mullah Omar.

September 11—A Humanitarian Failure

CIA Director George Tenet and FBI Director Robert Mueller have explained why they did not and could not predict the September 11 attacks, although there had for some time been indications that Osama bin Laden might try a major direct attack on the United States. Nor did President Bush or his Secretary of State Colin Powell or any other American political or military officials expect such a direct and massive attack.

But Peter Thomsen, a former special U.S. envoy to Afghanistan who in 1993 tried to persuade the U.S. government to help rebuild Afghanistan in order to protect it from extremists, gave the real explanation for what happened on September 11. He said that the United States had simply chosen to ignore Afghanistan during the 1990s: "We walked away."[7] And Secretary-General Annan observed that "There is a clear and ineradicable trail from the absence of engagement with Afghanistan in the 1990s to the creation of a terrorist haven there and to the attacks on the World Trade Center."[8]

After the Western Cold War victory over the Soviet Union and the withdrawal of Soviet forces from Afghanistan, the Afghans would have welcomed a Western presence and Western help in the reconstruction of their country. Such a presence and such help might well have prevented the domination of the Taliban. Americans at the time enjoyed enormous popular support in Afghanistan because American weapons and military aid helped defeat the Soviet occupation forces.

Afghanistan thus represented a major political and humanitarian disaster. Washington and other Western capitals chose to ignore it after the end of the Cold War because America's Afghan allies had become less important and less useful, just as they had chosen to let Yugoslavia come apart because its dissolution no longer represented a strategic hazard. The Afghan people had no choice but to accept others—including the Taliban.

Analysts and experts can debate whether plentiful Western humanitarian aid and a continuing Western commitment could have prevented the Taliban from taking power in Afghanistan. But one cannot doubt that a Western presence would have made Afghans less ready to support such anti-Western extremists and terrorists as bin Laden. Nature abhors a vacuum. The NGOs did their best but it could not be enough.

September 11 thus represented a humanitarian failure and an aid failure more than an intelligence failure. The terrorist attacks could have been prevented if Western leaders—and especially American leaders—had supported Afghanistan after the Soviet retreat. The United States and the West as a whole abandoned an ally when they thought they no longer needed that ally. They should not have been surprised when others took advantage of that opening.

bin Laden in Afghanistan

Osama bin Laden had played a prominent role in organizing aid to the Afghan Mujaheddin in their struggle against the Soviet invaders. In 1983 he established a special office in the Pakistani city of Peshawar, near the Afghan border, to recruit and to train volunteers for the Mujaheddin and to help finance their operations. The recruits came to be termed "Arab Afghans," volunteers from all over the Arab world who wanted to join the Mujaheddin. To coordinate their activities, bin Laden created al Qaeda ("The Base") in 1989.

Bin Laden returned to Saudi Arabia in 1990 after Soviet forces had been expelled from Afghanistan. But he turned against the Saudi government because it permitted U.S. troops to remain on what he regarded as sacred Muslim soil even after Iraq had been defeated in the Gulf War. The Saudi government then forced him to leave. This did not stop him from conducting terrorist operations, including an earlier bombing at the New York World Trade Center in 1993.[9]

Bin Laden moved to Sudan to continue his operations. He used his continuing contacts with the "Arab Afghans" to maintain the al Qaeda network, which by then operated in dozens of Arab countries—sometimes in opposition to the local government. The al Qaeda network, estimated to consist of more than 50,000 loyalists, remained under his influence and guidance although he did not try to exercise operational control over all its activities. Over time, bin Laden found Sudan increasingly uncongenial as well.

Clinton rejected the Sudanese government offer to turn bin Laden over to the United States in 1996, along with information about his terrorist network. Clinton did not want to do anything that might improve relations with Sudan, which he regarded as a "rogue state." American government lawyers also feared that bin Laden might become an embarrassment because they might be unable to prove that he had killed Americans or done direct damage to the United States.[10]

Bin Laden then moved to Afghanistan with his family and supporters and established himself in Kandahar with the support of Mullah Omar. In exchange, he helped to finance the Taliban. He also set up extensive training camps and storage facilities in the mountains of eastern Afghanistan in order to train Arabs for terrorist operations against the United States and against such Arab states as Algeria and Egypt. The Taliban grew to appreciate his presence and support so much that Mullah Omar rejected a Saudi request to expel bin Laden even though his refusal meant the loss of Saudi aid.[11]

Bin Laden made his intentions clear in February 1998, when he convened an al Qaeda meeting that issued a manifesto on behalf of what he called "The International Islamic Front for Jihad against Jews and Crusaders." The manifesto denounced the "occupation" for seven years of the "holiest of places in the Lands of Islam, the Arabian peninsula." It added a ruling that "to kill the Americans and their allies—civilian and military—is an individual duty for every Muslim who can do it in any country in which it is possible."[12]

The U.S. Central Intelligence agency had specifically targeted bin Laden by then and tried to watch his every move. Nonetheless, bin Laden launched his biggest operation to date, the bombings of the U.S. embassies in Nairobi and Dar-es-Salaam, on August 7, 1998, killing over 200 Americans and Africans while wounding thousands. American retaliatory strikes against bin Laden's hideouts in the mountains of Afghanistan killed over 20, many of them Pakistanis, but did not kill bin Laden himself. Washington demanded that Afghanistan turn him over if it wanted to receive any aid at all from the West. When the Taliban refused, the U.N. Security Council in October 1998 imposed sanctions on Afghanistan.

With that, the Americans wrote off Afghanistan even more, trying to isolate the Taliban and bin Laden. Only strictly limited humanitarian support continued. The Taliban watched relief agencies closely for any actions that it might regard as improper. For example, in August 2001, it arrested eight aid workers of the NGO Shelter Now International on suspicion of proselyting.[13]

The Western sanctions did not stop the Taliban from continuing to conduct weekly ceremonies of lashings and amputations in Kabul's football stadium to punish Afghans for violating the Taliban interpretation of Islamic law. But they did mean that the people of Afghanistan would have to suffer the loss of even more elements of a bearable existence.

The War

President Bush assembled significant support and a large coalition to attack bin Laden in Afghanistan after September 11. The NATO Council met and invoked Article 5 for the first time in its history, providing for all NATO states to come to the defense of the United States because it had been attacked. Two weeks later, the U.N. Security Council passed a resolution requiring all states to join the struggle against international terrorism.

Bush wanted to be sure that the military campaign would be effective. Secretary of Defense Donald Rumsfeld and the Joint Chiefs of Staff spent several weeks preparing for operations before beginning successful cruise-missile and fighter-bomber operations on October 7. The Americans mainly attacked Taliban-controlled cities such as Kabul, Kandahar and Jelalabad, as well as suspected al Qaeda bases in the mountains. British forces joined in the attack. To counter bin Laden's argument that the United States was the "murderer of Iraqis and Palestinians oppressed by Israel, America's friend," Bush pointed out that American forces had helped Muslim populations in Kuwait, northern Iraq, Somalia, Bosnia and Kosovo. He also worked closely with the government of Pakistan, where General Pervez Musharraf had seized power as president in a 1999 coup.[14]

A number of NATO members joined the U.S. attack against the Taliban and al Qaeda. Britain sent 4,200 troops as well as equipment; Germany sent 3,700; Canada sent 2,000; Australia sent 1,500. Italy and France also sent forces. Altogether, a total of 18 states either sent men and equipment, including naval and air units, to help destroy the Taliban and al Qaeda, or let American and other forces use their bases for operations.[15] The Northern Alliance, composed largely of Uzbek and Tajik tribal forces, seized Kabul in November and expelled the Taliban rulers.

Washington did not use NATO but kept total control. Many Pentagon officials remembered the difficulties they had experienced with General Wesley Clark as NATO commander during the Kosovo campaign (chapter 9) and did not want to have another semi-autonomous commander giving advice that the Pentagon did not want to hear. Highly trained U.S. Special Forces conducted many operations. On one of their operations, in the mountains of Tora Bora near the border with Pakistan, the Americans planned and hoped to kill or capture bin Laden. He escaped, reportedly because he had given his cell phone to a bodyguard whom the Americans then did follow and capture. But bin Laden was clearly on the run.

The American way of war did not always suit conditions in Afghanistan any more than in Kosovo and Serbia. War from the air, without a detailed knowledge of conditions on the ground, could and did kill innocent civilians in a war in which Taliban and al Qaeda soldiers did not wear distinguishing uniforms and often operated near small villages or in rugged terrain. All too often, American bombers flying at 15,000 or 30,000 feet relied on misleading electronic signals rather than on persons on the ground for targeting. In one case, U.S. fighters and helicopters attacked a wedding party and pursued civilians trying to run away from the scene. The U.S. aircraft may have thought that the spontaneous rifle fire customary at Afghan ceremonies had been intended to hit their aircraft. President Bush expressed "deep sadness" over the incident, although Rumsfeld pointed out that civilian casualties had to be expected when terrorists lived among civilians.[16]

The killings led at least some Afghans to question the value of having Americans as allies. They welcomed U.S. military actions against the Taliban but they felt that the Americans operated unfeelingly from the air and from distant killing machines. Pro-Western Afghans asked the Americans to be careful so that they would not lose the kind of political support they had first enjoyed.[17]

Afghan Political Reconstruction

Kofi Annan wanted to make sure that the political and humanitarian sides of the Afghanistan operation kept pace with the military. On October 15, he appointed Brahimi as his special representative for Afghanistan. He gave him "overall authority for the humanitarian, human rights and political endeavors of the United Nations in Afghanistan" and instructed him "to initiate preparations for transition to the post-conflict peace building phase in Afghanistan."[18] One month later, he appointed United Nations Development Program (UNDP) Administrator Mark Malloch Brown to lead and coordinate the recovery effort in Afghanistan under Brahimi's broad direction.

Brahimi worked for a political as well as economic transition. After a week of negotiations among various factions in Bonn, Germany, under his chairmanship, the Afghans on December 6, 2001, established an interim government with Hamid Karzai as interim head. Karzai, a prominent Pashtun tribal chief close to the old king, Zahir Shah, had fought the Taliban who had assassinated his father.

Karzai and the interim government assumed power in Kabul on December 22, 2001, but stated that they would assemble a *Loya Jirga*, a traditional Afghan council of tribal elders, to form a transitional government until elections for a permanent government could be held in two years. Brahimi worked with the transitional government to form an independent commission to convene the *Loya Jirga*. Many Afghans hoped for the return of their king, the 88-year-old Zahir Shah, who had ruled Afghanistan from 1933 to 1973 and who was living in exile in Italy.

Afghan politics still had a potentially ugly edge to them. In early April 2002, the Karzai government arrested several hundred members of an extreme Pashtun Islamic sect and charged them with plotting to overthrow the government. A month later, fighting erupted between rival Uzbek and Tajik groups in the northern city of Mazar-e-Sharif. In both cases, the government tried to make light of the incidents, but they showed that traditional tribal and personal rivalries lingered.[19]

The *Loya Jirga* itself reflected high hopes as well as ethnic tensions when it met from June 11 to 17, 2002. The choice of many delegates through a local selection process showed promise. So did the return of many Afghan intellectuals and professionals who had been in the West and who wanted to join in building a new government. But the former king, who had made a special effort to return in time for the meeting, could not assume a formal role because the Northern Alliance opposed him. Women emerged underrepresented. This led to protests from some groups, including Pashtuns, as well as from some expatriate professionals who had experienced Western democracy and wanted to see more of it at home.[20]

Karzai had done what he needed to do, carefully balancing the claims of various groups to give each its due and to keep them working with him. The Pashtuns might not be as heavily represented as their population would justify. On the other hand, they could rejoice that one of their own continued as interim leader. They could also be pleased that he had won the full backing of the United States and of Western donor states. Moreover, Karzai's foreign connections could give him a powerful hold over the government and even over other groups because of his control over the flow of funds.

Karzai chose to be careful. He moved very slowly. He took no extreme positions. And he saw the risks. In July 2002, only a few weeks after the *Loya Jirga*, he asked for a platoon of U.S. forces to provide security for him. Journalists speculated that he feared his defense minister and thus did not want to be protected by potentially disloyal Afghans.[21] Wherever the truth may lie, Karzai's request for U.S. security protection showed that Afghan political rivalries had not melted away in the glow of the *Loya Jirga* and the new government. The request appeared amply justified in September 2002, when Karzai only narrowly escaped assassination in one of three attempts on his life during 2002. When U.S. troops could not continue to protect him, Karzai hired a private American security firm.

Karzai and others saw reasons for hope. The Afghans had suffered 23 years of conflict and 2 million dead. They desperately wanted peace. No tribal leader would want the responsibility for starting a civil war, especially as no group could be sure who would win. The King returned to his royal palace after the *Loya Jirga* to add an element of stability, although the tribal rulers clearly did not want him to have political authority.

Nonetheless, 23 years of war had left a volatile and highly combustible mix. They had also left a sense that everybody needed to take care of their own before worrying about the country as a whole. Warlords did not like to take orders from Kabul. Karzai often found that his decrees did not carry in the countryside if he tried to move too far too fast, as when he tried to fire 15 provincial officials in November 2002. Brahimi and the U.S. government worked hard behind the scenes to assure continued warlord support for Karzai and the central government. American forces sometimes risked destabilizing Afghan unity because they cooperated closely with local warlords to arrange security for their bases and their soldiers. The NGO Human Rights Watch criticized the U.S. government for trying to win the friendship of some warlords by permitting them to engage in torture and other gross human rights violations.[22]

Karzai and Afghanistan as a whole had to hope, like the Bosnian and Kosovo governments in the Balkans, that time and the effects of peace and mutual discussions would widen their support. They could hope that a people tired of war and death might welcome a more stable existence in which they could lead a less precarious and more tranquil existence. For this, they would also want economic growth and some return to prosperity. They would need to have major infusions of outside help to rebuild their shattered infrastructure and to repair such ravages of war as disease, malnutrition and one of the lowest literacy rates in the world.

Bush also wanted to protect the United States better at home. He directed various U.S. intelligence and security agencies as well as the Immigration and Naturalization Service to make certain that terrorists could not enter the United States nor function there if they did enter. He created a new Department of Homeland Security under Tom Ridge to combine many agencies for better coordination.

An immediate effect, and a negative one, was much tighter control over the admission of refugees for resettlement—although none of the September 11 hijackers had been refugees. Due to the new security measures, the United States during 2002 admitted fewer than 30,000 refugees. This was the lowest number since the resettlement program had been started in 1980 and fell far behind the original plan to admit 70,000. Refugee admissions for 2003, not complete as of this writing, will remain at the same low level.[23]

More widely, the attacks of September 11 concentrated more public and government attention at home. With the nation having been attacked on its own soil for the first time in generations, most Americans wanted to make sure they were safe at home. Less attention and fewer civilian resources went abroad. The country did not turn isolationist but it concentrated more on domestic issues—and especially on security—than on any international happenings that did not need urgent attention.

Humanitarian Aid

As the American military campaign and Afghan political maneuvering continued toward the end of 2001 and beginning of 2002, the United Nations system and its affiliated NGOs wanted to feed the people of Afghanistan to get them through the war and the winter. NGOs had been forced to pull out their expatriate workers during the bombing campaign because the Taliban had threatened them. But the agencies had left their Afghan personnel in charge so that food and other relief shipments could continue as needed. Because of their long experience of working with only sporadic foreign support, Afghan aid personnel could work very effectively on their own. And Afghan NGOs, such as ACTED, continued their operations as before.

Karzai traveled to Washington and to other Western capitals to make his country's needs clear. At an initial Washington meeting, Western states pledged immediate aid and relief while promising long-term support once they knew what was needed. Powell stressed the importance of post-conflict relief and reconstruction aid.

Seeing a people at the edge of starvation at the beginning of winter, the appropriate U.N. and U.S. agencies as well as the NGO community began pouring in as much food as possible. Catherine Bertini, the head of the World Food Program (WFP), aimed for 2,000 tons a day. Andrew Natsios, Administrator of the U.S. Agency for International Development (AID), went to Afghanistan to assess the need and to support the WFP program. So did the European Union's Commissioner for Humanitarian Aid, Poul Nielson. Even in the midst of the bombing and fighting, dozens of Western and Afghan NGOs did what they could to help.

Ruud Lubbers, the U.N. High Commissioner for Refugees, sent truckloads of food and materials for tents to keep refugees and returning refugees as comfortable as possible during the upcoming winter. So did Brunson McKinley, the Director of the International Organization for Migration (IOM), which had become responsible for helping internally displaced persons in Afghanistan. Lubbers had earlier met with Taliban officers in Islamabad to ask them to stop looting relief supplies and to respect the safety of relief workers.

The WFP, the IOM, the Red Cross, CARE, the Iranian Red Crescent, Médecins sans Frontières, OXFAM, Save the Children and other agencies also sent food and other relief supplies. They sent it from Iran and Pakistan but could send only limited amounts from the north because the Uzbek government refused to open the "Friendship Bridge" that the Soviet Union had built. It was only on December 9, in response to a personal appeal from Secretary Powell during a visit to Tashkent, that the Uzbek government agreed to open the bridge.[24]

Not all relief supplies reached the needy. Local warlords seized some trucks or bribed their drivers to make off with some supplies. They also raided warehouses. But enough humanitarian aid in the form of food and blankets came through to make it possible for the Afghan people to survive the winter. Humanitarian organizations had long waited to take enough relief supplies into Afghanistan and did not want to miss the chance.

Although the immediate relief efforts for Afghans could help save countless lives, the leaders of the West and of the new Afghan government knew that the country needed long-term as well as short-term aid to overcome the effects of the long war. Bush promised that the United States would rebuild Afghanistan as it rebuilt Germany and Japan after World War II.[25]

Powell promised that the United States would avoid the mistakes of the 1990s. He and other Western foreign ministers agreed to rebuild the country and to help make Afghanistan a functioning state with a real economy and no more starvation. They consulted with Annan and the United Nations system to see what would need to be done.

The general situation needed no special studies. Afghanistan had endured a longer period of war than any European nation since the end of the Thirty Years' War in 1648. It had lost its civil society and its infrastructure, its institutions and its bureaucracy. Afghan illiteracy and infant mortality rates ranked among the highest in the world. Three years of drought had decimated its rural population. It needed and was beginning to receive humanitarian help of the most immediate kind but it also needed long-term development aid. It had to be rebuilt from the ground up to become a functioning member of the global economy.

Afghanistan had few all-weather roads and almost no bridges, water or sanitation systems, schools or hospitals, functioning office buildings or undamaged housing areas. One American correspondent, looking around at Afghan cities and at the countryside, said that "we might as well be doing nation-building on the moon."[26]

Malloch Brown and James Wolfensohn, the president of the World Bank, jointly outlined the reconstruction aid needed to bring Afghanistan into the modern world. They estimated that the country would require $1.73 billion for 2003 and $10.21 billion for the next five years, not counting immediate humanitarian support. Malloch Brown and Wolfensohn thought that humanitarian agencies and NGOs should supply short-term help. They expressed the hope that some expenses, like salaries for teachers, doctors and civil servants, could be paid from Afghanistan's own funds once the national economy recovered.[27]

To encourage action, Malloch Brown and Wolfensohn called a donor meeting in Tokyo January 20–21, 2002. At that meeting, they stressed the importance of long-term economic aid to help avert another Afghan humanitarian tragedy. A number of major states made important pledges (in millions of dollars):

- Iran (over the next five years): 560
- Japan (over the next two and a half years): 500
- The European Union (for the first year): 495
- The United States (for the first year): 297
- Saudi Arabia (over three years): 220
- Pakistan (over five years): 100
- India (line of credit): 100
- Great Britain (in 2002): 86
- South Korea (over two and a half years): 45

Smaller states, like the Scandinavians, also pledged support, although they contributed through the European Union as well as directly. No meaningful totals could be calculated because the pledges covered different time periods, but the pledges could have met basic needs during the next few years.[28]

The Afghan government found itself very disappointed when aid deliveries during 2002 and 2003 did not match pledges. In some cases, the appropriations process took longer than expected, as did designs for projects to be funded; in others, pledging states changed their minds when their economies slowed down; in yet others, pledging states found that their pledges had to be used for emergency aid rather than for reconstruction. As of the end of 2002, only $365 million had gone to reconstruction whereas $1.16 billion had gone to emergency humanitarian aid. The latter had to have the higher priority because it gave Afghans food, medical attention and shelter, but Afghanistan also needed roads and other infrastructure. Some of the more sophisticated Afghans noted that Western aid to their country amounted to only $42 a person over five years, whereas the West had given Kosovo, East Timor and Rwanda more than five times as much per capita.[29]

Karzai complained that foreign governments and NGOs spent much more on their own workers than on Afghans and that they seemed in more of a hurry to build up their offices than to get their work done. He said that the agencies had brought 2,000 staffers into Kabul and were paying them large salaries but were not yet doing enough outside Kabul where more was needed. He obviously needed to get early action outside Kabul to try to establish his authority and the image of a government that acted for its people. Some Afghans complained that U.S. action did not match U.S. rhetoric.[30]

International NGOs expressed particular frustration because they agreed with Karzai that they needed to work fast to give Afghans a sense of progress. But they complained about lack of security after aid workers suffered several attacks over the summer of 2002. They also complained that Afghanistan still made more money from the opium trade than any other export, just as Kosovo continued to make money from its heroin and prostitution trade instead of concentrating on growing food. Powell noted that by the fall of 2002 less than two-thirds of the promised aid had been delivered.[31]

The debates showed that the political and humanitarian impact of aid would not arrive in a hurry. Afghans would continue to feel cold and hungry, like victims of war, even after peace had arrived. But they could at least rejoice that they were not being killed as before.

Refugee Return

Ruud Lubbers and many relief agency heads had feared in the fall of 2001 that the bombing campaign and the intensified war would drive even more Afghans into Pakistan and Iran by the hundreds of thousands. They launched a special "donor alert" on September 27 to warn the international community that as many as 1 million Afghans might flee to Pakistan and another half million to Iran and to other states bordering Afghanistan. Lubbers set up special receiving centers in Pakistan. The U.S. Committee on Refugees, a Washington-based NGO that concentrated on protection as well as relief for refugees, warned the U.S. government that refugees should not be forced to return to Afghanistan in the middle of a military campaign. Like Lubbers, it feared being unprepared for a repetition of the 1999 flight from Kosovo. The U.S. government gave special emergency funds to a number of agencies to help refugees and other Afghans fleeing the war.[32]

Lubbers' fears proved to be exaggerated, in part because both the Pakistani and the Iranian governments refused to let refugees enter and in part because—as in Kosovo—many persons fled the bombing by hiding in the hills instead of leaving the country. Afghans also did not expect the military campaign to last very long. Therefore, fewer refugees than expected crossed the borders.[33] But Lubbers still felt he had to make a special appeal to Musharraf to let the neediest refugees, such as women, children and the aged, enter Pakistan. As in many wars, the humanitarians (like their charges) were trapped in the middle.

Perhaps 150,000 refugees fled to Pakistan, and they did so only by maneuvering over very forbidding terrain. As for Iran, the Iranian government set up reception centers and camps on the Afghan side of the border and worked with the International Organization for Migration and many international and Afghan NGOs to help the displaced Afghans there instead of letting them enter Iran.

The return of long-term Afghan refugees from Pakistan, Iran and elsewhere proved to be just as unpredictable. As in Kosovo, the U.N. High Commissioner for Refugees found it impossible to predict how many might return and how fast. His estimate came in low, as had happened in Kosovo. He had thought that perhaps 400,000 might return in the first wave during spring and summer 2002 and that close to 1 million might return in 2002 as a whole. But the number of returnees rose well above that estimate, with almost 2 million returning during the year as a whole.

Many Afghans wanted to get back quickly to rebuild their old houses before winter and to plant crops before the snows came. UNHCR gave each returnee family $100. But many families who wanted to return to their traditional homes found conditions in the countryside too insecure or still inhospitable. Hundreds of thousands had to remain in Kabul and its surroundings. There, relief—consisting mainly of food, blankets and basic building materials—could be delivered easily, and most returning refugees suffered no undue hardship.[34] A number of refugees did not want to stay in overcrowded conditions in Kabul. An estimated 100,000 quietly went back to Pakistan and Iran so as to try again in 2003 or later.[35]

The prospects for return to Afghanistan posed wrenching dilemmas for many middle-class Afghan refugees who had fled during the 1980s and had started careers in the United States or Western Europe. They felt the tug of home but they might have established themselves as lawyers or doctors in the West. They believed they could have an essential contribution to make to a new Afghanistan, and Karzai had appealed in those terms to the Afghan community leaders whom he had met during his visits to Washington and other Western cities. On the other hand, they had to think of their families and careers.

McKinley and the IOM established a special program to encourage the return of refugees from the West, and hundreds did return. They helped get the new Afghanistan off to a running start. But many other exiled Afghans might not make a definitive decision for years and would need at least one or two visits to Kabul before they would make that decision.

Peacekeeping Lite

Karzai had argued with the U.S. government from the beginning of the Afghan campaign about the size and mission of a peacekeeping force for Afghanistan. He began asking in December 2001 for major U.N. peacekeeping contingents to come to Afghanistan. He wanted peacekeepers throughout Afghanistan as a whole, not only in Kabul. Karzai even made his request in person to the U.N. Security Council. He believed that a U.N. peacekeeping force could bring security and could help unite Afghanistan. He especially wanted American troops among the peacekeepers because the Afghan people would have a better image of the Americans if they could see American soldiers in person instead of bombing from the sky. Brahimi supported Karzai's plea.

Western relief agencies, afraid that factional fighting and al Qaeda remnants could interfere with humanitarian aid shipments, also asked for U.N. peacekeepers. Officials of such NGOs as the International Rescue Committee and the Women's Commission for Refugee Women and Children came to Washington to plead that case.[36]

But President Bush did not want U.N. peacekeepers all over Afghanistan. Nor did he want to assign American soldiers to such duties. Neither did Rumsfeld, who thought that it would detract from the soldiers' readiness for combat duty. Washington officials derisively described peacekeeping as the kind of "nation-building" that the U.S. government resolutely rejected for Afghanistan. And Washington remained mistrustful of the United Nations, opposing U.N. "blue helmet" engagement in Afghanistan. If there was to be any force at all, it was to be a force of Western coalition troops and confined to Kabul itself. Karzai appealed for even token contingents to other cities as a sign of Western commitment to a united and peaceful Afghanistan and to make it more difficult for competing tribes and warlords to go their own way. Annan and Brahimi supported Karzai's plea for a nationwide peacekeeping force. They recalled that the West's peacekeeping efforts in Bosnia and Kosovo had paid off, with most forces able to leave after a few years.

Rumsfeld feared that peacekeeping throughout all of Afghanistan would require a major force of tens of thousands, perhaps as many as 100,000. He also feared that U.S. involvement in such a force could lead to significant American casualties. The U.S. military wanted no repeat of Somalia. They argued hard against what they termed "mission creep." Bush also let it be known that he regarded the war against terrorism as a global campaign, with Afghanistan only one part of it, and that U.S. troop commitments should be flexible.[37]

Despite these debates, the Western coalition did begin to form a small peacekeeping force consisting of the military contingents that several states had sent to Afghanistan. The force, called the International Security Assistance Force (ISAF), had about 8,000 soldiers, mainly British, French and German. Britain took command of the force in January 2002, after the Afghans had retaken Kabul. American troops did not join the force. ISAF soldiers had no U.N. mission and did not wear blue helmets. But they did have the authority to operate under their own command, independent of the Afghan government.[38]

Instead of an international force, Bush and Rumsfeld supported a program for training and equipping an Afghan national army of 80,000 that would be able to patrol and secure the entire country. American Special Forces as well as British and French troops began training that army. Germany in turn started to train an Afghan police force of 70,000. But the training programs proceeded painfully slowly. The Afghan army would have only about 10,000 men by the fall of 2003, plainly not enough to control the entire country, and many recruits left after basic training to seek more money elsewhere. None of the allied or Afghan leaders expected the army to be strong enough to perform nationwide peacekeeping duties before 2005 or 2006.[39] Washington said that it would send aid to equip and to pay the force, but Rumsfeld added that he expected other states to help to pay the bill.[40]

In accordance with earlier plans, Britain gave up command of ISAF in July 2002. It also withdrew many of its forces as the campaign against al Qaeda appeared to be winding down. Turkey took over command on June 20, 2002, and Germany followed later. Both assigned additional soldiers to the force to compensate for the British withdrawal. The Americans continued to insist that the force should not and would not operate outside Kabul. The U.S. intelligence agencies and special forces thought that separate arrangements with local warlords would help more in the war against al Qaeda than the Kabul government could.

Bush and Rumsfeld began to change their approach after the security situation did not improve during 2002. But they still did not want U.N. peacekeepers. Instead, the Pentagon began to deploy an American civil affairs force that might be able to fan out across major Afghan population centers.

General Richard Myers, Chairman of the U.S. Joint Chiefs of Staff, said this meant moving to "the next phase," which he called "the reconstruction phase." During that phase, several hundred American military officers would deploy to Afghanistan and would be assigned in small contingents to major Afghan cities in order to coordinate U.S. reconstruction efforts. They would not be peacekeepers in the traditional sense but would combine some security, military and political roles. They would, Myers pledged, not engage in "nation-building."

Myers said security would be left to local forces, presumably warlord armies, until the national army could cover the entire country, although the 7,000 American soldiers would continue to keep up their search for remnants of al Qaeda.[41] And the Americans continued to oppose a United Nations presence, which Karzai again requested on a visit to New York in late fall 2002. This left U.S. forces with conflicting priorities, primarily fighting al Qaeda and secondarily keeping Afghanistan at peace.

Afghanistan would not have a nation-wide U.N. peacekeeping force. NATO would have the peacekeeping task, but only around Kabul.

Rafael Robilard, the spokesman for 77 American and other humanitarian NGOs operating in Afghanistan, voiced their concern about the U.S. military civil affairs role. He said that the NGOs feared that it would mean military coordination of relief efforts, meaning that their humanitarian work might become part of a military campaign. It might expose them to attack and would also make Afghans look upon them less favorably than before. They would no longer be humanitarians but extensions of the military. It might pose problems for non-American NGOs who had come to serve a common humanity but not the American military.[42]

American civil affairs contingents raised a political problem as well, which U.N. troops would not have raised. Although the Pentagon stated that the U.S. forces would act in civil affairs roles, not traditional tactical military roles, Afghans and neighboring governments—such as the Iranian—might well regard them as a strategic U.S. presence. They would either welcome or oppose them as they would any other foreign force. The civil affairs officers introduced a potentially sensitive political concern that U.N. forces would not have introduced. They also appeared poised to perform more than humanitarian roles. And they would not be as effective as a U.N. peacekeeping force in helping Afghanistan return to a normal life.

Without an army and without peacekeepers, the Afghan government cannot control the country. Karzai is, at least for the moment, the mayor of Kabul, with the remainder of the country governed by traditional warlords whose main livelihood comes from smuggling, opium production, and local taxes. The NGOs often fear for their own safety, especially after an ICRC staff member was killed in April and after American and German soldiers were killed in May and June 2003. With international aid funding cut and with many resources being drawn to Iraq, Afghanistan may again fall a victim to neglect. The West might repeat its mistake of the 1990s, neglecting the future of Afghanistan as a state while Western forces concentrate on the capture of Osama bin Laden and his al Qaeda and Taliban associates.

In all the discussion about Afghanistan, Americans and others sometimes appear to be forgetting that Afghanistan is a country, not a battleground. And that the Afghans are a people who deserve to have a chance at reconstruction and at a normal life. How that normal life will come, and when, remains highly uncertain. But it will clearly not come soon. In the meantime, the Taliban and al Qaeda will have many chances to return.

The War of the Worlds

Afghanistan has become the epicenter of a new kind of war, although that war will range much further than any one country or even any one continent. It is a war against terror but also a war between two styles of sovereignty: a traditional Western style, which possesses people, land, currency and armed forces; and another style, a sovereignty of the cave, which reaches for deranged and perhaps desperate minds.

Al Qaeda differs from other terrorist movements in its global organization and its global aims. Most terrorists want local and often negotiable goals, be it independence, autonomy or some other immediate objectives. They normally end their terror when their political purposes are met and when those who support the terrorists enter a political process, whether in Ireland, in Kosovo, in the Middle East or in the former colonial states of Africa and Asia. But al Qaeda is not fighting for liberation. It has a wider purpose, more deadly and more pernicious than others.

Never has there been a more uneven contest. On the one side, the most powerful sovereign state the world has ever known—democratic, progressive and relatively open to the world. On the other, a self-proclaimed sovereignty with no governing power—hierarchical, conservative and sealed off from the world. It should be no contest. And yet it is, because neither can yet destroy the other. America cannot be defeated in battle. Al Qaeda cannot be defeated in the mind. American forces can strike al Qaeda at will but they must first find it. Al Qaeda can strike only rarely but its targets are all easily seen.

The West and especially the United States may need to fight a long and difficult war, well beyond Afghanistan. America and the West must assess their strategy thoughtfully. Finally, America and the West must not ignore or dismiss two of their principal potential allies, the peoples of the world and their humanitarian spirit. Those allies helped America and the West win the Cold War and will be at least equally needed in the war against terror. But American political and military leaders do not yet recognize that.

THIRTEEN

HUMANITARIAN CARE
FOR WAR IN IRAQ

PRESIDENT GEORGE W. BUSH ON MARCH 19, 2003, ordered American and coalition forces to attack Iraq. He had decided to depose the Iraqi dictator Saddam Hussein, to seize and to destroy Saddam's suspected weapons of mass destruction, and to convert Iraq into a peaceloving modern democratic state. Bush planned for a short war of two to three weeks and for a longer but still limited period of American administration over Iraq.

Bush had already made his decision to attack Iraq in the weeks after September 11, 2001. Most of his senior advisers, and particularly Vice President Dick Cheney and Defense Secretary Donald Rumsfeld, warned him that terrorists might use Saddam's weapons of mass destruction for an attack on the United States. They even considered the attack on Iraq more urgent than the campaign against al Qaeda, although they often linked the two.

Bush's father, President George H. W. Bush, had not tried to remove Saddam in 1991 after U.S. forces had expelled Iraqi forces from Kuwait (chapter 11). Instead, he had called upon the Shiite Muslims of southern Iraq and the Kurdish people of northern Iraq to rise up against Saddam. But he had not helped the Shiites or Kurds and Saddam's Revolutionary Guard divisions had slaughtered the insurgents. Over 200,000 Shiites had fled to Iran. Kurdish forces had tried to flee into Turkey but the Turkish army had blocked them at the border.

Bush had then protected the Kurds as "internally displaced persons" in Iraq and had carved out a special zone for them along the Turkish border. He had also asked Mrs. Sadako Ogata, the U.N. High Commissioner for Refugees, to give them legal protection and to distribute relief supplies to them. To help protect the Kurds and the Shiites against the Iraqi air force, Bush had instituted protected areas—called "no-fly" zones—in northern and southern Iraq. American and British fighter jets patrolled those zones to prevent Iraqi aircraft from attacking Kurds and Shiites from the air.

The U.N. Security Council had then passed a number of resolutions forbidding Saddam from developing or deploying weapons of mass destruction. The resolutions also imposed tough economic sanctions against Iraq. They forced Saddam to export Iraqi oil only through an "oil-for-food" program administered by the United Nations and through a government-controlled distribution system. They limited approved imports to food and essential humanitarian supplies. The sanctions curtailed most economic activity in Iraq but evidently did not weaken Saddam's control. They even reinforced Saddam because he administered food distribution and could use it to dispense favor or punishment as he wished.

The "oil-for-food" program did not provide fully enough nourishment for the Iraqi people. By 2003, when George W. Bush launched his attack on Iraq, chronic malnutrition affected one third of the people of Iraq, including children. The country had no reserves of food or other humanitarian resources. Hospitals could not get enough medicines for the people nor keep enough trained doctors and nurses. Moreover, Iraq's infrastructure gradually eroded because it could import few non-food and non-medical items.[1]

On the advice of Secretary of State Colin Powell and British Prime Minister Tony Blair, Bush decided to try to persuade the U.N. Security Council to approve an attack on Iraq. He asserted that Saddam's failure to comply fully with a U.N. inspection regime for weapons of mass destruction represented a serious breach of Iraq's international obligations and justified an attack. Blair particularly wanted U.N. approval of an attack because he thought that would help persuade a skeptical British public opinion to support a war against Iraq. He also hoped it would help legitimize an attack, which many states would otherwise perceive as unprovoked aggression.

Security Council members accepted the American and British arguments against Saddam's behavior but France, Germany and Russia did not want to grant explicit approval for an invasion. Therefore, Council members fudged the language. On November 8, 2002, the Council unanimously approved Resolution 1441, which threatened "serious consequences" if Iraq did not comply with Security Council resolutions supporting full inspection for weapons of mass destruction.[2] That resolution set the clock ticking toward war without specifically mentioning it.

Hans Blix, the principal U.N. weapons inspector for Iraq, reported several times to the Security Council in subsequent months. He repeatedly told the Council that Iraq was not cooperating fully with the inspectors but was complying in part, and that he had no current evidence of weapons of mass destruction although

Iraq had possessed them earlier.[3] This gave ammunition to both sides, and in retrospect appears to have been accurate.

Pentagon civilians, especially Deputy Secretary Paul Wolfowitz and senior consultant Richard Perle, scoffed openly at Blix's reports. They said that U.N. inspections were not tough enough to find the weapons of mass destruction that they knew to be there. But French President Jacques Chirac and German Chancellor Gerhard Schröder said that the inspectors were preventing any weapons production by their sheer presence and should be allowed to continue their work. Rumsfeld, determined to attack Iraq by early 2003, ordered U.S. troops into the Gulf region. Blair sent British forces.

Tony Blair then wanted to get another Security Council resolution specifically authorizing an attack on Iraq. He again needed it to persuade an increasingly skeptical British public.[4] Bush, who had called Resolution 1441 the "final test," acceded to Blair's wishes although he did not think he needed another authorization for war.

Blair's wish proved to be a mistake. Chirac and Schröder dug in their heels. Russian President Vladimir Putin joined them. They offered some compromises that would have delayed the invasion of Iraq by a month to give the inspectors more time to find weapons, but Rumsfeld did not want to delay an invasion because the onset of summer temperatures in Iraq would complicate military operations. Rumsfeld, angry that France, Germany and Russia blocked U.S. wishes, derided them as "old Europe." He praised Poland and other Eastern European states, which favored war against Iraq, as "new Europe."

Powell lobbied hard to win votes for a resolution authorizing war. Chirac lobbied hard against it and even threatened a veto. Dominique de Villepin, the French Foreign Minister, travelled to Africa to win the votes of undecided African Security Council members. Transatlantic relations hit a new low.

When all the Security Council lobbying had ended, Washington and London could not muster the nine votes needed for a Council majority.[5] They called off their effort to get a second resolution. As in Kosovo, the Americans would have to attack without U.N. authorization. This time they could not even claim NATO support, although many NATO states permitted some use of their facilities. But Bush and Blair decided to go ahead as a separate coalition with a few minor allies. Within a week, their forces were bombing and invading Iraq.

The Anglo-American coalition labored under a colonialist legacy. Great Britain, which had carved Iraq out of the former Ottoman Empire after World War I in order to unite the oil-rich Kurdish region around Mosul and Kirkuk with the Persian Gulf port of Basra, had been a hated colonial master there from 1921 until a military revolution in 1958. The United States had become identified with British policies because of their joint control over the Iraq Petroleum Company, which had developed and exploited Iraq's oil fields. Although many Iraqis would welcome the removal of Saddam Hussein's cruel dictatorship, they would not welcome a return to anything resembling colonial rule.

Tommy Franks and the American Attack

Bush and Rumsfeld designed a military campaign based on small elite forces and on the American advantage in technology. The American military, under orders from U.S. Central Command leader General Tommy Franks, moved quickly along carefully selected routes on which they could apply overwhelming force in decisive battles. They functioned with blinding speed, overwhelming air superiority and a mobility that the Iraqis could not match. At Rumsfeld's direction, U.S. and British forces remained small and highly professional. Bush and Rumsfeld did not want to send a large lumbering army.[6]

Bush did not want to bomb civilian targets such as bridges and power stations, as the U.S. Air Force had done in Serbia during the Kosovo war. He wanted to win the support of the Iraqis over the long run. American air and naval air forces tried hard to avoid excessive civilian casualties. The Pentagon selected its targets with the greatest of care. In that sense, the bombing of Iraq was more "humanitarian" than the bombing of Serbia. New precision bombs and missiles made it possible. Bush specifically commented that: "In this new age of warfare, we can target a regime, not a nation."[7]

The U.S. Army and the Marines also tried to avoid civilian casualties in their battle plans. They, as well as their British coalition partners, did not at first go directly into city centers where street fighting would kill masses of Iraqis—as well as coalition soldiers. Instead, they first concentrated on military camps and targets. Their attacks did cause some civilian casualties, but fewer than they had caused during the first Gulf war of 1991 as well as fewer than in Serbia.

Coalition ground forces fought few pitched battles. Iraqi forces—including the vaunted Republican Guard divisions that had been expected to fight to the last man—appeared to melt away before the American and British onslaught. Thousands of Iraqi soldiers surrendered as prisoners of war. Most of the others appeared to have gone home, taking their weapons with them.

On May 1, President Bush landed on the flight deck of the U.S. aircraft carrier *Abraham Lincoln* and announced that military operations in Iraq had ended. American and British forces had rid the world of Saddam Hussein and had liberated Iraq. Bush, Rumsfeld and other American leaders were confident that they were now on the way to a peaceful and democratic Iraq.

The real problems in Iraq began when the official coalition military campaign had ended. The small number of coalition forces could win a war but they could not conduct an occupation. Moreover, neither American nor British forces had been trained for civil administration. They had not expected such a total collapse of the Iraqi government and military. They needed to establish and administer an occupation regime, and they found that Iraqi administrative structures did not work for them as they had hoped. They had set out to destroy the Iraqi regime and found that they had succeeded all too well.

Rumsfeld had made general plans for a military government under General Franks as victorious military commander. He had planned to appoint a civil administrator, retired Lt. General Jay Garner, with a "consultative council" to be composed of Iraqi expatriate civilians who had opposed Saddam Hussein's regime and who had close ties to such Pentagon civilians as Wolfowitz and Perle. Garner had planned to install separate regional administrators for northern, southern and central Iraq. A retired U.S. Ambassador, George Ward, was to oversee humanitarian aid and would coordinate NGOs providing aid.[8]

Blair, who still hoped to gain some legitimacy for the war, wanted the United Nations to administer Iraq or at least to play an important role in the administration. He tried to persuade Bush of this at Camp David on March 27. He had even told journalists during a discussion of "post-conflict issues" that "there is no doubt at all that the United Nations has got to be closely involved in this process." Bush, still furious about the U.S. defeat in the Security Council, overruled him, announcing that he would only let the United Nations coordinate humanitarian programs.[9]

Kofi Annan feared a deep rift between the United States and the Arab world if Bush insisted that the United States or a Western coalition should occupy Iraq, especially if the occupation lasted for a long time. It would remind too many Arabs of the earlier British occupation. He thought a U.N. role, as in Afghanistan, Kosovo or East Timor, would actually serve Western interests. But several American journalists attacked Annan for alleged anti-American bias. He retreated, disappointed that the Americans had not understood that he had wanted to help them as well as the Iraqis.[10]

Bush and Rumsfeld wanted to keep control in American and British hands. They had little faith in the United Nations. But neither did they want U.S. forces to become bogged down in a drawn-out occupation or in peacekeeping. The U.S. Army had closed its Peacekeeping Institute at the Army War College in Carlisle, Pennsylvania, after Rumsfeld had become Secretary of Defense. Neither he nor Bush have wanted American troops to do nation-building.

The Pentagon did not want to send many U.S. forces to occupy Iraq. General Eric Shinseki, then chief of staff of the U.S. Army, had told a U.S. Congressional committee in February 2003 that an American occupation of Iraq would require several hundred thousand soldiers. Wolfowitz and Rumsfeld had denounced Shinseki for giving such a high figure. Wolfowitz had denounced Shinseki's figures as "wildly off the mark" and had said that the war and occupation would be a "cake-walk." They had thus committed themselves to a much smaller occupation force. They wanted to keep it well below 150,000 and had first hoped to bring it down to 30,000 by the end of 2003.[11]

Tommy Franks was not as good at winning the peace as he had been at winning the war, especially because he did not have enough forces for an occupation. As soon as the military campaigns ended, Iraq imploded into chaos. Looters roamed the streets, robbing everything in sight. They stole precious Mesopotamian antiquities from museums. They stole motors and wiring from most electrical installations. They looted ministries, business offices and private homes in a frenzy of theft and destruction. They also looted hospitals, removing vital medical equipment as well as supplies that the ICRC and others had stored to help war victims. The ICRC departed from its usual neutrality to appeal for American military protection of hospitals and clinics, but U.S. forces could not provide it. The American forces also ignored Iraqi civil servant appeals for help in running their offices and protecting their equipment.[12]

Under the Geneva Conventions of 1949, the American and British occupiers had the responsibility for maintaining civil order. But they had not prepared for that burden. They had not expected to act as police officers. They did not even go out on the streets. American civilian and military officials would not travel around Baghdad or beyond except under heavy military escort—which was not always available. They could not deal with the deteriorating situation and often did not even know what was happening outside their offices. They clearly had not prepared to administer Iraq and found themselves unable to cope with the rapidly deteriorating situation.

The Iraqi people, who at first welcomed the Americans for deposing Saddam, turned against the occupiers. They criticized the occupation forces for permitting the breakdown in security and they held Garner and his office responsible for the looting and widespread mayhem. They denounced Iraqi exiles sent to Baghdad by the Pentagon as puppets. They complained about lack of electricity, water, sanitation and other basic services. Some began to organize themselves to resist U.S. and British occupation forces.

The humanitarian aid that could have helped to change the mood of the Iraqi people was slow in coming because the U.S. government had not yet ended the sanctions regime that prevented American NGOs from functioning in Iraq (see below). American and other NGOs complained that the U.S. military were trying to do things that the NGOs could do better and faster, and that the military were not even consulting the NGOs or other international civilians.[13]

Throughout May and June, the Americans appeared to be losing control of Baghdad as mobs of looters, rioters and protesters dominated the streets. Members of Saddam's forces and intelligence services who had melted into the population began to ambush and attack American and British forces. By the end of July 2003, over 50 American and British servicemen had died in the occupation. An American general said that "the war has not ended."[14]

General John Abizaid, who replaced General Franks as head of the U.S. Central Command, in July blamed the deaths of coalition forces on members of Saddam Hussein's Baath party as well as on radical anti-American Islamist and criminal elements. He said that much of Iraq was stable and that American and other coalition forces would defeat the radicals and other opponents over time by energetic patrolling.[15] But the Iraqi resistance continued.

A June 24 incident in which Iraqi civilians killed six British soldiers illustrated the difficulties that the coalition faced in trying to establish peace. The British had been conducting house-to-house searches for weapons in a town near Basra when a mob of angry Iraqis set upon them and killed them in a police station. The Iraqis had resented the intrusion into their homes and family quarters. One man said: "You cannot forget that we are Shia Muslims. You cannot come into my house and see my wife."[16]

American and British forces were trained and sent to Iraq to fight a war. They knew how to shoot and to kill. But they were not trained as occupiers. Rumsfeld did not want to send military police battalions or trained peacekeepers. In particular, he did not want to ask the United Nations to run the kind of operations it had successfully managed elsewhere. But it became increasingly clear that the United States and its coalition partners might need more force to occupy a nation of 24 million than to defeat an army of 240,000.

Coalition troops became increasingly isolated from the Iraqi people and increasingly frustrated by their new role. They did not know how to deal with a sullen civilian population or how to conduct searches without offending people. The American and British forces, like the Iraqi people, began paying the price for this after May 1.[17]

Paul Bremer as Occupier

To turn the situation around, Bush appointed a former ambassador, L. Paul Bremer III, who had long served as a terrorism expert in the State Department and in private life. Bremer assumed the direction of the occupation authority, the Coalition Provisional Administration (CPA). He acted quickly and forcefully to give a sense of direction and command. But he made clear that he would not soon allow an Iraqi civilian government. He first wanted a new constitution, which might mean that there would be no Iraq government until 2004 at the earliest. In the meantime, he did comply with a U.N. resolution to establish an interim consultative and administrative body by appointing a governing council of 25 Iraqis who had no operational authority but could do some political consultation.

To prevent the coalition forces from becoming completely overwhelmed, the Pentagon asked about 70 states to send forces to join the occupation. More than two dozen states promised to send about 20,000 peacekeepers, with perhaps another 10,000 expected from other states. They would form what the Pentagon called "international divisions." As of this writing, a British division and a Polish division are to take over some responsibilities in central and southern Iraq. The Czech Republic, Denmark, El Salvador, Honduras, Italy, Lithuania, The Netherlands, New Zealand, Norway, Portugal, Romania, Spain and The Ukraine are to make contributions. The Pentagon still expects some from Australia, Bulgaria and Turkey. But a number of major states, including France, Germany, India and Russia, said that they would only consider sending troops after a U.N. resolution mandating a peacekeeping force. They might serve in such a U.N. force, but not in a Western occupation. Almost all the additional troops will need financial support, totaling perhaps $250 million, from the United States. Moreover, that level of foreign contingents will still not permit a drawdown of U.S. forces to the 30,000 level.[18]

The occupation of Iraq differs fundamentally from the peacekeeping operations that have generally been successful in the Balkans and in some other areas. Mainly, the occupying force has no international legitimacy. It is not under the United Nations, the European Union or NATO. Instead, it is an ill-disguised American-dominated force with a few minor coalition members supporting the Americans but hardly equal in influence—especially as Washington is paying their costs. Only Great Britain has a voice remotely matching that of the United States, although it remains possible that one or another major state may decide to send large forces and to seek appropriate influence if a formula can be negotiated.

This presents the Americans with a dilemma. On the one hand, they find it convenient to exercise unchallenged authority. Bremer reports directly to Rumsfeld, who likes to give his own orders and who appears to despise the United Nations. On the other hand, the Americans cannot shake their uncomfortable image as foreign occupiers. Nobody can easily accuse the United Nations or the European Union of colonial ambitions in the Balkans or elsewhere. But it is easy to accuse the Americans, especially in the Middle East and in a land where oil is the primary export. Iraqis will not believe, no matter how often and how sincerely they may be told, that Washington sent its forces to Iraq, and is now keeping them there, for the sake of the Iraqi people.

Bremer continued to argue, however, that the occupation would ultimately succeed. At the end of June 2003, after a visit to northern Iraq, he said:

It's just been damn hard. It's going to take a lot of money. It's going to take time. It's going to take dedicated people. We're just going to have to keep plugging away at it.[19]

With this, he voiced a determined commitment to continue the occupation and to try to transform it over time into a successful Iraqi government. Neither Bush nor Rumsfeld had wanted to do nation-building, but by the summer of 2003 they were doing just that.

The humanitarians would also have plenty to do for a long time, under difficult conditions. If the U.S. forces did not have the "cakewalk" that Wolfowitz had promised them, neither would the humanitarians.

Humanitarian Help for the People of Iraq

Iraq had stood for years at the edge of economic and humanitarian collapse although it had once possessed a modern economy and a modern society. Ever since the end of the Gulf War in 1991 and the introduction of U.N. and U.S. sanctions against Saddam Hussein, the Western world had systematically curtailed Iraq's access to most of the things that make life productive and livable. Even the "oil-for-food" program, which had given Iraq an opening to buy some food, medicines and other essentials, could not reduce the effect of the sanctions on ordinary Iraqis. Western limitations on what Iraq could buy, combined with Saddam's own manipulations, had left most Iraqis destitute, unable to get the kinds of medicines or other supplies they needed. For them, life had become almost unbearable.

The Iraqi people had become very vulnerable to the effects of any kind of disruption. Neither the people nor the government had any reserves.[20] Half of the people had no job. Most had sold whatever they possessed merely in order to get by. UNICEF believed that as many as a quarter of all children suffered from severe malnutrition. Many who had cheered the Americans had done so not only because they wanted to see the end of the regime but also because they wanted an end to misery and sanctions.

Expecting the American attack, the Iraqi government had used the "oil-for-food" program to distribute extra rations so that each household had at least a month of food in reserve. The World Food Program had also prepared for war by asking for special donations to be able to place reserve stocks near Iraq for immediate distribution during or after a war.

Medicine represented a more serious problem. Because of the U.N. sanctions and especially because of the even more severe U.S. sanctions, Western NGOs could not bring medicine or hospital equipment and supplies into Iraq. The "oil-for-food" program provided only the barest necessities and contained no provision for the kind of reserves that would be needed to help victims of war. Iraqi hospitals lacked virtually everything. The International Committee of the Red Cross had tried to maintain adequate supplies despite the sanctions, but it had not been able to do so. Nor could it import all the hospital equipment that a modern state would normally have. UNICEF pre-positioned emergency health kits for 900,000 Iraqis but nobody knew if that would suffice in war.

United Nations agencies began to sound the alarm by December 2002, as American preparations for war became ever more obvious. Kofi Annan warned the United States and the United Kingdom that under international law they would be responsible for the well-being of the people in the areas that they had conquered. The members of the U.N. Humanitarian Liaison Working Group tried to evaluate what would be needed to prevent a humanitarian disaster and to permit humanitarian agencies to meet immediate needs.

The humanitarian agencies initially asked for $2.2 billion for aid to Iraq. Donors met about $900 million and the "oil-for-food" program covered most of the remainder. In June 2003, the agencies asked for an additional $259 million, an amount that is also likely to be met.[21]

But the American government did not want to anticipate too much. Bush and Rumsfeld did not want to make the costs of a potential war clear in advance. They also expected a short war. Thus they did not provide any reserves of pre-funding, promising only to review the needs once they could assess them more clearly.

Mary McClymont, the president of InterAction, the Washington-based association of American and international NGOs, used a letter to President Bush on December 20, 2002, to voice the worries of the humanitarian community about the imminent war. She particularly stressed four NGO principles:

- Unhindered humanitarian access to those affected by the violence;
- Military respect for the independence and impartiality of humanitarian agencies;
- Civilian direction of any relief activities carried out or supported by the U.S. government; and
- Giving the United Nations the responsibility for coordinating humanitarian activities in Iraq.[22]

InterAction had organized an Iraq working group and wanted to prepare to coordinate humanitarian aid.

Humanitarian agencies particularly objected to the prospect of working under a military command. In the Balkans and in East Timor, they had worked under the general guidance of a U.N. senior representative. This gave them a neutral and clearly humanitarian status. It made it possible for them to operate everywhere and made them impartial in any conflicts that might arise between the people and the occupiers. But if they had to function under military direction, they might be attacked for being part of an occupation force.

The European Union agreed with the humanitarian agencies. Poul Nielson, the EU Commissioner for Development and Humanitarian aid, told the U.S. government that he would not coordinate his aid with a U.S. military occupation office. He would not compromise European aid by tying it to any military operation. He complained that U.S. forces in Afghanistan had tried to legitimize their security operations by delivering aid, and that this had jeopardized the safety of the humanitarians. He said that: "For the EU, it is about securing the independence and neutrality of what we are funding."[23] Many European NGOs have specific rules against operating with or for military forces and they would not have been able to function under U.S. or British military direction.

Secretary of State Colin Powell also agreed with the humanitarian agencies. He wrote to Rumsfeld at the end of March, saying that he wanted civilian control of the aid program. He pointed out that foreign governments and international aid agencies would not help a humanitarian effort directed by the U.S. military. He stressed that it should be managed by USAID disaster response teams. Supporting his wish, the U.S. Congress on April 8, 2003, wrote into the Iraqi spending bill a provision that the Department of State and USAID instead of General Garner's office would be responsible for directing humanitarian and other aid funds.[24]

The American NGOs had long faced a special problem. Under the sanctions regime against Iraq that Washington had spear-headed, American NGOs could not pay for any operations in Iraq. Even with the war looming over the horizon, they could not prepare for action. Non-American agencies could do more because the U.N. sanctions regime permitted humanitarian relief, but American sanctions did not. Thus, foreign NGOs like Médecins sans Frontières could do more for the Iraqis, as could the ICRC.

Sandra Mitchell, vice president of the International Rescue Committee's Washington office, appealed to the U.S. Senate Foreign Relations Committee in early March to lift the sanctions on Iraq so that American NGOs could legally prepare humanitarian programs for Iraq.[25]

Bush himself wanted very much to have American agencies lead the relief effort in order to show that the United States had a humanitarian attitude toward Iraq.[26] But the White House did not formally lift sanctions until May 27, 2003, four days after the U.N. Security Council had lifted its sanctions. This left many American NGOs unable to meet Iraq's humanitarian needs quickly after the official end of the fighting.[27]

Bremer's appointment has eased NGO fears about becoming too associated with the U.S. military. Although he reports to Rumsfeld, he remains a civilian official—not a former General like Garner. Recognizing NGO concerns, Ward drew the CPA organizational diagram to make clear that its director for humanitarian affairs has no command function over the humanitarian agencies but only a coordinating responsibility.

The United Nations and other humanitarian agencies moved quickly after the end of the major military campaigns. The World Food Program began feeding as many as 27 million Iraqis (four times as many as it had fed in Afghanistan). The ICRC distributed supplies to hospitals, although it at first restricted the amounts to prevent looting. They and other agencies tried to return the lives of ordinary Iraqis to normal as soon as possible.[28] Bremer also tried to return Iraqi life to normal, deciding to begin school programs and other routine economic and social activities and to restore full services as soon as it could be done. He also pledged a referendum on Iraq's future constitution.

To help define a United Nations role, Kofi Annan in June 2003 agreed to an American request to send Sergio Vieira de Mello to Baghdad as his special representative for four months. The U.N. High Commissioner for refugees, Ruud Lubbers, in turn sent Dennis McNamara as his special envoy to Iraq. Between the two of them, Vieira de Mello and McNamara carried more peacekeeping and nation-building experience (Bosnia, Kosovo, East Timor, etc.) than the entire American administration of Iraq. They kept a low profile, being careful not to supplant the role of the official U.N. humanitarian coordinator, Ramiro Lopes da Silva. Nonetheless, Vieira de Mello issued a statement that it would be good to give more political responsibility to the Iraqis at an early date.[29]

Annan made clear that United Nations concerns and obligations went beyond those of the occupiers. In a July 18 report on Iraq to the U.N. Security Council, he wrote that the occupiers should urgently establish a timetable "leading to the end of military occupation" in order to stem growing impatience in a "precarious, some believe deteriorating, security situation." He said that the United Nations could help to prepare elections, to write a constitution and to reform the judiciary (all tasks that the United Nations had done elsewhere). He added that many Iraqis "considered United Nations involvement essential to the legitimacy of the political process," noting that "democracy should not be imposed from the outside." Annan's comments probably drew on reports to him from Vieira de Mello."[30]

Iraq had also faced a potential refugee crisis before the onset of the military campaign. Even before Bush and Rumsfeld began their attack against Saddam Hussein, U.N. and non-governmental agencies had made preparations for massive flows of Iraqi refugees to Iran, Jordan and perhaps other neighboring states. They had also prepared for the possibility that many Iraqis would flee the cities to avoid bombing and would need some support in the countryside as internally displaced persons.

Having been denounced by Secretary of State Madeleine Albright in 1999 for not being ready to meet the needs of Kosovo refugees, the U.N. agencies had decided that they would get as ready as they could and that they would make their needs clear in advance. They wanted to respond immediately to humanitarian needs within and outside Iraq. They also wanted to alert the United States and other donors to what it might cost.

The Western leaders also remembered Kosovo, especially their own failure to provide aid for the agencies in advance. When Lubbers had said that he might need support for 1.5 million refugees, he received $27 million in donations. He prepared emergency food and other supplies for hundreds of thousands of refugees and internally displaced persons.

As it happened, no waves of refugees moved into neighboring states in the first weeks of the war. Several hundred thousand did leave Baghdad and other major cities but did not need immediate support. Most were able to find shelter with friends or relatives outside the major cities and away from the main scenes of battle.[31]

The return of earlier refugees nonetheless presented a problem. Over 200,000 Shiites who had fled from Saddam in 1991 remained in Iran. Tens of thousands of other refugees had fled to Jordan and Saudi Arabia, usually not remaining in camps but merging into the local population. All were expected to consider returning, but nobody could be sure how many would want to return quickly if at all. Moreover, they probably would not go back into any kind of camp situation—as in Afghanistan—but would want to go back to their homes.

As of this writing, refugee repatriation remains slow. Bremer does not want to encourage it because it could promote the early return of several hundred thousand more Shiites from Iran to Iraq, potentially giving Teheran an even bigger voice. But smaller groups and individuals have been returning from Syria, Jordan and Saudi Arabia. Many do not return under any program administered by UNHCR, preferring to move quietly and to settle back into their old neighborhoods. Many had fled from Saddam's dictatorship and are happy to be able to return freely.

The internally displaced persons are being helped by the International Office for Migration in the south and by a special U.N. office for Project Services in the Kurdish areas. There, major property problems remain between Arabs displaced by Kurds and Kurds displaced by Arabs during various phases of the wars in Iraq. Those will take time to resolve and could spark bitter arguments.

The U.N. agencies, the humanitarian NGOs and the occupation authorities have combined to ease the potential humanitarian crisis. More than 50 NGOs have begun to provide relief in Iraq. They include American, European and a number of

Red Crescent societies from various Arab states of the Middle East. In physical terms, despite the terrors of the war, Iraqi civilians find themselves relatively well provided with the kinds of basic support that the humanitarian agencies can provide quickly and expertly. Despite political and bureaucratic problems, many Iraqis can perhaps sense that their lives may begin to improve from the days of the sanctions and of the very restrictive "oil-for-food" program.

But the people of Iraq and the occupation authorities face a deeper problem. For the war has not truly ended. Elements of Iraq society, whether nationalists or Saddam loyalists, have begun a sustained resistance against the occupation forces. As the American, British and other occupiers begin their own campaigns of retaliation against those resistance fighters, a deeper humanitarian crisis looms. Relief supplies might be available, but peace and security are not. Although many parts of Iraq remain calm, others have sunk into warfare. Without neutral international peacekeepers, the risk of an anticolonial uprising remains very real.

U.N. Peacekeeping for Iraq

As the crisis in Iraq deepens, Washington appears to be stuck in a time warp with respect to the United Nations role. It has become focused almost exclusively on United Nations political and humanitarian functions without appreciating the potential for the U.N. peacekeeping function.

After the U.N. Security Council failed to endorse the U.S. and British attack on Iraq, President Bush denounced the Council. He cited the vote not as a failure of U.S. and British diplomacy but as a failure of the United Nations itself. Bush and the White House maintained that Washington had "tested" the United Nations and that it had flunked the test. They still supported and accepted the U.N. humanitarian function, but they wanted no part of U.N. peacekeeping despite Tony Blair's pleas for such a U.N. role.

U.S. officials cited such alleged past U.N. failures as the humiliation in Somalia, the genocide in Rwanda and the Serb killing of Muslims at Srebrenica in Bosnia. They forgot that an American General ordered the attack that failed in Somalia, that Belgian and French troops refused to support the United Nations in stopping the genocide in Rwanda and that Dutch and NATO peacekeepers followed their own separate instructions to ignore the genocide at Srebrenica. They also forgot a more recent string of successful U.N. peacekeeping and nation-building successes in the Eastern Slavonia province of Croatia, in Bosnia and Kosovo, in East Timor or in Cambodia and elsewhere (chapters 7–10).

In opposing U.N. peacekeeping in Iraq, Bush and Rumsfeld have ignored two crucial U.N. assets: credibility and experience.

Credibility, or legitimacy, already looms as the single most important element for any government in Iraq, a country deeply suspicious of all outsiders because of a long history of subjugation, colonialism and exploitation. The Iraqis appear much more ready to accept a U.N peacekeeping operation than what they increasingly see as an occupation by American, British and associated forces.

The United Nations could also recruit international forces who have had much more experience than U.S. soldiers at peacekeeping. Over the past 50 years, and especially the past 15, thousands of U.N. peacekeepers have served in dozens of crises. They know far more about how to function in such situations than the Americans. And many U.N. peacekeepers would have more experience than the forces that the United States has invited to join. International peacekeepers would also permit more American soldiers to come home. In short, an international peacekeeping force could save American lives.

Nonetheless, U.S. officials—and especially senior Defense Department civilians—remain deeply suspicious of any United Nations role in peacekeeping or in anything else. But this may prove to be a costly prejudice for the United States, and especially so for American soldiers who might be killed while doing tasks that U.N. peacekeepers could do at least as well, and probably more safely.

First Steps in Reconstruction

As U.S. bombing began, with over 5,000 bombs and 1,000 cruise missiles launched during the first two weeks of the war, Washington and others began to debate about who would pay for reconstruction. Bush and senior American officials said Washington could not be expected to pay for reconstruction by itself, especially because Congress might not authorize the tens of billions of dollars that would be needed. After all, the sanctions had been imposed by the United Nations. Moreover, U.S. officials, and especially Rumsfeld, insisted that Iraq would need income well beyond its potential oil export sales. Rumsfeld said other nations should help to pay.[32]

To try to decide what to do, potential donor states met in New York June 24 and 25 at a meeting hosted by UNDP administrator Mark Malloch Brown. The American delegation urged all European states as well as Russia, Japan and others to contribute. The states did not agree on specific financing targets, but suggested that Iraq reconstruction costs would dwarf the sums to be contributed for Afghanistan. The states did agree that they would hold a more formal pledging conference in October 2003.

Many potential donors are holding back on pledges because they feel reluctant to contribute to an American occupation. They would prefer an international administration, especially the United Nations, or a legitimate Iraqi government. At the very least, they want more power to be given to an international monitoring board established by the United Nations.

Some European states insist that the American-dominated CPA establish a separate fund controlled by an international institution. The European Union, usually a major contributor to humanitarian appeals, may be reluctant to contribute because it still resents Rumsfeld's charge that it represents "old Europe." A French official observed that: "There is a tendency on behalf of the coalition authorities to be too heavy-handed." Some donors have said that they would contribute only to a special "donor trust fund" independent of the occupation authorities. Therefore, although reconstruction funds will ultimately come, the amount that may be pledged and finally granted remains very uncertain.[33]

Other donors also hesitate because the United States has already granted or promised contracts to American companies for various reconstruction projects, including the oil fields, roads and other public works. Washington has asked three major American companies, Halliburton, Bechtel and Kellogg, Brown and Root, to undertake projects worth hundreds of millions of dollars to rebuild Iraqi oil fields and to do other construction work. The Americans have justified these contracts by recalling that the U.S. Congress requires the use of American firms for projects funded by the U.S. government. Given the security situation, some firms may even be reluctant to operate in Iraq. All this adds to the uncertainty.[34]

The Future of Iraq

Like Yugoslavia, Iraq has multiple ethnic and religious groups. Unlike Yugoslavia, which its own diverse peoples decided to form after World War I, Iraq was cobbled together by a foreign imperial power, Great Britain. London forced the Kurds in northern and the Shiite Muslims in southern Iraq to live under the control of a central Iraqi regime in Baghdad.

There is no guarantee that the different groups will now work together. In the northern areas, the Kurds welcome American and other occupiers as guarantors of Kurdish autonomy from Baghdad. Having been free of Sunni control for a dozen years in the "no-fly" zone, they do not want to obey the Sunnis again. They have already made clear that they want the future Iraq to be a loose federation with considerable autonomy for the Kurdish area, although they have not said what share they might want of the Mosul-Kirkuk area oil revenues. In the southern regions, the Shiites have been pleased about the end of Saddam's regime and they may think they have the right to rule because they are in the majority. In the center, the Sunnis actively oppose the U.S. occupation, especially because they have the most to lose.

Bremer and his team want to continue to run Iraq as a single entity although they have selected separate regional coordinators and different occupation forces for different geographic areas. They have made clear that they would not tolerate having the Shiites establish a separate Islamic region under Iranian influence. Fearing that the Turks would react violently to any kind of Kurdish separate identity, the Americans have also told the Kurds that they will remain part of Iraq.

As of this writing, the only part of Iraq's future that can be predicted with any confidence is a long, costly and potentially murderous foreign occupation. When U.S. Senators Richard Lugar, Chuck Hagel and Joseph Biden returned from a visit to Baghdad in late June, 2003, they predicted that the U.S. occupation would last for at least two years and perhaps as long as five. Given that peacekeepers remain in Yugoslavia five years after they had been predicted to leave, that may seem optimistic.[35]

Nor can anybody dare to predict how the occupation itself will proceed over the years ahead, especially during the brutally hot Iraqi summers. As of the middle of 2003, many Iraqis have already begun resenting the presence of American and other foreign forces although they might have been glad to have Saddam ousted. They complain that Americans promised democracy and brought occupation. They especially resent Bremer's decision not to permit early elections even at the local level.[36]

For their part, U.S. soldiers, ill-trained and uncomfortable as occupiers and as peacekeepers, complain to American journalists that they came to fight a war and not to be killed while acting as a police force.[37] They are also showing themselves to be trigger-happy, sometimes killing Iraqis who commit no greater offense than to drive past a road-block without noticing it.[38] That kind of opposition between occupiers and occupied could produce nasty incidents and a rash of humanitarian problems.

Conquest does not mean victory. Over the long term, almost anything seems possible in Iraq. It may be broken up, like Yugoslavia, although that now seems unlikely; it may descend into informally accepted separate enclaves, like Afghanistan; it may compel the retreat of foreign forces, as in Somalia; finally, and hopefully, it may emerge from foreign occupation like Germany, a united, federal and democratic state. A lot may depend on how the United States and its partners manage the occupation, on whether and how soon the American forces can capture or kill Saddam Hussein after having promised a huge reward for him, and on whether the United States and Great Britain invite the United Nations to play a meaningful role.

The humanitarian agencies are doing what they can to help the Iraqi people through whatever may lie ahead. They are providing food and medical aid, refugee care and resettlement, and a healing hand. Although the United Nations as a whole does not carry any official responsibility, its agencies and its personnel have helped to stabilize the humanitarian situation and have thus contributed a calming influence to the political debate that will proceed over the next several years.

The humanitarian NGOs can also take some satisfaction from the knowledge that they helped avert a humanitarian catastrophe during the last years of Saddam Hussein's rule and may be able to continue to do so during whatever will follow. They may well function in Iraq long after the American, British and other occupiers have gone. To date, they appear to have gained the respect and thanks of the Iraqi people.

The Gate of Fire

Iraq represents the archetype of the new type of humanitarian emergency, carrying the problems of the 1990s to a new level. It combines war, civil resistance, economic rehabilitation and humanitarian need. It is a highly dangerous crisis, for it is happening in the center of the renowned Middle Eastern powder keg. It also represents the first time since 1945 that a major Western sovereign state has launched an attack on another state without first having won the approval of the United Nations or of any other major international organization.

Humanitarian agencies can try to help as much as possible. They can distribute food and medicine and give all the people whatever level of care they may need for their immediate physical needs. That work remains essential. Until the end of the Cold War, it would often have been enough.

But in Iraq, as in other crises since 1990, the real humanitarian emergency goes beyond the humanitarian realm. Beginning in Bosnia and continuing in Kosovo, Somalia, Rwanda, Congo, Timor and Afghanistan as well as in other areas, humanitarians must now function in the midst of war and political upheaval. Their work is intimately linked with that upheaval. The agencies can serve the humanitarian conscience, but they cannot go beyond that. Others have to find solutions.

The crisis in Iraq, like the crisis in Afghanistan, has entered the realm that the sovereign states have reserved to themselves for hundreds of years, the realm of politics and war. The sovereign states have to date excluded humanitarian agencies and humanitarian considerations from that realm. They will make their own sovereign decisions, right or wrong. But they will need to think again if they do not want to face even more emergencies like those in Afghanistan and Iraq.

Kofi Annan had earlier said that the world had entered the new millennium through a "gate of fire." At the start of the millennium, that fire burned most luridly and most threateningly in Iraq. The humanitarians will try to help put it out, but they cannot do it alone. They may also, like Iraqis, Americans and others, find themselves consumed in the conflagration.

FOURTEEN

RECONNECTING WITH
THE HUMANITARIAN CONSCIENCE

NEVER SINCE THE DAYS OF HENRY DUNANT have humanitarians faced a more desperate situation than now, in the age of terror.

Humanitarian care has had a roller-coaster ride. Before 1850, it barely existed although its origins went back through centuries of humanist and religious philosophy. From 1859 to 1945, it only began to find a small role, mainly in caring for soldiers and prisoners of war. After 1945, humanitarians suddenly had more to do, as Western leaders helped the world to recover from war and supported wider humanitarian action, peacekeeping and refugee care. Humanitarians hit their high point.

After the Cold War, during the 1990s, humanitarian needs changed. Humanitarian care had to be given ever more often in the midst of crisis and upheaval in which both the victims and the caregivers might be at risk. The leaders of the West helped to foment some of these crises, or at least did not move quickly and firmly enough to prevent them. They began talking more about humanitarian care than actually doing it. Although they had infinitely more power to shape the world than during the Cold War, they permitted humanitarian emergencies to erupt from Yugoslavia to Africa. They provided humanitarian relief but did not try to solve the basic problems until thousands had died. They left too many crises to fester and to bleed. Humanitarians have thus now hit a low point.

Since September 11, 2001, Western leaders have shown a strange ambivalence. They continue to provide humanitarian relief, albeit in dwindling amounts. They also continue to support and to accept refugees, although also in dwindling amounts. But they have not tried to prevent, to contain or to solve the many crises that beset South Asia, Chechnya, the Middle East or major parts of Africa—although President Bush and the "Quartet" of the United States, the United Nations, the European Union and Russia are making another long over-due effort to arrange a peace settlement between the Israelis and the Palestinians.

The Conspiracy of Silence

A conspiracy of silence has set in. The sovereign political and military leaders of the world and of the West all too often regard the humanitarians as cleaning crews who will overcome or at least contain emergencies with relatively modest funding while the sovereigns feel free to go on to other quarrels that require greater resources and renewed vigor. As from the thirteenth to the twentieth centuries, the captains and the kings can go about their grand and proud paces and speeches without paying too much attention to the countless dead, wounded, maimed, dispossessed, starving and desperate victims they or others leave behind. The humanitarian organizations are to take care of the victims, and to make it appear as though no lasting damage has been done.

But time has not stood still. As the war in Iraq and the trials of the occupation have shown, the world cannot use its traditional humanitarian methods to meet the full range of needs spawned by recent humanitarian emergencies. The potentially imminent threat of a total collapse of Afghanistan underlines the point. New humanitarian problems are not like the old.

Humanitarian agencies can of course still offer care to the victims of war and upheaval. But they know that that is not enough. People do not need only water, food and medicine. They need some sense of stability, some notion of a future. They want to be able to plan for more than a day, let alone a week.

Therefore, political policy, diplomatic policy and security policy must also have a humanitarian goal. The West can no longer use the excuse that it cannot control what happens elsewhere because of Soviet power. In fact, the West can control what happens almost everywhere. But it needs to decide what to do with that control. And it especially needs to recognize that the range of humanitarian needs widens with the new type of humanitarian emergency. If the West does not realize that, there will be no end to crises and emergencies.

For it is becoming ever more true that every political crisis inevitably leads, sooner or later, to a humanitarian emergency. And every humanitarian emergency leads, sooner or later, to a political crisis. They must be handled at the same time, with each doing its share and each having its voice, if that vicious cycle is to be broken. Unfortunately, the sovereign states do not yet realize that.

Thus George W. Bush and L. Paul Bremer can say to Kofi Annan and Sergio Vieira de Mello that the Americans will take care of the big political decisions and that the U.N. agencies are to do the less important humanitarian work. They seem not to realize that they can never stabilize Iraq if the humanitarian situation does not improve and that the humanitarian situation will not improve if they do not find political solutions. Western leaders think that they can leave humanitarian problems to the humanitarians, not realizing that the modern type of humanitarian emergency can not be truly solved without correct political decisions, careful diplomacy and aid.

In the face of the new emergencies and the new needs, the leaders of the West have abandoned the humanitarian conscience. They have done so although many of their people, especially the young, continue to believe firmly that they should be helping those in need. The young—and others—choose to work for humanitarian agencies and NGOs despite the risks, but the political figures are turning their backs on them. They seem not to recognize what faces them.

The leaders of the world, and even the leaders of the West, believe that they can ignore the humanitarian conscience. Humanitarian crises do not carry much weight. They receive a dwindling amount of cash and some lip service but nothing more. The international agencies and the NGOs are to keep people alive as best they can but not to talk about problems.

Yet it is precisely the humanitarian failure of the West to help the Afghans, the Somalis and the Sudanese during the 1990s that enabled Osama bin Laden and his supporters to prepare the attacks of September 11. The lack of a continuing humanitarian response in those places fueled the crisis now faced by the West and the world. Humanitarian action would not only have helped the people who needed help. It would also have prevented a disaster. Worst of all, we do not know how many similar crises may be brewing.

The most deadly weapon of mass destruction is despair. Only humanitarian action can ease or end it. The world, and especially the West, cannot afford to keep backing away from its support for humanitarian action, or to back away any further from its support for humanitarian principles.

After the disaster of September 11 and the revelations about its origins, a return to the humanitarian conscience should guide everything that leading states do or consider doing. The range and the depth of the many humanitarian tragedies around the world has become too great and their human cost has become too high. And the impact of those tragedies on the world as a whole has become too important and too dangerous, as New York and Washington should have learned on September 11, 2001.

The "war on terror" often proclaimed in the West has no positive element. No Western leader has yet signalled any major international policy changes that could hope to prevent another September 11 or similar attacks. But the old policies have clearly failed, and there is no room for further complacency.

The humanitarian agencies and humanitarian NGOs cannot do everything, especially with dwindling resources and diminishing support. They can fulfill their assigned humanitarian tasks and help those who need help. They show high levels of courage and dedication every day. But serving the humanitarian conscience requires more than protection and relief, which the humanitarians can offer. It requires political will.

Only governments can prevent humanitarian problems or put an end to the conditions that lead to those problems. They alone can solve the problems that do arise. They should not expect the humanitarian agencies and the NGOs to do those things. They must themselves summon the strength and determination to prevent and to solve humanitarian problems. That is part of the new responsibility that comes with sovereignty after September 11, 2001.

Western leaders need to look at the world in a new way. They have usually seen globalization as an economic phenomenon, in which states impact on each other's economies. They have quaintly termed the world a "global village."

But globalization has become a humanitarian as much as an economic reality. Humanitarian tragedies can no longer be isolated in separate compartments. They cannot be ignored until some humanitarian agencies step in obediently to try to ease whatever pain has been caused. Tragedies have become part of the new field of battle.

Nor should the West continue to speak of the "global village." It sounds too sweet. Instead, the world has become a global city, with high rent districts and broad avenues as well as with back alleys and fetid slums teeming with the homeless, hopeless, criminal and diseased. And, of course, easy enough to get around so that no area is fully immune to what happens elsewhere.

Osama bin Laden and al Qaeda have drawn their support and some of their recruits from the slum sites of humanitarian tragedies, whether in Afghanistan or Sudan or beyond, and from groups revolted by those and other tragedies. If the states of the world want to deny bin Laden those slums, they must act. More important, they must act if they want to preserve their own sense of what is right.

Terrorism is a symptom. It is not only a danger in itself, but is a sign of a greater danger.

The states of the West face a stark choice. They can continue to act on the basis of their asserted sovereign rights, intervening when and where they choose, never looking back and counting on others to clean up behind them.

If the states make that choice, the twenty-first century will be a century of death like the twentieth—probably worse, for the old ills will have bubbled longer. Moreover, weapons will be more powerful and have a longer reach.

Or the states can follow the principles of the humanitarian conscience, trying to prevent and to end humanitarian tragedies and giving humanitarian action the priority it deserves.

In the searing heat of the new century and of the third millennium, the states really have no option. They must pay attention to the humanitarian needs of those who share the city. They must give humanitarian concerns a high place in the order of their own thinking.

After the end of the Cold War, the West now has both the opportunity and the responsibility to shape the world. It can keep that world as it has been, with sovereign states exercising their sovereign rights and thinking only of their immediate interests. Or it can introduce a new spirit, dedicating itself to the relief of suffering as a vital element of anything it does.

The West must let a new basic principle guide all national actions. Every policy must have a humanitarian purpose or at least a humanitarian element, and every action must take its humanitarian impact into account. Equally important, and perhaps more so, humanitarian goals should guide each policy.

Some may say that this sounds utopian. They may think they can continue as they have. But they should then ask how that has helped to bring the world into the age of terror, and they might think again.

Within that broad principle, several specific as well as several general steps must follow for the world, the West and especially for the United States as the leading nation in the world and the West.

The following must form the three main elements—diplomatic, military and economic—of a new and wider humanitarian agenda.

Humanitarian Diplomacy: The College of Conciliators

The single most important step toward a humanitarian world must be a much greater stress on active diplomacy. The world needs preemptive diplomacy more than it needs preemptive war.

In particular, the world needs humanitarian diplomacy—diplomacy specifically designated to solve or ease humanitarian crises. That kind of diplomacy should become a basic element of international action.

Literally dozens of major humanitarian tragedies could be avoided, ended or at least eased by intensified and sustained diplomatic efforts. But those efforts need senior personalities who can bring significant prestige, a proven record of service and a persuasive personality. And those personalities need the authority of the international community behind them, not only of one or a few states.

War, revolution and resistance follow a well-known dynamic. Hatred and frustration grow. Those who favor war win power. They hold on to that power by policies that justify their actions, keeping themselves in office and their nation at war. They avoid real negotiations. The war parties and the extremists on opposite sides win support for themselves and, ironically, for each other. The descending spiral continues unrelieved until all come to their senses many years and countless killings later.

Diplomacy also has its own dynamic. It may, of course, include impatience and frustration. But signs of progress can multiply and the peace parties can win more power and support. Those who want war can become discredited once the benefits of peace can be clearly seen. A mood for genuine reconciliation can grow on all sides.

But the road to peace takes more time than the road to war, although states normally grant more time to the warriors than to the peacemakers. In a classic case, President Bill Clinton and the Israelis and Palestinians tried to resolve the basic problems of the Israeli-Palestinian conflict in the last weeks of Clinton's tenure in 2000. But two weeks at Camp David could not resolve problems that had deepened for generations. So the fighting continued.

Major international problems cannot be solved in a week, in a month and perhaps even in a year. Nor can they be solved at the working level. They must be solved by the most senior figures on each side, either through direct talks or through others whom they trust.

A senior and respected person must take the first step, for no war leader can take it without risk. All must act in coordination.

Many wars now need diplomacy:

- The war between Israelis and Palestinians is perhaps the most difficult to resolve. Its roots go back to decisions taken a long time ago. It punishes both sides terribly. Israeli soldiers shoot Palestinian innocents, including women and children, as well as terrorists. The Israeli occupation dooms the Palestinians to that combination of bitterness and enforced idleness that fuels terrorist activities. The Israelis fare no better. Palestinian suicide bombers kill Israeli innocents, including women and children, as well as soldiers. Israelis are not under occupation, but they cannot lead normal lives any more than Palestinians can.
- The war in Kashmir, with roots almost as old, is also far from a solution. The Muslim majority in Kashmir will not accept Hindu rule. It offers support for terrorists, whether the terrorists infiltrate from Pakistan or grow up within Kashmir. Yet Pakistan and India to date appear more disposed to continue a stalemate of almost 60 years than to make a genuine breakthrough, although they risk nuclear war.
- The Christian majority in southern Sudan will not accept being ruled from the Muslim north, and the Muslim north will not accept southern secession. Hundreds of thousands and perhaps millions have died in one of the most futile wars of the twentieth century. And the people on both sides suffer the effects of the war, denying Sudan the chance to become prosperous from its oil.

- The Chechens will not accept continued Russian rule and Russian President Vladimir Putin will not grant them independence. Russian forces have destroyed the Chechen capital of Grozny and they routinely bomb Chechen villages. Chechen rebels have launched terrorist attacks and briefly captured a Moscow theater in November 2002.
- Countless African states have been left as "mini-empires" (chapter 11), with colonial boundaries that compel different ethnic groups, tribes and entire nations to live together in an uneasy coexistence prone to exploitation, tension and periodic outbursts of violence. From Angola to Nigeria to the Congo to the Ivory Coast, Sierra Leone and Liberia, hundreds of thousands have been killed or crippled.
- Several Asian states, including the Philippines, Indonesia and Sri Lanka, suffer from the same problem. Some wars have continued for decades. Every year, thousands die, whether in the southern Philippine islands, in Aceh in Indonesia or in Colombo in Sri Lanka.

Solutions can be found to virtually every conflict, bringing reconciliation, perhaps by a federal sharing of power and profit, and putting an end to human suffering. In every case listed above, most people on both sides, like most dispassionate observers, know the solution that can end the war. They could write it down on a scrap of paper.

But those engaged in the conflict have lost their ability to solve their own problems or even to start the process toward peace. They may think that they can win with just one more campaign or bomb. They may not be sure of what peace may bring. They may fear that peace will help opposition parties. They may think that war gives them greater security and greater prospects for governing than peace. In the meantime, humanitarian tragedies multiply.

Diplomacy, peace and humanitarian considerations must be linked. For often only a political settlement can put an end to humanitarian tragedies. And only an end to humanitarian tragedies will make a settlement last.

To generate a new dynamic of humanitarian diplomacy, the states of the world should establish a new College of Conciliators, a group of prestigious men and women who will be prepared to serve as diplomatic intermediaries.

Such a college should consist initially of no more than 25–30 figures, men and women who have retired from active public life and who would be available to help negotiate settlements for problems that nobody has yet solved. Former American presidents, senators or secretaries of state might be considered for membership, as well as European, African, Asian or Latin American leaders of similar experience.

The college should be attached to the United Nations, directly to the office of the Secretary-General. The Secretary-General could nominate persons to join it. So could national leaders. The Secretary-General or the U.N. Security Council should assign members of the college to various negotiating tasks after mutual consultation. They should be able to assign such members on their own initiative, whether invited by the parties or not.

Members of the College of Conciliators who have been assigned to a specific negotiation should be bound to stay with that negotiation until they succeed or until they conclude, with the concurrence of the Secretary-General, that nothing can be done.

The college could expand over time as needed, as it becomes effective and as other distinguished conciliators are nominated. Its members would not need to move to New York, remaining at their normal homes and offices, but should be available on call for consultations and perhaps for such meetings of the entire college as the Secretary-General or the Security Council may want to convene.

The members of the College would bring personal prestige, a record of accomplishment and a background of public life.

The nomination of a prominent and distinguished man or woman to a negotiating mission might break the ice. It would give leaders on both sides the opportunity—as well as the obligation—to formulate a real offer. It should make them react, and react seriously, because they cannot ignore such a person.

The personal prestige of the assigned conciliator would help find solutions. National leaders would find it easier to make concessions in response to a prestigious person than to what they regard as their opponent in a negotiating process.

Perhaps most important, such a person can find solutions that give all sides a chance to save their dignity. That may be the most crucial element in a negotiation. Only a prestigious outside party can provide a mutually acceptable formula for agreement.

The background in public life should have given conciliators some experience in solving "impossible" problems. They would know very well that successful negotiators and mediators need tremendous reserves of patience, tenacity and imagination. They must be prepared to come back to their talks several times and perhaps to involve other persons or organizations to help them, whether through peacekeeping, aid or other inducements to success. They must have the full support of the Secretary-General and of the Security Council to provide whatever may be needed.

The assignments of the College of Conciliators should be linked to humanitarian needs. Whenever the United Nations must send humanitarian aid or a peacekeeping force to help solve a humanitarian crisis, the College of Conciliators should be automatically seized with the issue and one or another member should be selected to follow it. He or she might not be the person finally chosen to try to negotiate, but should at least begin to offer suggestions as necessary to the Secretary-General and the Security Council.

The appointment of the College of Conciliators should make the selection of a negotiator more automatic than it is now. Under present circumstances, the Secretary-General or the Security Council must take the initiative to look for a negotiator and to appoint that person. Now the person would be already there.

Such an appointment would also end the common international practice of treating humanitarian action as an excuse for political inaction. All too often, the sovereign states decide that they have done enough for a crisis when they send humanitarian aid. But that should no longer be enough. Once a humanitarian crisis hits, the Security Council should send not only humanitarians but also somebody to try to solve it. The humanitarians should not be used as a band-aid to excuse diplomatic inaction.

The person would also bring credibility that national negotiators would not bring. When French Foreign Minister Dominique de Villepin negotiated a tentative solution to the Ivory Coast crisis in January 2003, rioters in the Ivory Coast capital of Abidjan accused him of serving French national interests. A person selected by the U.N. Secretary-General would not risk that kind of accusation.

Humanitarian diplomacy has a different motive and dynamic from ordinary diplomacy. Like other expressions of the humanitarian conscience, it wants to save lives. Many traditional negotiators may look at problems from a political or economic view. But humanitarian negotiators look at the tragedies that can be averted. They have a special mission. They want to promote reconciliation. They will try to find solutions that make it possible for different people to live together in peace. Richard Holbrooke's negotiations at Dayton brought peace. Not, perhaps, an enduring peace for generations, but a framework that can make an enduring peace possible by stopping the killing.

Diplomacy does not have the same appeal as military action. It does not offer the same ready—if false—promise of quick solutions. It compels leaders to look at their real interests, which they may not like to do. It forces some uncomfortable compromises and discourages demagogy. But it can often change the world far more effectively than military action.

In the hands of an effective College of Conciliators, diplomacy can provide a powerful humanitarian force. It can help solve rather than complicate problems. It can help parties to find peace, the ultimate humanitarian goal.

The College of Conciliators represents the diplomatic third of the new humanitarian agenda.

Peacekeeping: Forces in Reserve

The states of the world should begin urgently to put together a trained international peacekeeping force on a standby basis. Lakhdar Brahimi's 1999 report (chapter 11) offers a useful proposal for such a force. It offers many ideas that could be adopted at the United Nations and implemented within a year.

U.N. Secretary-General Kofi Annan would have no trouble recruiting forces. Over 80 states have offered contingents. Some of those states, like the Scandinavian states and Russia, are European; some, like China, India, Pakistan, Bangladesh and Nepal, are Asian; some, like Argentina, are Latin American; some, like Nigeria and Tunisia, are African; others, like Canada and Australia, have long-standing relations with the United Nations. Forces from these states, like the Jordanians and others, have served with distinction on dozens of United Nations peacekeeping teams.

The United Nations has sent over 50 peacekeeping contingents into crisis situations. In most cases, they have returned to their home countries within a year or two. In some, they had to remain longer. In others, they remain even after five decades. But they have always served with distinction and have mostly achieved what they set out to do. They have represented one of the most valuable contributions that the United Nations has made to the stability of the world community. They have scored countless successes, often unappreciated in the world at large. They have averted many wars and helped to end many others.

Secretary-General Boutros Boutros-Ghali proposed in 1992 in *An Agenda for Peace* that peacekeeping forces should be under the Secretary-General's command (chapter 7). But the Secretary-General is neither trained nor staffed for a command function. Command must go to a person with military experience. Moreover, only a person on site can exercise command, although the Security Council and the Secretary-General must keep supervisory responsibility.

The crisis in Afghanistan after 2001 has again underlined the need for such an international standby force. If that force had been readily available, the United States and others would not have needed a long and fruitless debate about whether or not to put a peacekeeping force throughout all of Afghanistan. The U.N. peacekeepers could have gone. They would have held Afghanistan together against local warlords and would have offered enough security to have permitted refugees to return all over the country.

Instead of the risky situation that now exists, where the entire country may be slipping out of the central government's hands and where it is taking years to assemble and train a united Afghan army, a U.N. peacekeeping force would have provided a unifying and pacifying element from the beginning. Such a force would have cost less than any purely Western force and would have permitted U.S. forces to concentrate on fighting al Qaeda.

The crises in the Congo, in the Ivory Coast, in Sierra Leone and in Liberia between 2000 and 2003 make the same point. An available international force would have offered an alternative to the disasters in those states. In the Congo, it might have held the country together. The contingent that was finally sent in the spring of 2003 may be both too little and too late. In the Ivory Coast, U.N. peacekeepers would have offered a more politically acceptable option than the French forces. Trained peacekeepers, sent quickly, might have hastened breakthroughs to peace in all those states. They would certainly have helped to save many lives.

The United States, the West and the United Nations might have avoided tragedy in Somalia, Srebrenica and Rwanda, if such a force had been in place and available during the 1990s. On the other hand, such experienced forces helped to carry out international intent in Eastern Slavonia and East Timor. Trained peacekeepers made a crucial difference between lives lost and lives saved.

A U.N. peacekeeping force would have helped to stabilize the postwar situation in Iraq during 2003. Peacekeepers have unquestioned international authority without the stigma of an occupation force. They can act firmly without generating the same kind of resentment as U.S. forces have encountered. They would have permitted the Americans to concentrate on their task of ferreting out Saddam Hussein and his loyalists. The peacekeepers would also have saved American lives. They could have performed many of the police and guard duties for which American forces are not trained or equipped. Fewer Americans would have been killed or wounded.

The Liberian crisis of spring and summer 2003 again shows the need for a trained standby U.N. peacekeeping force. Once Kofi Annan had been seized with the problem, he quickly appointed a seasoned Special Representative, Jacques Klein (chapter 8). But African peacekeeping forces took weeks to assemble and equip while Liberians were dying in a vicious civil war. Although President Bush had promised American peacekeepers, the conditions he imposed delayed those forces until after African troops arrived. A suitable African force could have, and should have, been ready within days, saving Liberian lives and reducing the need for U.S. peacekeepers.

The trained and specially commissioned international peacekeeping force, like the College of Conciliators, is designed to make the selection of a humanitarian instrument more automatic. Now, the Secretary-General or the Security Council has to look around for volunteer forces and to make sure they are right for the task. That can take time. If forces are trained, staffed and readily available, everything will work faster.

All states that volunteer potential U.N. peacekeepers should receive a complete set of training manuals, which they can use under the supervision of U.N. peacekeeping staff in order to prepare their troops for peacekeeping missions. They must show evidence that they have actually conducted such training for their forces. In addition, all should receive joint training for peacekeeping at the staff and command level down to junior officers and junior noncommissioned officers, preferably at a designated U.N. peacekeeping facility. The actual peacekeepers themselves, once selected, should receive accelerated training either before they go into the field or, if there is no time for that, a refresher course once they get there. They should be qualified to go wherever needed on short notice.

The United Nations cannot—and need not—have a permanent force, but it could have a small permanent staff and headquarters in the Department of Peacekeeping Operations. The staff should consist of about 50–100 officers and noncommissioned officers of various nationalities, and they should make certain that they keep themselves as well as the standby troops on the ready. A United Nations peacekeeping force should be able to assemble within hours. Its loyalty would be to the United Nations, not to any national command, and to the humanitarian mission it is sent to carry out. It would be fully in line with the original plans for the United Nations, plans then blocked by the Soviet Union.

Any such standby force should also receive training in civil and police affairs, as many will find themselves performing police functions rather than traditional military missions. Law-and-order functions constitute an important part of virtually all humanitarian operations. Yet few national police officers volunteer for peacekeeping police duties. Therefore, basic police work should be part of normal training for peacekeeping.

The best peacekeeping forces do not usually come from Western states. Western national forces showed time and again during the 1990s that they could not truly carry out peacekeeping missions. Western political leaders fear casualties above all else. They will commit forces but, like the Dutch in Srebrenica, the Belgians in Rwanda or the Americans in Somalia, will withdraw them as soon as they are really needed. Local terrorists can intimidate those forces and have done so. But U.N. peacekeepers have often accepted real risks. They have also reacted to those risks in ways that won respect and minimized further incidents, as in Eastern Slavonia and East Timor.

Moreover, most Western military forces clearly prefer to receive orders from their own rather than United Nations or even NATO commanders. Throughout Western peacekeeping operations in Rwanda, Somalia, Bosnia, Kosovo and Afghanistan, Western forces either received orders from their own national headquarters or confirmed international orders with their own national headquarters before obeying them. They only cited "U.N. orders" when it came time to shift the blame. No international peacekeeping force can function on that basis because no commander can be held responsible if he does not know that his orders will be obeyed. Forces from non-Western states are usually much more ready to follow U.N. orders and thus to do their mission.

Many large Western states do not train their forces for international missions. The Scandinavian and Canadians as well as a number of small states do it. They think in terms of international service. But most Western forces organize and train mainly for national or NATO missions heavy with armor and artillery or else for special missions. They are not programmed to conduct other types of operations effectively.

The American military are a case in point. They do not really want to conduct peacekeeping missions. The U.S. Army began training U.S. forces for such missions during the 1990s but the new U.S. administration in 2001 closed the principal training areas. Not being prepared or right for such missions, they should not be assigned to them.

The world remains unstable. Crises will come and go at regular intervals. It is time to begin preparing the kind of international forces that can meet those crises and perhaps even prevent them. Most of all, such forces should help make sure that no more massive humanitarian disasters follow.

A United Nations standby peacekeeping force represents the military third of the new humanitarian agenda.

Aid: The Ten Percent Formula

The U.S. government has forgotten the link between development aid and the humanitarian conscience. In 1947, Secretary of State George Marshall announced what has come to be known as the Marshall Plan, promising aid for European states to rebuild their economies. The Marshall Plan helped to end the postwar humanitarian crisis in Europe.

Aid can serve a humanitarian as well as an economic purpose. It can ease the crushing burdens of disease, famine and hopelessness that afflict all too many states in Africa, Asia and Latin America. It may not do it immediately, for many states have sunk so deep that it will take time for them to find hope again. But, given the chance, it will work.

Americans often complain that aid goes to corrupt regimes, only helps the elite by building them new palaces and is often lost entirely. But those problems can be fixed and have been to a large extent. They represent problems of management, not of basic purpose. If, for example, aid funds were managed by NGOs in conjunction with local national governments, the level of corruption could be brought under control.

The total current U.S. aid package, as shown by figures prepared for presentations to the U.S. Congress, shows a planning total (in the so-called "150" account) of about $25 billion per year during 2003 and 2004. The final figure will probably be closer to $21–22 billion after Congressional consultations.

Not all the aid has a direct humanitarian goal. The largest single amount (more than $4 billion) is for military aid, but that can help support peacekeeping. Less than $2 billion will provide humanitarian aid. And barely more than $100 million is to be spent on support for international peacekeeping missions.

President Bush has proposed an additional "Millennium Challenge Account" intended to boost total U.S. aid for states that qualify by making certain economic and political reforms. The amount is to begin at about $1.7 billion in 2003 or 2004 and is to rise to $5 billion by 2006 or 2007. He has also proposed a new AIDS package of $15 billion over a period of five years. These valuable ideas could theoretically raise U.S. annual aid totals to between $27 and $32 billion by 2007 or 2008, unless (as some fear) they will mainly substitute for other forms of aid. The amount and timing remain subject to Congressional approval, but they represent a step in the right direction.

The current aid total between $20 and $25 billion represents about 6 to 7 percent of the current U.S. military budget of around $350 billion, which will rise for the war in Iraq. But in humanitarian terms and in real terms during the war on terror, development aid and humanitarian aid do as much for American security as the military budget. They change the climate of thinking everywhere. They make America safer by making it harder for terrorists to operate.

The American government should adopt a simple formula: the total level of American aid, including development and humanitarian aid, should be at least 10 percent of the U.S. military budget. That would mean that the total American aid budget should rise to $35-$40 billion per year and perhaps more in future.

That may appear like a lot, but it is barely a third of one percent of the American gross domestic product. Every other Western democracy gives a greater proportion of its wealth. And, if the American aid is given to international organizations, it can become a multiplier factor, for others can be encouraged to give more.

The purpose of aid now matters as much as the amount. The American military, powerful and dedicated as it may be, cannot protect the American people in the war on terror. American military forces cannot be everywhere. American service men and women cannot watch every country, every city and every village. They need others to help them. They cannot win over those others by bombing them or by occupying them. Instead, they must win them over as friends. That is what aid can and will do.

American commentators like to speak of "failed states" and of how the developing world seems unable to repay World Bank or other international loans. But the main reason for their inability to repay is that Western states, and especially the United States and the European Union, prefer to subsidize their own food production and even their food exports than to buy from others. They effectively condemn the developing world to ask for aid in order to get any Western currencies because the West will not let them earn those currencies. The developed states of the world pay their farmers well over $300 billion in agricultural subsidies, more than the gross domestic product of sub-Saharan Africa, and the annual European Union subsidy for a cow is more than twice as high as the average income of a sub-Saharan farmer or worker. It is little wonder that the Africans cannot compete and that they are insisting that the upcoming Doha round of global trade negotiations should deal honestly with agricultural subsidies and tariffs.

Many countries in the developing world can produce only agricultural goods, but the West will not buy those goods and will even prevent them from being sold elsewhere by undercutting their prices. The West cannot then blame Africans or Caribbeans for failing to sell into Western or other markets. They have only themselves to blame if the developing world cannot repay its debts. They should treat foreign aid as a part of their own agricultural subsidy programs, for if they did not have those subsidies they would not need to provide as much aid.

All poverty is a human tragedy, even if not a strictly humanitarian one. But human tragedies can and often do become humanitarian tragedies. American aid, like other Western aid, should be directed to prevent or relieve real or potential humanitarian tragedies. Like other actions that affect the humanitarian world, it should be preemptive, not reactive.

The increase in American aid, added to what others are already paying, represents the final third of a new humanitarian approach.

These three elements must form a triad, working together to be truly effective. Humanitarian diplomacy must intervene if there is a crisis that might lead or that has already led to a humanitarian problem. Peacekeeping may be needed as well, and humanitarian aid as well as economic aid should be sent. All three elements should form integral parts of the totality of humanitarian action, supporting and extending whatever may be done by humanitarian agencies and NGOs working in the field. And humanitarian assistance in itself, as well as refugee support and admissions, must return to levels that truly meet the needs.

Costs of Inaction

One often hears that some proposals cost too much. It will certainly be heard against the cost of international peacekeeping or of the College of Conciliators, and particularly against any increase in the levels of U.S. aid.

Such arguments cannot seriously be made, however, after September 11, 2001. That single incident has cost far more than any proposal offered here would cost over dozens of years.

Moreover, the costs of September 11 cannot be dismissed as accidental. Nor can one say that September 11 would have happened no matter what the United States might have done. After all, as shown in chapter 12, the three states in which Osama bin Laden established his training sites, Afghanistan, Somalia and Sudan, had all been open and even friendly to the West. If the West, and especially the United States, had continued to provide aid for those countries, and if it had remained there, bin Laden would not have had the time or the bases to prepare his attack on the World Trade Center and the Pentagon.

The costs of American and Western failure have been incalculable. For New York City alone, estimates have run as high as $200 billion. For the American travel and airline industry as well as for American airframe manufacturers, the costs have probably risen to $100 billion already and may go higher. Although the American stock market would perhaps have declined even without the events of September 11, the shock of those events and their effect on a whole range of American companies have certainly run to astronomical figures. Some estimates for the total costs of September 11 have ranged to more than $400 or $500 billion.

Those estimates do not count the lives lost and the horror. Nor do they count the inconvenience suffered by millions of Americans and visitors, nor the diversion of U.S. resources and of U.S. attention from other pressing needs. In comparison, a few millions or even tens of millions of dollars spent in Afghanistan, Somalia, Sudan and perhaps elsewhere would have represented an incalculable bargain.

The same remains true today. In the unstable global city since September 11, international humanitarian care, international negotiations and international peacekeeping can help promote stability. Nothing can better serve the interests and the peace of mind of the American people and the people of other Western states, whose prosperity and safety depend upon such stability.

Solving crises through care or through negotiations, peacekeeping and aid is always cheaper than letting them continue or allowing them to provoke even deeper emergencies. It is also infinitely better for those who must live in the crisis area. The world owes it to them, as well as to itself, to explore every chance for peace.

The world should know by now that political and economic crises produce humanitarian emergencies. Humanitarian emergencies in turn produce political and military crises as well as terror. It is high time to break that cycle.

The Wider American Role

President George W. Bush has told the world that the United States will win the war against terror, and specifically against Osama bin Laden and al Qaeda.

The war on terror may last as long as the Cold War or the combination of the world wars. It may, like those wars, take many forms. But the war cannot be won defensively.

No nation, not even the strongest, can win a war *against* something. It can only win a war *for* something. The war that America must engage is not a war against terror or a war against bin Laden, but a war for greater humanitarian care and greater service to the humanitarian conscience. America should engage in that war, for that war is truly worth fighting and winning.

One day, bin Laden will be killed or captured or will die of natural causes. The humanitarian impulse and the humanitarian conscience will continue long after he is gone. They can make certain that he has no successors.

Americans must engage the world. They decided in 1947 with the Marshall Plan to go out into that world and to change it. They succeeded. They now face the same situation, a war against terror that, like the Cold War, cannot be won at home. Homeland security is only a small part of real security. Global battles will not be won by hunkering down.

Americans should take it upon themselves—as they have done before—to support humanitarian programs and other programs that will help the entire world. With their immense power, Americans set the tone, for better or worse. They may set that tone deliberately, deciding on the kind of world they want. Or they may set that tone inadvertently, not realizing the effects of what they do or of what their leaders say.

People all over the world watch the United States far more carefully than American leaders realize, and they notice what America does more than what it says. Americans must not think that nobody notices the suffering that Western state policies may cause or permit.

Secretary of State Madeleine Albright often described America as "the indispensable nation." With that, she acknowledged an awesome responsibility. September 11 did not change it.

The war against terror and against Osama bin Laden requires humanitarian policy even more than any other war. For bin Laden's sovereignty is the sovereignty of the shadow and of the darkened mind. He does not have buildings or guns to be destroyed. He has the loyalty of the deprived, the twisted and the enraged. They have become killers in his service and in his cause.

Nothing can be done to win him or his closest followers. They must be killed or captured or at least kept on the run so interminably that they can no longer carry out their plans. But other steps can be taken that can hurt him more.

The Chinese revolutionary Mao Zedong wrote that revolutionaries are like fish in the ocean: they depend on a congenial sea for survival and support. Bin Laden must find that the ocean has turned against him. If Bush's wish to protect America is to be carried out, bin Laden must find no welcome wherever he may turn. He must also find that young men no longer want to join the service of al Qaeda. America can win the war on terror only by removing the causes of that terror.

The American military can win any war and can certainly outgun al Qaeda. But bin Laden cannot be beaten fully by military means. He can be beaten only by convincing those who support him that he has misled them about America and about its allies. The West cannot end the hatred of those who would destroy it. But it can deny them a base.

A policy that engages the world and helps its citizens and that respects human life, one that people around the world will regard as humanitarian, will do more to dry up bin Laden's support than any amount of bombing.

Any teenager or sub-teenager who has seen the *Star Wars* epics or other science fiction movies can easily tell who are the villains. They fly overhead in space ships or aircraft and drop bombs or fire rockets. Or they appear in gigantic armored vehicles and shoot from the shelter of a tank. Those same viewers also know that the movie's heroes walk among the people. And they care for women and children and for the lost of this world. They are, in a sense, the humanitarians.

Americans cannot defeat bin Laden without stepping out of their space stations, their aircraft and their tanks. They cannot be only those who bomb, but must be those who help. They must walk among the people and they must understand and help the people. That is the only way to win the war on terror.

Some analysts deride a humanitarian policy as a soft and "unrealistic" strategy designed for idealists without true grit. But it is the opposite. Those who walk among the people and help them show genuine valor as well as idealism.

Since September 11, Americans have been practicing self-containment. They have isolated themselves behind new airline security devices, new immigration rules, new border controls, new immunizations and new rules and regulations. Those can be important. But they do not give true or lasting security. For that, one must go beyond the borders to help the people of the world.

A defensive policy and one without humanitarian content will definitely not defeat bin Laden. Nor will it project to the world the kind of image of real America that the American people would want to project.

We are no longer in the nineteenth century, but in the twenty-first. Old rules about military operations and Western domination no longer apply. If force must be used, it cannot succeed on its own. It must be surrounded—and tempered—by a framework of supportive humanitarian care.

America and its allies prevailed in the Cold War because they stood for more than the display and exercise of sovereignty and power. Generosity became part of strategy, perhaps unwittingly. The West proclaimed and practiced universal human- itarian principles that others understood, accepted and welcomed. Nothing could be more foolish than to abandon those principles now, when they are even more necessary than they were during the Cold War.

The governments of the West, and especially that of the United States, must follow the humanitarian conscience because it is right. But they must also recognize that it is essential to any success they hope to have. For the United States was once a beacon of humanism and humanitarian action, and it must return to that.

Coordinated Action

The world has come a long way since Solferino. But it has not yet come far enough. With tens of millions suffering as refugees or internally displaced persons, with tens of thousands being killed every year in international and internal wars, humanitarians and those who support them cannot in good conscience claim more than modest progress, especially when the new humanitarian crises have become even more difficult to solve than the old.

This century has begun as the old one ended, in grief and suffering. If it is not to be another century of death, the world—and especially the West—must serve the humanitarian conscience in everything it does. That, more than anything else, could make it a century of life.

Humanitarian care has become too important to be left to the humanitarians, as the crises in Afghanistan and Iraq have shown. Governments must give it the weight that it deserves, not ignore it or unctuously dismiss it as secondary or irrelevant. States must begin realizing that they must support humane principles and humanitarian action, for the days of absolute sovereignty and invulnerability are gone, and they are gone forever.

Humanitarian care is not a little separate engine, to be turned on when needed and turned off at will. It is part of a whole complex of supporting and supported actions. All must work together to solve problems.

The war on terror must have a humanitarian component if it is to succeed. A truly humanitarian policy can help to win that war. Real humanitarian action, on a large scale, can help in Afghanistan and elsewhere. Even when a humanitarian action does not have a political purpose, it has a political effect. And a policy that is right for its own reasons can be right for other reasons as well.

Humanitarians should welcome genuine diplomatic, peacekeeping and economic support. Humanitarians need to acknowledge that they can no longer succeed alone and cannot any longer think alone. Diplomacy, aid and peacekeeping policies can legitimately be used to help the humanitarian cause. Humanitarian care can have a wider effect precisely because it is not political, but there will be times when it will need and when it should have political support to succeed.

Mrs. Sadako Ogata, the former U.N. High Commissioner for Refugees, has said that humanitarian problems cannot be solved by humanitarians alone. That is correct. Of course, neither can they be solved by non-humanitarians alone. They must be solved by political leaders acting on a humanitarian basis and respecting humanitarian action. And they can be solved only when all work together to think of what the people may need.

The world is well past the days when sovereign states could ignore others and count on the humanitarians to clean up the mess they leave behind. Instead, the sovereign states need to avoid making such messes in the first place. If they act in a way that avoids humanitarian tragedies, they will be successful. If they act in a way that causes or inflames humanitarian tragedies, they will fail. And, most important, they will not protect the very sovereignty that they treasure.

Every policy should meet a simple test: does it serve a humanitarian goal? That must become a legitimate and accepted question that every policy must answer. If the answer is yes, the policy should be continued. If the answer is no, the policy should be put in question. It must either be dropped or changed.

The humanitarian conscience can complicate state policies. It demands attention to problems that states may not want to face. It can sometimes require action that one might prefer to avoid. If one chooses to avoid it, one can let a genocide happen in Rwanda or let Afghanistan again collapse. But every failure to face a humanitarian issue or to act in a humanitarian way will come back to haunt those who committed it.

Humanitarian actions in future, as in the past, must have a humanitarian and not a political motive and character. But humanitarian policy can constitute an essential element of stability and peace. Generosity and strategy do go hand in hand, as much now and in future as in the past.

Sovereignty, Humanism and Natural Law

The world is passing through a twilight zone where things cannot be seen clearly. No simple answers are at hand. But certain principles remain. Among them are the old principles of natural law and the doctrines of humanism and of human dignity, doctrines that preceded the nation-state and will outlive the nation-state.

Aristotle, Cicero, St. Augustine and St. Thomas Aquinas spoke to the heart. So did the great religious leaders, scholars and philosophers of the Far East and the Middle East. Their ideals touched something deep in the human conscience. Humanitarian action does the same. The West must now acknowledge natural law and the humanitarian conscience. If not, the international system will perish and the West with it.

The Abbé St. Pierre predicted in the middle of the eighteenth century that the world would have another 200 years of absolute sovereignty before finally rejecting it (chapter 2). Those 200 years ended around 1945, so it is high time to move on.

Humanitarian care, based on natural law, forms the link between the state and the universal order. The state that follows the humanitarian conscience and the humanitarian impulse, even at the cost of some sovereignty, will be heard and recognized. For any human suffering violates the common spirit of humanity.

The West has long touted its humanitarian principles and objectives. But it does not always act on a humanitarian basis. Humanitarian impulses do not determine state action as often as they should. Much of the world has respected and supported the West when it has followed its ideals. Those can have a powerful impact when they are clearly spoken and faithfully followed. At their best, they invoke a higher law and gleam with a common human aspiration.

The humanitarian conscience, nurtured by universal principles and going far beyond the dictates of sovereignty, should guide Western leaders all the time. Humanitarian policy should not be ignored until the last minute. Instead of giving humanitarian principles a pallid lip service, Western leaders should give the principles universal application. And they should tailor other policies to suit humanitarian purposes.

Do the states of the West want to recreate a Westphalian world, as it was between 1648 and 1859, without humanitarian care? Or do they prefer a world in which the humanitarian element plays an important role, as it began to do after 1859 and particularly did during the Cold War?

The humanitarian cause, the cause of a natural justice that transcends the narrow rule of states, has been a noble cause for millennia. The world responds to that noble cause. Never has the world needed it more than now.

No state, including the United States, can act alone and succeed. The humanitarian conscience does not thrive in isolation but in cooperation. It represents a universal set of values, universally understood. It is pervasive, always there, in all minds. We cannot have "à la carte" humanitarian care, giving it to some and not to others, if we want to emerge with true peace and stability from the age of terror.

The humanitarian conscience is now being neglected. Too many leaders, including the leaders of the West, have chosen to ignore it. But they cannot escape it. If the United States abandons it, or fails to serve it, we lose something of ourselves. We also give up the chance to link with a common spirit of humanity in other countries. We must re-connect with it, and quickly, for only that will bring real and lasting peace for this generation and for those who follow.

EPILOGUE:
AUGUST 19, 2003

A HUGE CAR BOMB DEMOLISHED THE UNITED NATIONS offices in Baghdad on August 19, 2003. It killed more than 20 persons, mainly United Nations employees, including Sergio Vieira de Mello.

Vieira de Mello's loss represented a genuine blow to the global humanitarian cause. He had served in many crises and had helped countless persons everywhere. He will be deeply missed, in Iraq and at the United Nations. And his humanitarian spirit will be missed as well.

The blast also killed another distinguished humanitarian, Arthur Helton, who had been a consistent advocate for refugees and asylum seekers and a consultant to the Council on Foreign Relations. He had also written many works on humanitarian topics.

The bomb again showed that United Nations and NGO employees as well as other humanitarians must increasingly accept risk as part of their mission. With al Qaeda having claimed "credit" for the blast, and with the United States now fully engaged in Iraq, one can only hope that the West will protect the people of Iraq and the humanitarians who work there as fiercely as it protects its own perceived interests. In an age of terror, the world cannot go back to 1859 when people were killed or maimed without any hope for help.

After the explosion, George W. Bush and Donald Rumsfeld reversed their attitude toward the United Nations because they realized that they needed international support. They began trying to get Security Council approval for a U.N. peacekeeping force under U.S. command. They also asked other states to help bear the costs of nation-building in Iraq.

The American effort to recruit allies underlined the importance of creating a U.N. standby peacekeeping force, as recommended in Chapter 14. Such a force would have made the peacekeeping and nation-building efforts in Iraq more automatic, more successful and less costly in American lives. It can, and should, still be established, and it should be established soon.

For the humanitarian cause, the situation remains desperate. If both the United States and al Qaeda treat Iraq as a battleground rather than as a country, the humanitarian situation can only worsen. Many innocents on all sides will remain terrorized and the people of the entire Middle East will continue to die.

The West, and especially the United States, must set a humanitarian example. Terrorists can ignore humanitarian needs, but the West cannot. The people of Iraq, long exhausted by sanctions and now trapped in a war they did not choose, desperately need a humanitarian alternative to conflict. They cannot be regarded merely as mute pawns in a struggle fought over their land and over their heads. That plays the terrorist game.

The West must offer the people of Iraq more than destruction. It must offer major programs of aid, relief and medical support to make up for the past thirty years and for the war. That will do more for the political stability of Iraq than any amount of bombing or patrolling.

When the needs of a people are subordinated to fighting a war, two things are certain: first, that the people will suffer; second, that the war will be lost.

The humanitarian organizations, with or without Vieira de Mello, cannot determine the future of Iraq. The people of Iraq must be given the chance to do that. But the humanitarians can help to make a real future possible once there is a humanitarian goal. Vieira de Mello died while trying to define one. Nobody else has yet defined it either. It must still be done, and fast.

As of this writing, and without a humanitarian alternative, the future of Iraq remains an open question. So does the future of the entire region. And the bombing of the U.N. offices in Iraq further complicates the process of bringing any aid to the suffering people of Iraq.

The leaders of the United States and of the entire West risk ignoring humanitarian needs as the world passes further into the age of terror. But the lengthening lists of the dead and wounded should remind those leaders that service to the humanitarian conscience has become more essential than ever, not only for the sake of others but also for the future of the West.

Resource Flows within the International Humanitarian System

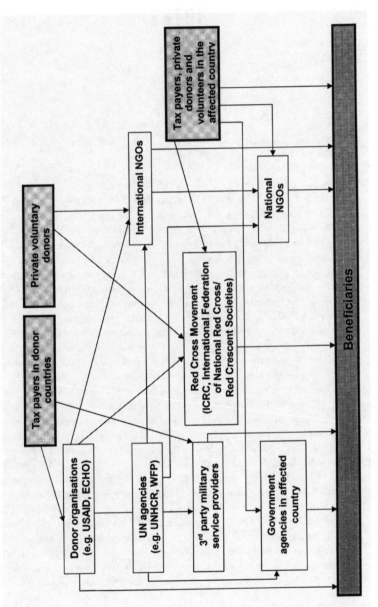

Reprinted with permission of John Borton, designer of the diagram.

NOTES

Chapter 1

1. *International Herald Tribune,* May 5–6, 2001, 2; UNHCR press release, September 28, 2000, 1–2.
2. Ibid.
3. InterAction, *Monday Developments,* May 28, 2001, 12.
4. Scott Anderson, *The Man Who Tried to Save the World: The Dangerous Life and Mysterious Disappearance of Fred Cuny* (New York: Doubleday, 1999), 17–34.
5. Ahmed Rashid, *Taliban* (New Haven: Yale University Press, 2001), 72.
6. Anthony Lake, "Honoring Relief Workers," *New York Times,* June 22, 2002, 19.
7. *Wall Street Journal,* April 25, 2000, 1.
8. James Bishop, Deputy Director of InterAction in Washington, provided this estimate of 65,000–75,000 on the number of full-time humanitarian professionals in the field. It is not possible for him or others to have a fully accurate number because those workers are employed by literally thousands of U.N. agencies, governments, Western and non-Western humanitarian NGOs or other religious and secular organizations. Moreover, the numbers change almost daily as crises wax or wane. But several other experts have confirmed the estimate as probably accurate for the number of full-time humanitarian professionals. If anything, the actual number may be higher than the estimate.
9. International Committee of the Red Cross, International Force in East Timor, International Organization for Migration, International Rescue Committee, International Security Assistance Force (in Afghanistan), Kosovo Force, Médecins sans Frontières, Stabilization Force, United Nations, United Nations High Commissioner for Refugees, United Nations Children's Fund, World Food Program.
10. Adam Roberts and Richard Guelff, eds., *Documents on the Laws of War,* 3rd ed., (Oxford: Oxford University Press, 2000), contains full listings and pertinent texts of principal laws of war including some humanitarian laws; Guy Goodwin-Gill, *The Refugee in International Law* (Oxford: Clarendon Press, 1983) and Louise Holborn, *Refugees: A Problem of Our Time* (Metuchen, N.J.: Scarecrow Press, 1975), volumes 1 and 2: passim, summarize pertinent international refugee laws; The International Committee of the Red Cross, *International Humanitarian Law* (Geneva: ICRC, n.d.) and *International Humanitarian Law: Answers to Your Questions* (Geneva: ICRC, n.d.) serve as summary guides to humanitarian laws and conventions.

Chapter 2

1. Leo Strauss, *Natural Right and History* (Chicago: University of Chicago Press, 1953), 120–135, contains an extended discussion of these principles.

2. Ernest Barker, "Translator's Introduction," Otto Gierke, *Natural Law and the Theory of Society, 1500 to 1800* (Boston: Beacon Press, 1957), xxxiv-xxxxviii.
3. Anthony Quinton, "Political Philosophy," Anthony Kenny, ed., *The Oxford History of Western Philosophy* (Oxford: Oxford University Press, 1994), 284–291.
4. Paul Gordon Lauren, *The Evolution of International Human Rights* (Philadelphia: University of Pennsylvania Press, 1998), 8–14.
5. Wallace H. Ferguson, "Toward the Modern State," in *The Renaissance* (New York: The Academy Library, 1953), 5.
6. St. Thomas Aquinas, "Summa Theologica, Question 94, On the Natural Law," Michael L. Morgan, ed. *Classics of Moral and Political Theory* (Indianapolis: Hackett, 1992), 482–483.
7. Michael Howard, *War in European History* (Oxford: Oxford University Press, 1976), 27–37.
8. Christopher Allmand, "War and the Non-Combatant in the Middle Ages," in *Medieval Warfare: A History*, Maurice Keen, ed., (Oxford: Oxford University Press, 1999), 254–55.
9. Ibid., 264.
10. Ibid., 268.
11. Theo Sommer, "Teure Frucht des wüsten Krieges," *Die Zeit*, October 22, 1998, 94.
12. Stephen D. Krasner, *Sovereignty: Organized Hypocrisy* (Princeton: Princeton University Press, 1999), 20–25.
13. Hugo Grotius, *De Jure Belli ac Pacis* (Cambridge: William Whewell, 1853), 1: 59, quoted in Howard, *War in European History*, 24.
14. Derek Heater, *The Idea of European Unity* (New York: St. Martin's Press, 1992), 31.
15. Ibid., 41–45.
16. *Castel de Saint-Pierre*, 49, quoted in Heater, *Idea of European Unity*, 88.
17. Lauren, *Evolution of International Human Rights*, 18, 31.
18. Quoted in Howard, *War in European History*, 81.
19. Except where otherwise cited, the bulk of the material about the Red Cross movement in this chapter is drawn from Caroline Moorehead, *Dunant's Dream: War, Switzerland and the History of the Red Cross* (New York: Carroll & Graf, 1998), 1–257; and from John F. Hutchinson, *Champions of Charity: War and the Rise of the Red Cross* (Boulder, CO: Westview Press, 1996), 11–276, with detailed passages or quotations cited separately where appropriate.
20. Henry Dunant, *A Memoir of Solferino* (Geneva: International Committee of the Red Cross, 1939), 19, 41, 44, 48, 51 and 61. There is some inconsistency in the spelling of Dunant's first name, with some spelling it in the English manner (Henry) and others in the French and French-speaking Swiss manner (Henri). This book uses Henry because that is the way Dunant himself spelled it in the first 1863 edition of his book.
21. Ibid., 124–128.
22. Trevor Royle, *Crimea: The Great Crimean War, 1854–1856* (New York: St. Martin's Press, 2000), 246–260.
23. Lauren, *Evolution of International Human Rights*, 58.
24. Hutchinson, *Champions of Charity*, 31–32, has text of the resolution.
25. Moorehead, *Dunant's Dream*, 22.
26. Ibid., 83.
27. Ibid., 142–147.
28. Ibid., 149–157.

29. Ibid., 155.
30. Ibid., 157.

Chapter 3

1. Misha Glenny, *The Balkans* (New York: Viking, 2000), 307–309.
2. Moorehead, *Dunant's Dream,* 178.
3. Hutchinson, *Champions of Charity,* 171.
4. J.M. Roberts, *A History of Europe* (New York: Allen Lane, 1997), 455.
5. Hutchinson, *Champions of Charity,* 256–276.
6. Moorehead, *Dunant's Dream,* 185.
7. Stéphane Courtois, "Introduction: The Crimes of Communism," in Courtois, Nicolas Werth, Jean-Louis Panné, Andrzej Paczkowski, Karel Bartosek, and Jean-Louis Margolin, *The Black Book of Communism,* trans. Jonathan Murphy and Mark Kramer (Cambridge: Harvard University Press, 1999), 6.
8. Moorehead, *Dunant's Dream,* 261, discusses Davidson's effort and the competition it represented for the ICRC.
9. Ibid., 273–280.
10. Ibid., 271–274, gives a summary of the plight of the returning prisoners of war.
11. Ibid., 291.
12. Günther Beyer, "The Political Refugee 35 Years Later," in Barry N. Stein and Sylvano M. Tomasi, eds., *Refugees Today,* Special Issue of *International Migration Review* (Spring-Summer, 1981), 28–30.
13. Louise W. Holborn, *Refugees: A Problem of our Time,* 1: 3–7; Tony Kushner and Katharine Knox, *Refugees in an Age of Genocide* (London: Cass, 1999), 65–100; Mendel R. Marrus, *The Unwanted* (New York: Oxford University Press, 1985), 40–82, discuss European refugees after World War I.
14. Holborn, *Refugees,* 1: 5–7. For detailed discussion of refugee movements between 1919 and the 1930s, as well as of various efforts to help refugees, see Marrus, *Unwanted,* 51–295; Claudena M. Skran, *Refugees in Inter-War Europe* (Oxford: Clarendon Press, 1995), passim; and Paul Frings, *Das Internationale Flüchtlingsproblem* (Frankfurt am Main: Verlag der Frankfurter Hefte, 1952), 15–56.
15. Neremiah Robinson, *Convention Relating to the Status of Refugees* (New York: Institute for Jewish Affairs, 1953), 2–3.
16. Moorehead, *Dunant's Dream,* 292–295, 411–412.
17. Courtois et al., *Black Book of Communism,* 7–10.
18. United Nations High Commissioner for Refugees, *The State of the World's Refugees, 2000: Fifty Years of Humanitarian Action* (Oxford: Oxford University Press, 2000), 15, which also contains further information about Nansen, McDonald and interwar refugee support.
19. Ibid.
20. Ibid., 310.
21. Ibid., 309.
22. Ibid., 320.
23. Ibid., 326.
24. Ibid., 316–328, reviews ICRC service in the Spanish Civil War.
25. InterAction, *InterAction Member Profiles, 1997–1998* (Washington: InterAction, 1997), 1–361; this book, in various editions, provides further information on the listed NGOs.

26. Moorehead, *Dunant's Dream*, 484, 486, 497; the Japanese germ warfare experiments are reported in *Financial Times*, August 28, 2002, 3; *New York Times*, September 4, 2002, 20.
27. Moorehead, *Dunant's Dream*, 392.
28. Ibid., 411.
29. For example, Jean-Claude Favez, *The Red Cross and the Holocaust* (Cambridge: Cambridge University Press, 1999); Arieh Ben-Tov, *Facing the Holocaust in Budapest* (Dordrecht: Henry Dunant Institute and Martinus Nijhoff Publishers, 1988).
30. *International Review of the Red Cross*, 271, July-August 1989, 394–397, contains the ICRC statement. David S. Wyman, *Abandonment of the Jews: America and the Holocaust, 1941–1945* (New York: Pantheon Books, 1984), points out that the Red Cross was not alone in failing to help Jews.
31. Michael Beschloss, *The Conquerors* (New York: Simon and Schuster, 2002), 56–68, 284–286.
32. Martin Malia, "Judging Nazism and Communism," *The National Interest*, Number 69, Fall, 2002, 69, citing Courtois et al., *Black Book of Communism*.
33. Anne Applebaum, *Gulag: A History* (New York: Doubleday, 2003); Samantha Power, *"A Problem from Hell": America and the Age of Genocide* (New York: HarperCollins, 2002); Harry Wu and Carolyn Wakeman, *Bitter Winds: A Memoir of My Years in China's Gulag* (New York: John Wiley and Sons, 1993).

Chapter 4

1. Lauren, *Evolution of International Human Rights*, 184.
2. James L. Carlin, *The Refugee Connection* (London: Macmillan, 1989), 9–18. The use of the term "United Nations" in UNRRA in 1943 did not mean the United Nations in the current sense of an international organization but in the World War II sense of the Allies.
3. Holborn, *Refugees*, 1: 46.
4. Holborn, *The International Refugee Organization* (London: Oxford University Press, 1956), gives the full history of the International Refugee Organization.
5. Holborn, *Refugees*, 1: 18–35.
6. Ibid., 1: 24.
7. Ibid., 1: 25–27.
8. Ibid., 1: 39.
9. UNHCR, *State of the World's Refugees, 2000*, 23.
10. Ibid.
11. Holborn, *Refugees*, 1: 151–174, and UNHCR, *State of the World's Refugees, 2000*, 18–26, give background on the U.N. Refugee Convention and the creation of UNHCR.
12. Hurst Hannum, *Guide to International Human Rights Practice*, third edition (Ardsley, N.Y.: Transnational Publishers, 1999), 3–18, for principles growing out of the war crimes trials.
13. William Korey, *NGOs and the Universal Declaration of Human Rights* (New York: St. Martin's Press, 1998), 29–50.
14. Lauren, *Evolution of International Human Rights*, 205–240, reviews the steps leading to the Declaration; quote from Mrs. Roosevelt is on 237; text and commentary in *Human Rights Today* (New York: U.N. Department of Public Information, 1998), passim.

15. Hannum, *Guide to Human Rights Practice,* 319.
16. United Nations, *The Blue Helmets,* third edition (New York: United Nations, 1996), 17–21, gives a summary report on U.N. observers in the Israeli-Palestinian conflict.
17. Pamela Aall, Daniel Miltenberger and Thomas G. Weiss, *Guide to IGOs, NGOs, and the Military in Peace and Relief Operations* (Washington: U.S. Institute of Peace Press, 2000), 52–57.
18. Boutros Boutros-Ghali, *An Agenda for Peace, 1995,* second edition (New York: United Nations, 1995), 57.

Chapter 5

1. Moorehead, *Dunant's Dream,* 569–578, reviews the POW treatment record and the ICRC role in the Korean War.
2. Ibid., 576.
3. Aaron Levenstein, *Escape to Freedom* (Westport, Conn.: Greenwood Press, 1983), 50–63, and Mark Dawson, *Flight: Refugees and the Flight to Freedom* (New York: International Rescue Committee, 1993), 27–37, review IRC assistance to Hungarian refugees.
4. Carlin, *Refugee Connection,* 41–61.
5. UNHCR, *The State of the World's Refugees, 2000,* 26–33, reviews the Hungarian exodus and especially the High Commissioner's role.
6. United Nations, *Blue Berets,* 175–199, contains information on peace-keeping operations reported in this section, unless otherwise cited.
7. Ibid.
8. Moorehead, *Dunant's Dream,* 617.
9. Ibid., 614–627, and David P. Forsythe, *Humanitarian Politics: The International Committee of the Red Cross* (Baltimore: Johns Hopkins, 1977), 181–196, have a review of ICRC operations in the Nigeria-Biafra conflict.
10. Moorehead, *Dunant's Dream,* 626.

Chapter 6

1. Henry Kissinger, *White House Years* (New York: Little, Brown, 1979), 438–439, 1474–1476.
2. Kissinger, *Years of Renewal* (New York: Simon and Schuster, 1999), 540–546.
3. U.N. High Commissioner for Refugees, *The State of the World's Refugees, 2000,* 81–82.
4. Kissinger, *Years of Renewal,* 533–534,
5. Ibid., 546.
6. More has been written about Indochinese refugees than about any other single group. Some useful references are Georges Condominas and Richard Pottier, *Les Refugiés originaires de l'Asie du Sud-Est* (Paris: La Documentation Française, 1982); Bruce Grant, *The Boat People* (Harmondsworth, England: Penguin Books, 1979); Lesleyanne Hawthorne, *Refugee: the Vietnamese Experience* (Melbourne: Oxford University Press, 1982); Gil Loescher and John Scanlan, *Calculated Kindness* (New York: Free Press, 1986) 102–169; William Shawcross, *The Quality of Mercy* (New York: Simon and Schuster, 1984); U.S. Department of State, *The Indochinese Refugee Situation,* Report to the Secretary of State by the Special Refugee Advisory Panel, August 12, 1981; and U.S. Department of State, *Report of the Indochinese Refugee Panel,* April, 1986.

7. Kissinger, *Years of Renewal*, 514–519.

8. *New York Times*, September 15, 2002, 10.

9. Andrew F. Smith, *Rescuing the World: The Life and Times of Leo Cherne* (Albany: State University of New York Press, 2002), 125–127.

10. Richard H. Solomon, *Exiting Indochina* (Washington: U.S. Institute of Press, 2000), 90.

11. UNHCR, *State of the World's Refugees, 2000,* 93–97.

12. Ibid., 97–102.

13. Ibid., 102.

14. Ted Robert Gurr, *Minorities at Risk: A Global View of Ethnopolitical Conflicts* (Washington: U.S. Institute of Peace, 1995), 326–363, lists ethnic groups in new African states.

15. Holborn, *Refugees*, 2: 830, 959–1396, contains an extended discussion of these and other African refugee groups during the 1950s, 1960s, and early 1970s.

16. UNHCR, *State of the World's Refugees, 2000,* 105–108.

17. UNHCR, *UNHCR Activities Financed by Voluntary Funds,* 1980, 58–65.

18. Robert Gorman, *Coping with Africa's Refugee Burden: A Time for Solutions* (Dordrecht, The Netherlands: Martinus-Nijhoff, 1987), covers these conferences in detail.

19. *Refugees* (January, 1987), 19; U.S. Committee for Refugees, *Shattered Land, Fragile Asylum* (Washington, U.S. Committee for Refugees, 1986).

20. *New York Times*, February 10, 1987.

21. *Refugees* (January, 1987), 8–10.

22. U.S. Congress, House of Representatives, *Reports on Refugee Aid* (Washington: U.S.G.P.O., 1981), 71–75; Said Azhar, "Three Million Uprooted Afghans in Pakistan," *Pakistan Horizon* (First Quarter, 1985), 60–68.

23. Refugees in Iran have attracted relatively little international notice. The best sources for information are following reports in the magazine *Refugees* (May, 1984), 11; (November, 1985), 19–21, 27; also, the U.N. High Commissioner for Refugees' annual reports to the Executive Committee since 1983 have provided information.

24. U.N. High Commissioner for Refugees, *Collection of International Instruments Concerning Refugees,* 2d. edition (Geneva: UNHCR, 1979), 247–273, contains texts of these conventions.

25. UNHCR, *Declaration of Cartagena* (Geneva: UNHCR, 1984), 34.

26. *Refugees* (March, 1986), 5.

27. U.S. Department of State, *Report of the Cuban-Haitian Task Force,* November 1, 1980, A–5 to A–18, gives background on the Cuban exodus. Selected articles on Cuban refugees appear in Carlos E. Cortes, ed., *Cuban Refugee Programs* (New York: Arno Press, 1980).

28. Ronald Copeland, "The Cuban Boatlift of 1980: Strategies in Federal Crisis Management," Loescher and Scanlan, *The Global Refugee Problem: U.S. and World Response,* special issue of *Annals of the American Academy of Political and Social Science*, vol. 467 (1983), 138–150.

29. *Refugees* (March, 1986), 38–39.

30. Ibid.

31. Ibid.; *Report of the Cuban-Haitian Task Force,* A–18 to A–26; Naomi Flink Zucker, "The Haitians versus the United States: The Courts as last Resort," in Loescher and Scanlan, *The Global Refugee Problem,* 151–162.

32. These statistics come from UNHCR reports to its Executive Committee and from the following issues of *Refugees* magazine: (October 1985), 17–18; (January 1986),

14–16; (May 1986), 27–28; (July 1986), 19–30; (August 1986), 19–31; (October 1986), 19–30.

33. *New York Times,* August 16 and 20, 1985, and November 3, 1986.

34. Aaron Levenstein, *Escape to Freedom,* 3–99; Malcolm J. Proudfoot, *European Refugees* (Evanston, Ill.: Northwestern University Press, 1956); and Marrus, *The Unwanted,* contain information on Eastern European refugees.

35. U.S. Department of State, *World Refugee Report, 1986* (Washington: U.S. Department of State, 1986), 63–65.

36. UNHCR, *UNHCR Activities Financed by Voluntary Funds,* 1986.

37. *Refugees* (December 1986), 22.

38. For detailed refugee statistics, one can consult UNHCR annual reports to the Executive Committee as well as special or regular appeals that the High Commissioner for Refugees may issue. One can also consult the annual U.S. Committee for Refugees *World Refugee Survey.* The former does not include the Palestinian refugee numbers but the latter does.

39. Holborn, *Refugees,* 1: 521.

40. Peter Willetts, "The Impact of Promotional Pressure Groups on Global Politics," in Peter Willetts, ed., *Pressure Groups in the International System* (New York: St. Martin's Press, 1982), 179–196.

41. For texts of ECOSOC documents and related papers, see Willetts, *Pressure Groups,* 201–215.

42. Aall, Miltenberger, and Weiss, *Guide to IGOs, NGOs, and the Military in Peace and Relief Operations* and the periodic United Nations High Commissioner for Refugees' *NGOs and UNHCR: Directory of Non-Governmental Organizations* contain more complete listings.

43. *The Economist,* January 20, 2000, 36.

Chapter 7

1. U.S. Committee for Refugees, *World Refugee Survey, 1991* (Washington: U.S. Committee for Refugees, 1991), 95–97; *World Refugee Survey, 1992* (Washington: U.S. Committee for Refugees, 1992), 96–100; UNHCR, *The State of the World's Refugees, 2000,* 211–218, are main sources for this section, supplemented by interviews with refugee officials in Geneva, April, 2001.

2. U.S. Committee for Refugees, *World Refugee Survey, 1991,* 4.

3. Gil Loescher, *The UNHCR and World Politics* (Oxford: Oxford University Press, 2001), 286–289.

4. UNHCR, *The State of the World's Refugees, 2000,* 166–167.

5. The United Nations Children's Fund, *Annual Report, 1990,* passim.

6. International Organization for Migration, *Report of the Director General on the Work of the Organization for the Year 1990,* April 30, 1991, Annex III.

7. See the annual *World Refugee Survey,* published by the U.S. Committee for Refugees, as well as reports of separate agencies, to follow funding levels and principal contributors year to year.

8. United Nations, *OCHA: What it is. What it does.* (New York: United Nations, n.d.), passim.

9. Boutros Boutros-Ghali, *An Agenda for Peace,* 2nd ed. (New York: United Nations, 1995), 39.

10. Ibid., 44.

11. Ibid., 58.
12. Ibid., 59–67.
13. United Nations, *Blue Helmets*, 231–265, 413–440, 659–665.
14. Ibid., 72.

Chapter 8

1. Warren Zimmermann, *Origins of a Catastrophe* (New York: Random House, 1999), 1–9.
2. Mischa Glenny, *The Balkans: Nationalism, War, and the Great Powers, 1804–1999* (New York: Viking, 2000), 360–366.
3. Ibid., 365.
4. Ibid., 360–366.
5. Susan L. Woodward, *Balkan Tragedy: Chaos and Dissolution After the Cold War* (Washington: Brookings, 1998), 82.
6. Ibid., 90.
7. Ibid., 104.
8. Zimmermann, *Origins of a Catastrophe*, 62.
9. Woodward, *Balkan Tragedy*, 98.
10. Robert C. DiPrizio, *Armed Humanitarians* (Baltimore: Johns Hopkins University Press, 2002), 117.
11. Ibid., 97.
12. Woodward, *Balkan Tragedy*, 120.
13. Ibid.
14. Ibid.
15. Ibid., 122.
16. Ibid., 108.
17. Ibid., 157–160.
18. Richard Holbrooke, *To End a War* (New York: Random House, 1998), 21.
19. Ibid., 161.
20. Woodward, *Balkan Tragedy*, 158.
21. Ibid., 184.
22. Woodward, *Balkan Tragedy*, 184; David Halberstam, *War in a Time of Peace: Bush, Clinton, and the Generals* (New York: Scribner, 2001), 88–89.
23. Woodward, *Balkan Tragedy*, 187.
24. Ibid., 184–187.
25. Ibid., 277.
26. Glenny, *The Fall of Yugoslavia: The Third Balkan War*, 3rd ed., (New York: Penguin, 1996), 143.
27. Glenny, *Balkans*, 172.
28. *Washington Times*, December 29, 2002, 10.
29. Glenny, *Balkans*, 230.
30. Woodward, *Balkan Tragedy*, 279–283.
31. Glenny, *Balkans*, 231.
32. Glenny, *Fall of Yugoslavia*, 228–229.
33. Bill Frelick, "Preventing Refugee Flows: Protection or Peril?," in U.S. Committee for Refugees, *World Refugee Survey, 1993* (Washington: U.S. Committee for Refugees, 1993), 9.
34. Ibid., 232–233.

35. Ivo H. Daalder, *Getting to Dayton* (Washington: Brookings, 2000), 9–10.

36. UNHCR, *The State of the World's Refugees, 2000*, 218–230, summarizes protection and relief operations in Bosnia and Kosovo during the wars there.

37. Ibid., 220.

38. William Shawcross, *Deliver Us from Evil* (New York: Simon & Schuster, 2000), 15–16.

39. Ibid., 28.

40. Jan Willem Honig and Norbert Both, *Srebrenica: Record of a War Crime* (New York: Penguin, 1997), passim, provide extensive description of the fall of Srebrenica and the crimes committed there.

41. Ibid., 6.

42. Daalder, *Getting to Dayton*, 43.

43. *Washington Times*, July 2, 2001.

44. Honig and Both, *Srebrenica*, 38.

45. Sadako Ogata, "The Interface between Peacekeeping and Humanitarian Action," in Daniel Warner, ed., *New Dimensions of Peacekeeping* (Dordrecht, Neth.: Martinus Nijhoff, 1995), 8.

46. Daalder, *Getting to Dayton*, 68.

47. *New York Times*, April 8, 2000, 4.

48. *Financial Times*, April 11, 2002, 7.

49. Holbrooke, *To End a War*, 99.

50. Ibid., 299.

51. Ibid., passim.

52. Pauline Neville-Jones, "Dayton, IFOR and Alliance Relations in Bosnia," *Survival*, Winter 1996–1997, passim, conveys the mood of the sessions and of Holbrooke's style.

53. Neville-Jones, "Dayton, IFOR and Alliance Relations," passim, and Holbrooke, *To End a War*, passim.

54. Daalder, *Getting to Dayton*, 157.

55. U.N. Mission for Bosnia and Herzegovina, *A Mandate Implemented* (Sarajevo: UN-MIBH, 2002); International Organization for Migration, *IOM and Assisted Voluntary Return (AVR)* (Geneva: IOM, 2002), 2.

56. Jacques Klein, Coordinator of U.N. Operations in Bosnia-Herzegovina, in a briefing at the U.S. Institute of Peace, Washington, D.C., March 12, 2002.

57. Ibid.

58. Ibid.

59. *Wall Street Journal*, January 10, 2003, 1; *Washington Post*, November 19, 2002, 17; *New York Times*, January 21, 2003, 8.

60. The following sources have been used here to summarize the United Nations operation in Eastern Slavonia: Derek Boothby, "Probing the Successful Application of Leverage in the UNTAES Operation," a paper prepared for the Roundtable Meeting on "Applying Leverage: Lessons from the United Nations Operations in Mozambique and Eastern Slavonia," sponsored by the Center for Naval Warfare Studies, U.S. Naval War College, United Nations Program, Yale University, and Center for the Study of International Organization, NYU School of Law and the Woodrow Wilson School of Princeton University, October 8, 1999; Christine Coleiro, "Legacy of the UN in Eastern Slavonia and Transitional Missions," unpublished thesis in Interdisciplinary Studies at George Mason University, Fairfax, Virginia, Spring semester, 2000; U.S. Department of Defense, "The main conditions that should be fulfilled in

order that future UN missions will have a reasonable chance of success," Defense Research Paper, n.d.

61. Holbrooke, *To End a War,* 233–270, and especially 233–240, 259–261, and 264–270.
62. Boutros-Ghali, *Unvanquished* (New York: Random House, 1999), 256.
63. Boothby, "Probing the successful Application of Leverage," 4.
64. Holbrooke, *To End a War,* 321.
65. Klein, "My Visit to Croatia and Serbia, December 28–31," Memorandum to the Secretary-General of the United Nations, January 5, 1996.
66. Major David Sterling Jones, USA, and Captain Paul J. McDowell, USAF, "Operation Little Flower: The United Nations Apprehension of an Indicted War Criminal," *Military Intelligence,* (April-June, 1998), 46–51.
67. Klein, "The Prospects for Eastern Croatia: The Significance of the UN's Undiscovered Mission," *RUSI Journal,* (April, 1997), 19–24; "The Security Council and the G8 in the New Millennium, assessing the Council's Performance: The View from the Field," Paper presented at the Fifth International Berlin Workshop, Stiftung Wissenschaft und Politik, Berlin, July 1, 2000; Defense Research Paper, "The main conditions that should be fulfilled in order that future UN missions will have a reasonable chance of success," unattributed, undated and unnumbered; Christine Coleiro, *Bringing Peace to the Land of Scorpions and Jumping Snakes: Legacy of the United Nations in Eastern Slavonia and Transitional Missions* (Cornwallis Park, N.S.: The Canadian Peacekeeping Press of the Lester B. Pearson Canadian International Peacekeeping Training Center, 2003), passim.

Chapter 9

1. Tim Judah, *Kosovo: War and Revenge* (New Haven: Yale University Press, 2000), 53.
2. Ibid.
3. Ibid., 74–75.
4. Julie A. Mertus, *Kosovo: How Myths and Truths Started a War* (Berkeley: University of California Press, 1999), 307; Glenny, *The Balkans,* 652.
5. Judah, *Kosovo,* 135–173, describes this situation.
6. Ibid., 182.
7. Ibid., 183.
8. Ibid., 164–196.
9. Strobe Talbott, *The Russia Hand* (New York: Random House, 2002), 302–303.
10. The Independent International Commission on Kosovo, *The Kosovo Report* (Oxford: Oxford University Press, 2001), 323.
11. Ibid., 322–323.
12. Stephen T. Hosmer, *Why Milosevic Decided to Settle When He Did* (Santa Monica, CA, USA: RAND, 2001), 12–18.
13. Quentin Peel, "A Cautionary Tale from the Kosovo War," *Financial Times,* January 14, 2003, 13.
14. Hosmer, *Why Milosevic Decided to Settle,* 212.
15. Judah, *Kosovo,* 224–225.
16. Michael Mandelbaum, "A Perfect Failure: NATO's War Against Yugoslavia," *Foreign Affairs* (September/October 1999), 4.
17. Talbott, *Russia Hand,* 303.
18. *Washington Times,* June 29, 2001.

19. Hosmer, *Why Milosevic Decided to Settle,* 19.
20. Judah, *Kosovo,* 235.
21. Ibid., 250.
22. Ibid., 240–241.
23. Ibid., 241.
24. Ivo H. Daalder and Michael E. O'Hanlon, *Winning Ugly: NATO's War to Save Kosovo* (Washington: Brookings, 2000), 112.
25. Wesley K. Clark, *Waging Modern War: Bosnia, Kosovo, and the Future of Combat* (New York: Public Affairs, 2001), 222, 249, 250, 255.
26. Clark, *Waging Modern War,* 299.
27. Judah, *Kosovo,* 256–258.
28. Clark, *Waging Modern War,* 269–271.
29. Ibid., 302.
30. *Washington Times,* November 21, 2001, 16.
31. Hosmer, *Why Milosevic Decided to Settle,* 79–90.
32. Ibid., 100.
33. *New York Times,* June 15, 1999; *Berliner Morgenpost,* August 9, 1999; and *Financial Times,* June 14, 1999, have reports on contacts in Berlin, Moscow and Belgrade.
34. Talbott, *Russia Hand,* 321–329.
35. *Financial Times,* June 14, 1999; *Berliner Morgenpost,* August 9, 1999.
36. The United States Institute of Peace in Washington has conducted many seminars on Kosovo peace and reconstruction. *New York Times,* December 29, 2002, 8, and *Financial Times,* December 31, 2002, 3, have summary reports of these and other activities in and about postwar developments in Kosovo.
37. Mandelbaum, "A Perfect Failure."
38. Glenny, *Balkans,* 657.
39. Adam Roberts, "The Laws of War After Kosovo," *U.S. Naval War College, International Law Studies,* 78 (2002), 401–432.
40. Most major American and European newspapers reported on the NLA attacks against Macedonia. Some of the most extensive stories, used as sources here, appeared in the *New York Times,* February 9, May 3 and May 8, 2001.
41. *Financial Times,* May 28, 2001.
42. Brenda Pearson, *Putting Peace into Practice* (Washington: U.S. Institute of Peace, 2002), 4–8.
43. *New York Times,* June 12, 2001.

Chapter 10

1. The principal sources for this discussion of Somalia are Herman J. Cohen, *Intervening in Africa* (New York: St. Martin's Press, 2000), 197–217; John I. Hirsch and Robert B. Oakley, *Somalia and Operation Restore Hope* (Washington: U.S. Institute of Peace, 1995); Terrence Lyons and Ahmed I. Samatar, *Somalia* (Washington: Brookings, 1995); Samuel M. Makinda, *Seeking Peace from Chaos: Humanitarian Intervention in Somalia* (Boulder: Lynne Rienner, 1993); Mohammed Sahnoun, *Somalia: The Missed Opportunities* (Washington: U.S. Institute of Peace, 1994); and United Nations, *The Blue Helmets,* 291–318. Specific citations from these sources, as well as from other sources, will be noted as appropriate.
2. Cohen, *Intervening in Africa,* 205–211.
3. Hirsch and Oakley, *Somalia and Restore Hope,* 111.

4. Ibid., 118.
5. Ibid., 126-127; Mark Bowden, *Black Hawk Down: A Story of Modern War* (New York: Atlantic Monthly Press, 1999), tells the story of the battle in detail.
6. Hirsch and Oakley, *Somalia and Restore Hope,* 129–132.
7. Much has been written about the Rwanda genocide of 1994. This section relies mainly on L.R. Melvern, *A People Betrayed: The Role of the West in Rwanda's Genocide* (London: Zed Books, 2000), which is the principal source unless other sources are cited. Beyond that, more specific sources include Glynne Evans, *Responding to Crises in the African Great Lakes,* Adelphi Paper 311 (Oxford: Oxford University Press, 1997); Scott R. Feil, *How the Early Use of Force might have succeeded in Rwanda,* A Report to the Carnegie Commission on Preventing Deadly Conflict (New York: Carnegie Corporation, 1998); Larry Minear and Philippe Guillot, *Soldiers to the Rescue: Humanitarian Lessons from Rwanda* (Paris: Development Center of the Organization for Economic Cooperation and Development, 1996); Scott Peterson, *Me Against my Brother: At War in Somalia, Sudan and Rwanda* (New York: Routledge, 2000); and *Report of the Independent Inquiry into the Actions of the United Nations during the 1994 Genocide in Rwanda* (New York: United Nations, 1999).
8. Mahmoud Mandani, *When Victims Become Killers: Colonialism, Nativism, and Genocide in Rwanda* (Princeton: Princeton University Press, 2001), passim, explores at length the ethnic tensions in Rwanda and the Belgian role in deepening them.
9. Melvern, *People Betrayed,* 17.
10. Ibid., 43–44.
11. *Report of Independent Inquiry,* 4–5.
12. *Globe and Mail,* Toronto, February 1, 1998, cited in Melvern, *People Betrayed,* 83.
13. *Report of Independent Inquiry,* 6–7; Melvern, *People Betrayed,* 91–93.
14. Melvern, *People Betrayed,* 96.
15. *Report of Independent Inquiry,* 10; Melvern, *People Betrayed,* 112.
16. Melvern, *People Betrayed,* 117.
17. *Report of Independent Inquiry,* 11–12
18. Melvern, *People Betrayed,* 122.
19. Ibid., 126.
20. Ibid., 132.
21. Ibid., 148.
22. Ibid., 148–155; *Report of Independent Inquiry,* 15–17; Feil, *Early Use of Force,* 7–10.
23. Melvern, *People Betrayed,* 163.
24. Ibid., 177–179.
25. Ibid.
26. Ibid., 202.
27. Romeo Dallaire, "Introduction," in Feil, *Early Use of Force,* v.
28. Dallaire, "The End of Innocence," in Jonathan Moore, ed., *Hard Choices: Moral Dilemmas in Humanitarian Intervention* (New York: Bowman & Littlefield under the auspices of the International Committee of the Red Cross, 1998), 85.
29. Melvern, *People Betrayed,* 189.
30. Ian Martin, "Hard Choices after Genocide," Moore, *Hard Choices,* 160.
31. Dallaire, "End of Innocence," 83–85; Martin, "Hard Choices," 163–166.
32. See *Report of Independent Inquiry,* 22–40, for conclusions.
33. For reviews of developments in the Congo and Rwanda toward the end of 2002, see *Financial Times,* April 3, 2002, July 27–28 and August 3–4, 2002; *Washington Times,* April 4, 2002 and January 2, 2003; and *New York Times,* December 18, 2002.

34. *New York Times,* June 7, 2003, 3.
35. Geoffrey C. Gunn, *East Timor and the United Nations* (Lawrenceville, N.J.: Red Sea Press, 1997), reviews the history of East Timor during Indonesian control and gives texts of appropriate U.N. resolutions and statements.
36. James Traub, "Inventing East Timor," *Foreign Affairs* (July/August, 2000), 76, is a source for the background history of East Timor, as are James Cotton, "Against the Grain: The East Timor Intervention," *Survival* (Spring, 2001), 127–130, and Astri Suhrke, "Peacekeepers as Nation-builders: Dilemmas of the UN in East Timor," *International Peacekeeping* (Winter, 2001), 1–20.
37. Traub, "Inventing East Timor," 78.
38. UNHCR, *State of the World's Refugees, 2000,* 236–237.
39. Ibid.
40. Ibid.
41. Traub, "Inventing East Timor," 83.
42. Cotton, "Against the Grain," 130–131.
43. Jarat Chopra, "The UN's Kingdom of East Timor," *Survival* (Autumn, 2000), 27–39.
44. Sergio Vieira de Mello, "Presentation to the National Council of East Timor," June 28, 2001, 13–15.
45. *Washington Post,* March 14, 2002, 24.
46. United Nations Security Council, "Report of the Secretary-General on the United Nations Transitional Administration in East Timor for the period from 25 July to 15 October 2001," October 18, 2001, 11–12.

Chapter 11

1. *Washington Times,* March 13, 2002, 3.
2. Public television, "The United Nations," January 7, 2003.
3. Annan, Address to the 54th Session of the U.N. General Assembly, September 20, 1999, United Nations press release, 2.
4. David Rieff, *A Bed for the Night* (New York: Simon & Schuster, 2002), 324; Ahmed Rashid, *Taliban: Militant Islam, Oil and Fundamentalism in Central Asia* (New Haven: Yale University Press, 2002), 108.
5. Gurr, *Minorities at Risk,* 326–363.
6. U.S. Committee for Refugees, *World Refugee Survey, 2002* (Washington; U.S. Committee for Refugees, 2002), 4–6.
7. Annan, Speech to U.N. General Assembly, October 6, 1999, U.N. press release, 1.
8. *New York Times,* June 28, 2002.
9. United Nations, *Brahimi Report: Panel on United Nations Peace Operations* (New York: United Nations, 2000); also, "UN Peace Operations: Past and Future," *Refugee Reports* (November, 2000), 11, has a summary and evaluation.
10. Adrian Wood, Raymond Apthorpe and John Borton, *Evaluating International Humanitarian Action: Reflections from Practitioners* (London: Zed Books, 2001), xv-xvi.
11. Ibid., 2–18.
12. ALNAP, *Humanitarian Action: Learning from Evaluation* (London: Overseas Development Institute, 2001), 31–40.
13. U.N. Office for the Coordination of Humanitarian Affairs, *Hope for the Future: Consolidated Interagency Appeals, 2003* (New York: UNOCHA, 2002), 5–6.

14. General Accounting Office, "Cost of Peacekeeping is Likely to Exceed Current Estimate," Briefing Report to the U.S. House of Representatives Committee on International Affairs, August, 2000, 10.

15. Dennis C. Jett, statement before the House Committee on International Relations, October 11, 2000, distributed at a meeting on international peacekeeping at the U.S. Institute of Peace, December 14, 2000.

16. Ruud Lubbers, "Opening Statement at the Fifty-third Session of the Executive Committee of the High Commissioner's Program," September 30, 2002, 2.

Chapter 12

1. Rashid, *Taliban*, 7.

2. Briefing by James Dobbins, Special U.S. Representative for Afghanistan, at the U.S. Institute of Peace, Washington, D.C., January 12, 2002.

3. This portion of the Afghanistan chapter, recounting the origins and early history of the Taliban, is based on Rashid, *Taliban*, 21–49.

4. Ibid., 135, 178.

5. U.S. Committee for Refugees, *World Refugee Survey, 2002* (Washington: U.S. Committee for Refugees, 2002), 144.

6. Rashid, *Taliban*, 65.

7. *Washington Post*, November 5, 2001.

8. *New York Times*, March 7, 2002, 10.

9. Rashid, *Taliban*, 128–142; Mark Huband and John Willman, "Holy War on the World," *Financial Times*, November 28, 2001, 6–7; Mark Huband, "Bankrolling bin Laden," *Financial Times*, November 29, 2001, 6–7.

10. *Washington Post*, October 3, 2001, 19; *Investor's Business Daily*, December 21, 2001, 18.

11. Rashid, *Taliban*, 138–139.

12. Ibid., 134.

13. Lydia Mann-Bondat, "Humanitarian Action in Afghanistan," unpublished paper presented at the Institute for the Study of International Migration, Washington, D.C, February, 2002, 10, 18.

14. *New York Times*, October 8, 2001, 1.

15. *New York Times*, November 6, 2001, 5.

16. *Financial Times*, July 6–7, 2002, 3.

17. *Financial Times*, July 22, 2002, 3; *New York Times*, July 21, 1.

18. Mann-Bondat, "Humanitarian Action in Afghanistan," 52–53.

19. *Washington Times*, April 3, 2002, 15, and May 2, 2002, 11.

20. These reports of the *Loya Jirga* and its results are based on *Financial Times*, April 18, 2002, 11; *New York Times*, June 18, 2002, 10, June 21, 2002, 25, and June 28, 2002, 8; *Washington Post*, June 21, 2002, 19; *Washington Times*, June 12, 2002, 15.

21. *Washington Post*, July 24, 2002, 14.

22. *Washington Post*, November 5, 2002, 22; *Financial Times*, November 6, 2002,

23. U.S. Committee for Refugees, *World Refugee Survey 2003* (Washington: U.S. Committee for Refugees, 2003), 252–253.

24. Reports of relief shipments and problems were carried by *Financial Times*, October 18, 2001, 7, and November 2, 2001, 2; *New York Times*, November 30, 2001, 4; and *Washington Post*, December 11, 2001, 18.

25. *New York Times*, December 26, 2001, 2.

26. Thomas L. Friedman, "The Talk of Kabul," *New York Times,* January 12, 2002, 19.

27. *New York Times,* January 22, 2002, 11; *Washington Times,* January 16, 2002, 7.

28. *New York Times,* January 22, 2002, 11.

29. InterAction, *Monday Developments,* November 11, 2002, 8; Kathy Gannon, "As Year Ends, Afghans Look Ahead," *Washington Times,* December 29, 2002, 8.

30. Ivo Daalder and James Lindsay, "It's Hawk vs. Hawk in the Bush Administration," *Washington Post,* October 27, 2002, 3.

31. *New York Times,* September 27, 2002, 13.

32. Mann-Bondat, "Humanitarian Action in Afghanistan," 30, 50, 55.

33. *New York Times,* October 31, 2002, 3, and November 8, 2001, 30.

34. Larry Thompson and Michelle Brown, "The Next Afghan Crisis," *Washington Post,* June 12, 2002, 31.

35. Gannon, "As Year Ends, Afghans Look Ahead," 8.

36. *New York Times,* November 22, 2001, 4; *Washington Post,* December 7, 2001, 31; *Washington Times,* November 17, 5.

37. Barnett Rubin, "Is America Abandoning Afghanistan?," *New York Times,* April 10, 2002, 25; *New York Times,* April 18, 2002, 15.

38. *New York Times,* January 5, 2002, 7.

39. *Financial Times,* May 24, 2002, 6.

40. *New York Times,* March 21, 14, and March 26, 2002, 12.

41. *New York Times,* October 25, 2002, 10.

42. *Washington Times,* December 11, 2002, 13.

Chapter 13

1. The following reports provide information on the humanitarian situation in Iraq on the eve of the war: Congressional Research Service, "Iraq War? Current Situation and Issues for Congress," February 20, 2003, 19–26; Sandra Mitchell, "Testimony before the U.S. Senate Foreign Relations Committee on Humanitarian Consequences Related to Iraq," March 11, 2003, 1–10; Mary McClymont, "Iraq Contingency Planning," *Monday Developments,* February 24, 2003, 1–7; Ray Buchanan, "Iraq: Moving from What to Why," *Monday Developments,* March 10, 2003, 7.

2. *New York Times,* November 9, 2002, 1.

3. *Washington Times,* January 28, 2003, 14, has typical Blix report.

4. *Financial Times,* May 29, 2003, 11.

5. *Financial Times,* February 14, 2003, 2.

6. Max Boot, "The New American Way of War," *Foreign Affairs,* July/August 2003, 41–45.

7. *Washington Post,* April 27, 2003, 7.

8. *New York Times,* March 25, 2003, 22.

9. *New York Times,* March 28, 2003, 12.

10. *New York Times,* March 30, 2003, 1–10.

11. Robert Novak, "Grumbles from Rumsfeld's Army," *Washington Post,* June 23, 2003, 21.

12. *New York Times,* April 14, 2003, 7; for a wider description of the looting and lawlessness, see International Crisis Group, *Baghdad: A Race Against the Clock,* June 11, 2003, 1–7.

13. *New York Times,* February 11, 2003, 11.

14. *Washington Post,* June 1, 2003, 6.

15. *Washington Times,* June 26, 2003, 3.
16. *Financial Times,* June 26, 2003, 3.
17. *Washington Post,* June 20, 2003, 1.
18. *New York Times,* May 3, 2003, 8, and June 19, 2003, 13; *Washington Post,* June 22, 2003, 20; *Financial Times,* July 3, 2003, 2.
19. *Washington Post,* June 30, 2003, 9.
20. *The Economist,* February 8, 2003, 16.
21. *Financial Times,* June 24, 2003, 4.
22. *Monday Developments,* January 13, 2003, 1.
23. *Financial Times,* March 31, 2003, 4.
24. *Monday Developments,* April 14, 2003.
25. *Humanitarian Times,* March 13, 2003, 1.
26. *Washington Post,* March 27, 2003, 34.
27. *Washington Post,* May 28, 2003, 16.
28. *Financial Times,* June 25, 2003, 11.
29. *Wall Street Journal,* June 25, 2003, 3.
30. *Financial Times,* July 19/20, 2003, 3.
31. *Monday Developments,* April 28, 2003, 1.
32. *Financial Times,* March 26, 2003, 5; *New York Times,* March 28, 2003, 13.
33. *Financial Times,* June 4, 2003; *Wall Street Journal,* June 25, 2003, 1–3; *Washington Post,* June 26, 2003, 16.
34. *New York Times Magazine,* June 22, 2003, 32–37; *Financial Times,* June 27, 2003, 1.
35. *New York Times,* June 23, 2003, 1; *Washington Post,* June 20, 2003, 1, 15.
36. *Washington Post,* June 28, 2003, 20.
37. *Washington Post,* June 16, 2003, 1.
38. *New York Times,* July 3, 2003, 10.

INDEX